ELIZABETH AND MARY

ROYAL COUSINS, RIVAL QUEENS

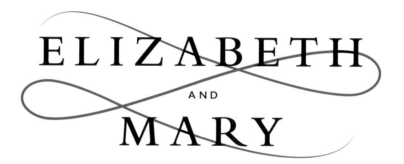

ELIZABETH
AND
MARY

ROYAL COUSINS, RIVAL QUEENS

Sponsored by
The Sir John Ritblat Family Foundation

Edited by Susan Doran
British Library lead curator: Andrea Clarke
British Library curators: Alan Bryson and Karen Limper-Herz

First published in 2021 by
The British Library, 96 Euston Road, London NW1 2DB

Text © the contributors 2021
Images © the British Library and other named copyright holders 2021

British Library Cataloguing-in-Publication Data
A catalogue record is available from the British Library

ISBN 978 0 7123 5348 9 (HB)
ISBN 978 0 7123 5353 3 (PB)

Designed and typeset by Ocky Murray
Picture research by Sally Nicholls
Printed in the Czech Republic by PB Tisk

This publication accompanies the British Library exhibition
Elizabeth and Mary: Royal Cousins, Rival Queens

**This exhibition was made possible thanks to
the generous sponsorship of the Sir John Ritblat
Family Foundation.**

The British Library would also like to thank
The John S Cohen Foundation and all supporters
who wish to remain anonymous

This catalogue has been kindly supported by
The Strathmartine Trust

THE
STRATHMARTINE
TRUST

CONTENTS

CURATOR'S PREFACE

Andrea Clarke

Almost 500 years on, the story of Elizabeth I and Mary, Queen of Scots continues to fascinate and enthral. It is a story of two women whose lives were indissolubly connected, for not only were they fellow sovereign queens but also, as Mary reminded Elizabeth in countless letters to her, 'both of one blood, of one country and in one island'.

Elizabeth and Mary: Royal Cousins, Rival Queens is the first major exhibition to consider these two iconic female rulers together, putting them both centre stage and giving them equal billing. Using original documents, the exhibition takes a fresh and revealing look at the compelling story of two powerful queens, bound together by their shared Tudor inheritance and rivalry for the English and Irish thrones, whose complex, turbulent relationship dominated English and Scottish politics for thirty years.

Despite having been united many times on stage and screen, in real life the two women never met face to face; instead their relationship was played out at a distance, much of it by letter. It is these thrilling documents, written in the queens' own hands and in their own words, that form the narrative backbone of the exhibition and enable visitors to step back into their world and to understand how from amicable beginnings and sisterly affection, their relationship turned into one of suspicion, distrust and betrayal.

The exhibition also explores how Elizabeth and Mary's stormy relationship reflected a much broader story. Set against the background of England and Scotland deeply divided between Protestants and Catholics, and a Europe torn apart by religious conflicts and civil wars, it reveals how their battle for dynastic pre-eminence within the British Isles became inseparable from national religious struggle and England's unsettled relationship with Scotland, France and Spain. Remarkably, many of the themes woven through the exhibition narrative, such as Anglo-Scottish relations, international diplomacy and Europe, state surveillance and espionage, still have a deep relevance today.

Two-thirds of the exhibits are drawn from the British Library's outstanding collection of early modern manuscripts, historical documents and printed material. Elizabeth and Mary's autograph letters are accompanied by state papers, diplomatic reports, speeches and letters written in cipher. Beautiful maps, drawings and woodcut engravings illustrate key moments and events.

The early modern period is the first in British history to be so thoroughly documented in manuscripts, letters and state papers. To choose a relatively small number of exhibits from the many hundreds of thousands of such documents held at the British Library has been no easy task. I am therefore delighted that while the exhibition has been in preparation, the Library has digitised 600 of its early modern manuscripts, half of them with the generous support of Mark Pigott, KBE, KStJ. Online access to these digital images, along with enhanced catalogue records created by Amy Bowles, Jessica Crown, Clarck Drieshen and Tim Wales, will not only enable visitors to continue to explore and enjoy many of the exhibits beyond the confines of the exhibition gallery, but also provide an enduring and valuable resource for anyone interested in the early modern period.

As well as showcasing the Library's world-class collections, the exhibition is further enriched with a number of exceptional paintings, jewels, textiles, maps, drawings and objects borrowed from private and public collections across the UK and Spain. I am extremely grateful to Her Majesty The Queen for graciously lending two portraits of Mary, Queen of Scots, as well as to all the private individuals (both named and anonymous) and public institutions listed on p. 10 who have willingly and generously lent their precious works for display.

As lead curator of the exhibition, I owe a debt of gratitude to many people. The project has benefitted from an excellent exhibition advisory group, and I offer heartfelt thanks to Charlotte Bolland, Jane Dawson, John Guy, Katy Mair, Alison Rosie and Sebastiaan Verweij for their enthusiastic support and invaluable scholarly and curatorial advice over the past three years. Numerous other individuals have helped with research enquiries and facilitated loans, and I am particularly grateful to Peter Barber, Ulrike Hogg, Philip Mould, Matthew Payne, David Starkey, Edward Town and Mary Wellesley.

I wish to thank all the authors who have contributed essays and entries to this publication, and especially Susan Doran, who has thoughtfully and skilfully shaped and edited the volume. I am also grateful to Abbie Day and John Lee of British Library Publishing, who have steered the catalogue expertly through the press, to Sally Nicholls for her picture research, to copy-editor Rob Davies, and to Ocky Murray, who has designed the catalogue.

The exhibition was designed by Robin Clark of Hara Clark, in association with graphic designer Helen Lyon of studio HB and lighting designer David Robertson of DHA Lighting Designs. The audio-visual elements were produced by Chris Owens of Clay Interactive, and Elizabeth and Mary's tombs and effigies have been recreated by Michael Whitely. Jana Dambrogio and Dan Starza Smith have generously shared their time and expertise to help create a video on the fascinating subject of letterlocking. It has been a pleasure to work with them all.

The exhibition was delivered by a large team at the Library and I am particularly grateful to Conrad Bodman, Head of Culture Programmes, Alex Kavanagh, Exhibitions Manager, Susan Dymond, Interpretation Manager, Janet Benoy and Hannah Kershaw, Exhibitions Assistants, Alexa McNaught-Reynolds, Conservation Exhibitions and Loan Manager, Hazel Shorland, Loans Co-ordinator, Christina Duffy, Conservation Research Imaging Scientist, and Sandra Tuppen, Heritage Made Digital Portfolio Manager. I would also like to thank all of the many other colleagues I have worked with in Collection Care, Collections and Curation, Commercial Services, Corporate Affairs, Design, Development, Digital Marketing, Events, Heritage Made Digital and Imaging Services, Learning, Marketing and Visitor Services, as well as all the members of the Library's exhibition project board.

I also wish to recognise the advice, support and encouragement that I have received from Claire Breay, Kristian Jensen and Scot McKendrick, as well as the help of my colleagues in Ancient, Medieval and Early Modern Manuscripts, especially Calum Cockburn, Kathleen Doyle, Charmaine Fagan, Julian Harrison, Eleanor Jackson, Pauline Thomson, Peter Toth and Anna Turnham.

My largest debt of gratitude, however, is to my two co-curators, Alan Bryson and Karen Limper-Herz. As Exhibition Project Curator, Alan has worked tirelessly, helping to intellectually shape the exhibition, locate and research objects, and select and organise the exhibits, always with the utmost dedication, enthusiasm and reassuring calmness. The exhibition has benefitted greatly from Karen's expertise on sixteenth-century printed books and more broadly from her vast curatorial experience and steadfast commitment and support.

Finally, I am deeply thankful to Sir John Ritblat for his generous sponsorship of the exhibition. I am also grateful to The John S Cohen Foundation, The Strathmartine Trust and all supporters who wish to remain anonymous for grants that have supported the development of the exhibition and catalogue.

CONTRIBUTORS

Simon Adams retired from Strathclyde University in 2011 as Reader in History and is presently completing his biography of Elizabeth I. He has published *Leicester and the Court* (2002), *Household Accounts and Disbursement Books of Robert Dudley, Earl of Leicester* (1995) and eighty articles and essays, the latest in 2017.

Stephen Alford is Professor of Early Modern British History at the University of Leeds. He is the author of six books on the Tudor period, including *Burghley: William Cecil at the Court of Elizabeth I* (2008) and *The Watchers: A Secret History of the Reign of Elizabeth I* (2012).

Amy Blakeway is a lecturer in Scottish History at the University of St Andrews. She has published widely on sixteenth-century Scotland, including on Anglo-Scottish relations, and is the author of *Regency in Sixteenth-Century Scotland* (2015). She is a regular contributor to BBC Radio Scotland's *Time Travels* and collaborated with the British Library in supervising this exhibition's PhD student, Anna Turnham.

Charlotte Bolland is Senior Curator, Research and 16th Century Collections at the National Portrait Gallery, London. She has co-curated a number of exhibitions including *The Real Tudors* (2014), *Les Tudors* (2015) and *The Encounter* (2017), and has published on portraits of Henry Howard, Earl of Surrey and Lady Margaret Beaufort. She is currently working on a large-scale survey project of Tudor portraiture with the Paul Mellon Centre and the Yale Center for British Art.

Alan Bryson is a Project Curator at the British Library. He works on the reigns of Henry VIII and Edward VI, with a particular interest in relations between the crown and the nobility and gentry. He co-edited *Bess of Hardwick's Letters* (2013) and *Verse Libel in Renaissance England and Scotland* (2016).

Andrea Clarke is Lead Curator of Medieval and Early Modern Manuscripts at the British Library. She co-curated the Library's exhibition *Henry VIII: Man and Monarch* in 2009, and *Leonardo da Vinci: A Mind in Motion* in 2019. She is the author of *Love Letters: 2000 Years of Romance* (2011) and *Tudor Monarchs: Lives in Letters* (2017).

John Cooper is Reader in History at the University of York. A graduate of Merton College, Oxford, he is Principal Investigator of the AHRC projects 'St Stephen's Chapel, Westminster' and 'Listening to the Commons', in partnership with Parliament. His book *The Queen's Agent: Francis Walsingham at the Court of Elizabeth I* (2011) was serialised on BBC Radio 4.

Susan Doran is Professor of Early Modern British History at the University of Oxford and Senior Research Fellow at Jesus College and St Benet's Hall, Oxford. She has written numerous books, including *Mary Queen of Scots, An Illustrated Life* (2007) and *Elizabeth I and Her Circle* (2015). This is the fourth exhibition catalogue she has edited.

Thomas S. Freeman is the co-author of *Religion and the Book in Early Modern England: The Making of John Foxe's 'Book of Martyrs'* (2011), and the co-editor of six essay collections on early modern British history and historical films, including *The Tudors and Stuarts on Film* (2009) and *Biography and History in Film* (2019).

John Guy is a Fellow of Clare College, Cambridge. His many books include *Mary Queen of Scots* (2018) and *Elizabeth: The Forgotten Years* (2016). He has presented and contributed to numerous television documentaries and appears regularly on BBC Radio's flagship cultural programmes. The 2018 film *Mary Queen of Scots* was adapted from his biography.

Paulina Kewes is Professor of English and Fellow of Jesus College, Oxford. She has published extensively within and across the fields of early modern literature and history – political, religious, and intellectual – as well as traditional boundaries of period and language. She is completing a monograph entitled *Contesting the Royal Succession in Reformation England: More to Shakespeare* for Oxford University Press.

Karen Limper-Herz is Lead Curator, Incunabula and Sixteenth Century Printed Books, at the British Library. She is Hon. Secretary and Vice-President of the Bibliographical Society of London and a faculty member of the Rare Book School, University of Virginia, USA. She was co-curator of the *Georgians Revealed* exhibition at the British Library in 2013.

Alec Ryrie is Professor of the History of Christianity at Durham University, Professor of Divinity at Gresham College, London, co-editor of the *Journal of Ecclesiastical History* and a Fellow of the British Academy. His books include *Being Protestant in Reformation Britain* (2013), *The Age of Reformation* (2009, 2017) and *Unbelievers: An Emotional History of Doubt* (2019).

Arthur Williamson, a historian of early modern Europe, has produced a number of books, most recently *Apocalypse Then: Prophecy and the Making of the Modern World* (2008). His research concerns the intellectual foundations of secular culture, and he is currently engaged in a large-scale study of political thought under the title, *'The Nation Epidemicall': Scotland and the Rise of Social Theory*.

AG Anna Groundwater, National Museums Scotland

AT Anna Turnham, University of Kent and British Library

AGB Amy Bowles, British Library

BC Barrie Cook, British Museum

ET Edward Town, Yale Center for British Art

JC Jessica Crown, British Library

JD Jane Dawson, University of Edinburgh

MB Michael Bath, University of Glasgow

PA Philip Attwood, British Museum

TW Tim Wales, British Library

LENDERS

The British Library would like to thank the following institutions and individuals for their assistance and generous loans to the exhibition:

Her Majesty The Queen

Archivo General de Simancas, Spain: Isabel Aguirre Landa, Agustín Sánchez Marchán

The American Trust for the British Library

The Bodleian Libraries, University of Oxford: Helen Copping, Ellen Hausner, Maddy Slaven

British Museum, London: Jill Holman, Rachel King

The Duke of Buccleuch & Queensberry, KBE, KT and the Trustees of the Buccleuch Chattels Trust: Kathryn Price

The Chequers Trust: Rodney Melville

Edinburgh University Library: Jill Forrest, Anna Hawkins

Lord Egremont, Petworth House: Alison McCann

Historic Environment Scotland, St Andrews Cathedral Museum: Sara Charnley-Sellar, Ross Irving, Beth Spence, Rona Walker

Lambeth Palace Library, London: Fiona Johnston, Giles Mandelbrote

The National Archives, Kew: Katy Mair, Kate Narewska, Ishwant Sahota, Ruth Selman

National Library of Scotland, Edinburgh: Ulrike Hogg, Sally Todd

National Museums Scotland, Edinburgh: Rebecca Drummond, Anna Groundwater, David Forsyth

National Portrait Gallery, London: Charlotte Bolland, Sean Crawford

National Records of Scotland, Edinburgh: Linda Ramsay, Alison Rosie

National Trust, Hardwick Hall: Susan Paisley, Nigel Wright

Parochial Church Council of St Mary's Church, Preston St Mary, Suffolk: Janet Martin

Private Lenders

The Marquess of Salisbury, Hatfield House: Vicki Perry, Sarah Whale

The Scottish Catholic Heritage Collections Trust (Blairs Museum): Bishop Joseph Toal, Mary McHugh, Amy Miller, Elinor Vickers

Victoria and Albert Museum, London: Silvija Banic, Sara Mittica

Waddesdon (Rothschild Family): Naomi Richards, Pippa Shirley, Colette Warbrick

CONVENTIONS

Names: The spelling 'Stuart' is used for Mary, Queen of Scots' second husband Henry Stuart, Lord Darnley, while the spelling 'Stewart' is used for all Scots. Established English versions of foreign names such as William of Orange and Philip II of Spain are used but otherwise foreign names are given in the form used by the individual, for example, François Clouet. Foreign titles have been anglicised.

Spelling: The original spelling and orthography of manuscripts and printed texts have been retained in quotations in entries. For ease of reading, contractions have been silently expanded. The spelling and capitalisation of book titles and quotations have been modernised in the essays. Translations and reconstructions of missing or damaged text as well as inferred details in imprints are given in square brackets.

Dates: Dates are given in the old style Julian calendar, which was in use in England and Scotland in the sixteenth century. However, it is assumed that the calendar year began on 1 January, not on 25 March (Lady Day) as was customary in this period. Life dates are included in the index.

SCOTLAND

Perth ●

Stirling ● ● Lochleven

Linlithgow ● ● Edinburgh

Berwick

● Durham

York ● ENGLAND

● Sheffield

Tutbury ● ● Wingfield

Chartley ●

● Fotheringhay

GAELIC IRISH

● Dublin

IRELAND

Woodstock ● London ●

● Tilbury

THE NETHERLANDS

● Antwerp

● Calais ● Brussels

● Paris

LORRAINE

FRANCHE-COMTÉ

FRANCE

SAVOY

The kingdom of Scotland

The kingdoms of England and Ireland

The Gaelic Irish lordships

The kingdom of France

The territories of Philip II of Spain

NAVARRE

SPAIN

PORTUGAL

FAMILY TREE

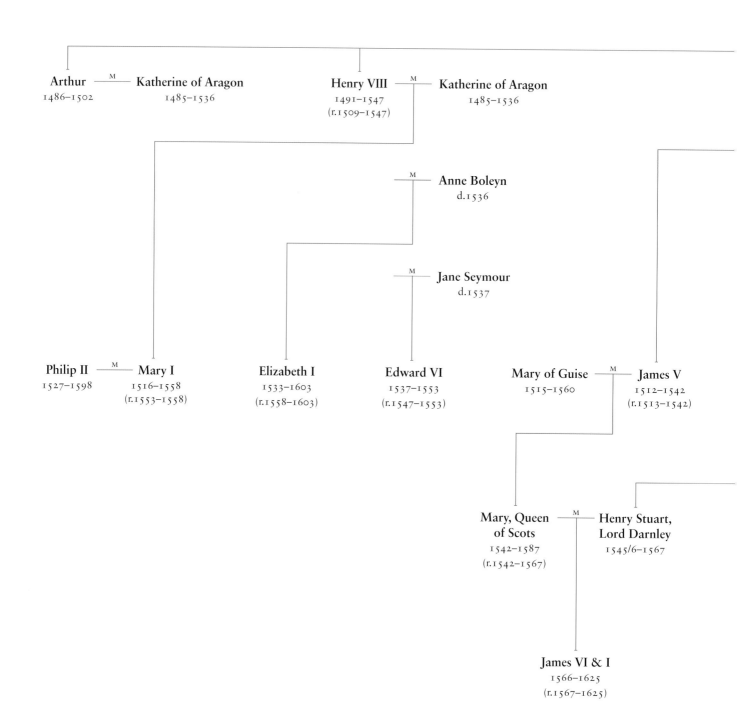

Edmund Tudor
d.1456
— M —
Margaret Beaufort
1443–1509

Arthur
1486–1502
— M —
Katherine of Aragon
1485–1536

Henry VIII
1491–1547
(r.1509–1547)
— M —
Katherine of Aragon
1485–1536

— M —
Anne Boleyn
d.1536

— M —
Jane Seymour
d.1537

Philip II
1527–1598
— M —
Mary I
1516–1558
(r.1553–1558)

Elizabeth I
1533–1603
(r.1558–1603)

Edward VI
1537–1553
(r.1547–1553)

Mary of Guise
1515–1560
— M —
James V
1512–1542
(r.1513–1542)

Mary, Queen
of Scots
1542–1587
(r.1542–1567)
— M —
Henry Stuart,
Lord Darnley
1545/6–1567

James VI & I
1566–1625
(r.1567–1625)

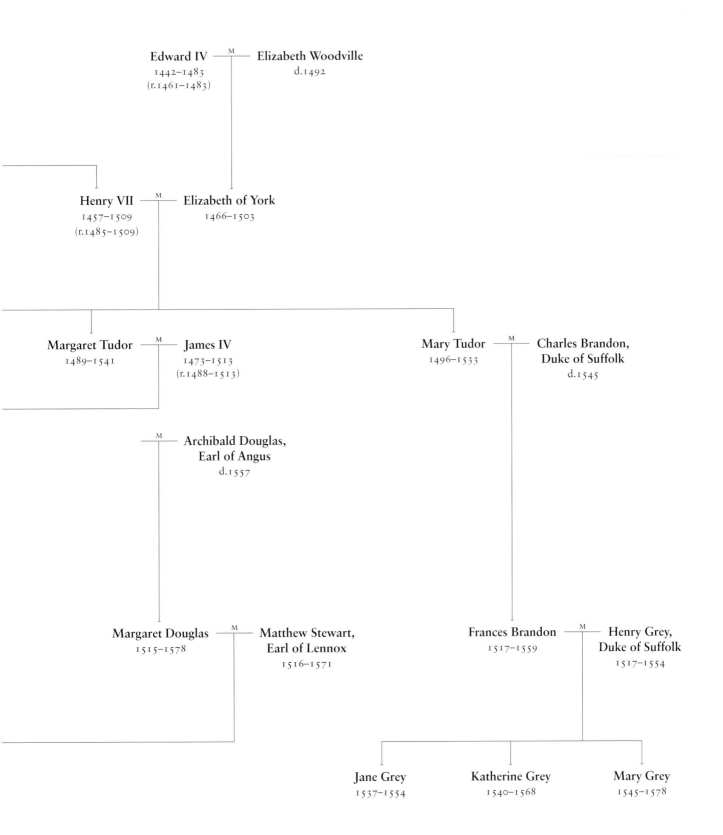

Edward IV — M — Elizabeth Woodville
1442–1483   d.1492
(r.1461–1483)

Henry VII — M — Elizabeth of York
1457–1509   1466–1503
(r.1485–1509)

Margaret Tudor — M — James IV
1489–1541   1473–1513
                      (r.1488–1513)

Mary Tudor — M — Charles Brandon,
1496–1533   Duke of Suffolk
                      d.1545

M — Archibald Douglas,
     Earl of Angus
     d.1557

Margaret Douglas — M — Matthew Stewart,
1515–1578   Earl of Lennox
                      1516–1571

Frances Brandon — M — Henry Grey,
1517–1559   Duke of Suffolk
                      1517–1554

Jane Grey   Katherine Grey   Mary Grey
1537–1554   1540–1568   1545–1578

Your good Sistar and Cousin

Elizabeth R

Vostre tres desolee plus proche Cousine et
affectionnee sœur

MARIE R

INTRODUCTION

John Guy

'Mary Queen of Scots got her head chopped off' – still a children's skipping rhyme in Scotland – is one fact about Elizabeth I and Mary that everyone knows. It is a story where we can be confident of the final scene at Fotheringhay, but might struggle to appreciate the ins and outs of the preceding drama.

This book, like the exhibition it accompanies, seeks to refresh and retell the story of these remarkable women, using the original sources and the latest research – the many thrills and spills along the way may make you want to believe it could all have ended differently. It is a story of how the infinite curiosity these two 'British' queens had for one another turned to mutual suspicion and ended in lethal enmity: a tale of the inwardly wary, outwardly sisterly friendship of two women 'so nearly tied' to each other 'in blood and neighbourhood', as Elizabeth later put it, that they had once exchanged verses and lovers' tokens as if contemplating 'marrying' each other (cat. 107). It is a story of how sovereign rulers who never met were forced to conduct their relationship through their letters or the speeches of their ambassadors.

And it is a story about the very different ways in which Mary and Elizabeth set about dealing with the vexed question of marriage. Mary married three times, Elizabeth never. Both queens, at different times, had their reputations called into question for alleged sexual indiscretions.

As the daughter of James V of Scotland and his second wife, the French noblewoman Mary of Guise, the Scottish queen was the granddaughter of Henry VIII's elder sister Margaret and thus Elizabeth's cousin. She had the virtue of being incontestably legitimate, whereas at the precise moment Elizabeth was conceived, Henry VIII's marriage to her mother Anne Boleyn was clandestine and bigamous. From the beginning, Elizabeth and Mary had much in common by way of rank, education and privilege. Each believed she had been called to rule her country by God. Each was the only other woman on the planet who could guess what it was really like to be in the other's shoes. And yet their characters and experiences from childhood onwards differed profoundly.

Mary was generous, charismatic and far more politically astute than she usually receives credit for – she was notably successful in Scotland for the first four years of her personal rule until she married Henry Stuart, Lord Darnley – but could be too trusting. Gregarious as well as glamorous, she rarely stood on ceremony as long as her 'estate regal' was respected. She was a natural conversationalist – 'no plain speech seemeth to offend her, if she think the speaker thereof to be an honest man'. Although devoutly confident in her Catholicism, she retained her stance as a tolerant *politique* for Scottish audiences even for the bulk of her nineteen-year imprisonment in England.

Elizabeth was always steelier and more reserved, forged in the fire of her tribulations during the reigns of her half-brother Edward VI and half-sister Mary I. Particularly searing were her experiences in Edward's reign, when her stepfather, the seductively handsome, recklessly ambitious Sir Thomas Seymour, molested her, and after Sir Thomas Wyatt's Rebellion early in Mary I's reign when, terrifyingly, she was arrested, sent to the Tower of London, then held under guard at Woodstock in Oxfordshire for almost a year.

Unlike Elizabeth, the young Scottish queen – with a notable exception when she was 4¾ – enjoyed a charmed and secure youth. In fear of abduction by the English after the Battle of Pinkie (1547), her mother smuggled her by night to Inchmahome Priory, a remote spot on an island in the Lake of Menteith – but within a year she would be shipped to the safety of France. Brought up at the French court in unashamed luxury under the watchful eye of Henry II and her Guise uncles, Mary largely coasted through her education apart from poetry and music, preferring riding and outdoor sports. Other passions included dancing and embroidery, so that at Holyroodhouse, after her return to Scotland in 1561, she danced almost every night, often until after midnight, for which she would be castigated by the Calvinist preacher John Knox, who saw it as a depravity 'more like to the bordell[o] than to the comeliness of honest women', an invitation to idolatry and sexual transgression.

Elizabeth, unlike Mary, was bookish as a teenager: she spent much of her time reading – her favourites seem to have been Italian and French

MARY WAS GENEROUS, CHARISMATIC AND FAR MORE POLITICALLY ASTUTE THAN SHE USUALLY RECEIVES CREDIT FOR

texts. She often read the Bible and occasionally wrote verses. At Woodstock, she passed her time reading and translating the Latin classics. As a fully mature adult, she made line-by-line translations from Latin into English from Tacitus's *Annals* and 'The Consolation of Philosophy' by the early sixth-century writer Boethius. Although she was a Protestant, her beliefs retained many traditional elements such as veneration of the cross, and after her accession she would set up a crucifix in the Chapel Royal, to the disgust of more radical Protestants.

Encouraged by Robert Dudley, her dashing favourite and Master of the Horse, Elizabeth grew to enjoy outdoor sports, chiefly hunting, along with the theatre. Never much interested in horses as a teenager, she took a keener interest in her late twenties, when she demanded her agent in Antwerp, Sir Thomas Gresham, send her a Turkish riding horse from Germany, along with large quantities of silk stockings and 'collars' for her 'headpieces of silk'. Like Mary, she loved music and dancing, and was herself an accomplished performer at the virginals.

MARY'S FIRST LETTER TO a foreign prince was addressed to Elizabeth's half-sister Mary I. Written in French, it is neatly copied out between lines carefully etched into the paper by a stylus. 'May it please God', penned the young queen of Scots in her very best handwriting, 'there shall be, if God pleases, a perpetual memory of two queens having been joined together at one time in this Isle in inviolate amity as they also are in blood and near lineage'. But when in 1558 Mary married the Dauphin Francis and a year later became queen consort of France, everything changed. By then, Elizabeth was crowned queen of England and Ireland, and her chief minister and backstairs fixer, Sir William Cecil, feared what he saw as the colonising project of the Catholic Guise family, who sought to subsume England and Scotland as part of a 'Franco-British' empire. As Mary was the cornerstone of the Guise dynastic project, Cecil demonised her as his – and Protestant England's – most dangerous adversary. His mantra became Elizabeth's 'safety': he took this line from the moment one of Mary's uncles, Charles of Guise, Cardinal of Lorraine, ordered the royal arms of England to be quartered with those of Scotland and France on his niece's armorial badges and escutcheons (cat. 32).

TO ASSUME THAT MARY WAS ELIZABETH'S MORTAL ENEMY FROM THE BEGINNING OF THE STORY IS COMPLETELY FALSE

And yet, to assume that Mary was Elizabeth's mortal enemy from the beginning of the story is completely false. For much of the time before Anthony Babington's plot to kill Elizabeth in 1586, both 'British' queens were, as it might whimsically be said, fully paid-up members of the women monarchs' trade union.

Mary began to stake out her position even before her first husband, Francis II, died in December 1560. Addressing Sir Nicholas Throckmorton, then English ambassador to France, in August of that year, she said she was impatient to find out more about her 'sister queen' and hoped to make a fresh start in their relations. To this end she would send Elizabeth her portrait, providing the English queen would reciprocate. It was a generous gesture, even if Mary's curiosity about her cousin's true height and appearance partly lay behind it. Declaring herself to be 'the nearest kinswoman she hath, being both of us of one house and stock', Mary called for Elizabeth's 'amity' on the basis of their kinship ties: 'for we be both of one blood, of one country and in one island' (cat. 37).

This was to be a constant refrain of Anglo-Scottish diplomacy after Mary's return to Scotland in August 1561, because her ambition was always to reach a pact with Elizabeth. She wanted Elizabeth to recognise her as her lawful successor should the English queen not marry and have a child. And for much of the time, that was what Elizabeth wanted too. In return, Mary offered to renounce her immediate dynastic claim to the English throne. It was a reasonable, generous offer – one that the ever-vigilant Cecil interpreted as a sign of weakness, causing him to double the stakes. From 1559 onwards, Cecil had an almost messianic Protestant vision of a largely unified British Isles in which Scotland would become a satellite state of England, with Mary excluded from power (cat. 31). When debating the English succession, he put religion ahead of dynastic right, whereas Elizabeth took the opposite approach.

During her personal rule in Scotland (1561–7), Mary proved herself to be a risk-taker, most obviously so in a crisis, although her resolve during the revolt led by her half-brother, James Stewart, Earl of Moray, in protest against her marriage to Darnley in 1565 paid off handsomely. Proving herself to be a warrior queen, she mounted her horse, riding astride at the head of her army, sporting a steel cap on her head and a pistol in her saddle holster. Even John Knox was forced to admit her gallantry. 'Albeit the most part waxed weary,' he wrote, 'yet the Queen's courage increased man-like so much, that she was ever with the foremost.'

Mary routed her rebels. She dealt courageously with the Rizzio plotters in 1566, and a few months later began the most dangerous phase (in Cecil's eyes) of her diplomacy with Elizabeth. It took place after Mary gave birth to her son, the future James VI and I, coming to a head in mid-December around the time Mary held a glittering three-day fête at Stirling to celebrate the infant's baptism. As the negotiations inched forward, Elizabeth went over the heads of her councillors. In what very nearly concluded five years of dynastic duelling, she and Mary discussed terms through their ambassadors for a new treaty of 'inviolable amity'. By the start of 1567, Elizabeth was closer than she had ever been to acknowledging Mary's rights as heir presumptive in England.

Only the first British Gunpowder Plot which resulted in Darnley's murder in the early hours of 10 February 1567 extinguished hopes of this rapprochement. From the moment shortly after 2 am, when the great 'crack' of the explosion roused the citizens of Edinburgh from their beds, things could only go downhill. In May, Mary hastily married James Hepburn, Earl of Bothwell, thereby embroiling herself in the sex scandal of the century. Since it was all but certain that Bothwell's men had lit the fuse setting off the explosion, Mary's third marriage fostered suspicions that she might have colluded in the murder plot, even perhaps been Bothwell's illicit lover while still married

DURING HER PERSONAL RULE IN SCOTLAND, MARY PROVED HERSELF TO BE A RISK-TAKER, MOST OBVIOUSLY SO IN A CRISIS

to Darnley. Soon Mary was on trial in the court of public opinion, pilloried in a propaganda campaign masterminded by Darnley's bereaved relatives (cat. 64). By the middle of June, rebels had imprisoned her in the island-castle of Lochleven near Kinross, intent on deposing her.

Her forced abdication followed in July. At first she refused to sign the documents. Seeing her hesitate, Lord Lindsay of the Byres threatened her –

MARY'S THIRD MARRIAGE FOSTERED SUSPICIONS THAT SHE MIGHT HAVE COLLUDED IN THE MURDER PLOT

as Mary's supporters later claimed – that 'if she would not subscribe, he had command to put her presently in the tower'. Only then did a terrified Mary sign. Elizabeth was outraged. She instinctively aligned herself with her fellow monarch, believing that what Mary's enemies had done was abhorrent. They had imprisoned and deposed an anointed queen: a crime against God that was still more heinous than Darnley's assassination, whoever had been behind it.

Elizabeth sent Throckmorton as her crisis ambassador to Scotland to demand Mary's restoration (cat. 68). For much of their time, Elizabeth and Cecil worked more or less harmoniously together – but not where Mary was concerned. So it was that Cecil covertly issued Throckmorton with the only terms on which Mary might be restored. She was to be stripped of her authority, which would be vested in a council of Protestant nobles. She might be styled queen, but only nominally. And at the end of the document, Cecil jotted down these words: 'Athalia interempta per Joas[h] regem' – 'Athalia was killed so that Joash could be king'. It is one of the most revealing comments he ever made. A quotation from the Second Book of Chronicles in the Old Testament, it is one of the very same texts used by Knox to justify the use of armed resistance against 'idolatrous' female rulers. When Cecil made that jotting, he saw the hand of God in history. He read the biblical text (as Knox had done) as a prophecy applying to Mary.

IN MAY 1568 MARY escaped from Lochleven, but her forces were defeated at the Battle of Langside and she fled in a fishing boat across the Solway Firth to appeal for asylum and Elizabeth's aid. Had she stayed in Scotland, she could have capitalised on the growing divisions among her opponents. After the regent Moray was assassinated in 1570, a resurgent queen's party might have enabled her to triumph – but not by remote control from England. Mary's flight was her biggest mistake: it precipitated a crisis in England, where Cecil rightly feared that the northern, still overwhelmingly Catholic counties could rise in her support. And yet the Bothwell marriage comes a close second in the disaster stakes. Given Mary's dire predicament after Darnley's assassination, her decision to take as her 'protector' the one noble consistently loyal to her and her late mother (and who was financially solvent and able to muster an army) is explicable – but marriage was a different matter. The trouble was that Bothwell refused to take no for an answer.

Here we approach the crux. In the sixteenth century, women rulers were damned if they married and damned if they did not. If they did marry, their husbands would expect to become king, as Darnley and Bothwell did – elbowing their wives to the side and triggering a power struggle with ministers and councillors. And yet, if women rulers refused to marry and settle the succession by having a child, their dynasty died with them. Personal choice was decisive: as Mary protested shortly before her wedding to Darnley, 'Not to marry, you know it cannot be for me. To defer it long, many incommodities ensue.' Later, justifying her marriage to Bothwell, she said that her country, 'being divided in factions as it is, cannot be contained in order unless our authority be assisted and set forth by the fortification of a man'.

Elizabeth, by contrast, seems to have resolved never to marry, despite official protestations to the contrary. Even while embroiled in a burgeoning sex scandal herself in 1559–60 while canoodling with the (then) married Robert Dudley, she was dropping hints of her intention to stay single. As she told parliament in 1559, 'And in the end this shall be for me sufficient, that a marble stone shall declare that a queen, having reigned such a time, lived and died a virgin' (cat. 46). Psychologically, she may well have had serious doubts about marriage – not surprisingly, given that her father beheaded her mother after accusing her of adultery and incest, and the abuse she received as a teenager. Nothing, we may suspect, mortified her more than the rumours prevalent when she was 15 that she was pregnant by her stepfather.

GIVEN THE DRAWBACKS OF communicating solely through correspondence or intermediaries, Mary always believed that if she and Elizabeth could only meet and talk woman to woman, they could settle their differences. Such an encounter came tantalisingly close in 1562. Arrangements were made for a meeting at York. And yet so little did Cecil trust his own queen not to make concessions that he was determined to block the idea, and succeeded after the troops of Mary's uncle, Francis, Duke of Guise, travelling from Joinville to Paris, opened fire on several hundred Huguenots worshipping in a barn in Vassy, leaving twenty-three dead. Sir Henry Sidney, Dudley's brother-in-law, had the unenviable task of travelling to Edinburgh, to tell Mary of the cancellation.

Despite Mary's many appeals to Elizabeth for reconciliation, notably one she wrote on Christmas Day 1571 while in custody in Sheffield (cat. 84), she never got her way – but there is a final tease. One of the highlights of this book and exhibition is a rediscovered letter Elizabeth wrote on 31 October 1584 – part of a cache of forty-three documents unseen in public since 1762 – in which she opened her mind, if not her heart, to Mary (cat. 107). Signing at the top with her customary flourish, Elizabeth addressed her letter to Sir Ralph Sadler, Mary's new gaoler, who was to read it aloud to her. In it, Elizabeth levelled sharp criticism against her cousin's suggestion that she should set aside the 'jealousy and mislike' she felt for her, blaming Mary alone for the breach.

MARY ALWAYS BELIEVED THAT IF SHE AND ELIZABETH COULD ONLY MEET AND TALK WOMAN TO WOMAN, THEY COULD SETTLE THEIR DIFFERENCES

'For she herself knoweth (wherein we appeal unto her own conscience) how great contentment and liking we had for a time of her friendship'. All the same, Elizabeth held out an olive branch: her goodwill, she continued, was not yet utterly spent despite Mary's 'sundry hard and dangerous courses held towards us'. Should Mary wish, she should send Claude Nau, one of her secretaries, to her 'to acquaint us with such matter as she shall think meet by him to impart unto us'. He was to bring with him such proposals 'as might work upon good ground a thorough reconciliation between us, which as she seemeth greatly to desire, so should we also be most glad thereof' (cat. 107).

ELIZABETH HELD OUT AN OLIVE BRANCH: HER GOODWILL WAS NOT YET UTTERLY SPENT

Nau did have an audience with Elizabeth; alas no progress was made. But Elizabeth's letter reveals how far she was genuinely torn: outwardly icy, inwardly longing almost as much as her Scottish cousin for a settlement, as her later extreme reluctance to condemn Mary to death even after the Babington affair confirms (cat. 123). A meeting of the two queens during the winter of 1584–5 – had it taken place – may well have ended in acrimony, but to us today, the mere prospect of it still counts among British history's greatest 'what ifs?'.

whither he sayes ...
... me to go to ...
the ... was, and ...
caused the Nurse to
... that I ...
... it is as good ...
... age and as ...
... But when I had
to the said ...
... late and ...
... where as yet ...
of the noble ... of
... man at his ...
countrey It is ...

The Early Years

1533–1560

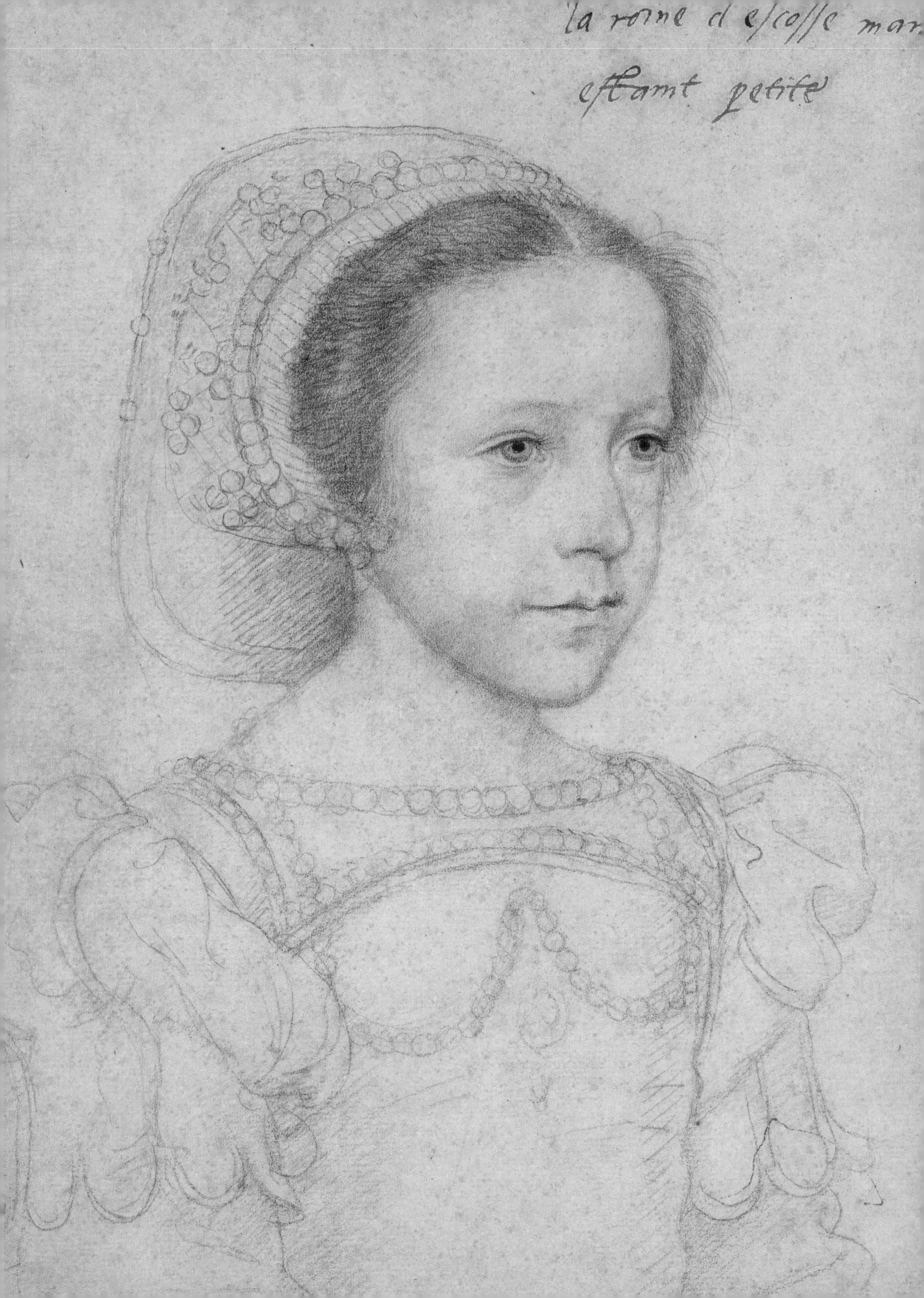
la roine d escosse mar
estant petite

2

ELIZABETH, 'HIGH AND MIGHTY PRINCESS OF ENGLAND' AND MARY, QUEEN OF SCOTS

Alan Bryson

Elizabeth I was born on 7 September 1533 at Greenwich Palace, the first child of Henry VIII and his second wife, Anne Boleyn. She was baptised three days later, named after both her grandmothers. Towards the end of the ceremony the Garter King of Arms cried aloud, 'God of his infinite goodness, send prosperous life and long, to the high and mighty Princess of England Elizabeth', in effect proclaiming her heir presumptive to the throne. At that moment Mary, Henry's daughter with Katherine of Aragon, was displaced as illegitimate.

Elizabeth was the granddaughter of Henry VII and his wife Elizabeth. As Earl of Richmond, Henry had been the leader of the house of Lancaster during the later stages of the Wars of the Roses against the house of York. On 22 August 1485, he defeated and killed the Yorkist Richard III at the battle of Bosworth. Afterwards he married Richard's niece, Elizabeth of York, greatly enhancing his own claim to the throne and uniting the red rose of Lancaster and the white rose of York (cat. 1). They had four surviving children, their second son becoming Henry VIII.

The island of Great Britain was divided between the kingdoms of England and Scotland. However, England claimed suzerainty (overlordship) of Scotland, using its claim as grounds for the domination of Britain. For centuries, the Scots successfully resisted English invasions, forming the 'Auld Alliance' with France, England's long-standing enemy. In return for its support, France used Scotland as a back door to neutralise England whenever the two countries were at war. To draw the Scots away from the French, England oscillated between offering inducements and resorting to coercion. The triangular politics connecting France, England and Scotland shaped relations between the contending British kingdoms until 1560. Additionally, kings of England were first lords, then (after 1541) monarchs, of Ireland. However, throughout the sixteenth century much of Ireland was ruled by Gaelic chieftains, many of whom only nominally recognised English authority or rejected it altogether.

England was wealthier and more powerful than Scotland. Around the time of Elizabeth I's birth, its population was about 2.5 million to Scotland's more than 500,000, and its crown revenue was twenty-one times higher. Anglo-Scottish relations were not universally hostile. In a period of economic expansion and rapid population growth, much trade passed between the two

> FOR THE REMAINDER OF HIS REIGN HENRY ALWAYS ACKNOWLEDGED ELIZABETH AS HIS DAUGHTER

kingdoms, and significant numbers of Scots emigrated south. The great majority of English and Scots were native born. Nonetheless, 'strangers' (immigrants) settled in both countries, either because they filled a labour gap or because they brought valuable skills. Most of these immigrants originated from neighbouring countries. Individuals from further afield, like the Spanish goldsmith Martín Soza, who was probably a *converso* (a Jewish convert to Christianity) and became sheriff of York, or the African trumpeter John Blanke, who served Henry VII and Henry VIII, were exceptional.

WITHIN MONTHS OF SUCCEEDING to the throne in 1509, Henry VIII married his brother's widow, Katherine of Aragon. They had a daughter and three sons, who were all miscarried, stillborn or died prematurely, before the birth of Mary in 1516. Recognising that they would have no more children, Henry stopped sleeping with Katherine in 1524. In order to marry his new love Anne Boleyn, he took the first secret steps in May 1527 towards obtaining an annulment – a declaration that no legal marriage had taken place. Interpreting Leviticus 20:21 ('If a man takes his brother's wife, it is an unclean thing: he has uncovered his brother's nakedness: they shall be without children') to mean that Katherine and he had suffered divine punishment, Henry petitioned to overturn the papal dispensation of 1503 that had permitted their marriage. Unfortunately for him, in 1527 Katherine's nephew, the Holy Roman Emperor Charles V, had invaded Italy and his mutinous army sacked Rome, leaving Pope Clement VII with little choice but to play for time by delaying legal proceedings on the king's 'Great Matter'.

As his legal impasse grew, Henry focused on overturning papal primacy as his only means of freeing himself from Katherine. Led by Thomas Cranmer and Thomas Cromwell, his government moved in a revolutionary direction, fundamentally reshaping the relationship between Church and state. The Reformation parliament passed a series of acts between 1529 and 1536 that broke with the papacy and founded an independent Church of England. The 1533 Act of Appeals declared that 'this realm of England is an empire, and so hath been accepted in the world, governed by one supreme head and king'. The following year, the Act of Supremacy recognised that Henry had always been Supreme Head of the Church and gave him almost unlimited power over it. All this was forced through because of the king's domineering will. But it was only possible because England had one of the most centralised systems of government in western Europe, one in which much power was concentrated on the person of the king, who was expected to rule directly.

While Henry hesitated over whether marriage to Anne could be valid while Katherine lived, it was probably Anne who forced the matter in autumn 1532 by agreeing to consummate their relationship after exchanging vows. Once she became pregnant, they were secretly married in January 1533. A few months later, Henry and Cromwell pushed the Act of Appeals through parliament and Cranmer declared Henry's marriage to Katherine invalid. A heavily pregnant Anne was crowned queen that summer. As the birth of Henry and Anne's child approached, letters were prepared announcing 'the deliverance and bringing forth of a prince'. These had to be amended to read 'princess' when a girl was born instead (cat. 2).

Elizabeth was Henry's third surviving child. He had one acknowledged bastard, Henry Fitzroy, and he and Anne must have expected that they would be blessed in future by the birth of healthy sons. Two miscarriages – both male – followed, bringing about Anne's fall from power. In May 1536 she was tried for adultery with multiple men, including her own brother, George Boleyn, Viscount Rochford. Although she defended herself courageously and persuasively against the charges, conviction was a foregone conclusion and Anne was beheaded on 19 May. A few days later Henry married one of her former ladies-in-waiting, Jane Seymour. The 1536 Succession Act confirmed the annulment of both his previous marriages, made his daughters Mary and Elizabeth illegitimate, and explicitly excluded both from succeeding to the throne. It also empowered Henry to limit further the succession in future by letters patent or his will, signed with his own hand. Yet while Anne's name was effaced for the remainder of his reign, Henry always acknowledged Elizabeth as his daughter.

Although Henry had broken with Rome, he had not broken with Catholicism. Indeed, he was hostile to the Lutheran heresy spreading across northern Europe. But Protestant beliefs shaped the English Reformation, in particular the drive to diminish the wealth and power of the Church and to attack the cult of saints – both of which were motivations for the dissolution of the monasteries. The publication in 1539 of the Great Bible (cat. 24), moreover, made the Word of God widely available in English. Most significantly, even after the birth of a legitimate son, Edward, with Jane Seymour in 1537, Henry never sought reconciliation with Rome. His royal supremacy would be his permanent legacy. Yet he remained Catholic until the end, unlike a growing number of his subjects, who embraced Protestantism.

Mary, Queen of Scots was born on 8 December 1542 at Linlithgow Palace, the third child of James V and his second wife, Mary of Guise. Six days later, in a state of physical and mental exhaustion, James died, most likely of dysentery or cholera. Mary was baptised the following month, named for her mother and, because she had been born on the Feast of the Immaculate Conception, for the Virgin Mary.

Mary's grandfather, James IV, had reversed decades of Anglo-Scottish hostility by signing the Treaty of Perpetual Peace in 1502 and the following year marrying Margaret, elder daughter of Henry VII and Elizabeth of York. Peace was short-lived, however, and Scotland was drawn into the growing conflict between England and France. In support of the Auld Alliance, James invaded England in 1513 but was defeated and killed at the Battle of Flodden, leaving the 1-year-old James V to succeed him. Through his mother, James V had a claim to the English throne, and this fact more than any other shaped his often acrimonious relationship with his uncle, Henry VIII. With too little to show from courting Henry, who would not acknowledge him in the English succession, James gravitated towards France. In 1538 he married Mary of Guise, eldest child of Claude, first Duke of Guise, and Antoinette de Bourbon. They had sons in 1540 and 1541, but both died young.

In 1542, war broke out between England and Scotland. What was intended as an opportune raid into northern England by the Scottish army proved disastrous when it was trapped and forced to surrender at the Battle of Solway Moss. James died within weeks. Henry seized this golden opportunity in summer 1543 to compel the Scots to accept the Treaty of Greenwich, which ended the war and arranged a marriage between Mary, Queen of Scots and Henry's heir apparent, Edward (cat. 8). It guaranteed Scottish independence and made provision for any offspring to succeed to the realms of England, Ireland and Scotland.

As was traditional, Mary was brought up with her mother at Stirling Castle. She had been removed from the custody of James Hamilton, second Earl of Arran, who was then regent. Arran, a great-grandson of James II, had himself recognised as heir presumptive and backed the English alliance. During an audience with the English ambassador, Sir Ralph Sadler, in March 1543 Mary of Guise denied Arran's claims that her daughter was sickly, Arran's implication being that Mary's reign would be short and he would soon succeed as king. She convinced Sadler; on being shown the infant, he wrote to Henry, 'it is as goodly a child as I have seen of her age and as like to live with the grace of God' (cat. 7). Mary of Guise was determined to safeguard her daughter's crown and preserve French interests in Scotland.

Over the course of 1543, Scottish enthusiasm for the treaty waned. By the time Mary was crowned queen at Stirling Castle on 9 September, Arran had reconciled with Mary of Guise. The Scots openly repudiated the treaty at the end of the year. Henry retaliated by sending an army the following spring under the command of his brother-in-law, Edward Seymour, Earl of Hertford. Hertford looted and torched Edinburgh, Holyrood Abbey and Holyroodhouse (cat. 9). The following year he led another massive raid into Scotland.

AFTER ANNE'S EXECUTION, ELIZABETH had been neglected by her father. Nonetheless, he summoned both his daughters to court from time to time, as for example when they participated in the baptism of their brother, Edward. Between 1536 and 1542 Elizabeth resided with one or both siblings.

Following Henry's marriage to Katherine Parr in summer 1543, Mary joined the new queen's household, but Edward and Elizabeth continued to live together until almost the end of the reign.

In 1544 Edward's household was reorganised and his formal education began in earnest under one of Cambridge's brightest humanists, John Cheke. This reorganisation had a profound impact on Elizabeth's own education and religion. Until then, Katherine Ashley had taught her needlework, deportment, manners and music, while John Picton seems to have begun her studies in French, Italian and perhaps Latin. In 1545, partly through Cheke's influence, the Cambridge scholar William Grindal was appointed to teach Elizabeth the *studia humanitatis*. This focused on learning grammar, history, moral philosophy and, above all, rhetoric (the art of persuasion) by reading the classical authors who first perfected it. To that end Elizabeth was taught Latin and Greek, but the aim was translation and not to teach her original composition such as befitted a future king.

Elizabeth made a number of translations as New Year's gifts, including one in December 1545 of Katherine Parr's *Prayers and Meditations* from English into Latin, French and Italian. She gave this translation to her father (cat. 12). After Grindal's death, she petitioned for a suitable replacement and the brilliant Latinist Roger Ascham was appointed. Jean Belmaine taught French to Edward and Elizabeth, and Giovanni Battista Castiglione continued her Italian. She knew some Spanish too. Grindal and Belmaine were responsible for forming Elizabeth's beautiful italic hand, possibly along with Castiglione. The fruit of her education was a remarkable fluency in speech and writing that served her brilliantly throughout her life.

Henry could have had little doubt about the Protestant leanings of Edward and Elizabeth's tutors. Perhaps he hoped, because of the decisive role education might play in shaping Edward's religion, that his choice of Cheke would safeguard the royal supremacy against Rome. And so it proved. Edward and Elizabeth – unlike their sister Mary – grew up Protestant. Elizabeth's religion seems to have been influenced also by Katherine Parr. Elizabeth practised a distinctly pre-Reformation form of piety, focused on prayer, especially in veneration of the cross, at variance with the more advanced Protestantism of her brother.

As a precaution against Henry dying on campaign in a new war against France, the 1544 Succession Act restored Mary and Elizabeth to the succession but did not legitimate them – both remained the king's acknowledged bastards. Henry died in January 1547 after a long illness, having written his last will the previous month (cat. 10). While repeating the existing provisions for the succession, the will placed the offspring of his younger sister, Mary, before those of his elder, Margaret – thus overlooking but not excluding the claim of Mary, Queen of Scots. The new King Edward VI was only 9, and leadership passed to a regency government headed by his uncle, Hertford, who was promoted to Duke of Somerset.

In summer 1547 Somerset invaded Scotland once more, destroying Arran's larger army at the Battle of Pinkie on 10 September (cat. 11).

MARY OF GUISE
WAS DETERMINED
TO SAFEGUARD HER
DAUGHTER'S CROWN
AND FRENCH INTERESTS

He established a series of garrisons in southern and eastern Scotland. An accompanying propaganda campaign heralded the benefits if Edward and Mary married: this godly union, as the English saw it, would unite the British Isles under one monarchy. The Scots turned to France for aid and in August 1548 Mary fled there for safety. Responding positively, Henry II of France sent an army to Scotland and negotiated the Treaty of Haddington with the Scots, whereby his heir, the Dauphin Francis, and Mary were betrothed. Two years later, the English were forced out of Scotland by a French-led army.

After Edward's accession Elizabeth lived in Katherine Parr's household, where the widowed queen's new husband, Thomas, Lord Seymour, was unduly solicitous towards her. On one occasion Katherine helped him as he cut Elizabeth's dress 'in a hundred pieces' as they all frolicked in the garden; on another, she found Elizabeth 'in his arms'. Elizabeth was sent away to form her own household, headed by Thomas Parry and Katherine Ashley, servants she could trust absolutely. She turned at this time for counsel and support to one of the rising stars in her brother's government, William Cecil. In 1549, for example, he suggested to her that she style herself 'Elizabeth, King Edward's sister' as a means of emphasising her royal status without overtly reclaiming the forbidden title of princess.

Edward VI's reign moved the Reformation onwards, attacking images and introducing two prayer books, the first replacing the Mass with an English communion service, but one sufficiently ambiguous so as not to alienate most Catholics, the second unmistakably Protestant. Unlike her sister Mary, Elizabeth embraced the religious changes. Nonetheless, when it became clear in spring 1553 that Edward was dying, he – perhaps on the advice of the most powerful man in his government, John Dudley, Duke of Northumberland – excluded both his sisters from the succession as bastards in order to prevent the Catholic Mary from becoming queen. Instead he named their cousin, the Protestant Lady Jane Grey, who was the granddaughter of Henry VIII's younger sister Mary. Again, the claim of Mary, Queen of Scots was ignored.

NORTHUMBERLAND'S COUP QUICKLY collapsed in the face of overwhelming support for Mary, who was joined by her sister Elizabeth on her triumphal entry into London. After her coronation, however, Mary I kept Elizabeth at arm's length. Mary's first parliament reversed the annulment of her parents' marriage and began dismantling Henry and Edward's reformations. Her decision to marry her cousin, Philip of Spain, triggered Wyatt's Rebellion in January 1554, which aimed to depose Mary in favour of Elizabeth. Despite denying involvement and pleading for an audience with her sister, Elizabeth was imprisoned in the Tower of London and then at Woodstock in Oxfordshire (cats 18, 20). She defended herself against charges of treason with steely resolve and the government was eventually forced to release her. For the remainder of the reign Elizabeth was watched closely but, like Cecil, outwardly conformed to Catholicism, as the drive for reconciliation with Rome culminated in the burning at the stake of 284 Protestants, Cranmer among them (cat. 26). In 1557 England and Scotland joined the war between Philip and Henry II of France on opposing sides, but there was little fighting on the Anglo-Scottish border.

Mary and Philip's marriage proved childless. Recognising that Elizabeth was, in effect, heir apparent, Philip saw to it that she was rehabilitated and tried to make her marry his cousin, Emmanuel Philibert, Duke of Savoy. Resisting the match, Elizabeth bided her time. In November 1558, as Mary lay dying, Philip's ambassador described how 'there is not a heretic or a traitor in all the kingdom who has not joyfully raised himself from the grave in order to come to [Elizabeth's] side', Cecil most prominent among them. Three days after her accession, Elizabeth made Cecil her Principal Secretary.

Elizabeth was crowned at Westminster Abbey on 15 January 1559 by Owen Oglethorpe, Bishop of Carlisle, because more senior, Catholic prelates were unacceptable to her. As was customary, she wore her hair loose, symbolising her fertility; she also wore the coronation robes made for her sister Mary five years earlier. During her procession through London the previous day, several pageants had greeted her as a Protestant queen who would free the realm from Catholicism (cat. 23). A week later parliament assembled for the purpose of re-establishing Protestantism. This legislative programme was resisted by the Catholic bishops and lords, and only after government pressure did parliament pass the Act of Supremacy restoring the royal supremacy and the Act of Uniformity establishing a new Protestant prayer book, largely based on Edward VI's second one but allowing for a belief in the 'corporeal presence' (cat. 27). Office holders had to swear an oath to Elizabeth as Supreme Governor of the Church, thus excluding many Catholics from public life. Curiously, Elizabeth never attempted to amend her father's final Succession Act, which had confirmed her illegitimacy.

ON THE ARRIVAL OF Mary, Queen of Scots in France, Henry II dismissed most of her Scottish servants and had her brought up with his children as a devout Catholic, monitored closely by his wife, Catherine de' Medici, his mistress, Diane de Poitiers, and Mary's grandmother, Antoinette de Bourbon. Mary learned the French language and French court protocol. By the time her mother visited in spring 1550, she could write French fluently. It would become her first language.

Mary had separate tutors – Claude Millot and Antoine Fouquelin – from both the dauphin and his siblings. Her education was more courtly than academic, developing her considerable abilities in music, singing, dancing, needlework and horsewomanship. She was being trained as Francis's consort rather than as queen of Scots. On one occasion Millot praised Mary's height, beauty, virtue and grace, but not her learning. In 1553 her uncle, Charles of Guise, Cardinal of Lorraine, decided that, as a reigning queen, she should study rhetoric. To that end she was taught Latin and perhaps a little Greek. In the preface to his work *La Rhétorique Françoise* (1557), Fouquelin commended Mary's progress in learning languages (cat. 16). After her return to Scotland, she was able to deliver an oration to parliament in 1563 'with a very good grace' but was apparently unable to hold her own on other occasions in argument against the Protestant reformer John Knox.

Henry II boasted 'I have pacified … Scotland, which I hold and possess with such authority and obedience as I do in France,' but he also sought a 'perpetual union' with England through Mary's claim to the English throne. In 1554 Arran was persuaded to surrender the regency to Mary of Guise, in return for French recognition as heir presumptive (cat. 15). In April 1558, however, Mary, Queen of Scots secretly gifted her crown to Henry, along with her right to the English and Irish successions, if she should die without legitimate offspring. This agreement excluded Arran. Five days later, Francis and she were married on a magnificent scale at Notre-Dame Cathedral. When the newlyweds quartered the coat of arms of England with their own, they directly challenged Elizabeth's right to rule (cat. 32).

Although Scotland was a personal monarchy, with authority vested in the

Mary, Queen of Scots and her husband Francis II, who were married on 24 April 1558 and became king and queen of France in July the following year.

Hours of Catherine de' Medici.
Bibliothèque Nationale de France,
Paris, MS NAL 82.

15-year-old queen, Mary's secret gift to Henry had still been illegal. Scottish resentment towards the French was growing, especially among the vocal minority of Protestants. In response, John Hamilton, Archbishop of St Andrews, led Catholic reform of the Kirk and ordered a halt to the persecution of Protestants but could not bridge the confessional divide. Matters came to a head in 1559 when, following an iconoclastic sermon delivered in Perth by Knox, a group calling themselves the Lords of the Congregation rebelled against the regent, Mary of Guise; she played for time by granting freedom of worship, while appealing for French military aid.

SCOTTISH RESENTMENT TOWARDS THE FRENCH WAS GROWING

At this critical moment, Henry II died from a wound incurred when jousting and Francis became king of France at the age of only 15. Cecil – whose thinking on the British dimension to English foreign policy had been formed under Somerset – pushed for military intervention to eject the French from Scotland in support of the Lords of the Congregation (cat. 31). Elizabeth's army joined the Lords in laying siege to the strategically important port of Leith, where the French army was bottled up. The garrison surrendered when reinforcements from France failed to arrive (cat. 35). With France itself sliding into religious conflict, in July 1560 the Guise family negotiated the disadvantageous Treaty of Edinburgh. By its terms the Lords of the Congregation would govern jointly with Mary, Queen of Scots and the French army would withdraw. Mary, whose mother had just died, was not consulted. Led by Knox, the Scottish parliament immediately adopted the Protestant Confession of Faith, ended the pope's authority and banned the Mass. Cecil felt vindicated: 'the best worldly felicity that Scotland can have is either to continue in a perpetual peace with ... England or to be made one monarchy with England as they both make but one isle divided from the rest of the world'.

3

QUEENSHIP AND GENDER

Susan Doran

British history would have been very different had Mary, Queen of Scots and Elizabeth I been born male. Almost certainly Elizabeth's mother Anne Boleyn would have avoided execution while she, as a he, would have been first in line for the throne after the death of Henry VIII.

With no reigns of Edward VI and Mary I, the English Reformations would have taken another course. In Scotland Mary, as a prince, would not have been such a great matrimonial prize so there would have been no Rough Wooing, no royal flight to France and possibly no Lords of the Congregation, since they were in part reacting to the subjection of Scotland to France following Mary's marriage to the dauphin.

Counterfactuals aside, what was the relevance of their gender in British history? How did it affect the two queens' lives and reigns? Obviously, the birth of a girl was a setback to both sets of parents: the dying James V reputedly said his dynasty which came with a girl would end with a girl; Henry VIII, who had put such great store on siring a son, tried to be more sanguine but his disappointment was palpable (cat. 2). Nonetheless, although queenship was thought undesirable, neither child was barred from the throne because of her gender. Mary became a queen regnant when 6 days old and Elizabeth, aged 10 years, was brought back into the succession by act of parliament, a position that was restated in her father's will of December 1546 (cat. 10). Salic law, which excluded females from dynastic succession, did not apply in sixteenth-century Britain, as it did in France.

Despite this, the fiery Protestant preacher John Knox denied the right of women to rule in *The First Blast of the Trumpet against the Monstrous Regiment of Women* (1558). This prohibition was on the grounds that female rule disobeyed God's law, since women's subservience to men was ordained in Genesis and upheld by the Apostle Paul. Moreover, in Deuteronomy 17:15, Knox explained, God had laid down that kings should be men 'chosen from thy brethren'. Ancient writers, continued Knox, agreed. Aristotle, for example, taught that women's nature made them unsuitable for leadership since they were weak, foolish, impatient, inconstant, cruel and 'phrenetic'. Female rule, therefore, was the 'subversion of good order, of all equity and justice'.

Although Knox presented this as a universal rule, his targets in 1558 were 'our mischievous Maries', the Catholic queen of England and regent of Scotland. Hence, when the Protestant Elizabeth came to the throne, Knox quickly backtracked and argued that 'God's great mercy maketh that lawful unto her, which both nature and God's law deny to all women'. Naturally according to Knox, this divine dispensation did not apply to the Catholic Mary, Queen of Scots. As recorded in his *History of the Reformation*, the preacher told Mary during an interview at Holyroodhouse: 'If the realm finds no inconvenience from the government of a woman, that which they approve shall I not further disallow than within my own breast, but shall be as well content to live under Your Grace as [the Apostle] Paul was to live under [the tyrannical Emperor] Nero.' Knox also claimed that Mary's response to his hectoring in this and similar interviews was to burst into tears, thereby betraying her female weakness and validating his point of view (cat. 44).

Knox's repudiation of female rule was later endorsed by the humanist scholar George Buchanan, another strict Calvinist. Buchanan used historical arguments rather than scripture in making his case. His aim, though, was the same: to justify resistance to Catholic rulers who happened to be women. So, in *The History of Scotland* (written in the 1560s but first published in Latin in 1582), he vindicated Mary's deposition in part by asserting that Scotland was an elective monarchy that excluded queens regnant. As was to be expected, those who supported Mary took the opposite tack. John Leslie, Bishop of Ross, Mary's loyal long-term servant, not only defended her reputation and attacked her deposition but also provided a refutation of Knox's denunciation of female rule (cat. 103). Of course, Catholics who opposed Elizabeth I on religious grounds could not employ the same arguments as either Knox or Buchanan, for they had approved her half-sister's right to rule and the potential Catholic replacement for her was also a woman. They preferred to label her, instead, as a tyrannical and ungodly queen, such as Jezebel and Athalia in the Old Testament, who were removed by God.

How prepared were Elizabeth and Mary to rule? As royalty, they had both been offered first-class educations in the liberal arts, Latin and modern languages. Elizabeth also learned Greek. Yet unlike Prince Edward of England,

> WOMEN'S NATURE MADE THEM UNSUITABLE FOR LEADERSHIP SINCE THEY WERE WEAK, FOOLISH, IMPATIENT, INCONSTANT, CRUEL AND 'PHRENETIC'

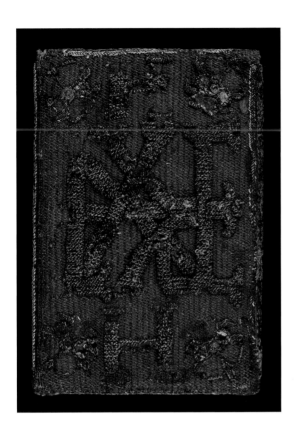

A binding embroidered by Elizabeth as the cover for her trilingual translation of Queen Katherine Parr's *Prayers and Meditations* (cat. 12). Her father's initials are entwined with those of her stepmother in the centre, and a white rose, the emblem of her paternal grandmother, is stitched in each corner.

British Library, Royal MS 7 D x.

their education was not designed to prepare them for government. From the evidence we have, Mary's immersion in the classics was limited, while Elizabeth used her foreign languages to focus on translations of prayers and devotional works (cat. 12) until it seemed likely that she would succeed her half-sister as queen; only then did her Latin tutor Roger Ascham start training her in Ciceronian rhetorical composition and Greek oratory. Furthermore, Elizabeth and Mary were both taught traditional 'feminine' skills such as embroidery: Elizabeth's handiwork can be seen in the ornate covers of the books she presented to her father and stepmother Katherine Parr as New Year's gifts (cat. 12). Mary's skill is evident in the needlework she undertook while under house arrest in England (cat. 96).

Once they began their rule, both queens assumed all the powers and prerogatives of their male predecessors. At their coronations they were anointed, a ritual that transformed them from private individuals into public figures with divinely bestowed powers of majesty, even sanctity. Hence Elizabeth could perform the ritual – customary in England and France – of touching for the 'king's evil' in order to miraculously heal sick people of scrofula. More mundanely, both queens discussed matters of state with their councillors and interacted with foreign ambassadors. When it came to religion, Elizabeth assumed the title of Supreme Governor of the English Church in 1559, in preference to her father and half-brother's title of Supreme Head, possibly because of her gender but more likely because she wanted her half-sister's Catholic bishops and clergy to stay in post and swear the Oath of Supremacy, a tactic that in fact did not work (cat. 27). In any event, Elizabeth behaved as a supreme head in issuing royal injunctions, demanding conformity to the 1559 Prayer Book and suspending her Archbishop of Canterbury, when he refused to obey one of her orders and defied her authority.

FOR HER PART, MARY, Queen of Scots decided it would be unwise to provoke another rebellion by undermining the Protestant settlement of August 1560 and challenging the Scottish Kirk. Instead, as agreed with her counsellors, she heard Mass privately in the Chapel Royal. Her particular assertion of royal authority lay in mounting successful political and military operations against disobedient nobility, both the Earl of Huntly in 1562 and the Earl of Moray and Duke of Châtelherault in the Chaseabout Raid of 1565. At the same time, like Elizabeth, Mary presided over a magnificent court, an essential feature of Renaissance monarchy.

Mary's gender, however, disadvantaged her when she married in Scotland. She chose Henry Stuart, Lord Darnley, for a seemingly sound reason, namely to forward her claim to the English succession, but his attractive appearance and her desire to show independence from Elizabeth were also powerful inducements. It was a terrible error. Once wed, Darnley refused to play a secondary role to his wife. It had previously been agreed that the government would be in their joint names, his appearing before hers on documents and on one existing coin (cat. 56). However, after the wedding, Mary's name was placed first on new coins and he demanded greater prestige and power, not least by being granted the crown matrimonial (making him co-sovereign and giving him the right to keep the throne if she died childless), which Mary rebuffed. Charming before their marriage, he was afterwards quarrelsome and abusive, demanding obedience from his wife and seeking to upstage her as a champion of the Catholic Church. Mary's response was to downgrade her husband. His name now appeared second not first in state papers and on inscriptions of coins. When he was invested with the chivalric Order of St Michael in February 1566, Mary refused him the right to bear royal arms. The conflict between queen and king encouraged faction and ended in two murders.

Worse was to follow with Mary's marriage to James Hepburn, Earl of Bothwell. What prompted the union is disputed, but it does seem likely that she consented to marry the earl only after he had abducted and raped her at Dunbar. Perhaps, because her female honour was compromised, she did not allow the other lords to rescue her from Bothwell. Mary's own justification for the marriage was also gendered, since she claimed she could not continue to rule without the 'fortification of a man' (cat. 65). The result of the Bothwell marriage was sexist abuse and a full-scale rebellion. When Mary was taken back to Edinburgh as a prisoner in June 1567, people in the crowd cried out 'burn the whore'. Typical of the propaganda against Mary was a placard displayed on the streets of Edinburgh that depicted her as a crowned bare-breasted mermaid (a mermaid was then associated with a prostitute) holding a whip made from a dolphin's fin (the dolphin standing for dauphin) and beneath her a hare with the Hepburn crest inside a circle of seventeen swords.

Elizabeth avoided such matrimonial conflicts and political unrest by not marrying. Like her half-sister she had come to the throne as a single woman because her uncertain status as a bastard made her an unattractive matrimonial prospect. On her accession, Elizabeth declared herself married to the realm and afterwards turned down the suitors for her hand. Yet it is debatable how far the issue of gender influenced the rejections. Although it is possible that fear of losing power might have motivated her to remain single, there were also strong religious and political obstacles to marriage with the most viable candidates

A placard displayed in Edinburgh after Mary's surrender at Carberry Hill in July 1567. Denouncing Mary as adulterous, it represents her as a crowned mermaid and John Hepburn, Earl of Bothwell (IH) as a hare.
The National Archives, Kew, SP 52/13 no.60.

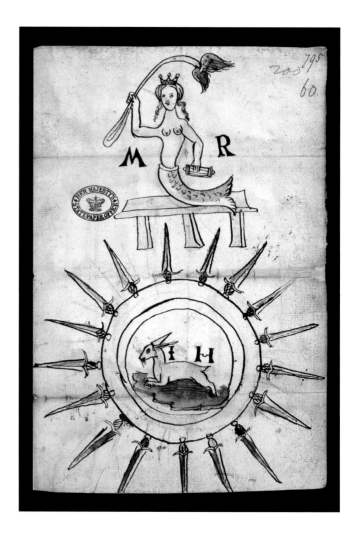

on offer, whether the Catholic princes – Archduke Charles of Austria and the brothers of the French King Charles IX – who demanded a public Mass, or the relatively low-born Protestant subject Lord Robert Dudley, who was suspected of murdering his wife. Whatever the cause, by avoiding the problems of an unpopular and divisive marriage, Elizabeth had to face those of an uncertain succession.

Like Mary, but with less damaging consequences, Elizabeth was subjected to accusations of sexual misconduct. Similarly slandered as a 'naughty woman' and a whore, Elizabeth was repeatedly said to have been the lover of Robert Dudley and borne his bastards. As late as 1585, a woman from Surrey was prosecuted for saying that 'the queen is no maid, and she hath had three sons by the Earl of Leicester'; in 1590, a widow from Essex upped the number of bastards, alleging that two of them were alive and the others burned to death, wrapped up as they were 'in the embers in the chimney which was in the chamber where they were born'. Such comments, made in public, were intended to harm the queen's reputation at a time when chastity was the feminine ideal. Furthermore, a lack of self-control over sexual appetite associated Elizabeth with the licentious and tyrannical queens of myth such as Semiramis.

Elizabeth's virginity might have been questioned in some quarters, but it proved a useful device for courtiers to exploit in the enhancement of her image. When the prospect of her marrying diminished, poets associated her with the powerful classical goddesses Diana and Pallas-Minerva. Painters, likewise, depicted her with an emblem that conveyed her power as a Virgin Queen, the crescent moon of Diana, a sieve connecting her to the vestal virgin Tuccia, and the unspotted white ermine. At a time when England was threatened by a Spanish invasion led by Philip II, the imperviousness of Elizabeth's natural virginal body stood for the impregnable body politic of England. In the patriarchal sixteenth century, it was to be expected that sovereign queens would face difficulties because of their gender. Elizabeth largely overcame them; but the question remains whether it was her gender or bad judgement that undid Mary.

Shared Tudor Inheritance and Childhoods

Elizabeth I and Mary, Queen of Scots were both descended from Henry VII and his wife, Elizabeth of York. Born in 1533, Elizabeth was their grandchild, the daughter of Henry VIII by his second marriage to Anne Boleyn. Nine years younger, Mary was Henry VII and Elizabeth of York's great-grandchild, the granddaughter of their elder daughter Margaret by her first marriage to James IV of Scotland. Mary was the only surviving child of James V and Mary of Guise.

Elizabeth was heir presumptive to the throne at her birth, owing to the bastardisation of her elder half-sister Mary, Henry's daughter by his first marriage to Katherine of Aragon. However, Elizabeth was likewise bastardised and demoted when Anne Boleyn was executed in May 1536. Henceforth she was known as the Lady Elizabeth and rarely came to court before Henry's last marriage to Katherine Parr in 1543.

Mary Stewart succeeded as queen of Scotland when her father James V died on 14 December 1542. Henry VIII immediately attempted to force through a marriage between her and his only son Prince Edward. Known as 'the Rough Wooing', the diplomatic and military interventions in Scotland to achieve this end dominated Anglo-Scottish relations until Mary was whisked off to France in the summer of 1548 and the English had to admit failure.

1

Union of Henry VII and Elizabeth of York
Poem in praise of Henry VII's marriage to Elizabeth of York, by Giovanni Gigli, c.1487.
British Library, Harley MS 336, f. 70r.

Henry, Earl of Richmond's victory over Richard III at the Battle of Bosworth on 22 August 1485 brought an end to the Wars of the Roses, which had been fought for decades between the feuding houses of York and Lancaster. Richmond was crowned King Henry VII, the first monarch of a newly established Tudor dynasty, on Sunday 30 October 1485. Henry, who on his mother's side claimed Lancastrian descent, married Elizabeth of York, eldest daughter of Edward IV and niece of Richard III, on 18 January 1486. The unification of the rival houses of York and Lancaster was symbolised by the Tudor rose – created by combining the white rose of York and the red rose of Lancaster.

This Latin epithalamium – or verses written in praise of the royal couple – was composed by Giovanni Gigli of Lucca, papal official, diplomat and future Bishop of Worcester, and is thought to be the only surviving contemporary literary work celebrating the marriage. The border decoration shows a white greyhound, associated with Henry's father Edmund Tudor, Earl of Richmond, supporting a banner bearing the arms of Henry VII. The flowering rose-plant illustrates the union of the white and red roses from which both Elizabeth I and Mary, Queen of Scots were descended as granddaughter and great-granddaughter respectively of Henry VII. It was this shared Tudor inheritance that led to Elizabeth and Mary's intense rivalry. AC.

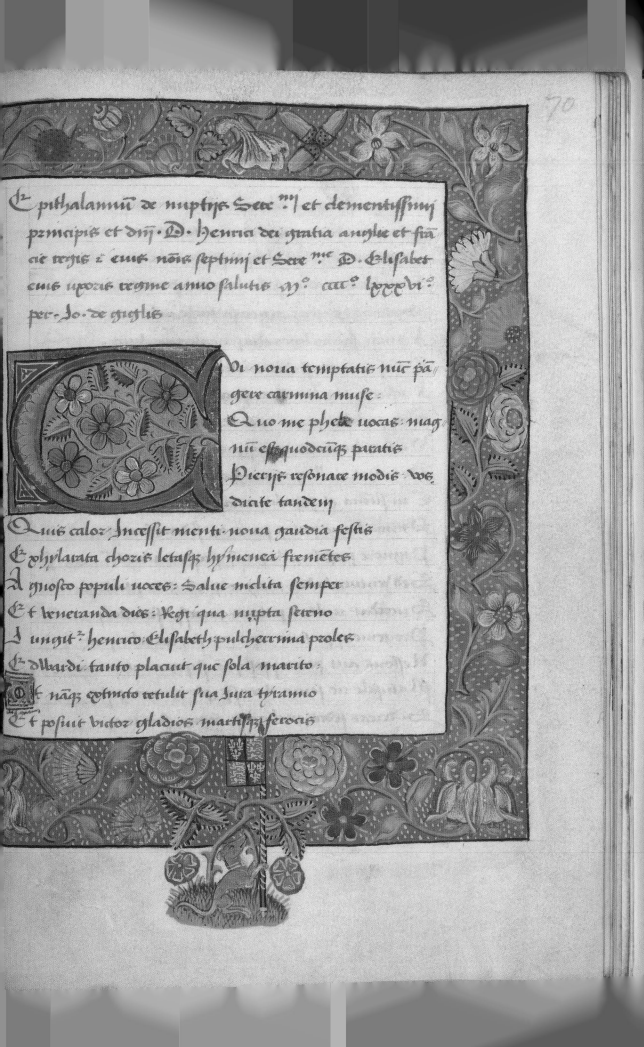

Epithalamiū de nuptijs Sere.mi / et clementissimi
principis et dñi · D · Henrici dei gratia anglie et frā
cie regis i eius nōie septimi et Sere.me D · Elisabet
eius uxoris regine anno salutis M̄° · cccc° lxxxvi°
per · Jo · de Gigliis ·

Ui noua temptatis nūc pā
gere carmina muse:
Quo me phebe uocas: mag
nū est quodcūq̃ paratis
Pieryses resonare modis: ve
dicite tandem

Quis calor Incessit menti · noua gaudia festis
E xhylarata choris letasq̃ hymenea frementes
A gnosco populi uoces: Salue inclita semper
E t ueneranda dies: Regi qua nupta sereno
J ungit˜ henrico Elisabeth pulcherrima proles
E dwardi tanto placuit que sola marito
E t namq̃ coniuncto retulit sua Jura tyranno
E t posuit uictor gladios martisq̃ ferocis

2

The Birth of Princess Elizabeth

Letter from Anne Boleyn, 7 September 1533, Greenwich Palace.

British Library, Harley MS 283, f. 75r.

In the summer of 1533, as the birth of Henry VIII and Anne Boleyn's child approached, Sir John Russell wrote to Viscount Lisle, Lord Deputy of Calais, that he had not seen the king 'meryer of a great while than he is now'. Henry's greatest desire was for a male heir and the court astrologers and physicians were predicting the birth of a son. The king believed that his first marriage to Katherine of Aragon, widow of his elder brother Arthur, had contravened divine law and that her failure to provide a healthy male heir had been a clear sign of God's wrath. Now, after breaking with the Roman Catholic Church in order to make Anne his wife and queen, Henry was certain that he was going to be blessed with a longed-for son, whom he planned to name Edward or Henry.

Anne gave birth to a daughter around 3 pm on Sunday 7 September 1533 at Greenwich Palace. Dozens of circular letters, such as this one, had been prepared in advance by the royal clerks to announce 'the delyueraunce and bringing furthe of a prince' and requiring the recipient 'to praye for the good helth prosperitie and contynuell preseruacion of the said prince'. Written in Anne's name, the letters had already been sealed with the queen's signet (signet letter) but before the letters could be dispatched to the nobility, leading gentry and the courts of Europe, the word 'prince' had to be hastily amended with the addition of an 's' in order to announce the birth of a 'princes [princess]'.

Anne and Henry were bitterly disappointed with the sex of the baby. The pageants and jousting tournament that had been planned to celebrate the birth of a male heir were cancelled. A *Te Deum* was, however, sung in the royal chapel to thank God for the safe delivery of the baby girl. Three days later, she was named Elizabeth after her two grandmothers, Elizabeth of York and Elizabeth Howard, in an elaborate christening in the Church of the Observant Friars at Greenwich.

Although Elizabeth was proclaimed the king's first legitimate child and heir, Roman Catholics, who refused to accept the validity of Henry and Anne's marriage, considered her a bastard, conceived out of lawful wedlock. Years later, her reign would be shaped by Catholic challenges to the legitimacy of her authority to rule. AC.

3

**Henry VIII, Prince Edward, Princess Mary,
Princess Elizabeth and Will Somer**

Unknown artist, mid-seventeenth century.

This rare Tudor family portrait is a copy of an earlier lost work that was probably painted during the reign of Edward VI. The boy king occupies the centre of the composition, whilst his sisters stand off to the side. The fifth figure has been identified as the court fool Will Somer, who served Henry VIII and Edward VI. He also had a place at Mary I's court and attended Elizabeth I's coronation. Somer was included in a number of group portraits of the Tudor royal family. This raises the question as to whether his presence was intended to serve as a marker of continuity, or to offer the key to an allegorical interpretation of the images. As a later copy without a readily recognisable source, it is difficult to assess the image of Elizabeth, but it provides a glimpse of her as a young woman who was about to endure some of the most difficult years of her life as she moved from the sidelines to the centre of the English court. CB.

4

Anne Boleyn

Queen Elizabeth's locket ring, c.1575.

The Chequers Trust.

This mother-of-pearl ring opens to show the enamelled busts and miniature portraits of two women. One is a profile of Elizabeth I as she looked in the mid-1570s; the other is probably a full-face depiction of Elizabeth's mother, Anne Boleyn, since the likeness is very similar to a portrait medal of her made in 1534. Inside the ring there is a small oval plate of gold ornamented in enamel, with a phoenix rising in flames from an earl's coronet.

When closed, the bezel bears the monogram 'ER', the E made of six table-cut diamonds set over the R of blue enamel. Elizabeth may have been given the ring as a gift from Edward Seymour, Earl of Hertford, since the phoenix was an emblem of his family as well as a device which she used.

Although Anne was executed in May 1536, convicted of adultery and incest, this ring suggests that Elizabeth did not accept the guilty verdict and found ways to honour the memory of her mother. Her subjects followed her lead and many portraits of Anne were commissioned and displayed during Elizabeth's reign. SD.

Inscribed left: IACOBVS QVINTVS SCOTTORVM. REX /
ANNO. AETATIS. SVE. / 28; inscribed right: MARIA.
LOTHORINGIA. ILLIVS. IN. SECVNDIS. NVP / TIIS.
VXOR. ANNO AETATIS SVE. 24; inscribed below:
FATHER AND MOTHER / OF MARY QUEEN OF SCOTS.

5

James V and Mary of Guise

Unknown artist, sixteenth century.

National Trust, Hardwick Hall, NT 1129152.

This double portrait commemorates James V and Mary
of Guise as the parents of Mary, Queen of Scots. Mary of
Guise was the daughter of a duke and a great favourite of
Francis I of France; James was the grandson of Henry VII
of England and the only child of James IV and Margaret
Tudor to survive infancy. Both widowed at a young age,
their marriage in 1538 strengthened the alliance between
France and Scotland. However, it was marked by tragedy:
their two sons died and, following the defeat of the Scots
by the English at the Battle of Solway Moss in 1542, James
became ill, living only long enough to learn that his and
Mary's third child was a daughter.

The artist probably used individual portraits that were
created around the time of their marriage as sources for
the composition; Mary holds a carnation, which was often
used as a symbol of betrothal. Tall, with auburn hair and
grey eyes, Mary cast aside colourful clothing after James's
death and wore mourning black for the rest of her life,
ruling Scotland as regent in her daughter's stead from
1554. CB.

6

Wooden Panel from Linlithgow Palace
Mid-sixteenth century.

National Museums Scotland, Edinburgh, H.KL 61.

This oak panel once decorated a chamber in Linlithgow Palace, West Lothian, the birthplace on 8 December 1542 of Mary, Queen of Scots. Dating either to the final years of the reign of her father, James V, or to her own reign, it displays the royal arms of Scotland twice; the arms below have been deliberately defaced. The arms above show a lion rampant, surmounted by the crest bearing the sword of justice in its right paw and the saltire of Scotland in its left; those below include the fleur-de-lis of France. The arms above show thistles, plants that had been associated closely with the Stewart monarchy since at least 1470. The panel combines medieval and sixteenth-century decorative elements (the flanking pillars have Gothic crocket finials, while the busts of warriors are characteristically Renaissance and similar to the 'Stirling heads' carved for the ceiling of Stirling Castle between 1540 and 1542); and it is evidence of the wealth and sophistication of the Stewart court.

James V carried out substantial building work at Linlithgow during the 1530s, employing French masons and craftsmen, alongside Scots, to complete a magnificent statement of his successful kingship. His palace shared a number of characteristics with French royal residences. It was a symmetrical and uniform courtyard building, dominated by a large fountain dating to about 1535, with richly painted decorative sculptures on the exterior walls. The King's Side, containing his hall, presence chamber and bedchamber, appears to have been located in the western range, and the Queen's Side – where the royal nursery lay – was probably in the northern range. AB.

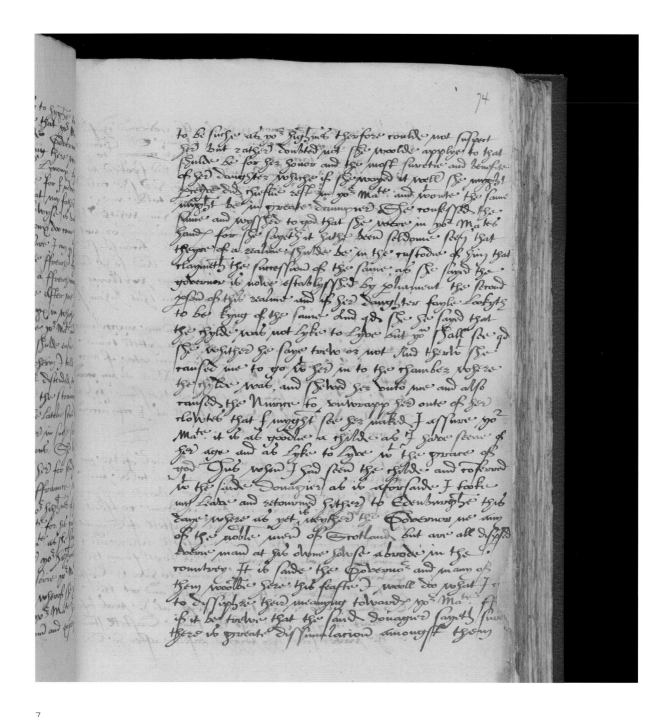

74

7

Mary, Queen of Scots as a Babe in Arms

Letter from Sir Ralph Sadler to Henry VIII, 23 March 1543,
Edinburgh.

British Library, Additional MS 32650, f. 74r.

In the summer of 1542, war broke out between England
and Scotland after Henry VIII failed to persuade his nephew
James V to break with King Francis I of France and the Roman
Catholic Church. Henry won a spectacular victory at Solway
Moss in Cumberland in November, when many Scottish
nobles and lairds were captured. When James died after a
short illness on 14 December, leaving a 6-day-old girl, Mary, as
his successor, Henry saw a golden opportunity and proposed
marriage between her and his heir, Prince Edward. To that end,
Sir Ralph Sadler was sent as ambassador in March 1543.

In his first audience with the dowager queen, Mary
of Guise, at Linlithgow Palace, Sadler 'founde her most
wyllyng and conformable'. She even told him that 'the
coniunction and vnyon of bothe thies Realmes in one'
was God's work, but she warned that the regent of
Scotland, James Hamilton, second Earl of Arran, would
never consent to the marriage, in particular because one
of Henry's demands was that Mary be brought up at the
English court. She denied Arran's claims that 'the chylde
was not lyke to lyve', taking Sadler to the royal nursery
to prove it. Mary of Guise 'shewed her vnto me and also
caused the Nurice to vnwrapp her oute of her clowtes
that I myght see her naked'. 'I assure your Maieste it is as
goodlie a childe as I have seene of her age and as lyke to
lyve with the grace of god.' AB.

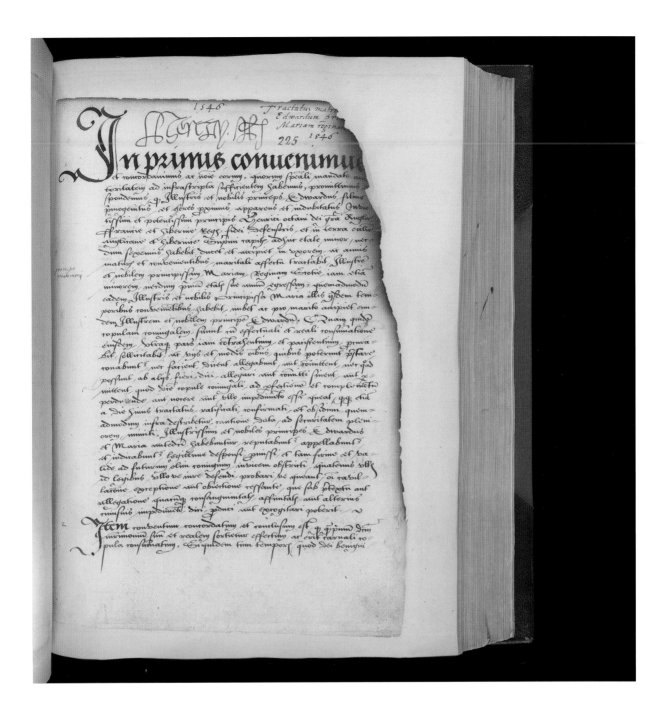

8

The Treaty of Greenwich

Marriage treaty between Prince Edward and Queen Mary of Scotland, signed by Henry VIII, 1 July 1543, Greenwich.

British Library, Cotton MS Vitellius C xi, f. 225r.

It was eventually agreed that the marriage between the young Mary, Queen of Scots and Prince Edward would take place as part of the Treaty of Greenwich. This is the first page of the articles of the treaty of marriage, signed by Henry VIII. At some point the document has been incorrectly dated to 1546, but the text refers to Edward being not yet 6 years old (*necdem sexennis*) and Mary as not yet 1 (*necdum primum etatis*), dating it to 1543. The main terms of the marriage treaty were that Mary should remain in Scotland until the wedding had taken place, although Henry could send English household servants to attend on her 'for the purpose of [her] better education'; she should be sent to England at her tenth birthday; and after consummation of the marriage she should receive dower lands valued at £2,000 a year, which would be doubled on Henry's death. Most importantly, following the dynastic union 'the kingdom of Scotland shall continue to be named and called the kingdom of Scotland and observe all its royal laws and legitimate liberties'. AC.

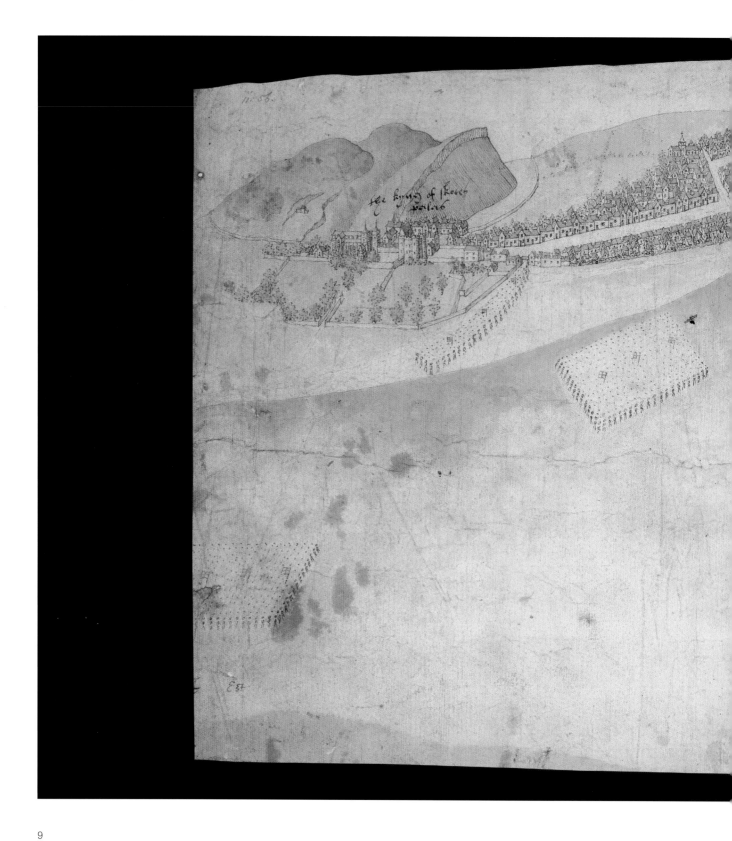

9

The Rough Wooing

Richard Lee, bird's-eye view of Edinburgh, May 1544.

British Library, Cotton MS Augustus I.ii.56.

Opposition to the Treaty of Greenwich grew in Scotland over the summer of 1543, and its government repudiated it in September. In response, Henry VIII appointed his brother-in-law, Edward Seymour, Earl of Hertford, as lieutenant-general for the invasion of Scotland, which took place in late spring 1544. Hertford broke with military convention by launching an amphibious assault, landing his army unopposed near Leith in Midlothian on 4 May. Edinburgh fell the following day, after Hertford had refused terms of surrender, saying 'he was sent thyther by the kinges hyghnes

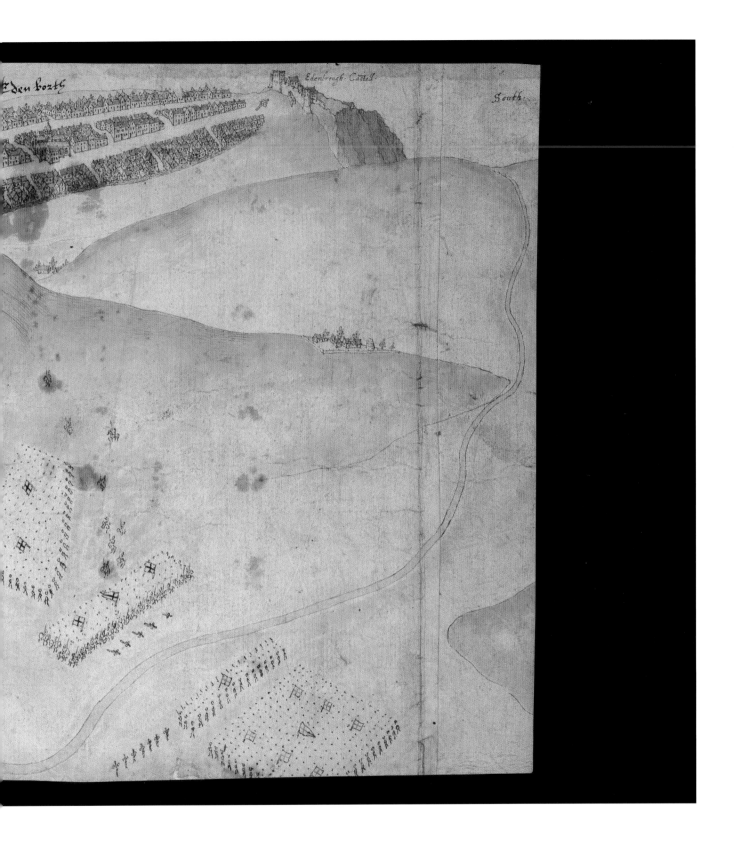

to take vengeaunce of their detestable falshed'. Edinburgh, Holyrood Abbey and Holyroodhouse were looted and put to the torch, 'so that neither within the wawles nor in the suburbes was lefte any one house vnbrent', but the castle proved impregnable. On 15 May Hertford broke camp, burned Leith and made overland for England, leaving a path of destruction in his wake.

This bird's-eye view, the first realistic depiction of Edinburgh, was probably drawn during the invasion by the military engineer Richard Lee to be presented to the king on his return. It shows the English army advancing towards the town from the north-west and entering by the Watergate. The now-lost right-hand side of the sheet depicted Leith. Hertford knighted fifty-eight men during his 1544 campaign, Lee among them. AB.

The Young Elizabeth and Mary

Both Elizabeth and her half-sister Mary were brought back into the succession by parliamentary statute and their father's will. Henry VIII died on 28 January 1547 to be succeeded by his 9-year-old son, Edward VI. During his reign (1547–53), Elizabeth became the subject of scandal because of the accusations that her new stepfather, Thomas Seymour, had tried first to seduce and afterwards to marry her. Her Protestantism returned her to royal favour, though not enough to prevent Edward from diverting the succession to Lady Jane Grey, a great-granddaughter of Henry VII. This attempt to exclude Edward's half-sisters failed and soon after his death Mary I took the throne, but her restoration of the Roman Catholic Church put Elizabeth in serious danger, especially after the rising of Sir Thomas Wyatt in January 1554. Nonetheless, Elizabeth survived two months in the Tower of London and almost a year under house arrest in Oxfordshire to become queen of England and Ireland on 17 November 1558.

During the English invasion of Scotland in Edward VI's reign, Mary, Queen of Scots lived for the most part in the stronghold of Stirling Castle, but she was moved to Dumbarton Castle in February 1548 and from there she was taken to France in August. Mary of Guise stayed in Scotland to watch over her daughter's interests.

10

Henry VIII's Disputed Will
Henry VIII's last will and testament, 30 December 1546, Whitehall.
The National Archives, Kew, E 23/4, ff. 8v–9r, 16v.

Aged 55, Henry VIII became gravely ill in late December 1546 and told his councillors on the twenty-sixth that he wanted to make changes to his existing will of 1544. Finding that document unsatisfactory, he ordered his Secretary Sir William Paget to draft a new one. Henry's immediate concern was to revise the names of the men who would comprise his heir's regency council. As far as the immediate succession was concerned, Henry made no changes. He retained the place of his two daughters, though they were legally still bastards, in the line of succession, just as he had in his third Act of Succession of 1544. However, he did add a new provision that set aside the strict rules of hereditary descent. He stipulated that the offspring of his younger sister Mary (who had been married to Charles Brandon, Duke of Suffolk) would succeed if all his children died without issue. The Scottish line of his elder sister Margaret was therefore omitted by default, and Mary, Queen of Scots was implicitly excluded from the succession.

Mary, Queen of Scots and her supporters later denied the validity of the will on the grounds that Henry had not signed it himself. Since September 1545, his clerks had impressed a facsimile of his signature (a dry stamp) on most documents to save him the trouble of signing all state papers. This mattered for two reasons: the first was an important legal technicality, as the 1544 Succession Act had authorised Henry's will with the words 'signed with his most gracious hande'; the second was that the will might have been forged. Nonetheless, most Protestants under Elizabeth who wished to exclude Mary from the throne fell back on the will as one of their main arguments. Henry VIII, they believed, had rightly excluded Margaret's descendants because they were aliens and as such were prohibited from holding English property by common law.

In late 1566, Elizabeth offered to recognise Mary as heir presumptive in return for Mary's recognition of her as the legitimate queen of England. On 2 January 1567, Mary accepted this proposal provided that Henry's will was subjected to a judicial examination in order to prove the signature was a dry stamp and the will invalid. Almost certainly a review would have taken place had not the murder of Mary's estranged husband, Henry Stuart, Lord Darnley, on 10 February put an end to the two queens' negotiations. SD.

shall holly remayne and com to our sayd doughter Elizabeth
and to the heyres of her body Lanfully begotten vppon
condicion that our sayd doughter Elizabeth after our
deceasse shall not marry nor take any person to her
husband withowt the assent and consent of the privye
Consaillours and others appointed by vs to be of consaill
to our sayd doughter prince prince Edward or the most
pt of them or the most pt of suche as they as
shalbe then on lyve thervnto before the said mariage
had in writing sealed with their seales which
condicion we declare Limitt appointe and will by these
pte shalbe to the said estat of our said doughter
Elizabeth in the said imperiall Crown and other
the premisses Limitt and appointed And if it shall
fortune our said doughter Elizabeth to dye within
Issue of her body Lawfully begotten we will that after
our deceasse and for defaute of issue of the
severall bodyes of vs and of our said sonne prince
Edward and of our said doughters Mary and
Elizabeth Lanfully begotten We will then the the
said imperiall crown and other the premisses after
our deceasse and for defaute of suche of the
severall bodyes of vs and of our said sonne prince
Edward and of our said doughter Mary

Elizabeth Lanfully begotten shall holly remayne and com
to the heyres of the body of the Lady Fraunces
our neyce eldest doughter to our Late Sister the
Fraunces Lanfully begotten And for defaute
of suche issue of the body of the said Lady
Fraunces we will that the said imperiall
crown and other the premisses after our deceasse
and for defaute of issue of the severall bodyes
of vs and of our sonne prince Edward and
of our doughters Mary and Elizabeth and
of the Lady Fraunces Lanfully begotten shall
holly remayne and com to the heyres of the bodye
of the Lady Elyanor our neyce second doughter
to our said Late Sister the Frenche Quene
Lanfully begotten And if it happen the said
Lady Elyanor to dye within issue of her body
Lanfully begotten we will that after our deceasse
and for defaute of issue of the severall bodyes
of vs and of our said sonne prince Edward
and of our said doughters Mary and Elizabeth
and of the said Lady Fraunces and of the said
Lady Elyanor Lanfully begotten the said imperiall
crown and other the premisses shall holly remayne

finally this present writing in paper we ordeyn and
make our Last will and testament and will the
same to be reputed and taken to all intentes and
purposes for our good strong vaillable most p feit
and Last will and testament and do dreame
all other willes and testamentes made at any tyme
by vs to be void and of non effect In witnes
whereof we have signed it with our hand in our
Palaice of Westm the thirtythe day of december
in the yere of our Lord god a thousand fyve hundred
fourty and six after the computacion of the churche
of england and of our reygn the xxxviij and herrto
we being present and called to be witnes have written
theis present with our owne hand

HENRICUS R
John Gate
E HARMAN
Wyllyam Saynthbarbe
Henry Nevell
Richard Coke
David Vincent
W Clerk

Derest vncle by your lettres and reporte of the messenger, We haue at good length vnderstanded to our great comfort, the good succese, it hathe pleased god to graunt vs against the Scottes by your good courage and wise forsight, for the With and other the benefites of god heaped vpon vs, like as We ar most bounden to yeld him most humble thankes, and to seke by al Waies We mai, his true honour, So do We giue vnto you, good vncle our most hartie thankes, praying you to thanke also most hartelie in our name our good Cosin therle of VVarwike, and all the otheye of the noble men, gentlemen, and others that haue serued in this iournei, of Whose seruice they shall all be Well assured, We Will not (god graunte vs lief) shew our selfes vnmindfull, but be redy euer to consider the same as anie occasion shall serue. yeuen at our house of Oatlandes, the eighteneth of September.

your good neuew

Edward.

11

The Occupation of Scotland

Letter from Edward VI to Edward Seymour, first Duke of Somerset,
18 September 1547, Oatlands.

British Library, Lansdowne MS 1236, f. 16r.

The Earl of Hertford was unable to capitalise on his invasions of Scotland in 1544 and 1545. However, in early 1547, he became Lord Protector and Duke of Somerset and invaded Scotland once more, destroying a larger Scottish army at the Battle of Pinkie on 10 September, a defeat known in Scotland as 'Black Saturday'. Eight days later Edward VI wrote to his 'derest vncle'. 'We haue at good length vnderstanded to our great comfort, the good succese, it hathe … pleased god to graunt vs against the Scottes by your good courage and wise forsight,' he declared. Somerset's victory was celebrated widely at home and news of it spread rapidly abroad. In an effort to revive the 1543 Treaty of Greenwich, Somerset now established a series of garrisons within Scotland, stretching along the border and up the east coast as far as Dundee and Broughty Craig in Angus. Hand in hand with this military occupation went a propaganda campaign trumpeting the benefits of so godly a union between the Protestant Edward and the Catholic Mary. One example even declared, 'both the Realmes thus vnited shal bere the name of grete britayn which is no newe name but thold name [of] them booth'. The Scots turned to the French for support, sending Mary to safety in France in August 1548, where she would remain for thirteen years. Thanks to the French intervention, England had to dismantle the garrisons and withdraw from Scotland in 1550. AB.

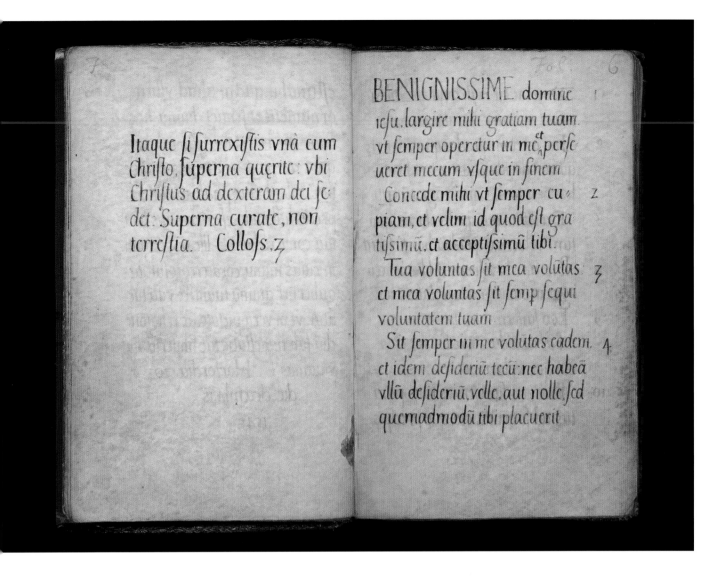

Itaque ſi ſurrexiſtis vnà cum
Chriſto, ſuperna quęrite: vbi
Chriſtus ad dexteram dei ſe-
det. Superna curate, non
terreſtia. Colloſ.z

BENIGNISSIME domine
ieſu, largire mihi gratiam tuam,
vt ſemper operetur in me̅ et perſe-
ueret mecum vſque in finem
  Concede mihi vt ſemper cu-
piam, et velim id quod eſt gra-
tiſſimū, et acceptiſimū tibi.
  Tua voluntas ſit mea volūtas,
et mea voluntas ſit ſemp ſequi
voluntatem tuam
  Sit ſemper in me volūtas eadem,
et idem deſideriū tecū: nec habeā
vllū deſideriū, velle, aut nolle, ſed
quemadmodū tibi placuerit

12

Elizabeth's Translations

Elizabeth's translation of Katherine Parr's *Prayers and Meditations*, 1545.

British Library, Royal MS 7 D x, ff. 5v–6r.

Elizabeth's education in foreign languages was put to good use in this New Year's gift to her father in December 1545. Written in her neatest hand, the book is a 117-page translation into Latin, French and Italian of English prayers and meditations assembled by Henry VIII's sixth and last wife, Katherine Parr. The volume had been printed in two editions the previous June, and Elizabeth used the second one as her text.

The book reflected Katherine's evangelical spirituality, which she passed on to Elizabeth. It contained no prayers for the dead nor any mention of the Catholic saints, but instead emphasised the importance of scripture in religious devotions and the need for a personal relationship with God without intermediaries. Elizabeth's tutors at this time – William Grindal and Jean Belmaine (who also taught Edward) – shared this reformist outlook and were probably appointed through the influence of Katherine and Archbishop Thomas Cranmer.

The Latin preface to the translation is the only surviving letter from Elizabeth to her father. Wisely she praised the king, but she also accentuated her status as his daughter; it was, she explained, 'a most suitable thing that this work … an assemblage by a queen as subject matter for her king, be translated into other languages by me, your daughter, who by this means would be indebted to you not only as an imitator of your virtues but also as an inheritor of them'. The book was bound in an elaborate embroidered cover, showing the initials of Henry and Katherine entwined in the centre of both covers in gold and silver threads and a white rose, the emblem of Elizabeth of York, in each corner (p. 37).

This was not the only translation of devotional texts that Elizabeth presented to her family. That same New Year, she gifted to Katherine the first chapter of John Calvin's *Institution de la Religion Chrestienne*. On 31 December 1544 she gave Katherine her English prose translation of Marguerite de Navarre's devotional verse composition in French under the English title *The Glass of the Sinful Soul*. In December 1547, her gift to Edward VI was a Latin translation of one of the Italian sermons of Bernardino Ochino, then a Protestant exile in England. Once queen, Elizabeth displayed her proficiency in foreign languages both in interactions with ambassadors and on visits to the universities, where she made addresses in Latin. SD.

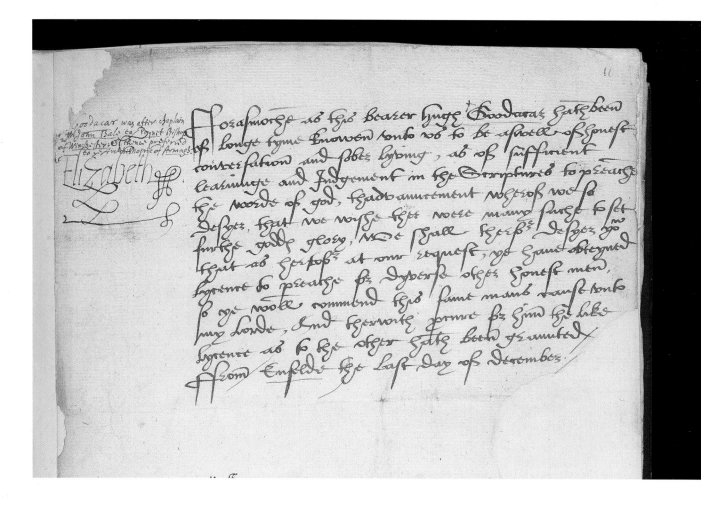

13

Elizabeth and William Cecil

Letter from Elizabeth to William Cecil, 31 December 1547, Enfield.

British Library, Additional MS 70518, f. 11r.

In December 1547, Elizabeth wrote to one of the rising stars in Edward VI's government, William Cecil, who had been in the service of the Lord Protector, the Duke of Somerset, since the spring. She petitioned Cecil to obtain a licence to preach for Hugh Goodacre who 'hath been of longe tyme knowen vnto vs to be aswell of honest conversation and sober lyving, as of sufficient learning and Iudgement in the Scriptures to preache the worde of god, th'advauncement wherof we so desyer, that we wishe ther were many suche to set furthe goddes glory'.

Goodacre was probably one of Elizabeth's chaplains and, by getting him licensed to preach, she hoped to advance his career in the Church. Although she was not successful in her immediate aim in writing to Cecil, Goodacre prospered. In October 1552, he was nominated as Archbishop of Armagh through the influence of Thomas Cranmer, Archbishop of Canterbury, and consecrated using the Protestant rite in Dublin the following February.

During Edward VI's reign, Elizabeth's own Protestant piety was shaped not only by Goodacre and her tutors but also by Katherine Parr, in whose household she lived for much of 1547 and early 1548. This letter contains one of the earliest examples of her famous italic signature. It is also the first evidence of contact between Elizabeth and Cecil, written when she was 14 years old. AB.

14

The Young Elizabeth

Unknown artist after William Scrots, sixteenth century.

Private collection.

Painted following Elizabeth's restitution to the English line of succession towards the end of Henry VIII's reign, the portrait by William Scrots (p. 92) offers a striking encounter with the teenage princess. Dressed in crimson and the lavish 'tissued' cloth of gold that was restricted to the royal family, she holds the viewer with a steady gaze as her finger marks her place in the small book in her hands. The prominence of books in the composition offers a visual reminder of her learning. As already seen, aged 12, she had translated her stepmother Katherine Parr's published *Prayers and Meditations* into Latin, French and Italian, and composed an accompanying Latin dedication, as a gift for her father (see cat. 12).

This portrait is a near contemporary copy. The original commission may have been instigated by Elizabeth's stepmother Katherine Parr, who took a keen interest in portraiture and had her own portrait produced by Scrots. The provenance of this copy suggests that it may have been commissioned by a member of the Seymour family. CB.

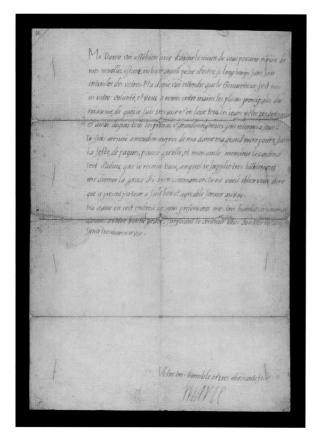

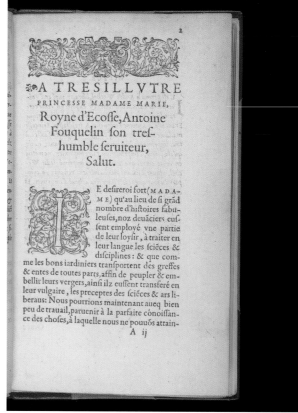

15

Mary, Queen of Scots in France

Letter from Mary to Marie de Lorraine (Mary of Guise),
[April 1554]. Meudon in the Île-de-France.

National Library of Scotland, Edinburgh, Acc. 7818.

16

Mary's Education

Antoine Fouquelin, *La Rhétorique Françoise*, Paris,
printed by André Wechel, 1557.

British Library, 236.b.3., f. 2r.

In France, the 5-year-old Mary was placed under the
guardianship of her maternal grandmother, the formidable
Antoinette de Bourbon, Duchess of Guise, matriarch of one
of the most powerful aristocratic families in France. As the
future queen consort of France, Mary was a valuable political
asset and Antoinette ensured that her granddaughter was
raised as a French Catholic princess, under the close control
of her Guise relatives.

It was decided that the young queen should be raised in
the French royal household with the dauphin and his siblings
to immerse her in French court protocol and culture and,
with the exception of her governess, Lady Janet Fleming,
Mary's Scottish household was replaced with French
aristocratic maids and companions. A pretty and vivacious
little girl, Mary charmed everyone and became the darling of
the French court. Henry II, her future father-in-law, conferred
pre-eminent status on her, giving her precedence over the
French princesses on official occasions.

In 1554, the 11-year-old Mary wrote this letter to her
mother in her native French tongue and a neat italic script,
informing her that she had travelled to Meudon to visit her
grandmother at Easter, when she would receive the Eucharist
for the first time. She also congratulated her mother, who had
recently replaced the Earl of Arran as regent of Scotland, a
regime change that would result in French hegemony over
Scotland. AC.

When Mary arrived in France in 1548, she was educated
together with all the royal children, and her education was
overseen by her future mother-in-law, Catherine de' Medici;
Diane de Poitiers, chief mistress of King Henry II; and
Charles of Guise, Cardinal of Lorraine, Mary's uncle. The
arrangement was unusual, but it provided an opportunity for
Mary and her future husband, the Dauphin Francis, to meet
in a less formal yet supervised setting. Mary was to be fully
educated in French and her education to be more courtly
than academic, as was thought appropriate for a future queen
consort of France.

In 1553, however, her uncle decided that Mary required
her own household and also needed to have a grounding in
classical education. She was, after all, a queen in her own
right, not merely Francis's consort. She was then taught Latin
and perhaps basic Greek and also began to learn Italian
and Spanish. In the preface to his *La Rhétorique Françoise*,
written when Mary was about 15, her tutor Antoine
Fouquelin praised her learning and accomplishments in
French, Latin and Greek. KL-H.

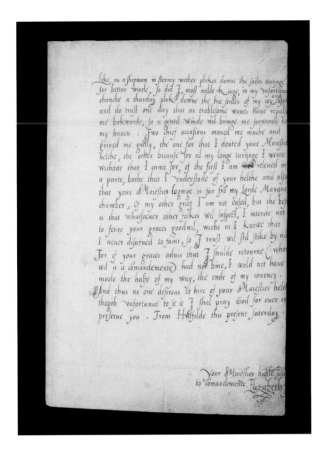

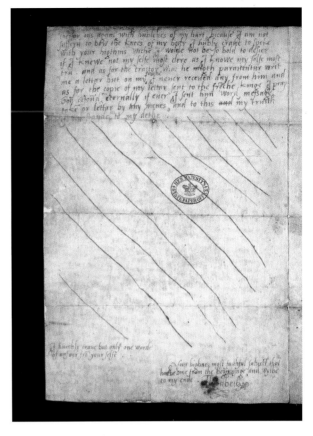

17

The Death of Edward VI

Letter from Elizabeth to Edward VI, [February 1553]. Hatfield.

British Library, Harley MS 6986, f. 23r.

In February 1553 Elizabeth penned this letter to her half-brother Edward VI, having been prevented from visiting him due to his declining health. Written in her elegant humanistic italic hand, the letter is beautifully composed and showcases the future queen's masterful use of language as well as her fondness for expressing herself metaphorically. To convey her disappointment at being prevented from seeing her brother, Elizabeth likened herself to 'a shipman in stormy wether' repulsed backwards by 'troblesome waues' and forced to 'pluk downe the hie sailes of my ioy and comfort'. Her distress is understandable, for she and Edward were close in age and shared a genuine affection for each other, having spent some of their childhood together. Elizabeth assured Edward that she would ignore the circulating rumours that she was no longer in his favour, and instead trust that 'your graces goodwil, wiche as I knowe that I neuer disarued to faint … wil stil stike by me'.

Despite the confidence she expresses here, Elizabeth would have been right to be suspicious. When it became clear that Edward's illness was terminal, he and John Dudley, Duke of Northumberland, decided to alter the line of succession to prevent the king's resolutely Catholic half-sister, Mary Tudor, from succeeding to the throne and undoing the Protestant Reformation. Edward's handwritten 'Device for the Succession' excluded both Mary and Elizabeth in favour of their cousin, the Protestant Lady Jane Grey. Against all the odds, on 19 July 1553 Mary became England's first ruling queen. AC.

18

Elizabeth in Danger

'The Tide Letter' from Elizabeth to Mary I, 17 March 1554, Whitehall.

The National Archives, Kew, SP 11/4/2, f. 3Av.

Arrested by her half-sister Mary I because of suspected involvement in Wyatt's Rebellion, Elizabeth was brought to Whitehall from her home in Ashridge in Hertfordshire in February 1554. She remained a virtual prisoner in the palace until ordered to the Tower of London on 17 March. Terrified that she would be summarily condemned and executed, Elizabeth begged permission to write to Mary.

Pleading her innocence, Elizabeth played upon Mary's sense of honour by citing the 'olde sayinge that a kings worde was more than a nother mans othe' and reminding her of her 'laste promise and my last demaunde' not to be condemned 'without answer and due profe'. Expressing humility throughout the letter, Elizabeth put her signature at the bottom of the last page slightly towards the right, a placement that showed deference to a superior. But as this left a space in which enemies might insert a forged confession, she scored through the remainder of the page. Her last words professed her innocence as she signed off: 'Your highnes most faithful subiect that hath bine from the beginnynge and wylbe to my ende.'

Elizabeth wrote the letter very slowly in the hope that the tide of the River Thames would have turned by the time it was finished so that her boat would be unable to pass under London Bridge towards the Tower without running aground. Hence the letter is called 'the Tide Letter'. The journey to the Tower was indeed postponed until the next day, but Mary refused her half-sister an audience. SD.

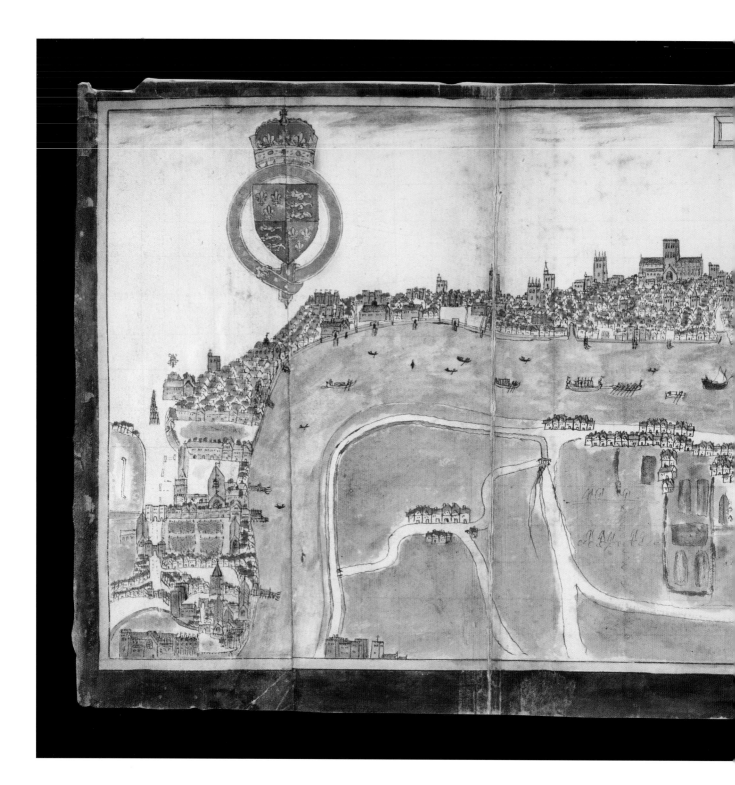

19

Elizabethan London

William Smith, profile and bird's-eye view of London, Southwark, and Westminster, 1588.

British Library, Sloane MS 2596, f. 52*r.

When Elizabeth was taken to the Tower, London was the largest city in England, with about 70,000 inhabitants. It was at the forefront of political, economic and cultural life, home to the court and parliament. By the time Elizabeth died in 1603, its population had grown to about 200,000, making it the largest city in western Europe after Paris.

William Smith was a herald and topographer who compiled his 'Particuler Description of England' between 1568 and 1603. His six years in Nuremberg in the 1570s and contact with leading German cartographers influenced his map-making. The 'Particuler Description' is complete with prospects and bird's-eye views of many of the principal cities and towns, and armorial bearings. In this panorama, ultimately derived from a large view by the Flemish artist

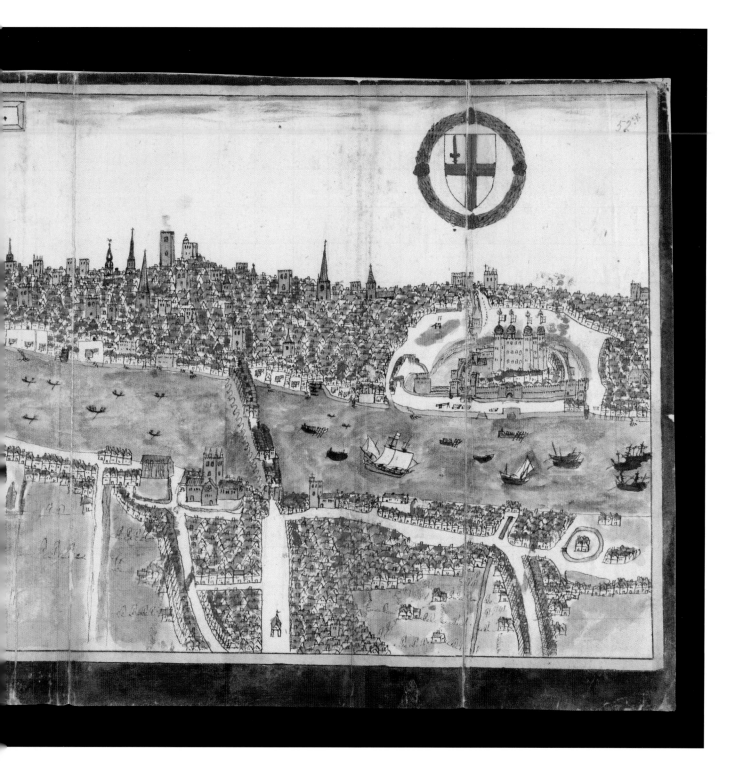

Antonis van den Wijngaerde of about 1540, Smith created
a profile view from the south of London and a bird's-eye
view of Westminster in Middlesex and Southwark in Surrey.
Prominent landmarks include St Paul's Cathedral, London
Bridge, the wharves, stairs and cranes on the Thames, and
the Tower of London; on the South Bank, which was still
surprisingly rural, St Mary Overy, Winchester Palace and
the two bear-baiting gardens; Charing Cross, Whitehall and
Westminster Abbey on the far left, where the river bends
south; and Lambeth Palace opposite. AB.

20

Elizabeth, a Prisoner at Woodstock

Letter from Sir Henry Bedingfeld to the privy council,
4 July 1554, Woodstock.

British Library, Additional MS 34563, ff. 39v–40r.

Elizabeth was released from the Tower in May 1554 and
sent to Woodstock in Oxfordshire in the custody of Sir
Henry Bedingfeld and 100 soldiers. Bedingfeld was one
of Mary I's trusted supporters, who took great care in
guarding his prisoner. Elizabeth observed Mass during her
imprisonment in the hope of appeasing her Catholic half-
sister. She also wrote to Mary, but in early July Bedingfeld
told her that the queen 'ys not plesed that [she] sholde
moleste hir … with any more off [her] colorable lettres'.
Elizabeth replied, 'yt ys lyke that I shall be offered [less]
then euer any prisoner was in the tower', for at least they
were 'suffered to open their mynde'. Later that day she

repeated her complaint that she was not allowed to protest
her innocence before the queen: 'I muste nedes continew
this lyff withoute all hoope worldelye / hollye restyng
to the troth of … my cause and that before godde to be
opened / armyng my self ageynst what so euer shall happen
to remayn the quenes true subiecte, as I haue done duryng
my lyff.'

Bedingfeld was also concerned about communication
between his prisoner and the outside world and he
complained to the government about 'the daylie repare off
my ladys graces seruants' to the Bull Inn in Woodstock,
where Thomas Parry, her household treasurer, was staying,
'beeng mannye more then haue cause to repare hyther for
any prouision'.

Elizabeth was released from custody in April 1555.
Years later, in 1586, she made a comparison of her
imprisonment with that of Mary, Queen of Scots. AB.

Mary's French Marriage

On 19 April 1558 the 15-year-old Mary, Queen of Scots was betrothed to the 14-year-old Dauphin Francis in the great hall of the new Louvre Palace in Paris. Five days later they were wed in the Cathedral of Notre-Dame. It was the first time a dauphin had been married in Paris for over 200 years, and the wedding was magnificent. Mary was led into the church by Henry II and her young cousin the Duke of Lorraine towards the end of a long, colourful procession.

The French royal family followed behind. Mary wore a bejewelled white dress – despite the fact that white was traditionally the mourning colour of the queens of France – and her long train was borne by two young girls. Her jewels included a diamond necklace and a golden coronet studded with pearls, rubies, sapphires and other precious stones. The courtier Pierre de Bourdeille, Seigneur de Brantôme described her as 'a hundred times more beautiful than a goddess of heaven … her person alone was worth a kingdom'. The wedding was followed by a procession, watched by the Parisian crowds, moving towards the Palais de Justice where a grand banquet was held with dancing far into the night.

The marriage was not just an opportunity for Henry II to display royal magnificence; it also advanced his imperial ambitions. Scotland would be absorbed into France, and his daughter-in-law might also stake a claim to the English and Irish thrones after Queen Mary I's death.

21

Mary, Queen of Scots

François Clouet, *c*.1558.

The Royal Collection / Her Majesty Queen Elizabeth II, RCIN 401229.

This portrait was probably produced to mark Mary's marriage to the Dauphin Francis, with the gesture of placing a ring on the fourth finger of her right hand acting as a reference to the marriage ceremony. However, a similar gesture is also seen in other portraits of monarchs, where it has been interpreted as a means of portraying the assumption of authority. It is therefore possible that the image alludes to Mary's attempt to claim the royal title and arms of England in 1558 as much as her enhanced status as dauphiness of France.

François Clouet drew the Scottish queen on a number of occasions during her childhood at the French court; he was painter to the king and was commissioned by the queen, Catherine de' Medici, to produce chalk portraits of the children in her family so that she could monitor their progress. CB.

22

The Marriage of Mary, Queen of Scots

Marriage articles of the dauphin and Mary, Queen of Scots,
19 April 1558, the Louvre in Paris.

National Library of Scotland, Edinburgh, Adv.MS.54.1.2 (1).

Letters patent for the marriage of the dauphin and Mary were
drawn up at Fontainebleau in the Île-de-France on 16 March
1558. These began by reiterating how the Scots had agreed
to the marriage as far back as July 1548, during the French-
led siege of Haddington. The letters patent stipulated that
Mary should be given away by her grandmother, Antoinette
of Bourbon, and eight Scottish commissioners, including
her half-brother, Lord James Stewart, and John, sixth Lord
Erskine (later Earl of Mar). Both men would go on to govern
Scotland during James VI's minority.

On 4 April 1558 Mary made a secret deed of gift to
Henry II. In consideration of his aid 'against the English,
the old and inveterate enemies of her predecessors and her',
Mary gifted the Scottish crown and her right to the English
and Irish crowns to the French king and his successors,
should she die without legitimate issue. In two further secret
documents of the same date she agreed to repay Henry's
costs in defending Scotland against the English invasion of
1547–50 and confirmed that the secret deed of gift could not
be overturned subsequently by the Scottish parliament. All
three secret documents were illegal under Scots law.

These marriage articles were read out on 19 April 1558
before the court at the Louvre, after which Francis and
Mary plighted their troths and exchanged wedding rings.
The articles were then witnessed by the French marriage
commissioners, Jacques Bourdin, Sieur de Villeines, Côme
Clausse, Sieur de Marchaumont, and Claude de l'Aubespine.
The marriage took place on a magnificent scale at Notre-
Dame on 24 April. AB.

Elizabeth I's Accession and Religious Settlement

Despite the ambitions of Henry II and the claim of Mary, Queen of Scots, Elizabeth I succeeded to the English and Irish thrones easily. After her coronation in January 1559, she had two main objectives: first, to end her half-sister's war against France; and second, to overturn the religious status quo in England. Both objectives were secured in April 1559. On the third of that month the Treaty of Cateau-Cambrésis was signed, binding England, France and Scotland to remain at peace for at least eight years. To Elizabeth's regret it also left Calais (captured by France in January 1558) in French hands. Shortly afterwards, the Acts of Supremacy and Uniformity passed through parliament. The Act of Supremacy gave Elizabeth the title of Supreme Governor of the Church of England and henceforth officials had to swear allegiance to her as such. When all but one of the Catholic bishops refused to take the oath, they were removed, and Protestants took their place. The Act of Uniformity compelled everyone to use a new English Prayer Book, which was largely based on the 1552 Book of Common Prayer, although some traditional rituals remained. Consequently, Elizabeth's religious settlement proved to be too Protestant for some and not Protestant enough for others.

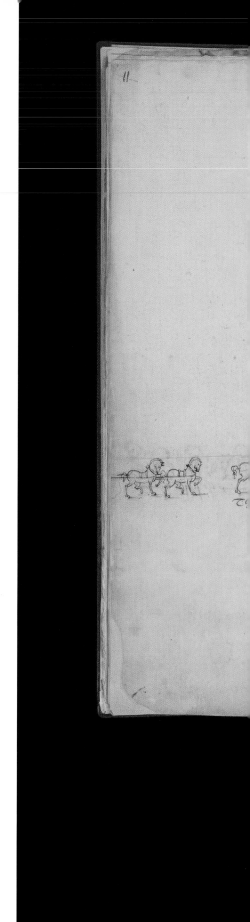

23

Elizabeth's Coronation

Pen and ink drawings of the coronation procession on
14 January 1559.

British Library, Egerton MS 3320, ff. 4v–5r.

Elizabeth's coronation took place at Westminster Abbey
on 15 January 1559, two months after her accession on
17 November 1558. The date was chosen as auspicious by
the astrologer Dr John Dee. Elizabeth was crowned by Owen
Oglethorpe, Bishop of Carlisle, because more senior bishops
– all Catholics – refused the honour, thinking there would be
no elevation of the host (a Catholic ritual) during the English
service. In fact, historians are uncertain as to whether the Mass
was celebrated at all during the ceremony.

This drawing comes from a book of twenty-four folios
which also includes a plan of the central space in the Abbey
for the coronation. One of the heralds probably drew up the
book for Elizabeth's Principal Secretary, Sir William Cecil. The
folios reproduced here show part of the traditional procession
that took place the day before the coronation when Elizabeth
travelled from the Tower to Westminster Abbey through
London. It was lightly snowing yet Elizabeth sat in an open litter
under a canopy held up by two knights on each side. Robert
Dudley, her Master of the Horse, rode immediately behind her
and led the palfrey of honour. During the procession Elizabeth
passed by and sometimes stopped at pageants put on by the
City, several of which hailed her as a Protestant queen who
would remove idolatry from the realm. SD

24

King Henry VIII's Great Bible

The Byble in Englyshe, [London], printed by
Edward Whitchurch, 1540.

British Library, C.18.d.10., title page.

Until 1536 most Bibles were in Latin and they were read and
interpreted by members of the clergy. After the break from
Rome, Henry VIII approved the printing of a new vernacular
Bible to give his lay subjects direct access to the scriptures.
The first two English translations – the Coverdale Bible and
Matthew's Bible – were deemed inaccurate. Consequently,
in 1538 Henry VIII's chief minister Thomas Cromwell and
Archbishop Cranmer commissioned the English reformer
Miles Coverdale to produce a better translation which would
become the authoritative version. In the same year, Cromwell
issued an injunction ordering every parish to buy a copy of

an English Bible and place it in 'sum convenient place' for all
to see and read.

First printed in April 1539, what became known as the
Great Bible appeared in six editions (more than 9,000 copies)
by 1541. New editions continued to be printed under Elizabeth
despite the production of other translations (the Geneva Bible
in 1560 and Bishops' Bible in 1568). The woodcut title page
was used to communicate a visual message about Henry VIII's
new role as the Supreme Head of the Church, independent
of the pope's authority in Rome. The illustration visually
reinforces the idea that Henry is receiving the Word directly
from God before passing it on to the clergy via Cranmer, and to
the laity through Cromwell. This special copy – later inherited
by Elizabeth I – was printed on vellum and illuminated. Its
inscription says that it was presented to Henry VIII by the
London haberdasher Anthony Marler. KL-H.

25

Reformation of the Word

Wooden triptych of the royal arms, English school, 1547–53, with additions made during Elizabeth I's reign.

Parochial Church Council of St Mary's Church, Preston St Mary, Suffolk.

This painted wooden triptych of the royal arms was made for Preston St Mary in Suffolk, perhaps originally to replace an altarpiece. It is inscribed on the inside at the base, 'ELIZABETHA . MAGNA . REGINA . ANGLIAE [Elizabeth the Great, Queen of the English]'. The inscriptions on the outside make clear the close association during the English Reformation between idolatry and iconoclasm: 'Before the Eternall thou shalt have no other/ God in any likeness whatsoever to bowe down/ and to worship it' (Exodus 20:2–3). Other biblical passages hammer home the point (Exodus 34:14; 1 Corinthians 6:9–11; 1 Corinthians 10:7–10).

The triptych is a rare survival of royal arms designed to hang within a parish church. Such arms were first set up during Henry VIII's reign to symbolise his role as Supreme Head of the Church of England. This triptych dates to Edward VI's reign, when the rood (the sculpture of the crucifixion before the high altar) and many images were cast down throughout the realm.

The monogram 'E[dwardus] R[ex] [King Edward]' appears either side of the lion crest; his badge, a sun in splendour, is at top right, and the supporters, the lion and dragon, are his. The biblical quotations may have been added in Elizabeth's reign, along with her title, which is displayed prominently at the bottom. The arms trace the Tudor lineage from Edward the Confessor, Edward the Martyr, the legendary Trojan Brutus and others, reinforcing the Tudors' right to rule. AB.

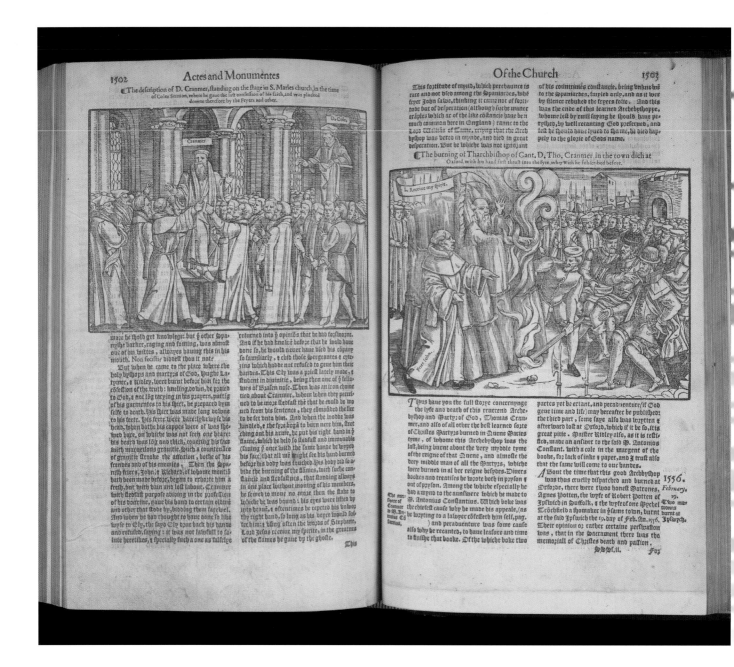

26

Foxe's Book of Martyrs

John Foxe, *Actes and Monuments of these Latter and Perillous Dayes, Touching Matters of the Church*, London, printed by John Day, 1563.

British Library, G.12101., pp. 1502–3.

'Foxe's Book of Martyrs' is a work of propaganda in which the world is depicted as clearly divided into good and evil. It captures the reversal of Protestant fortunes under the Catholic Mary I and details the persecution of Protestants during her reign. The Protestant scholar and martyrologist John Foxe had been exiled to the continent from 1554 to 1559 and made the completion of the *Actes and Monuments* his main aim when he returned to England. Foxe used original archival material and incorporated oral evidence to write his histories. The book had a large geographical and chronological scope and drew on continental Protestant martyrologies, but the focus of the first edition was on Church history from the fourteenth-century reformer John Wycliffe to the accession of Elizabeth.

Foxe worked closely with the printer John Day and together they produced a large folio volume with woodcuts, first published in 1563. It was printed in English and thus very accessible. The project had high-level support: Sir William Cecil gave permission for Day to hire more foreign press workers than were commonly allowed and Day had monopolies for books that would be guaranteed to earn him revenue. The book was immediately popular, was intended to be displayed in parish churches and had a huge impact on the Protestant identity of Elizabethan England, with four revised editions being published during Foxe's lifetime. This opening shows woodcuts of the trial and execution of Archbishop Thomas Cranmer in Oxford in 1556. KL-H.

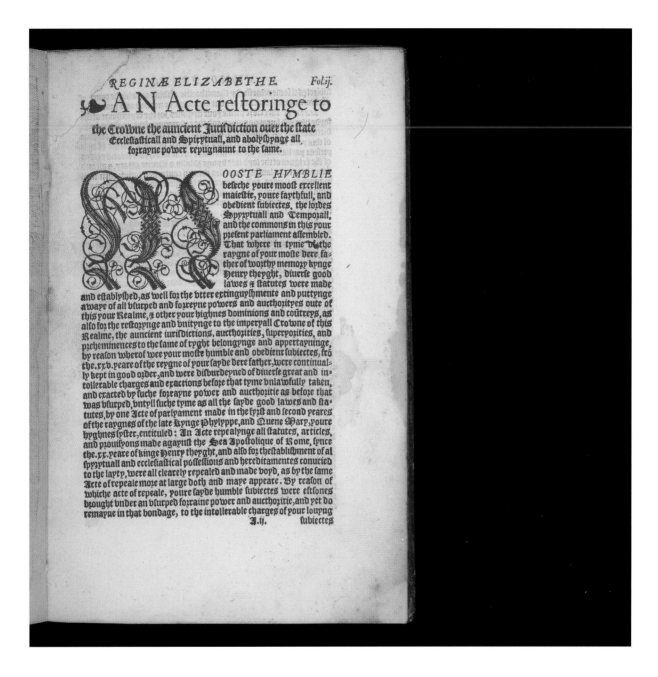

REGINÆ ELIZABETHE.   Fol.ij.

A N Acte reſtoringe to

the Crowne the auncient Iuriſdiction ouer the ſtate
Eccleſiaſticall and Spirytuall, and aboliſhynge all
foꝛrayne power repugnaunt to the ſame.

OOSTE HVMBLIE
beſeche youre mooſt excellent
maieſtie, youre fapthfull, and
obedient ſubiectes, the loꝛdes
Spꝛytuall and Tempoꝛall,
and the commons in this your
pꝛeſent parliament aſſembled.
That where in tyme of the
rapgne of pour moſte dere father of woꝛthy memoꝛy kpnge
Henry theyght, diuerſe good
lawes & ſtatutes were made
and eſtabliſhed, as well foꝛ the vtter extinguiſhmente and puttynge
awape of all vſurped and foꝛrepne powers and aucthoꝛityes oute of
this your Realme, & other pour highnes dominions and coūtreps, as
alſo foꝛ the reſtoꝛrynge and vnitynge to the imperpall Crowne of this
Realme, the auncient iuriſdictions, aucthoꝛities, ſuperpoꝛities, and
pꝛreheminences to the ſame of ryght belongynge and appertaynynge,
by reaſon wherof wee pour moſte humble and obedient ſubiectes, frō
the.xxb.peare of the rergne of pour ſapde dere father, were continual-
ly kept in good oꝛder, and were diſburdeyned of diuerſe great and intollerable charges and exactions befoꝛe that tyme vnlawfully taken,
and exacted by ſuche foꝛrapne power and aucthoꝛitie as befoꝛe that
was vſurped, vntyll ſuche tyme as all the ſapde good lawes and ſtatutes, by one Acte of parlpament made in the ſyꝛſt and ſecond peares
of the rapgnes of the late kpnge Phylppe, and Quene Mary, youre
hyghnes ſyſter, entituled : An Acte repealynge all ſtatutes, articles,
and pꝛouiſpons made agaynſt the Sea Apoſtolique of Rome, ſynce
the.xx.peare of kinge Henry theyght, and alſo foꝛ theſtabliſhment of al
ſpꝛytuall and eccleſiaſtical poſſeſſions and hereditamentes conueied
to the laytp, were all clearely repealed and made voyd, as by the ſame
Acte of repeale moꝛe at large doth and maye appeare. By reaſon of
whiche acte of repeale, youre ſapde humble ſubiectes were eftſones
bꝛought vnder an vſurped foꝛraine power and aucthoꝛitie, and yet do
remapne in that bondage, to the intollerable charges of pour louyng
A.ij.   ſubiectes

27

The Act of Supremacy 1559

'An Acte restoringe to the Crowne the auncient Jurisdiction
ouer the state Ecclesiasticall and Spirytuall', in *Anno Primo
Reginæ Elizabethe*, London, printed by Richard Jugge
and John Cawood, 1599.

British Library, C.83.e.3., f. 2r.

Elizabeth's first parliament assembled on 23 January 1559 with
the main purpose of establishing, in the words of Lord Keeper
Sir Nicholas Bacon, 'an uniforme order of religion'. A single bill
of supremacy and uniformity passed the House of Commons
but was vigorously resisted in the Lords, where twenty Catholic
bishops and one abbot were sitting alongside some Catholic
peers. Undeterred, Elizabeth and her Protestant councillors
decided to try again. During the Easter recess two bishops
were imprisoned, and when parliament met in April several
other bishops were inexplicably absent. This time, two separate
bills of supremacy and uniformity were introduced, and the
supremacy statute passed by twenty-one votes to eighteen.

There is evidence that the queen and her council had not
expected the uniformity bill to get through. The supremacy
bill therefore encompassed a repeal of the heresy laws and
communion in both kinds (i.e. the laity would henceforward
be offered wine as well as bread at communion), measures
that would be expected in a bill imposing uniformity of
worship. Another significant change from Henry's statute
was that Elizabeth would be 'Supreme Governor' rather
than 'Head' of the Church. The change in title implied that
the queen would not interfere in spiritual matters; this was
marginally more acceptable to Catholics.

This is Elizabeth's personal copy of the 1559 Act of
Supremacy. SD & KL-H.

28

The Bishops' Bible

The Holi Bible, London, printed by Richard Jugge, [1569].

British Library, G.12188., title page.

Matthew Parker, Archbishop of Canterbury, was critical of the 1560 Geneva Bible, the most popular edition of the Bible among English Protestants at the time, because of its Calvinist marginal notes and commentaries. In 1568 Parker was instrumental in persuading Elizabeth that a new translation was required and oversaw a group of bishops who revised the text of the Great Bible. Parker hoped that this new Bible would receive a royal seal of approval, but Elizabeth never formally authorised it. Soon to be known as the Bishops' Bible, it was used officially in parish churches, but the Geneva Bible remained more popular for private study and worship.

The first edition of the Bishops' Bible was printed by Richard Jugge in 1568. It is a beautifully printed folio volume with woodcuts, maps and its own set of Protestant marginal notes. A second revised folio edition was published in 1572. This 1569 quarto edition was printed for private devotion. The title page was illustrated by Frans Hogenberg, a Protestant exile from the Netherlands. It shows Elizabeth as Supreme Governor of the Church, seated on her throne in a similar pose to that of her father, Henry VIII, on the title page of the Great Bible (cat. 24). She is surrounded by female personifications of Justice, Mercy, Prudence and Fortitude. She is being crowned by Justice and Mercy, who carry the sword of the Spirit and the Bible. Below the title is a minister preaching to his congregation. This copy is printed on vellum and the title page has been illuminated. KL-H.

The Scottish Reformation and English Intervention in Scotland

Following a sermon delivered in Perth by John Knox on 11 May 1559, an iconoclastic riot erupted in the town and rapidly spread. To suppress what had become a full-scale rebellion led by the Protestant Lords of the Congregation, Mary of Guise, now the Scottish regent, obtained military aid from France. By November it looked as if the rebellion would be crushed and Catholicism fully restored. Playing on Elizabeth's fears of French domination in Scotland, Sir William Cecil persuaded her to intervene. In January 1560 she ordered a navy to the east coast of Scotland to blockade reinforcements from France arriving by sea; then, in the spring, she reluctantly sent a substantial army over the border to assist the rebels. Although the fighting ended in stalemate, the English won the peace: the Treaty of Edinburgh of July 1560 removed French troops from Scotland. Additionally, the Lords of the Congregation governed Scotland until the return of Mary, Queen of Scots the following year; and the Scottish parliament in August ended the pope's authority, adopted a Protestant Confession of Faith and banned the Mass.

29

False Idols

Carved stone head, thirteenth century.

Historic Environment Scotland, St Andrews Cathedral Museum, SAC/x/24.

On Sunday 11 June 1559, John Knox preached in
St Andrews, Fife, a sermon on Christ's cleansing of the
Temple, after which the city's altars, paintings, murals,
sculptures, carved woodwork, stained glass and even the
tombs of the cathedral, friaries, parish kirk and university
colleges were cast down.

Almost certainly this head is what is left of a full-length
figure of Christ that was probably toppled at this time and
thrown down the latrine, along with sculptures of St Andrew
and a king of Scots (perhaps Malcolm IV, who founded the

cathedral). All three were rediscovered during an excavation
of the cathedral's great drain in August 1894, when they
were found in the post-medieval archaeological deposits.
The cathedral, which was the largest church ever built in
Scotland, was abandoned in 1561 and quickly fell into ruin.

Carved in the thirteenth century, the Christ figure was
worked in fine-grained sandstone. Traces of red pigment
suggest it was once highly coloured. The back of the head
is relatively unfinished, indicating that the figure was set
against or within another feature, such as a niche. One of the
most remarkable surviving examples of medieval religious
sculpture in Scotland, the St Andrews Christ is beautifully
and sensitively carved, sharing similarities with French
thirteenth-century sculpture. AB.

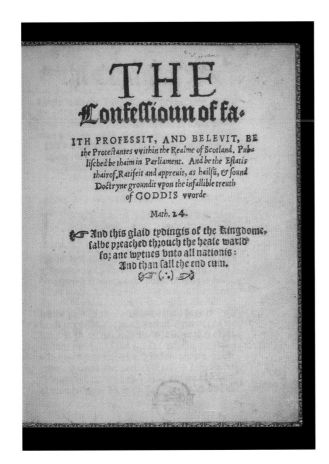

30

The Scottish Reformation

The Confessioun of Faith Professit, and Belevit, be the Protestantes vvithin the Realme of Scotland, Edinburgh, John Scott, 1561.

British Library, G.11837., title page.

The *Confessioun of Faith* was a statement of Protestant doctrine written for the August 1560 parliament by a committee of six, including John Knox, and printed the next year. Its parliamentary acceptance amid scenes of Protestant fervour marked a public declaration of Scotland's new religious alignment and was later regarded as the pivotal moment of its Protestant Reformation. The unusual presence of many Protestant lairds at that parliament cowed Catholic opposition to the *Confessioun* and other Acts banning Roman Catholic worship and outlawing papal jurisdiction. However, Mary refused to ratify either the *Confessioun* itself or the other legislation.

In the next months the same committee composed the *Buke of Discipline*, a blueprint for a new Kirk that called for radical changes to worship and religious organisation. Drawing upon existing ecclesiastical wealth, the committee wanted full funding for the Reformed Kirk, universities and adequate poor relief. As well as dismantling the Catholic Church as an institution, this ambitious plan would have disrupted royal and noble finances. Many of the *Buke*'s proposals were slowly implemented at parish level, but the dispute over resources took decades to resolve. This left the new Protestant Kirk looking highly vulnerable at the start of the 1560s, especially with the return of a Catholic queen. JD

31

British Unity and the Problem of Mary, Queen of Scots

Memorandum by Sir William Cecil, 31 August 1559.

British Library, Lansdowne MS 4, f. 26r.

Sir William Cecil composed his memorandum at the end of August 1559, almost four months after the Lords of the Congregation had rebelled against the regent, Mary of Guise. After a number of military standoffs, the Congregation forced her to grant freedom of worship. Meanwhile, Cecil was the driving force behind secret negotiations with them for an Anglo-Scottish amity that would fundamentally challenge the sovereignty of Mary, Queen of Scots. This amity could only be achieved, Cecil thought, if the French were expelled from Scotland, the Scots supported the Reformation and, most critical of all, Mary and her husband Francis II accepted the new political and religious situation. 'In primis it is to be noted that the best worldly felicitie that Scotland can haue is either to contynew in a perpetuall peace with the kingdom of Ingland or to be made one Monarchie with England as they both make but one Ile deuided from the rest of the world,' he wrote.

What Cecil was proposing was that the Congregation should govern Scotland with Mary's consent. Should she obstruct or resist them, the Scottish Parliament 'may committ the Gouuernance therof to the next heyre of that croune binding the same also to obserue the Lawes and Auncient rights of the Realme'. In other words, Cecil already countenanced the deposition of Mary. AB

32

The False Arms of Scotland, France and England

The arms of Mary, Queen of Scots and the French dauphin, and
of Scotland, France and England, sent from France, July 1559.

British Library, Cotton MS Caligula B x, ff. 17v–18r.

When Elizabeth I inherited the English throne, Henry II of
France quickly disputed her title and asserted Mary's claim to
the crown of England. His daughter-in-law, he implied, was a
more legitimate monarch than the bastard, heretical daughter
of Henry VIII. Mary and Francis began to style themselves
as 'King and Queen Dauphins of Scotland, England and
Ireland', and Mary's cloths of estate, silver plate, seals and
medals were decorated with a new armorial, which quartered
the arms of England with those of Scotland and France.

Alarmed by such provocative behaviour, Sir Nicholas
Throckmorton, the English ambassador in France, sent
this sketch of the 'Armes of Scotland and England' to Sir
William Cecil as evidence of Mary's heraldic pretensions.

Surmounted by a closed imperial crown, the armorial
shows the combined arms of Mary, Queen of Scots and the
dauphin on the dexter side and the arms of Scotland, France
and England on the sinister side. Accompanying verses
describe the drawing as:

> The Armes of Marie Quene Dolphines of france
> The nobillest Ladie In earth, for till advance
> Off Scotland quene / and of Ingland also
> Off Ireland als / God haith providit so.

Cecil, who interpreted the arms as a serious threat to
Elizabeth's authority, noted on the reverse that they were the
'false armes of scotl[and] fr[ance] engl[and] Iuly 1559'.

In July 1559, Henry II died from an injury sustained in a
jousting tournament and the dauphin and Mary became king
and queen of France. The danger posed by Mary, now queen
of Scotland and France, increased. AC.

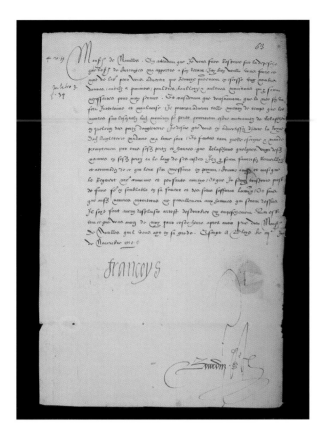

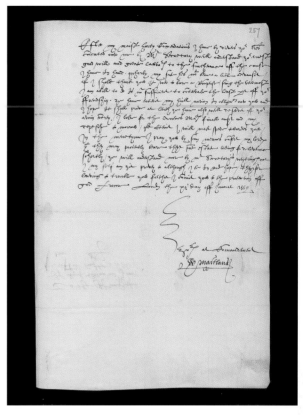

33

French Intervention in the British Isles
Letter from Francis II to Antoine de Noailles,
4 November 1559, Blois.
British Library, Additional MS 89368.

34

The Treaty of Berwick, 1560
Letter from William Maitland of Lethington to Sir Ralph Sadler
and Sir James Croft, 11 January 1560, London.
British Library, Additional MS 33592, f. 257r.

In this letter Francis II informed his ambassador in England, Antoine de Noailles, that a shipment of French arms and munitions was sailing for Scotland in support of Mary of Guise to be used against the Lords of the Congregation. 'I desired to write this letter to let you know that I am presently sending to Scotland a quantity of arms, trenching tools, powder, bullets and other munitions which are required for my service there,' the king wrote. If the ships were forced into an English port due to the weather, Noailles was to petition Elizabeth to permit them to continue their voyage to Scotland, once it was safe to do so, even though she was secretly supporting the Scottish rebels. Francis was therefore putting Elizabeth in a difficult position, because she was bound to uphold the Anglo-French peace of Cateau-Cambrésis of April 1559 by not supporting rebels against his wife, Mary, Queen of Scots.

Anglo-French relations had been strained during the summer by the fact that Francis and Mary incorporated the arms of England into their armorial (see cat. 32), making public Mary's claim to be Elizabeth's heir presumptive. The English government took this to be further evidence of French ambitions to dominate the British Isles. The fleet was, in fact, driven back by bad weather, taking shelter in French ports. AB.

Between 1554 and 1559, William Maitland of Lethington served as Principal Secretary to the Scottish regent, Mary of Guise. However, in November 1559 he joined the Lords of the Congregation, who had rebelled against her religious and pro-French policies. Maitland was appointed ambassador and sent to England to persuade Elizabeth to offer financial and military aid to the Congregation.

Writing in Scots to Sir Ralph Sadler, Warden of the East and Middle Marches, and Sir James Croft, Captain of Berwick-upon-Tweed, Maitland thanks them for 'zour ernest good will and greate lawboris to the furtherance off the cause I haue in hand'. 'Ze haue enterit my haill nation In obligation onto zow and I hope It shall prove at lenth ze haue also weill deservit off zour awin countrey.' From London, Maitland petitioned Sadler and Croft, who were stationed on the Scottish border, to 'comfort my lordis [of the Congregation] yet they may paciently beare theyr present estate'.

Elizabeth I was initially opposed to supporting the Protestant rebels against their rightful sovereign; she disliked John Knox and his radical Protestantism and was reluctant to spend money on military intervention. Cecil, however, favoured supporting the Congregation to encourage religious change and eliminate French power in Scotland, and he managed to bring the queen round to his way of thinking. Just over a month after Maitland wrote this letter, the Treaty of Berwick was signed between Elizabeth and the Congregation, securing a military alliance against the French. AT.

35

English and French Intervention in Scotland

'THE plat of Lythe with thaproche of the Trenches therevnto. And also the great Ordynance there in placed as it was at The daye of the Surrender'. Unknown military engineer, bird's-eye view of Leith, July 1560.

By kind permission of Lord Egremont, Petworth House, West Sussex.

Elizabeth I's kinsman Thomas Howard, fourth Duke of Norfolk, commanded the English invasion of Scotland in late March 1560 in support of the Lords of the Congregation against Mary of Guise. On 6 April the English and the Congregation laid siege to Leith, which the French, under the command of the veteran Henri Cleutin, Sieur d'Oysel, had fortified into a bastion. They breached the south rampart but failed to storm it on 7 May. Nevertheless, with no sign of reinforcements, the garrison was forced to capitulate on terms. An unknown military engineer drew a large bird's-eye view of Leith, orienting the north to the bottom and the east on the left-hand side. Leith, the bastion and the siege works are meticulously depicted at the bottom; Holyrood Abbey, Holyroodhouse, Edinburgh and its castle are at the top.

The Treaty of Edinburgh was agreed on 6 July. Its main terms were that the English and French would leave Scotland, the fortifications at Leith would be demolished, a privy council would be chosen jointly by Mary, Queen of Scots and the Congregation to govern the realm, and Elizabeth was recognised as rightful queen of England and Ireland. This treaty, in effect, ended the 'Auld Alliance' between France and Scotland, laid the foundation for the Anglo-Scottish 'Amity' and, above all, ensured the preservation of the Scottish Reformation. AB.

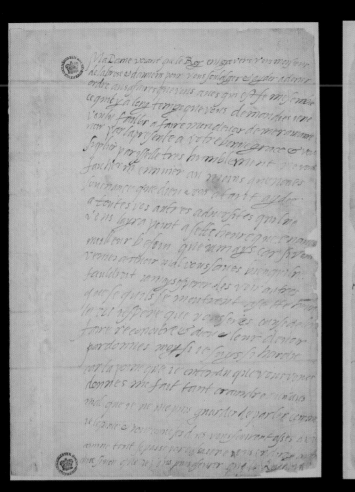

36

Mary of Guise Hopes for Support

Letter from Mary, Queen of Scots to Mary of Guise,
[late March?] 1560.

National Records of Scotland, Edinburgh, SP13/85.

Mary wrote this letter to her mother in her own hand. She told Mary of Guise that she wished she could take some of her misfortunes on herself and prayed 'may God aid you so much in your adversity'. The dowager queen of France, Catherine de' Medici, 'did us the honour to weep so much on hearing news of your troubles', Mary said. She assured her mother that her husband Francis II, 'is so keen to help you that it should reassure you, because he has so promised me,

that I will not let him forget'. She ended her letter by wishing her mother a 'very happy and long life'.

Mary of Guise had sent urgent appeals for further military assistance from France but none was forthcoming, in part because her homeland was sliding into religious civil war. Instead, her brothers – Francis, second Duke of Guise, and Charles, Cardinal of Lorraine – negotiated the disadvantageous Treaty of Edinburgh with England and the Congregation in July in order to extricate the French from Scotland. On 7 June Mary of Guise summoned the leaders of the Congregation and other nobles to her at Edinburgh Castle, urging them to maintain the 'Auld Alliance' with France. Four days later, she died after a long illness. AB.

s. Hibernia

S. Swly   Ellan Iwilla   As Owin Nehasnugh   Carndeburg

Loagh Na...   ORONZA   cetrokill
port inusse   Ellon Na.   Griroth
    Kerza   ILA   Scoloza
Ragh/ma   Duneveg   MVLL

                            ARRIVRA

mull of Kentire   Karay Gegay
    Diamard   Gyre   saudell   Knapdale   Loyrn
    phadda
    Santa   skipinic   L. fien   Ert of Ardgaill

Dunbritan frith

ull of Galoway   corswell   AREN
                        Arggra   Ardguile
    Ailza   Braid Alba
sallet   S. Rian
Glenlus   Lamla
aye of Glen   carlton   Ordmuig
    S. Trincohla noth   Galoway   Carpet
    whithorn   wigton   ayre   Barge
    Cref   Nyss   Ani   Batzenoth
        Lynwar   Ert o...
            Lord Knighton   Cluns
    Kirkbrig
    Mididuo
    AIAVCLL   Dunpuck   Lothean
    Carlil   peblis
                Marche   S. tubs head
                    Berwik   Read head
                            Fiffis nes

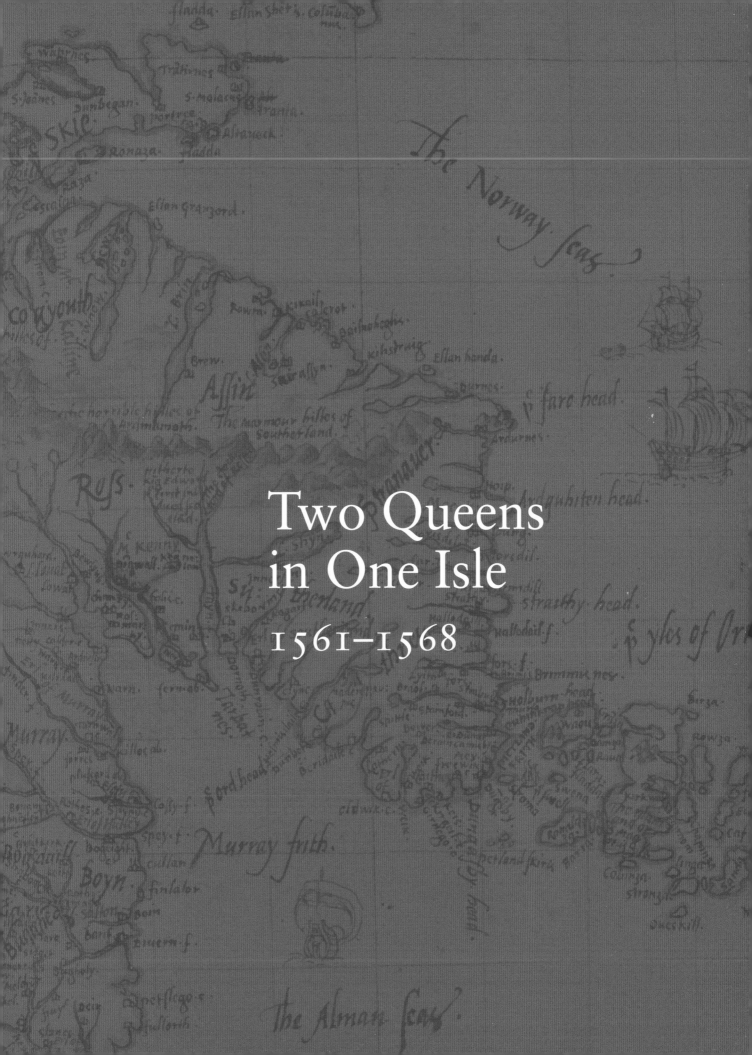

Two Queens
in One Isle
1561–1568

4

TWO QUEENS IN ONE ISLE (1560–8)

Simon Adams

The death of Francis II on 5 December 1560 brought radical changes to both Mary's life and the government of France. Catherine de' Medici, who moved swiftly to become effective regent for her son, the 10-year-old Charles IX, had no love of the Guises, no personal affection for Mary nor any interest in Scotland.

There was no doubt that Mary would return to Scotland, but the question was whether she should accept the 1560 religious settlement there or try to overturn it by force. Both her half-brother Lord James Stewart and her Guise uncles advised her to take the peaceful route. As for Elizabeth and her councillors, they vacillated over whether it would be better to separate Mary from her uncles or keep her an absentee in France. Elizabeth was adamant, however, that Mary should first ratify the 1560 Treaty of Edinburgh as a demonstration of good will. Refusing to permit her to travel to Scotland through England until she did so, Elizabeth forced Mary to take the riskier sea route to Leith, where she arrived on 19 August 1561.

Mary immediately proclaimed that she would maintain the religious status quo until a new settlement was made by parliament. This interim would include freedom for her and her household to retain the Mass. Yet she did not propose a new settlement in any of her three parliaments. It quickly became clear that she was less concerned with the government of Scotland than with her place in the English succession.

In September 1561, Mary's ambassador William Maitland of Lethington saw Elizabeth at Hertford Castle and warned her that the Treaty of Edinburgh was now obsolete. In its stead he proposed a new treaty in which Mary would recognise Elizabeth as queen (thus surrendering any immediate Catholic claim) in exchange for recognition as her heir. Elizabeth refused, citing various political reasons against naming an heir, including her own experience in her sister's reign. From subsequent discussions with Cecil and Lord Robert Dudley, Maitland learned that Elizabeth was not averse to a personal meeting the following summer, an idea Mary had proposed in the spring. But there were worries that the meeting could backfire, and so planning for it proceeded cautiously.

On 6 July 1562 it was finally agreed that the queens would meet at either York or Nottingham between 20 August and 20 September. However, on 16 July an outbreak of hostilities in France (in what became the First War of Religion) caused Elizabeth to postpone the meeting to the following summer. Plague in England then made that meeting impossible, and when Elizabeth attempted to revive it in 1564, Mary for mysterious reasons was not interested. Mary was studiously neutral during the First War and instead undertook a controversial royal progress through north-eastern Scotland as far as Inverness that led to the destruction of the leading Scottish Catholic nobleman, George Gordon, fourth Earl of Huntly, in the Battle of Corrichie on 28 October 1562. Despite the poor weather Mary was ebullient, claiming to enjoy a soldier's life. The sickly adolescent not believed to live long (the subject of much political speculation in 1559–60) was now an athletic, near-Amazonian woman.

Having intervened in the French War of Religion, Elizabeth summoned a parliament for January 1563. She had, however, suffered a serious attack of smallpox the previous October, and this brought the question of marriage and the succession to the fore. In 1561 she had rejected a marriage to Eric XIV of Sweden and dismissed one to Dudley on the grounds that as Master of the Horse he was her servant. The House of Commons now petitioned her to settle the succession; the petition was strongly anti-Catholic, so by implication hostile to Mary and in favour of the probable Protestant candidate, Lady Katherine Grey. Appreciating that she had painted herself

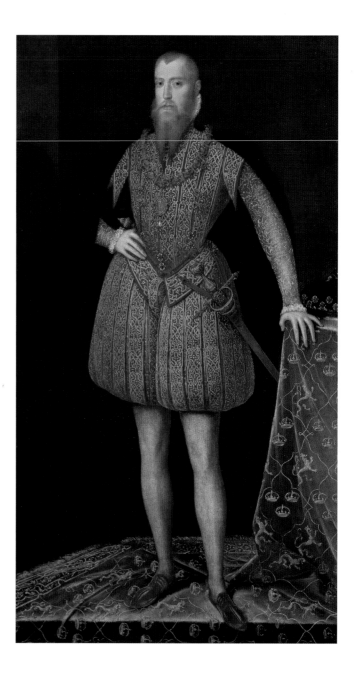

Eric XIV, King of Sweden, who sought the hand of both Elizabeth I and Mary, Queen of Scots.

Steven van der Meulen, 1561. Nationalmuseum, Stockholm.

into a corner, Elizabeth announced that she was in fact prepared to marry. In the autumn, cautious advances were made to revive an earlier proposal of Archduke Charles of Austria, cousin of Philip II of Spain.

The English succession debates made Mary's remarriage more pressing. By the end of 1561, her desire to marry Philip II's heir Don Carlos became known, but this marriage faced a number of barriers. Not only could Don Carlos not leave Spain, but his behaviour after suffering a head injury in 1562 raised questions over his sanity. Moreover, he was earmarked for marriage elsewhere. Nonetheless, Mary initiated direct negotiations for Don Carlos in the summer of 1563 through her personal secretary Pierre Raulet. Raulet was a central figure in her inner household, one of the French and Italian servants she brought with her or who, like the Savoyard musician David Rizzio, joined her later. It is not clear how much Maitland knew of these negotiations. Philip II vacillated over Mary's marriage proposition during the winter of 1563–4 but in the summer decided that she should marry the Archduke Charles, not his son. Precisely when Mary learned of his decision is unclear.

During the parliament of 1563 Elizabeth began hinting that she preferred Mary to marry an English husband. In August she followed this with a warning that if Mary rejected her advice she might not be able to protect her title to the succession (cat. 51). In March 1564 she formally nominated Lord Robert Dudley. Mary did not reject him out of hand but requested clarification of the terms of the marriage. Elizabeth appreciated that she had not helped her case by describing Dudley as her servant and on 29 September created him Earl of Leicester. The result was an Anglo-Scots conference at Berwick in November to discuss what the marriage would involve. The Scottish representatives stated that parliamentary recognition of Mary's title was essential.

Meanwhile, in September 1564, Matthew Stewart, Earl of Lennox, returned to Scotland after a long period of exile in England. Despite rumours that he and his wife (a granddaughter of Henry VII) were seeking to marry their son Henry, Lord Darnley to Mary, Elizabeth allowed the young man to visit Scotland. He met Mary on 17 February 1565. The next month, Elizabeth informed Mary in answer to the Berwick conference that she could not make a declaration on the succession until she had resolved her own marriage. Mary reacted furiously to Elizabeth's letter and by early April she was showing Darnley open affection (cat. 53). She then sent Maitland to inform Elizabeth that without parliamentary recognition Leicester was not suitable and that since Elizabeth had objected to foreign alternatives, she had found Darnley 'not

James Stewart, first Earl of Moray, the illegitimate half-brother of Mary, Queen of Scots who became James VI's regent after her deposition and was assassinated in January 1570.

Hans Eworth, 1561.
Private collection.

unmete [unsuitable]' and requested her approval for their marriage. Darnley was of the blood royal of both England and Scotland – he was also as tall as she was. But he was a divisive figure in Scotland, thanks to the rivalry between the Lennoxes and Hamiltons over the succession to the royal house of Stewart. He was also regarded with suspicion by James Stewart, now Earl of Moray, and his Protestant allies.

Elizabeth was furious at what she considered deception by the Lennoxes. She returned Maitland in early May 1565 with her willingness to assent to any husband other than Darnley, but while he was en route Mary announced she would go through with the marriage regardless. On 15 May she created Darnley Earl of Ross. By June, James Hamilton, Duke of Châtelherault, had allied with Moray against the marriage, but the two lords were unable to win popular support. Despite their opposition, Mary had her marriage celebrated with the Catholic rite on 29 July. Although it was agreed that the government would be in the joint names of the king and queen, she did not grant Darnley the crown matrimonial (see also pp. 34–9).

On 6 August 1565 Mary outlawed Moray and his allies (cat. 57). In what became known as the Chaseabout Raid, she pursued them across central Scotland until they arrived at Dumfries on 5 September and requested military assistance from her English cousin. Elizabeth had already sent them some money but, although her privy council supported military intervention, she preferred a French proposal of joint mediation. Mary, although now in the first stages of pregnancy, refused mediation and marched on Dumfries. In early October the lords retired into England.

Mary's apparent success had created its own tensions. She had recalled a number of exiles, mainly Catholics, but also James Hepburn, Earl of Bothwell, whom she appointed lieutenant general for the march on Dumfries, a command Darnley had expected. In December 1565 she allowed Châtelherault to retire to his French estates, but Moray was summoned to appear before a parliament to be held the following March. This was another setback for Darnley, for whom the Hamiltons were the main enemy. He refused to sign the safe-conduct for Châtelherault, forcing Mary to have a stamp made of his signature. It was believed the stamp was in the custody of David Rizzio, who had succeeded Raulet as Mary's personal secretary at the beginning of the year. He was also believed to be encouraging Mary's intransigence. The treatment of Moray seriously worried Mary's Protestant supporters, but the trigger for political instability was Darnley's jealousy of Rizzio's intimacy with the queen. At the beginning of February 1566 he appealed to his relatives – Lords Ruthven and Lindsay and the Earl of Morton – to aid him 'to be revenged' on Rizzio. They also agreed to assist Darnley to obtain the crown matrimonial, in return for which he promised to restore the exiled lords and ratify the 1560 religious settlement.

James Hepburn, Fourth Earl of Bothwell and Duke of Orkney, Mary's third husband.
Anonymous painter, 1566.
Scottish National Portrait Gallery PG 869.

On the evening of 9 March 1566, Darnley and his allies burst into the queen's chamber in Holyroodhouse and stabbed Rizzio to death. Three days later the effectively imprisoned Mary won over Darnley and they escaped to Dunbar. Joined by Bothwell and other supporters, they then marched on Edinburgh. On 21 March Mary agreed a general settlement in which Morton, Ruthven and Lindsay were accused of Rizzio's murder and Darnley proclaimed innocent; Mary also agreed to remit the outlawry of Moray and the Chaseabout lords. Morton and Ruthven fled to England, where Ruthven died, but not before writing a detailed and documented account of the conspiracy that challenged Mary's own description, especially whether her life had actually been in danger.

MARY'S ADVANCED STATE OF PREGNANCY PROVIDES AN IMMEDIATE MOTIVE FOR HER DESIRE FOR A PEACEFUL SETTLEMENT

Mary's advanced state of pregnancy provides an immediate motive for her desire for a peaceful settlement. The birth of Prince James on 19 June 1566 made this no longer necessary, and by the autumn Mary's estrangement from Darnley had become public. So too had her partiality for Bothwell – even if it was exaggerated in later accounts. In December there was a discussion at Craigmillar Castle between Mary, Moray, Maitland, Bothwell and the Earls of Argyll and Huntly over a divorce from Darnley and its possible effects on the legitimacy of Prince James, though the rival accounts disagree on the positions taken.

The birth of James exacerbated the English succession debate. For financial reasons Elizabeth needed to recall the prorogued parliament of 1563 in October. With no result of her promise to marry, since her negotiations with the Archduke Charles had stalled, she faced pressure from both Houses to settle the succession (cat. 59). On 5 November 1566 she snapped back in a famous speech that concluded 'it is monstrous that the feet should direct the head'. She also declared, 'I thank God I am indeed endued [endowed] with such qualities that if I were turned out of the realm in my petticoat, I were able to live in any place in Christendom.' Mary would also use this trope from the Italian poet Boccaccio the following year. But, after the parliament, Elizabeth made some significant concessions. She offered to resolve the succession with Mary and initiated a new effort to negotiate the archducal marriage. The Earl of Sussex left for Vienna at the end of June 1567, after some debate over the concessions she was prepared to make.

Elizabeth's negotiations with Mary were halted by the murder of Darnley at Kirk o' Field in Edinburgh (cat. 63) in the early morning of 10 February 1567 – an event that was even more disputed than the death of Rizzio. Mary's problem was that revenge for Rizzio's death made her the prime suspect, as Elizabeth immediately warned her. Her subsequent actions did not establish her innocence. As well as only going through the motions in investigating Darnley's murder, she did not disguise her closeness to Bothwell. On 19 April he persuaded the lords assembled for the parliament to sign the 'Ainslie's Tavern Bond' agreeing to his marriage to the queen (Mary's role is disputed). On 21 April Mary went to Stirling; on her return she was 'abducted' by Bothwell and taken to Dunbar. There was immediate suspicion she had gone to Stirling to regain possession of the prince from

IHS

Iudge and zevenge my cause o lord

The Darnley Banner depicting the corpse of Darnley together with his son, James, calling for divine retribution. Carried by the Confederate soldiers at Carberry Hill, it was also displayed afterwards, opposite the house where Mary was staying in Edinburgh.

The National Archives, Kew, MPF 1/366.

his guardian John Erskine, Earl of Mar, but Mar had refused to surrender him. On 1 May, four earls – Mar, Morton, Athol and Argyll – signed a bond to protect the prince, pursue the king's murderers and rescue the queen. By 8 May, four more earls and ten barons had joined what became known as the Confederate Lords.

Mary and Bothwell returned from Dunbar on 6 May and she created him Duke of Orkney six days later. They were married in a Protestant service at Holyrood on 15 May, before a small congregation. On 28 May she announced that she and the duke would conduct a circuit to administer justice (a justice ayre) in the Borders, but they were surprised by the Confederates at Borthwick Castle on 10 June. Bothwell escaped to Dunbar, and the following night Mary followed him in disguise as a man. With a small army assembled from local lairds, they advanced on Edinburgh but were confronted by the Confederates at Carberry Hill on 15 June (cat. 66). To avoid bloodshed and enable Bothwell to escape, Mary surrendered herself to the lords.

THE CONFEDERATES' PROBLEM WAS that they had rescued a queen who did not want to be rescued. On 18 June she was transferred to Lochleven Castle (cat. 67). Three days afterwards (according to Morton's later testimony) some letters and sonnets written by Mary to Bothwell – which are now known as the 'Casket Letters' – were discovered, and news soon circulated in London that incriminating material had been found. The Casket Letters shed no light on Kirk o' Field itself, but they are evidence that Mary brought Darnley to Edinburgh in concert with Bothwell and that his later abduction of her was collusive. The letters also give Mary another motive for wishing Darnley dead – freedom to marry Bothwell. Though the process is murky, the result was that Mary resigned the crown to her son on grounds of ill health in 'letters of demission'. She signed and sealed the demission on 24 July together with the nomination of Moray as regent for James, who was crowned at Stirling on 29 July. In 1568 Mary declared she had been intimidated into signing; and in the 1580s she claimed to have been suffering from exhaustion following a miscarriage. More interesting is the possibility that she hoped that by demitting office she would be freed to live privately with Bothwell and then found it was out of the question.

Moray's acceptance of the regency made him now the pivotal figure in Scotland. He visited his half-sister on several occasions during the autumn, but she apparently refused to repudiate Bothwell. Bothwell had escaped by sea, first to Orkney and then to Norway, where he was 'interned' by Frederick II of Denmark in September. Moray also summoned a parliament in the name of James VI that met in December. Its extensive legislative programme included ratifying the 1560 religious settlement and passing a statute that declared that the incriminating Casket Letters justified the Confederates' actions. Yet no further action could be taken over Mary until Bothwell could be brought to trial in Scotland.

This stalemate left Mary imprisoned, but on 2 May, thanks to careful planning by her supporters, she escaped and was able to reach Hamilton Castle in Lanarkshire (cat. 69). There she apparently repudiated her abdication. On 13 May her largely Hamilton army marched westward to escort her to Dumbarton. Moray was then in Glasgow and intercepted her at Langside (at that time a village south of the Clyde). After her army collapsed, Mary immediately fled south and outside Dumfries announced she would go to England. With a party of fourteen men and one woman she crossed the Solway Firth in a fishing boat, landing at Workington in Cumberland on 16 May. She informed Elizabeth of her arrival on the following day (cat. 71).

Elizabeth had been unable to exert any influence over the fast-moving events in Scotland in the summer of 1567. She opposed the demission, despite her doubts about Mary's innocence (cat. 68), but her attempt to orchestrate another Anglo-French mediation was aborted by the outbreak of the Second War of Religion in September 1567. Elizabeth's leading councillors warned that given the wider situation in Europe Moray was the best ally she had. The succession was another issue. Mary's Protestant rival Lady Katherine Grey died on 17 January 1568, and in February the marriage negotiations with the Austrians collapsed. Mary's claims had not been repudiated in the demission and Elizabeth now had the exiled queen thrust upon her.

5 'BOTH THE FAIREST LADIES IN THEIR COUNTRIES':

ELIZABETH AND MARY'S ENCOUNTERS THROUGH PORTRAITURE

Charlotte Bolland

'She desired to know of me, what colour of hair was reputed best; and whether my Queen's hair or her's was best; and which of the two was fairest. I answered, The fairness of them both was not their worst faults. But she was earnest with me to declare which of them I judged fairest. I said she was the fairest Queen in England, and mine the fairest Queen in Scotland. Yet she appeared earnest. I answered, They were both the fairest ladies in their countries.'

When the Scottish ambassador James Melville visited the English court in 1564, he found that Elizabeth was eager to learn more about her cousin. Having previously shown him a portrait of Mary in her possession, Elizabeth quizzed him about Mary's hair, her height, her skin and her dancing ability (cat. 52). This curiosity was reciprocated. Two years earlier Mary had keenly questioned the English envoy Thomas Randolph after finally receiving a portrait from Elizabeth, asking: 'How like is it unto the Queen your Mistress's lively face?' In the 1560s, as unmarried queens regnant, each offered the other their closest point of comparison, but they would only ever encounter each other by proxy: through the reports of their ambassadors, the gifts that they gave each other, and, most powerfully, in the portraits that they exchanged.

Elizabeth and Mary's portrait exchanges served the practical purpose of informing each about the other's appearance, while also allowing for the performance of intimacy and devotion. The model for this may have been set for them at an early age by the strong interest in portraiture demonstrated by the maternal figures in their lives. Elizabeth's stepmother Katherine Parr was probably responsible for the commissioning of the half-length portrait of the princess by William Scrots that marked her rehabilitation in the eyes of her father Henry VIII, whilst Catherine de' Medici commissioned François Clouet to make a number of portrait drawings of her future daughter-in-law Mary during the course of her childhood at the French court, in order to monitor the young girl's health (p. 24). However, from such similar foundations, their personal iconographies followed very different trajectories, with Elizabeth's artists and courtiers creating ever more iconographically rich images of the queen, whereas Mary's image gradually distilled into the likeness of a queen in eternal mourning that would proliferate after her death.

The young Elizabeth wearing a gown of crimson and gold, fabrics that were reserved by the sumptuary laws to the royal family.

William Scrots, *c.*1546. Royal Collection Trust / © Her Majesty Queen Elizabeth II 2021.

Elizabeth was well aware of the power of portraits to stand proxy for her presence, writing to her half-brother Edward VI in 1551 that she hoped that 'when you shall look on my picture, you will vouchsafe to think that as you have but the outward shadow of the body before you, so my inward mind wisheth that the body itself were oftener in your presence'. Intriguingly, this letter suggests that Elizabeth was much more reticent in the presentation of her portrait than in the demonstration of her learning, as she notes that 'for the face, I grant, I might well blush to offer, but the mind I shall never be ashamed to present'. Any personal reluctance to sit for her portrait was only exacerbated by the precariousness of her position during the reign of her half-sister Mary I, and the uncertainty of the early years of her own reign. As a result, the earliest image that Mary, Queen of Scots saw of her cousin may have been of the type that prompted Catherine de' Medici to interrupt the English ambassador in frustration as he described Elizabeth, stating that 'after what everyone tells me of her beauty, and after the paintings of her that I have seen, I must declare that she did not have good painters'. This is likely to have been one of the simple images of Elizabeth attired in black that were produced in the late 1550s. The negative reception of her early portraits may lie behind the decision of Elizabeth's privy council to draft a proclamation that sought to regulate the production of the queen's image in 1563. Although there is no evidence that this was put into effect, the 1560s saw a marked shift in Elizabeth's imagery, with the production of more portraits for the pragmatic purpose of marriage negotiations (cat. 60).

By contrast, the vivid colour and lavish jewels of the earliest painted portrait of Mary to survive attest to her status as queen of Scotland and future queen of France (cat. 21). Painted by Clouet, this small image shows Mary in a carnation dress, standing before a striking blue background.

Mary's placement of a ring on the fourth finger of her right hand suggests that the portrait was produced to mark her marriage to the dauphin in 1558. It forms part of the Royal Collection and may have been presented as a gift to Elizabeth. Mary certainly initiated an exchange of portraits with her cousin in 1560, informing the English ambassador Sir Nicholas Throckmorton that 'because the one of us cannot see the other, I will send her my picture, though it not be worth the looking on' and extracting a promise that the English queen would reciprocate, 'for I assure you, if I thought she would not send me hers she should not have mine' (cat. 37).

However, Elizabeth appears to have been unable, or unwilling, to send her portrait, and the following year, Mary was indignant that she had still not received Elizabeth's image, remarking to the ambassador that: 'You know I have sent mine to the Queen, my good sister, according to my promise but have not received hers.' In delaying the sending of her portrait, Elizabeth was flouting the conventions of reciprocity that governed gift-giving in the sixteenth century and risked appearing to be deliberately snubbing her cousin. Years earlier, her father Henry VIII had responded immediately with gifts of portraits of the royal family after Francis I sent portraits in miniature of his sons to the English court, whilst Henry VII had been forced to recruit a new court artist after he was unable to reciprocate when portraits were sent to him by the Duke and Duchess of Burgundy.

It was not until July 1562 that Elizabeth's portrait arrived in Scotland. The long delay was reported to have been due to the artist's ill health, indicating that it was a special commission. It may have been made by the miniaturist Levina Teerlinc, who was the only artist recorded as regularly producing portraits of Elizabeth in the early years of her reign. Teerlinc was the daughter of the Flemish illuminator Simon Benninck and, after entering Henry VIII's service in 1546, she went on to serve each of his children, receiving an annual salary of £40 as a court painter. Her earliest documented portrait of Elizabeth was painted in 1551 and it is possible that this was the portrait that Elizabeth 'blush[ed] to offer' to her brother when she wrote to him from Hatfield that year. During Elizabeth's reign, Teerlinc presented a number of small portraits to the queen as gifts at New Year; none of these have been securely identified, but Teerlinc may have been responsible for the early miniatures of Elizabeth that survive in the Royal Collection. A miniature would have been of a practical scale to transport to Scotland and would have facilitated the protestations of devotion that each queen wished to make. The scale of miniatures created an intimate encounter with the sitter, as the recipient was forced to bring the portrait close to their face for inspection. Their passage from hand to hand also brought a performative element to their viewing, as they could be revealed through unwrapping; presented to another viewer or withheld from prying eyes; worn concealed within a jewel; or pinned to clothing with the portrait on display for all to see. On this occasion, Mary used the encounter

IN DELAYING THE SENDING OF HER PORTRAIT, ELIZABETH WAS FLOUTING THE CONVENTIONS OF RECIPROCITY THAT GOVERNED GIFT-GIVING IN THE SIXTEENTH CENTURY

with Elizabeth's portrait to state to the English ambassador Randolph, 'let God be my witness, I honour her in my heart, and love her as my dear and natural sister': a message reinforced by the gift of a ring with a heart-shaped diamond that she sent to Elizabeth as thanks for the portrait.

Elizabeth mirrored this exchange with the Scottish ambassador James Melville in 1564. She took him into her bedchamber and showed him a number of miniatures wrapped in paper that she kept within a little cabinet; among them was a portrait of Mary that she took out and kissed in the ambassador's presence, causing him to adventure 'to kiss her hand, for the great love therein evidenced to my mistress'. This could have been Clouet's image of Mary in pink, or possibly a portrait commissioned specifically for Elizabeth following Mary's conversation with Throckmorton in 1560. If made at that date, it would most likely have shown her wearing white mourning (*en deuil*) for her father-in-law and mother, as seen in an oil portrait of Mary by Clouet that entered the Royal Collection in the seventeenth century (cat. 38). As Clouet was an adept miniaturist, it is possible that a smaller version of this composition was originally sent to Elizabeth. Given that Elizabeth's conversation with Melville centred on the possibility of Mary marrying Robert Dudley, an image of Mary in mourning would certainly have been more appropriate to the context than a celebration of her first marriage.

MARY SEEMS TO HAVE favoured miniatures; however, inventories suggest that rather than keeping them within the intimate spaces of her bedchamber as Elizabeth did, she preferred to wear them. An inventory of her jewels from 1566 describes an enamelled mirror on a cord with a metal tip, which opened like a watch to reveal an image of 'la Royne d'Angleterre' among a group of figures inside, and the inventory compiled for probate after her execution in 1587 describes 'a book of gold enamelled containing the pictures of the late Scottish queen, her husband and her son'. Both of these were likely to have been worn around the waist, and were probably made by a French painter in enamel and oils, Jean de Court, whom Mary had retained in her service even after her return to Scotland. It is therefore unsurprising that during her captivity in England she sought to continue this patronage. In January 1575, she wrote to the exiled Archbishop of Glasgow to request that four of her portraits in gold cases be sent to her secretly from France which she could then give to her supporters. By this point, however, de Court had become *peintre du roi* following the death of Clouet, and it is possible that no portraits were made. As a consequence, Mary was forced to turn to an English artist for the first time. This resulted in perhaps the closest encounter between the cousins, through the eyes of the artist who portrayed them both: Nicholas Hilliard.

Hilliard's portraits of Mary and Elizabeth allow for direct comparison of the two queens and their self-presentation. Given their questioning of their respective ambassadors, it seems unlikely that they would have failed to exploit the occasion for the 'discreet talk' that Hilliard advised could 'shorten the time and quicken the spirit, both in the drawer and he which is drawn' whilst a miniature was being made. Certainly, even the lightest conversation about their choices of clothing and jewels would have provided

(left) **Elizabeth I**

Nicholas Hilliard, c.1580–5.
Royal Collection Trust / © Her Majesty
Queen Elizabeth II 2021.

(right) **Mary, Queen of Scots,**
while she was captive in the
household of George Talbot,
Sixth Earl of Shrewsbury.

Nicholas Hilliard, c.1576.
Royal Collection Trust / © Her Majesty
Queen Elizabeth II 2021.

rich subject matter. Both commonly wore black and white, but whilst these were Elizabeth's favoured colours and worn by her champions in the tiltyard, for Mary they were a marker of her mourning for Darnley. Her preference had been pointedly reinforced by Elizabeth years earlier: when Mary fled to England and asked if Elizabeth might send her some gowns as she had only the clothes she stood up in, Elizabeth's response was to send black velvet, black satin and black taffeta. Similarly, the simple crucifix that Mary chose to be depicted wearing, positioned high around her neck so that it would still be seen in the close-cropped composition, seems to stand in deliberate contrast to the lavish jewels and pearls with which Elizabeth chose to be adorned in her portraits by Hilliard.

The circumstances by which Mary's sitting with Hilliard was arranged are not known. Mary was evidently seeking to have miniatures made, and her mother-in-law, Margaret, Countess of Lennox, could have acted as a conduit to the artist: she was in regular contact with Mary and had sat for Hilliard in 1575. However, given Hilliard's close ties to the English queen at this point, it is perhaps more likely that it was Elizabeth who took the opportunity to capture Mary's likeness. As Mary was her prisoner, there would be no pressure to reciprocate and give Mary the opportunity to critique her image, and of all those involved in the politics of the 1570s, it was surely Elizabeth who would be most eager to contemplate the Scottish queen's portrait and hold it in her hand.

Mary's Return to Scotland

In December 1560 Francis II died as the result of an ear infection, and consequently Mary had to return home. She arrived at Leith on a dank foggy morning in August 1561, a week earlier than expected, so only a handful of people, including Lord James Stewart, were waiting to greet her. Soon afterwards she was welcomed properly, and bonfires were lit in Edinburgh.

Before her arrival, Mary had agreed to make no alteration to religion in return for the right to hear a private Mass in her chapel, and on 25 August she issued a proclamation upholding the religious status quo until a parliament should settle the matter. The following Sunday John Knox preached a sermon denouncing the queen's idolatry and the reintroduction of the Mass in the Chapel Royal. As a result he was summoned before Mary and on 4 September was given his first audience with the queen.

37

Two Queens in One Island

Letter from Sir Nicholas Throckmorton to Elizabeth I, 22 August 1560, Melun in the Île-de-France.

The National Archives, Kew, SP 70/17, f. 81v.

Throckmorton was appointed English ambassador to France in May 1559 with instructions to disrupt the 'Auld Alliance' and to seek the restitution of Calais to Elizabeth. On 18 August 1560 he had an audience with Mary, Queen of Scots' uncle, Charles of Guise, Cardinal of Lorraine, in which they discussed ongoing negotiations over the ratification of the Treaty of Edinburgh and the arrival in England of King Eric XIV of Sweden (p. 84), as a suitor to Elizabeth. Throckmorton then had a brief audience with Francis II, after which he was conducted to Mary, 'accompanied with her ladyes and gentlewomen in very good order set about the chamber'. Usually Mary was accompanied during audiences with ambassadors by either her mother-in-law, Catherine de' Medici, or her uncles, and she would follow their lead in a carefully rehearsed fashion. This was her first solo audience, which she carried off both skilfully and graciously.

Throckmorton spoke to Mary 'in Englishe', 'wherunto she answered in Scottishe'. She told him she would follow her husband's direction regarding the treaty. She then spoke earnestly about Elizabeth, saying she expected the English queen to stop supporting Scottish rebels against her. 'And thoughe I be her suster because I am a Quene, as she is, which name worketh kindnes betwixt susters, yet tell her, there is more betwixt her and me, for we be both of one blood, of one countrey, and in one ylande, and by that tyme she haue made profe, she shall finde my frendshippe, more honnorable and to stand her in more stede, then the amity of my subiectes being Rebellis.' Here, she skilfully reminded Throckmorton of her strong claim to be heir presumptive to Elizabeth, framing it in the language of kinship, amity and unity. Her Guise uncles expressed similar sentiments: Elizabeth and she were 'bothe Queens, yn [one] isle, nere Kynswomen & yn maner off [one] language', they informed Throckmorton; and this kinship became the keystone of Mary's policy towards England for the remainder of her reign.

Mary had heard that Elizabeth was 'bothe a wise and very faire lady'. Because they could not meet in person, she proposed that they exchange portraits. She then said to Throckmorton, 'I perceive youe like me better when I loke sadly then when I loke merily; for it is told me youe desired to haue me pictured, as I ware the dueil.' The *deuil blanc* was the white mourning dress Mary had just recently put off, having worn it for her mother (cat. 38). AB.

nerest kinswoman, she hathe, being bothe of us of one house and
stock, she Quene my good sister coming of the brother and I
of the sister, So as being issued out of the same stock, I love
the same stock she lovethe, and assuredly can as ill beare inurie
as she can, and therfore I pray her to judge me by her self,
for I am sure she woold ill beare the disgrace, and disobedience
of her subiects, which she knowethe myne have shewed but now,
and write unto her from me, that as I am her nerest kinswoman
So I will for my part in all my dinge make it good, loking
for the like at her handes, and that we may se the resting of
us shall shewe moost kindnes to other, and I pray your maiestie
Embassadors (as sir) write unto her that I have once forgiven,
and forgoten the faultes of my subiects for her sake, and at her
request, trusting that she wille contented, if they feel theie
duties greased, they may be made to leme to know it, onely
that they shall receive no comfort at her handes, but rather
that she wille helpe me to have obedience of them, And though
I be her suster betause I am a Quene as she is, owing never
woorldes kindnes betwixe susters, yet tell her, there is more
betwixe her and me, for we be bothe of one blood, of one
countrey, and in one ylande, and by that tyme she have made
profe, she shall finde my frendshipe, more honorable and
to stand her in more stede, then the amitie of my subiects
being rebellis: Now (as sir) my mother is dead, whilste she
lived, I was ever troubled to the rare of her countrey, and
now I must be troubled to the rare of it my self, and tell
her I pray you that sayng we can not one of us see an
other, nor speak together, that yet we may use that kindnes
together, that dothe please ethe other, whilst we be absent,

38

Mary, Queen of Scots

François Clouet, c.1560–1.

The Royal Collection / Her Majesty Queen Elizabeth II, RCIN 403429.

Over the course of little more than eighteen months, Mary lost her father-in-law Henry II, her mother Mary of Guise, and her husband Francis II. Plunged into formal grieving, she returned to Scotland in 1561 wearing the white veils of French court mourning, which the poet Pierre de Ronsard described as billowing 'fold upon fold like a sail in the breeze as the wind drives the boat forward'.

Mary's appearance *en deuil blanc* was captured by Clouet in a drawing in the Bibliothèque Nationale de France,

perhaps commissioned as another family record by the bereaved Catherine de' Medici. The *deuil* encompassed a wired cap that was pressed flat on the crown of the head with a white gauze veil that fitted tightly in pleats at the chin. Clouet also made paintings of Mary in mourning; this version entered the Royal Collection in the seventeenth century during the reign of Charles I.

The public praise of Mary's pallor by poets and ambassadors perhaps suggests that James Melville chose his words particularly carefully during his audience with Elizabeth in 1564, when on repeated questioning about which queen was fairest, he finally conceded that Elizabeth was 'whiter' than Mary (see cat. 52). CB.

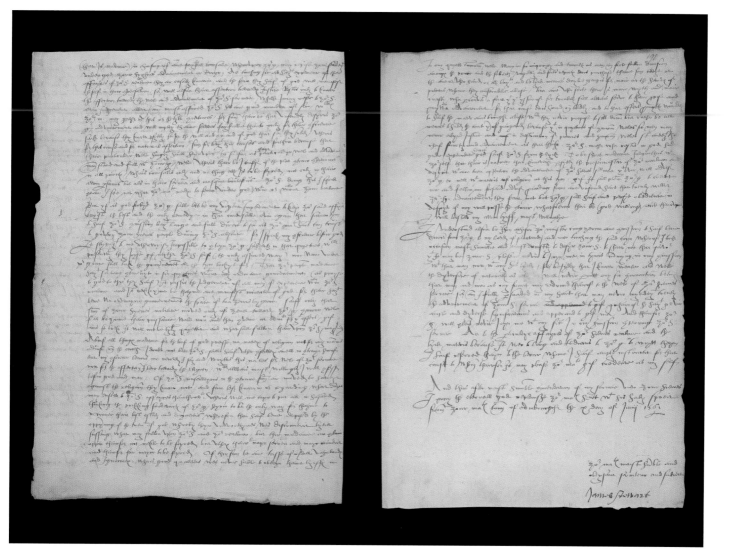

39

Mary Reaches a Détente

Letter from Lord James Stewart to Mary, Queen of Scots,
10 June 1561, Edinburgh.

British Library, Additional MS 32091, ff. 190v–191r.

Lord James Stewart was the illegitimate son of James V and
his mistress, Lady Margaret Erskine, which made him half-
brother to Mary, Queen of Scots. One of the leaders of the
Lords of the Congregation, following the death in December
1560 of Mary's husband he accepted that she must return to
Scotland and sought a rapprochement with her. He visited
her in France in spring 1561 to 'fully grope … her mynd'.
They spent five days discussing Mary's homecoming. Stewart
promised to defend her right to hear the Catholic Mass in
private, to support her government and to advance her claim
to be recognised as heir presumptive to Elizabeth I. In return,
Mary agreed to make no alteration to religion.

Once back in Scotland, Stewart wrote this long letter of
counsel to Mary in June, in which he reminded her 'abuif
all thingis madame for the luif of god presse na materis
of religion not for ony mannis aduise on the earthe'. He
also explained that her petition for Catholic toleration had
been ignored, because her Protestant subjects continued
'sa ernistlie bent vpon ane reformation of sic [such]
abuses'; and he counselled her to maintain friendship
towards England.

In another letter, sent to Sir Nicholas Throckmorton,
Stewart described how he had returned to Edinburgh
to find 'the wikked papistis' gathered in strength, 'wha
braggit (as mycht be) to sett oup the messe again'. They
quickly dispersed on learning that Mary had agreed to
recognise the state of religion as established. She quickly
came to depend on Stewart and on her Secretary, William
Maitland of Lethington. AB.

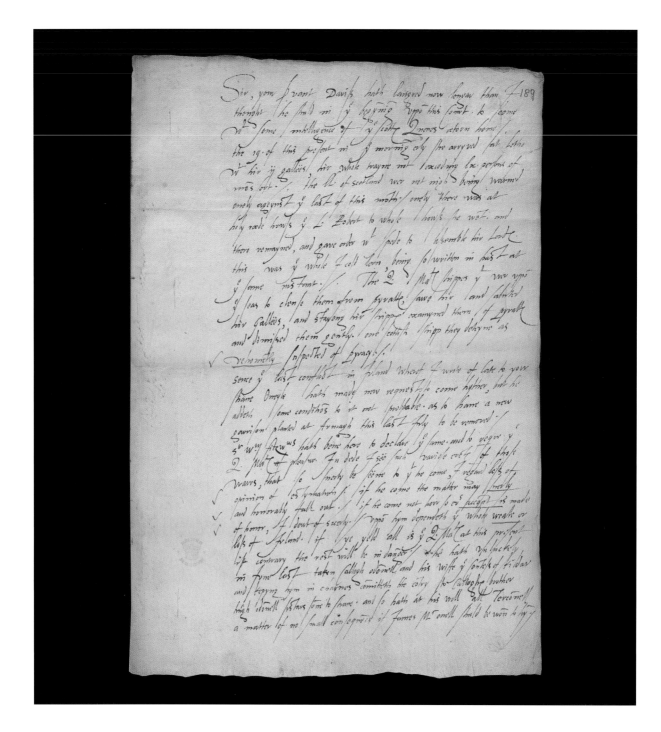

40

Mary's Return to Scotland

Letter from Sir William Cecil to Sir Nicholas Throckmorton,
26 August 1561, Bishop's Stortford.

British Library, Additional MS 35830, f. 189r.

In July 1561, Mary requested permission from Elizabeth I
to return to Scotland through England. Elizabeth refused,
because Mary would not ratify the Treaty of Edinburgh, and
insisted that she must 'doo those thynges that by hir promiss
under hir hand and seal she is boun[d]'. In this letter, written
in his distinctive italic hand, Sir William Cecil recounted to
Throckmorton how Mary arrived on 19 August at Leith by
sea, with 'hir whole trayne not exceding lx. [sixty] persons

of mens [mean] sort'. For some in Scotland, Mary's return
was unwelcome. John Knox later described the same event
in his *History of the Reformation*, noting how there 'was
never seen a more dolorous face of the Heaven, then was at
her Arrivall'.

Elsewhere in the letter, Cecil updated Throckmorton on
other unfolding domestic issues, reporting that the heavily
pregnant Lady Katherine Grey remained in the Tower of
London. The Protestant great-granddaughter of Henry VII and
possible heir presumptive to Elizabeth, Katherine had secretly
married Edward Seymour, Earl of Hertford. Infuriated, the
queen imprisoned her and had the marriage judged unlawful.
Once born, her son was declared a bastard. AT.

41

William Cecil, first Lord Burghley

[Arnold Bronckorst?], 1573.

By kind permission of the Most Hon. the Marquess of Salisbury, Hatfield House.

Inscribed: 15 AB 73

Appointed Principal Secretary in the opening days of
Elizabeth's reign, Sir William Cecil remained a trusted advisor
to the queen until his death. Only Robert Dudley, Earl of
Leicester, could rival his influence. Surviving images suggest
that his portrait was widely circulated, and in its production,
he seems to have followed the approach that he advocated
for the queen in a draft proclamation from 1563, which

attempted to regulate her portraiture, giving one artist a
sitting in order to create an approved portrait that could be
reproduced over time.

The earliest version of this portrait type likely pre-dates
Elizabeth's accession, as Cecil is depicted without his symbols
of office. In this version, which is dated 1573 at the base
of the column, Cecil holds the white staff of his office as
Secretary and wears the insignia of the Order of the Garter,
to which he was elected in 1572. The 'AB' monogram in
the inscription has been associated with the artist Arnold
Bronckorst; however, the paint handling and inscription are
very different in style from Bronckorst's signed portrait of
Oliver St John, first Lord Bletso. CB.

42

Cecil and the British Isles

Laurence Nowell, the Nowell-Cecil Atlas, *c*.1564–5.

British Library, Additional MS 62540, ff. 3v–4r.

In June 1563 the antiquarian Laurence Nowell wrote to Cecil with a proposal to map England and Ireland more accurately than ever before in order to aid Cecil in his office as Principal Secretary, 'besides especially I marvel at the way you take delight in small maps'. It was probably the following year that Nowell produced this pocket map, 'A general description of England & Ireland with the costes adioyning', using ink and coloured wash on parchment. At the time of its creation it was perhaps the most accurate map of the British Isles available. Nowell has portrayed himself reclining on a pedestal at the bottom left, holding an empty purse in his left hand. The inscription on the pedestal is taken from Hesiod's *Works and Days*, line 96 ('only hope remained there in an unbreakable home within, under the rim of the great jar, and did not fly out at the door', after Pandora opened her box). Cecil is depicted seated on an hourglass at bottom right, arms folded, possibly in an expression of impatience. One of Cecil's dogs is seen barking at Nowell. This is perhaps a jest on Nowell's part over the fact that the atlas remains incomplete until Cecil can pay for the rest of the work.

Cecil used this and other atlases and maps to help him comprehend the British context to government policy. Nowell's 'general description' was more strategically focused than previous maps, especially in its representation of political geography. It went as far north as the Western Isles of Islay and Jura and Angus on the Scottish mainland, as far east as Flanders and as far south as Normandy and Brittany. On the back there is a list of the posts from London to Scotland, essential information during the shuttle diplomacy of the 1550s and 1560s. Cecil folded his atlas in half vertically in order to keep it in his pocket, ready for use at all times. He was still consulting it at his death in 1598. AB.

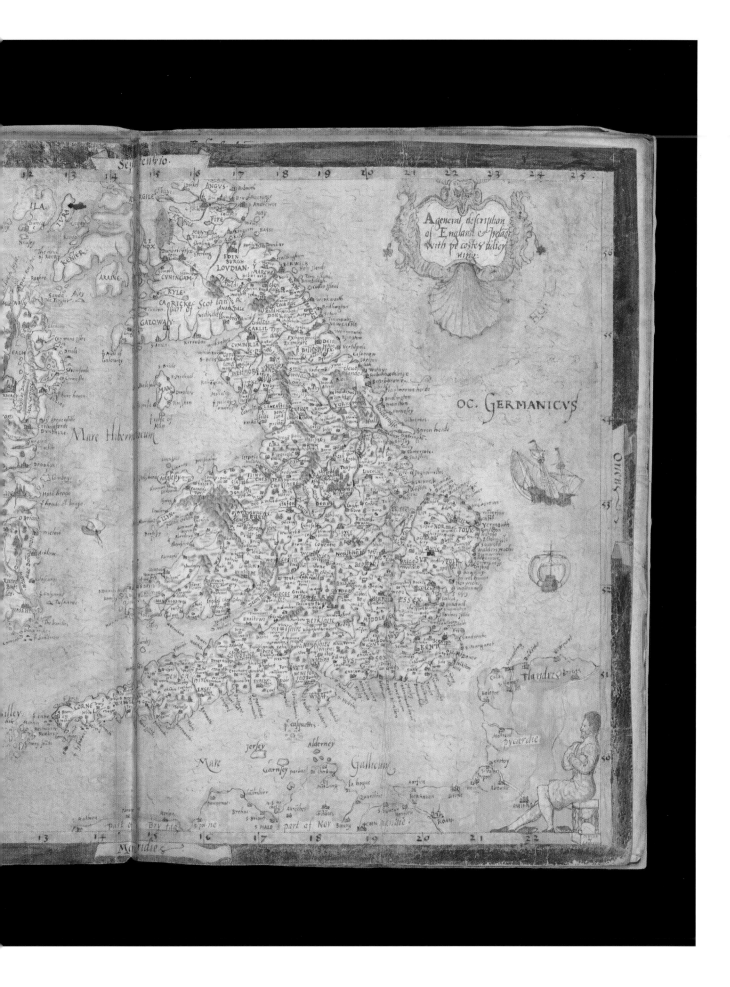

43

Marian Scotland

Laurence Nowell, map of Scotland, c.1564–5.

British Library, Cotton MS Domitian A xviii, ff. 98v–99r.

This map is part of a codex which contains other maps and prose by Laurence Nowell. By early 1563 he was living in Cecil's London house as tutor to his ward, Edward de Vere, seventeenth Earl of Oxford. Much of the codex can be dated to about 1564 because Nowell has noted where Robert Dudley, Earl of Leicester's principal estates lay in a map he made of the English midlands. Dudley was elevated to the peerage in 1564.

Nowell's map of Scotland was the most accurate produced to date, with west to the top, as was occasionally found at the time. Probably based on now lost manuscript maps and charts of the 1540s and 1550s in Whitehall Palace, it is even superior to the one he made in the Nowell-Cecil Atlas of c.1564–5 (cat. 42), which it presumably post-dates. Nowell recorded the most important burghs and castles in his map, including Edinburgh, Leith, Stirling, Perth in Strathearn, St Andrews, Dumbarton in the Lennox and Glasgow; the principal routes through the marches; and the centres of power of the Scottish nobility and Highland chieftains – all essential information for Cecil to formulate government policy in a British context. It is uncertain what purpose was intended, but the map seems to have been produced primarily for personal use, and scholarly curiosity was almost certainly an important element. Elsewhere in the codex, Nowell made brief notes on Scotland's geography and transcribed relevant passages from the fourteenth-century chronicler Ranulf Higden's *Polychronicon*, as well as creating detailed maps of England with supposedly Anglo-Saxon placenames. AB.

The ylc

ed hebrides

TREY.
COLLE.

Carndeburg

MVLL

Lochenubuer

Brard Alba

Batzenoth

GOWREA

Fiffis Nes

Read head.

Barri
mac Neil

Colt bang

Harry

Lewis
Mac Leod Lewis

Stornway

fladda

Ellan Shot's

SKIE

S. Joanes

portree

Altaueck

Ronaza

Fladda

Ellan granzord

Coryouth

The horrible hilles of
Brimhmoth

Assin

The marmour hilles of
Southerland

Ross

Stranauer

Mac ky

Ardquhiten head

M. Kenny

thenland

Erl of southerland

Ca Athney

Murray

Borough

Murray frith

Boin

finlator

Boyn

The Norway seas

y faro head

Ardquhiten head

strathy head

yles of Orkney

Brimmit ney

Holsburn head

Birza

Rowsa

The Alman seas

Buguthon Nes

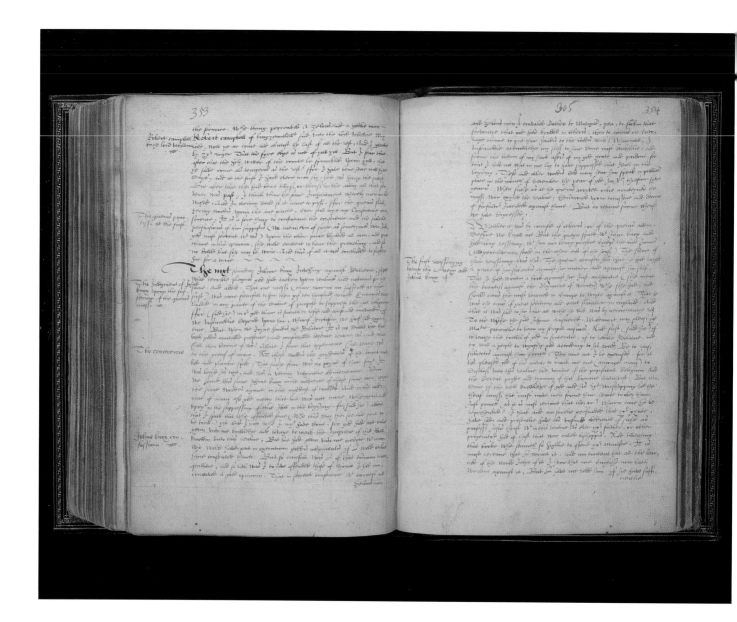

44

John Knox's First Audience with Mary

The manuscript of John Knox's *The History of
Reformation* (1566).

Edinburgh University Library, Laing MS III 210, pp. 353–4.

John Knox recounted his audiences with Mary, Queen of
Scots in his *History* and it provides the only source for
what was discussed. This section of the *History* was written
in 1566 when Knox had withdrawn from Edinburgh to
Ayrshire. His disillusionment was reflected in the side-notes
and digressions from the narrative to highlight lessons to be
learned from the years 1561–5.

Knox's first royal audience took place on 4 September
1561, shortly after the initial celebration of Mary's private
Mass at Holyrood. His account emphasised the split that
the concession created among Scottish Protestants, with
Lord James Stewart leading the 'courteours' blocking those
demanding the end of 'idolatrie' in the Chapel Royal. When
preaching in St Giles', Edinburgh, on 'the nixt Sonday' Knox
had declared that one Mass 'was more fearful to him then
gif ten thousand armed enemyes war landed' to overturn
Protestantism. That sermon provoked 'the first reassonyng
betwixt the Queyn and Johne Knox' when Mary taxed
the preacher with raising her subjects in rebellion against
her mother, Mary of Guise, and herself. They argued over
Knox's 1558 tract *The First Blast of the Trumpet against the
Monstrous Regiment of Women* and the authority of a queen
regnant. After further debate over whether the Protestant or
the Catholic Church was the true one, this audience ended on
civil terms. JD.

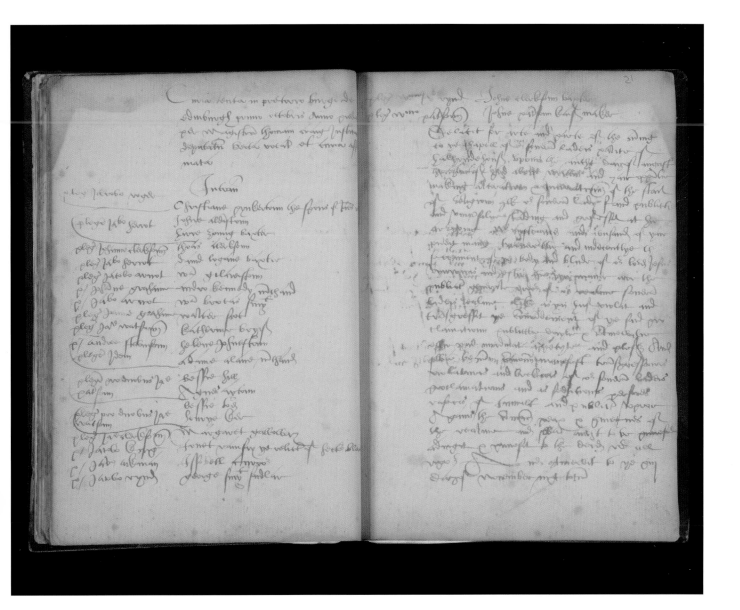

45

Marian Catholicism

Justiciary Court indictment, 1 October 1563.

National Records of Scotland, Edinburgh, JC1/12, ff. 20v–21r.

Just as John Knox had feared, many Catholics began joining Mary and her household at Mass in the Chapel Royal. Twenty-six inhabitants of Edinburgh were indicted at the Justiciary Court on 1 October 1563 and charged with attending the chapel at Holyroodhouse on 8 August, 'and [th]air oppinlie making alteratioune & innovatiovne of the stait of religioun quhilk our soueran lady fand publiclie and vniuersalye standing and professit at hir arryving', by celebrating Mass. Mary was in Stirling at the time.

The accused included merchants such as Adam Allan and Cuthbert Murray, the smith William Brocas, the saddler George Smyth and the cutler John Paterson, and ten women, among them Katherine Bryce, Helen Johnston and Isobel Currer. The husbands of Bryce, Johnston and Currer (James Watson, Andrew Stevenson and James Aikman respectively) entered pledges on their behalf. All three men were nominally Protestants. Watson and Stevenson were actually burgh councillors. Many of the twenty-six accused were related.

Although it was ordered that the men and women indicted 'aucht to be … adiugit & punesit to the deid with all rigour', they seem to have escaped with minimal punishment. Most of the merchants, for example, were still in trade two years later. AB.

Marriage and Succession

Parliament petitioned Elizabeth to marry or name a successor during the early years of her reign. The queen had many suitors – especially from abroad – but showed no inclination to marry any of them, and observers thought that she was hoping to wed her Master of the Horse, Sir Robert Dudley. In the parliament of 1563, the pressure mounted because Elizabeth had almost died of smallpox the previous October. At the close of the session, Elizabeth answered their petitions with the announcement that she was prepared to marry even though as a private woman she would have preferred to remain single. There was no question of Elizabeth naming a successor. Not only did she fear the consequences of a named heir waiting for – perhaps even hastening – her death, but also Protestant MPs would not accept Mary, Queen of Scots as heir presumptive. Their open rejection could only endanger Anglo-Scottish relations.

46

The Succession

Elizabeth I's answer to a petition of the House of Commons, 10 February 1559.

British Library, Lansdowne MS 94, f. 29v.

On 4 February 1559 MPs began debating the succession. Two days later a delegation of the House of Commons petitioned the queen to marry so that she might have a child and thereby settle the succession. This is a contemporary copy of her answer, which was read out to the Commons on 10 February. She told them 'that from my yeares of vnder standing ... I happelie chose this kynde of life in which I yet lyve [virginity] which I assure yow for myne owne parte, hath hitherto best Contented my self and I truste hath bene most acceptable to god'. If any 'Could have drawne or dissuaded me from this kynd of life I had not now remayned in this estate wherin yowe see me. But Constant have allwayes Contynved in this determynacion.' The queen did not rule out marriage but asserted that she would be bound by God's providence and not by parliament or public opinion. Her marriage was one of the *arcana imperii* or 'mysteries of state', discussion of which by her subjects she would not tolerate.

As to the second half of the Commons' petition, Elizabeth told them that she took it in good part that they did not seek to limit the crown by making her name a successor. She would make no such determination now, she said, but believed that God would choose 'a fitt governor' to succeed her. 'And in the end this shalbe for me sufficient that a marble stone shall declare, he[re] l[ieth Elizabeth which] reign[ed] a tym[e a virgin] & dyed a virgin.' AB.

or determyne harme to my self, wherewith the realme may or shall haue
iuste cause to be discontented. And therefore put that cleane out of
your heades. ffor I assure you what credett my assurance may haue
with you I can not tell but what credett it shall deserue to haue
the sequele shall declare. I will never in that matter conclude any
thing that shalbe preiudiciall to the realme. ffor the weale, good
estate and safetie whereof I will never spare to spend my life. And wheras yo shes
my sepulchre shalbe to lieth vppon I trust he shalbe as carefull for
the realme and you. I will not saie as my self because I can not
so reasonablie determyne of any other but at the least wayes, by my
good will and desire, he shalbe such as shalbe as carefull for
the preservacion of the realme and you as my self. And albeit it
might please almightie god to contynew me still in this mynde to
lyve out of the state of mariage, yet it is not to be feared, but he
will so woorke in my harte, and in your wisedomes as good provision
by his helpe may be made in conuenient tyme, wherby the realme
shall not remayne destitute of an heyre that may be a fitt gouernor
and paraduenture more beneficiall to the realme then such ofspring
as may come of me. ffor although I be never so carefull of your
well doinge and mynd euer so to be, yet may my issue grow
out of kynde, and become parhappe vngracious. And in the
end this shalbe for me sufficient that a marble stone shall declare that a Queene having reigned such a tyme lived and dyed
a virgen. And here I end and take your douinges in so good
parte, and geue you for the same all effectuall my harte thankes more yeth
for your zeale and good meaninge then for your petic̃õns

Feb, 10 1559/60

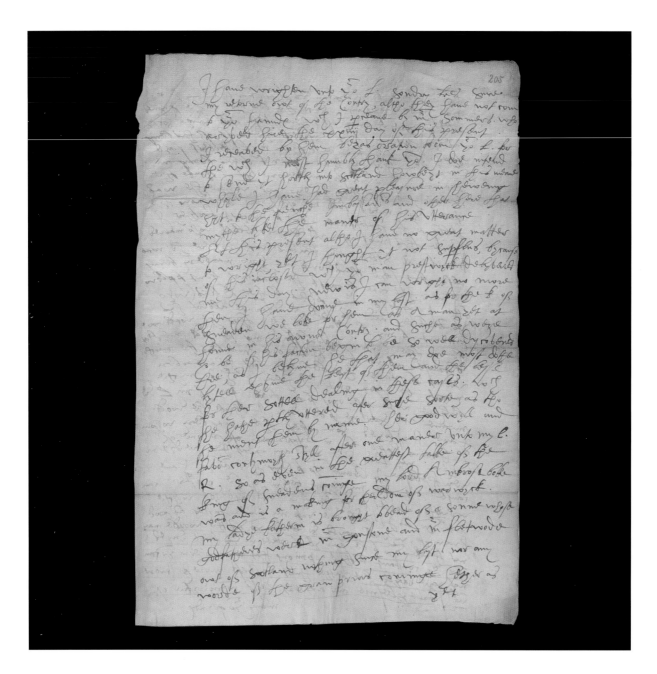

47

My Lord Robert

Letter from Henry Killigrew to Sir Nicholas Throckmorton,
28 September [1561], London.

British Library, Additional MS 35830, f. 205r.

During the early years of her reign, Elizabeth received
marriage proposals from Philip II of Spain, the Archduke
Charles of Austria, several foreign dukes and Henry
Fitzalan, twelfth Earl of Arundel. The Lords of the
Congregation also proposed a marriage between Elizabeth
and the Protestant James Hamilton, third Earl of Arran,
second in line to the Scottish throne, in order to strengthen
ties with England.

In September 1561 the diplomat Henry Killigrew sent
this newsletter to Sir Nicholas Throckmorton, the queen's
ambassador in France, and reported that people were
eagerly anticipating the arrival of Eric XIV of Sweden (p.

84), who had renewed the proposal he made to Elizabeth
during Mary I's reign and was believed to be travelling to
England to woo the queen in person. The marriage would
have united England with another Protestant kingdom,
but Killigrew confided that he did not think Elizabeth was
interested because 'her goodwyll and favour contynwyth
styll after one maner vnto my L[ord] R[obert]'.

Although Elizabeth seemed to enjoy being courted by
foreign suitors, she was deeply in love with the dashing and
athletic Dudley, who – despite being married – was soon
suspected of being the reason why Elizabeth ultimately
rejected all other marriage candidates. In September 1560
Dudley's wife died in mysterious circumstances. Eventually
cleared of any involvement, Dudley sought to win the
queen's hand, but after much agonising Elizabeth decided
that she could not risk her reputation nor jeopardise her
hold on power by marrying him. AC.

48

Robert Dudley, Earl of Leicester
Steven van der Meulen, *c*.1561.

Robert Dudley, Earl of Leicester, was Elizabeth I's favourite, accumulating offices and honours from the beginning of her reign, many of which are referenced in this portrait. He wears a jewelled medal of St George around his neck, signifying his status as a knight of the Order of the Garter, the insignia of which encircles his coat of arms in the upper right corner. His elevation to an earldom in 1564 resulted in the addition of the earl's coronet above the coat of arms, whilst the collar of seashells in the upper left was added following his invitation to join the French chivalric Order of St Michael in Elizabeth's stead in 1566.

Dudley was one of the most active patrons of the arts in England in the sixteenth century. He sat for his portrait to numerous artists and these images were widely disseminated. New scholarship has suggested that the spur for the commissioning of this portrait may have been the presentation of a portrait of Eric XIV of Sweden to Elizabeth in June 1561 as part of marriage negotiations (p. 84). The Flemish artist, Steven van der Meulen, had travelled to Sweden with an English merchant, John Dymocke, in the hope that the creation of the portrait would support his request for English denizenship. Dudley – as a rival for the queen's hand – may have commissioned a portrait from the same artist to offer the queen the opportunity to make direct comparison of her suitors. Van der Meulen only had a brief career in England; he was granted denizenship in 1562 but died the following year. ET.

his unckle

But ther can be no ~~never~~

~~dowar~~ dowar ... than princes word ~~...~~
~~...~~ to kep unspotted for my part ~~I was one that~~
wolo be lothe that ~~that wich kips~~ the marchants credit
from crasi shulde be the cause that princes ~~...~~ shulde
merite blame and so ther honor quaild ~~and sins~~ a answer therfor
I wil make ~~...~~ and thes it is ~~the~~
the two ~~...~~ that you ~~...~~ in many wordes
coteined thes two thinges in sorti, my mariage and
my successar of wiche two the last I thinke is best ba
toched and of the other a silent thoght may serve for
I had thoght it had bine so desired as ~~not none~~
other trees blossomes shuld have ~~...~~ bine ~~...~~
or ~~...~~ had bine denied yo consent, to thé last thinke
not that you had mevd this desire if I had bine
a time so fit and it so ~~...~~ to be ~~p donvinced~~ thi
oretches of the cause therfor and wei of your
retournes dothe make mi say that wiche I thinke
the wise may yis that as a shot time for
so longe a cotinuance ought not passe by
rote as many teleth tales even so as
cause by coference with the lerned shal
show ... matter worthy utterance for
your behofes so shal I gladly pursue
your good after my dayes ~~...~~
my prayers ~~...~~ meane to linger
my liuing thrive And this mochi more
than I had thoght wil I adde for your
cofort I have good record in this place
that other ~~...~~ have bine thoght of
behauche for your good as mochi
for my surty no les wiche
presently colde have bine ...
had not bine in quiet offerd but I hope I
shal die with nunc dimittis wiche
can not be without I se some ...
of your folowing surty after my graue
bones

49
Nunc Dimittis

Elizabeth I's answer to the House of Commons and Lords' petition that she marry, delivered by the Lord Keeper, Sir Nicholas Bacon, 10 April 1563.

British Library, Lansdowne MS 94, f. 30r.

In October 1562 the issue of the succession became a matter of urgency when Elizabeth contracted smallpox. Believing her life to be in danger, she instructed that, in the event of an interregnum, Dudley should be named protector of the realm. The queen recovered but the episode served as a stark reminder that the survival of the Tudor dynasty and the security of Protestant England depended on an unmarried female monarch, without a named heir. Elizabeth's ministers feared that her death would trigger a war of succession between rival claimants Mary, Queen of Scots, heir presumptive by hereditary right, and Lady Katherine Grey, a descendant of Henry VIII's younger sister Mary and rightful heir according to Henry VIII's will.

The following year, the Houses of Commons and Lords petitioned the queen to marry and name a successor. This is Elizabeth's draft response, written in her atrocious cursive or 'business' hand, which had replaced the elegant italic hand of her youth. The multiple corrections provide evidence of the considerable care that the queen, a master of rhetoric, took over the wording of the speech. The final version was delivered on her behalf and in her presence by Lord Keeper Sir Nicholas Bacon, at the prorogation of parliament on 10 April 1563. Elizabeth made it clear that she reserved the right to choose whether she would ever marry but also insisted that she had *not* determined *not* to marry: 'if any here dowte that I am as it wer by vowe or determination bent neuer to trade that life put oute that heresie your belefe is awry for as I thinke it best for a privat woman so do I strive with my selfe to thinke it not mete for a prince and if I can bend my wyl to your nide [need] I wyl not resist suche a mynde'.

On the matter of the succession, Elizabeth was equally non-committal but assured parliament that she wished to die peacefully, which could only happen if the succession had been secured: 'I hope I shal die in quiet with nunc dimittis wiche can not be without I se some climpes [glimpse] of your folowing surty after my graved bones'. *Nunc dimittis*, meaning 'Lord, now lettest thou thy servant depart in peace', is a quotation from the Song of Simeon in the New Testament (Luke 2:29–32). AC.

The Question of Marriage

In early 1562 Mary was hoping for a personal meeting with Elizabeth at which her right to the succession would be agreed. But the interview was postponed, and indeed never took place. After this disappointment, Mary's thoughts turned to marrying again, and her ambassador opened up informal negotiations with the Spanish ambassador for a match with Philip II's son, Don Carlos. However, Elizabeth warned that a foreign marriage would be viewed as a hostile act and proposed Lord Robert Dudley as an alternative suitor. To make him a suitable rank to marry a queen, she created him Earl of Leicester in 1564. However, when Elizabeth made it clear that she still would not recognise Mary as her heir even if this marriage took place, the Scottish queen looked elsewhere for a husband. Her eyes fell on her second cousin Henry Stuart, Lord Darnley, a grandson of Margaret Tudor and another great-grandchild of Henry VII. Despite Elizabeth's strong disapproval, the marriage took place on 29 July 1565 in the Chapel Royal at Holyroodhouse. The following day, the heralds proclaimed Darnley's new title as king of Scotland.

Elizabeth was not the only one to object to the marriage. When Darnley's title was proclaimed, it was greeted with silence. Worse still, a few months before the wedding, James Stewart, Earl of Moray, withdrew from court in disgust and refused to obey Mary's repeated summons to attend. When Mary put him 'to the horn' [outlawed him], he raised troops and attempted a rebellion, known as the Chaseabout Raid. Elizabeth refused him military help, and as a result he fled over the border and sought asylum in England.

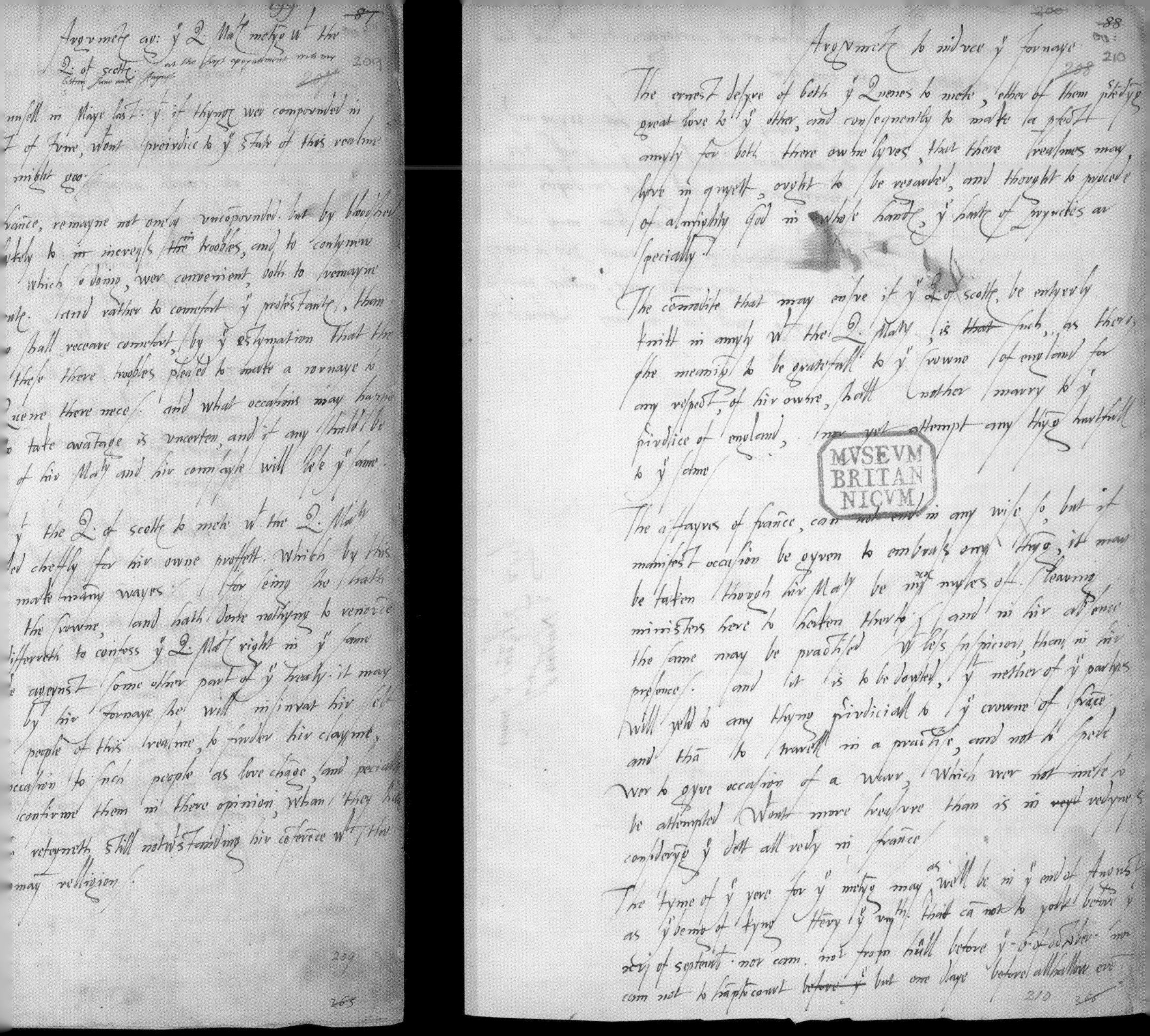

50

Meeting of the Two Queens

Sir William Cecil, pro and contra memorandum, 30 June 1562.

British Library, Cotton MS Caligula B x, ff. 209r and 210r.

Mary, Queen of Scots repeatedly declared her great desire for friendship and a face-to-face meeting with Elizabeth I in the hope of obtaining public recognition of her right to the succession. In January 1562, Elizabeth responded positively and, despite Cecil's strong reservations, officials began to prepare for a meeting in York that summer. Two months later, however, the troops of Mary's uncle, Francis, second Duke of Guise, massacred Huguenots at Vassy, sparking the First War of Religion between the Guise-led Catholics and the Protestants led by Louis, Prince of Condé.

This 'pro and contra' memorandum, setting out arguments for and against Elizabeth meeting Mary, is one of

hundreds penned by Cecil to help him structure his thoughts on a range of key issues and policies. The second point states that the situation in France now made the interview untenable because the Guises would 'receave comefort by ye estymation that the Q. Maiesty is in these there troobles pleased to make a iornaye to mete with the Quene there nece'. Furthermore, the meeting would be to Mary's profit because she would use it to 'insinvat hir self to somes sortes of people of this realme to furder hir clayme' to the throne.

Arguments in favour included 'the ernest desyre of both ye Quenes to mete, ether of them pretendyng great love to ye other, and consequently to make a perfect amyty for both there owne lyves'. In July 1562, Elizabeth committed military aid to the Protestant cause in France and the projected meeting between the two queens was postponed. AC

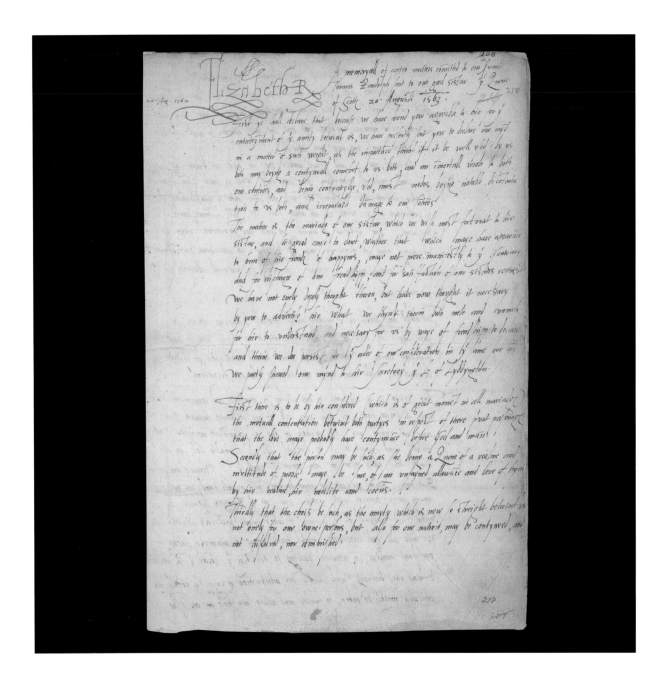

51

Two Queens, One Amity

Instructions for Thomas Randolph, 20 August 1563.

British Library, Cotton MS Caligula B x, f. 218r.

Thomas Randolph had been in Scotland since September 1559, when he became heavily involved in the clandestine English support for the Lords of the Congregation. He remained there as Elizabeth I's diplomatic agent, although he was never accredited ambassador. In August 1563 he was issued new instructions by the queen. His main task was to foster the amity between Elizabeth and Mary, Queen of Scots at a time of strained relations due to English intervention in France's First War of Religion. The best way of achieving this, Elizabeth thought, was if Mary followed her counsel regarding her choice of husband. Having 'depely thought theron', she told Mary to consider first 'the mvtuall contentation betwixt both partyes in respect of there privat

personages'; in other words, whether or not she was in love. 'Secondly that the person may be such, as she being a Quene of a realme and mvltitude of people, maye be sure, of an vnfayned allowance and love of hym by hir realme, hir nobilite and comens.' Third, and most important, Mary's choice of husband should not undermine amity with England. She warned Mary against following the counsel of her uncle, Charles of Guise, Cardinal of Lorraine, who was conducting secret marriage negotiations at this time with Archduke Charles of Austria, the third son of the Holy Roman Emperor, Ferdinand I. Elizabeth saw such a match as a grave threat to her throne and warned Mary against it, saying she would not recognise her as heir presumptive in such circumstances. Mary coolly received Elizabeth's message on 1 September, saying to Randolph that she would answer it in due course. Randolph wrote to Cecil, 'I knowe not yet her graces lykyng of the matter'. AB.

52

The Fairest Ladies of their Courts

Sir James Melville's autograph memoirs, c.1600.

British Library, Additional MS 37977, ff. 33v–34r.

Elizabeth I's proposal that Robert Dudley would make a suitable husband for Mary, Queen of Scots caused great offence and coincided with a deterioration in relations between the two queens. In late September 1564 Mary sent her envoy James Melville on a nine-day visit to London, primarily to smooth matters over with Elizabeth but also to treat secretly with Margaret, Countess of Lennox 'to purches leawe for [Darnley] to pass in Scotland'. Melville's autograph memoirs, which cover the years 1564–94, provide a detailed account of his daily meetings with Elizabeth and a fascinating insight into her preoccupation with her Scottish cousin and the human curiosity and rivalry which lay at the heart of their relationship.

During Melville's first audience with Elizabeth, she requested an update on the Dudley marriage proposal, keen to point out that 'sche estemed him as hir brother and best frend, whom sche suld have married hir self, had she not been determined to end hir lyf in virginite'. Instead, 'sche wissit that the quen hir sister suld mary him, as metest of all vther, and with whom sche mycht find in hir hart to declaire the quen second personne'. Elizabeth required Melville to stay to witness Dudley being ennobled as Earl of Leicester. He wryly observed that as Dudley kneeled before the queen, 'sche culd not refrain from putting hir hand in his nek, to kitle [tickle] him smylingly'. On another occasion, in Elizabeth's private chambers, the Scottish ambassador was 'accidentally' shown a miniature of Dudley, labelled 'My lordes picture'. Elizabeth declined his request to take it for Mary as 'sche had bot that ane of his'.

Over the course of his visit, Elizabeth bombarded Melville with questions about Mary's appearance. When quizzed about which of the two queens was fairest, he tactfully replied that both were 'the fairest ladyes off thar courtes, and that the quen of england whas whytter, bot our quen was very lusome [attractive]'. On hearing that Mary was taller, Elizabeth retorted that Mary 'was ouer heych, and that hir self was nother ouer hich nor ouer laich'. Further questions about Mary's accomplishments followed and Elizabeth was interested to hear that she played the virginals 'raisonably for a quen'. Later that evening, Elizabeth had a courtier take Melville to a gallery where she was playing the virginals 'excellently weill'. The ambassador probably anticipated what was coming and when Elizabeth demanded to know which queen played the virginals better, he 'gaif hir the prayse'. AC.

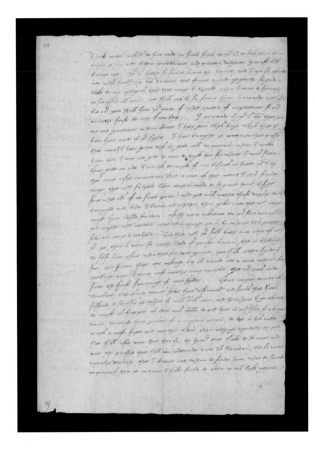

53

The Darnley Match

Letter from Thomas Randolph to Sir Henry Sidney,
31 March 1565, Edinburgh.

National Library of Scotland, Edinburgh, Adv.MS.1.2.2.24.

In this letter to Sir Henry Sidney, Thomas Randolph begins
by expressing frustration over the failure of the marriage
negotiations between Mary, Queen of Scots and Dudley,
now Earl of Leicester, whom Elizabeth I had put forward
as an acceptable alternative to a foreign prince. 'I have
broughte yt ... vnto that passe, that nowe that I have gotten
thys Q[ueen's] good will to marrie whear I wolde have her I
cane not gette the man to tayke her, for whome I was suter.'
Randolph then described Mary: 'ther is nowe so myche added
of perfet beautie, that in beholdinge the self same persone ...
you shall nether fynde that face nor feuter [feature], shape
nor makinge, but all torned into a newe nateur farr excellinge
anye (our owne moste worthye [Queen] onlye excepted) that
euer was made since the firste framynge of man kynde'. If
Elizabeth would recognise Mary as heir presumptive, she
would have her 'devotion'.

Randolph described Mary's favourable reception of her
kinsman, Henry Stuart, Lord Darnley, who had arrived at
court from England in February 1565: 'Ther is latelye ...
come vnto vs the yonge lustie longe lorde that loked euer
so loftie in the Courte whear he wente. I knowe not what
alteration that the syghte of so fayer a face dayelye in presens
maye worke in our hartes.' Randolph ended his letter to
Sidney by telling him how marginal a figure John Knox had
become. AB.

54

Henry Stuart, Lord Darnley

Cast by Domenico Brucciani, after unknown artist.
Electrotype of the alabaster figure of Henry Stuart,
Lord Darnley, on the tomb of his mother, in Westminster
Abbey (*c*.1560–5).

National Portrait Gallery, London, 359.

Mary, Queen of Scots' decision to make Lord Darnley her
second husband initially appeared to be a good choice. He
was handsome, well educated and accomplished, a fine
horseman and an excellent dancer, musician and poet. More
importantly, he was English born and had an excellent
dynastic pedigree for he had both English and Scottish
royal blood in his veins. Darnley's mother was Margaret
Douglas, Countess of Lennox, daughter of Henry VIII's elder
sister Margaret Tudor by her second husband, Archibald
Douglas, sixth Earl of Angus. His father, Matthew Stewart,
fourth Earl of Lennox, was a descendant of King James II
of Scotland. Mary and Darnley's marriage therefore united
their hereditary rights to the English throne and as a result
strengthened Mary's claim to the succession.

This small figure of Darnley is a replica of his effigy on
the elaborate tomb of his mother, which was erected by her
grandson James I in the south aisle of Henry VII's chapel in
Westminster Abbey. Dressed in armour, ruff and mantle, with
a crown placed above his head, Darnley is shown as a weeper
– in profile, kneeling and with his hands clasped in prayer.
His effigy in Westminster Abbey looks over to the magnificent
white marble tomb of Mary, Queen of Scots. AC.

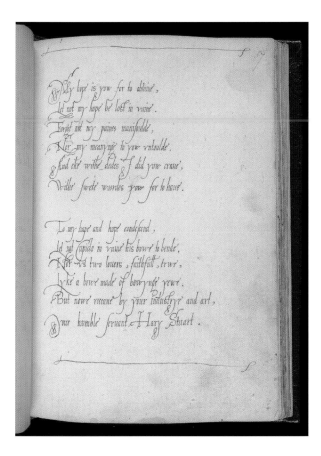

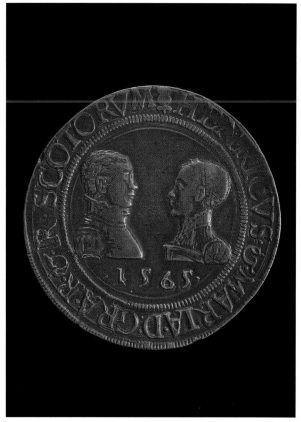

55

Darnley's Poem

Verses by Henry Stuart, Lord Darnley, written in his own hand, probably to Mary, Queen of Scots, beginning 'My hope is yow for to obtaine', 1565.

British Library, Additional MS 17492, f. 57r.

This manuscript contains a unique copy of a love poem, written in Darnley's own hand, 'My hope is yow for to obtaine, / Let not my hope be lost in vaine'. The twelve-line poem was probably composed between February and May of 1565 during his courtship of Mary. Soon afterwards, the queen made him Earl of Ross in a ceremony held at Stirling Castle. The promotion was the first public indication of the engagement between Mary and the nobleman.

These verses are found in the Devonshire Manuscript, a poetic miscellany originally compiled during the 1530s and early 1540s by several women at the court associated with Anne Boleyn. In addition to copies of poems by Geoffrey Chaucer, Thomas Hoccleve and Sir Thomas Wyatt the elder, the volume contains verses by Darnley's mother the Countess of Lennox, and her then husband Lord Thomas Howard, possibly exchanged in the Tower of London in 1536 during the couple's imprisonment for their unsanctioned secret marriage.

Darnley's poem, added around thirty years later in his elegant italic hand, asks Mary to 'forget not my paines manifoulde, / Nor my meanynge to yow untoulde'. Comparing the steadfast affection of 'us two lovers' to the bending bow of Cupid, Darnley ends by entreating his reader, 'But now receave by your industrye and art, / Your humble servant Hary Stuart'. AGB.

56

The Married Couple

Silver marriage ryal of Henry and Mary, King and Queen of Scots, 1565.

British Museum, London, 1849,0626.1.

The obverse of this coin shows uncrowned busts of Henry and Mary face to face, with the date, and surrounded by their names and titles as king and queen of Scots, placing Henry's name first, in the normal usage of the privy council. The design was one previously used by married ruling queens in Castile, Navarre and England and during Mary's marriage to Francis II of France. The reverse of the coin is traditional, with the Scottish royal arms between two thistles, but with a novel legend QVOS DEVS CONIVNXIT HOMO NON SEPARET, derived from Matthew 19:6 and familiar from the marriage service, 'Whom God has joined together, let not man put asunder'.

The only contemporary comment on the coin is from Thomas Randolph, the English ambassador, writing to William Cecil. He asserts that it was quickly withdrawn because it was unpopular. Certainly, a new non-portrait version of the ryal, now with two fractional denominations, was ordered in December 1565 in a document making no reference to the marriage ryal. This now placed Mary's name first. Randolph may have been correct, although it is also possible that he misunderstood or misrepresented the purpose of the first ryal, which may have been a ceremonial piece to be distributed at the wedding on 29 July.

This coin is now known from only two specimens. Weighing an ounce of fine silver, it was worth thirty shillings Scots, and was the first silver coin of its size in Scotland. BC.

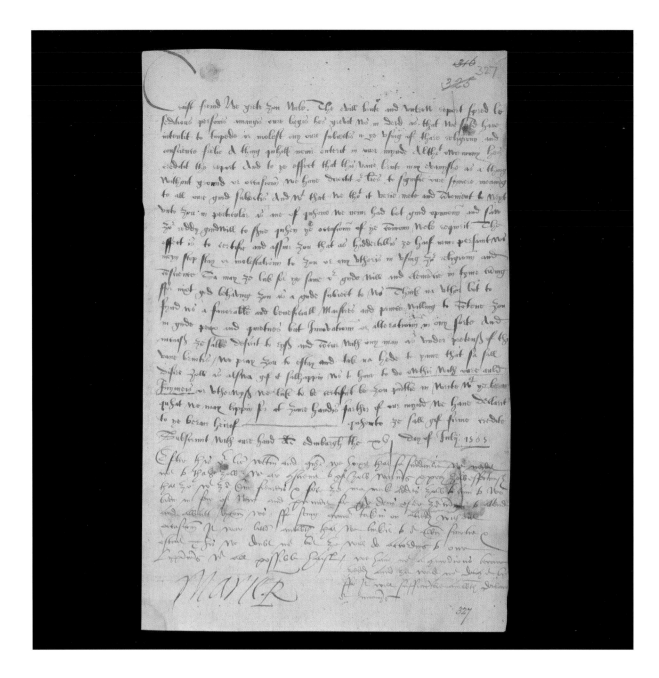

57

The Chaseabout Raid

Letter from Mary, Queen of Scots to an unknown addressee,
16 July 1565, Edinburgh.

British Library, Cotton MS Caligula B x, f. 327r.

In the weeks before her marriage to Lord Darnley, Mary
tried to appease her Protestant subjects by reissuing the 1561
proclamation upholding the religious status quo and making
clear that her Mass remained a personal one. But the marriage
reopened old political feuds between the Lennoxes and the
Hamiltons, who made common cause with James Stewart,
Earl of Moray, against the queen and Darnley. Although
Elizabeth I reacted angrily to the Darnley match, she could
offer little material support to James Hamilton, Duke of
Châtelherault, and Moray when they rebelled in August.

Mary wrote to her leading subjects for support against
the rebels. 'The evill brute and vntrew report spred be

seditious personis amangis oure legis hes grevit ws in
deid as that we suld haue intentit to Imbede [impede] or
molest ony oure subiectis in the vsing of thare religioun
and conscience frelie, a thing quhilk neuer enterit in
oure mynde'. 'Gif it salhappin [shall happen] ws to haue
to do owthir with oure auld Inymeis [the English] or
vtherwyss', Mary commanded her subjects to serve her
with all their power.

Most people ignored the rebel attempts to sow religious
division and backed the queen. Both sides took to the field
in the Borders late in August, manoeuvring inconclusively
against each other – and lending the rebellion its subsequent
name, the Chaseabout Raid. Châtelherault and Moray
found themselves heavily outnumbered, though, with many
of their own kinsmen and allies even serving Mary against
them. They were left with no choice but to seek asylum in
England early in October. AB.

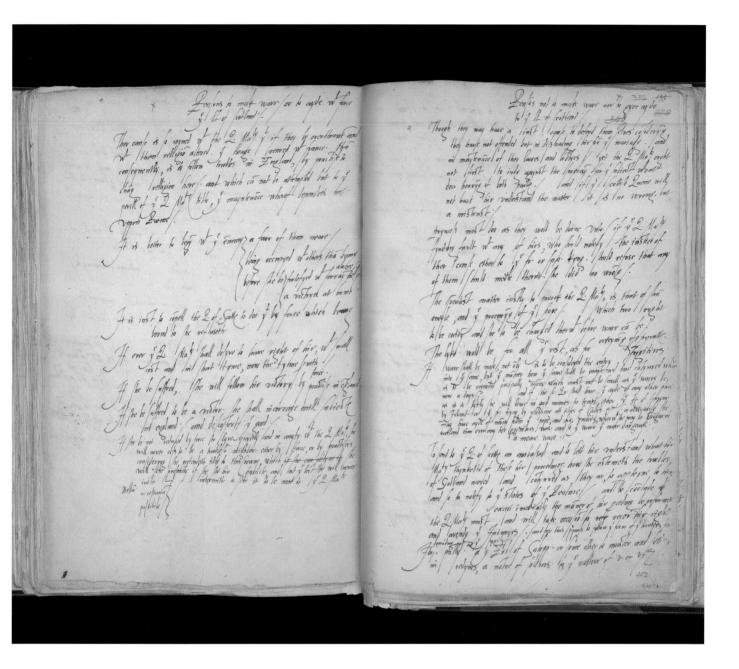

58

Constraints on English Intervention

Memorandum by Sir William Cecil, 24 September 1565.

British Library, Cotton MS Caligula B x, ff. 351v–352r.

In his usual manner when faced with problems (see cat. 50), Sir William Cecil set down in this memorandum the arguments for and against the continuation of amity between Elizabeth I and Mary, Queen of Scots. Reassessing their relationship, Cecil started with what impact Mary's refusal to ratify the 1560 Treaty of Edinburgh and her claim to be recognised as Elizabeth's heir presumptive had. It would be better, he argued in this classical rhetorical exercise, which was a product of his humanist training in government, if Elizabeth married and settled the succession through her male offspring.

The main focus of Cecil's memorandum was to explore reasons for invading Scotland in support of the Chaseabout rebels. These included that 'ther cause is so ioyned with the Q[ueen's] Maiesty that if they be overthrowne and with them relligion altered, the leage renved with france than consequently, is to follow troubles in England'. If Mary was not forced to back down against the rebels, she would be free to interfere in English politics, in particular by pressing more forcefully her claim to be recognised as heir presumptive, but also 'by practise to chang relligion here'. Reasons against invasion included not interfering in a conflict between Mary and her subjects without hearing from both parties first.

The 'meane waye' was for Elizabeth to send an ambassador to Mary to air her grievances, to threaten direct intervention and to support the rebels in some other, less open way. Cecil decided against putting the case for invasion before the queen and the privy council, not least because of 'the lack of disposition in the Queen's Maiesty to allow of warr'. AB.

I love so muche counterfeiting and hate so muche dissembling that I may not suffer you depart without that my admonitions may shewe your harmes and cause them vnseen perill. Two hath haue blinded the yees of the lokers one in this present cession so farforth as your pretince of bating the haue done some good. And these be succession and liberties. As to the first, the princes opinion and good wyll ought in good order haue bine felt in other sort than in so publik a place be vttered it had bine convenient that so waighty a cause had had his original from a princes consideration not of subiects laboured orations out of suche mouthes wiche what the be time may teache you knowe and ther demerites dyd make them acknowledge how the haue done ther lewde indevour to make all my realme suppose that ther care was muche whom myn was none at all. Ther handeling of this doth well shewe the being ignorant how fit my graunt shall be to suche a demand mani in one thing or ther imparfet dealings be excused for I think this be the first time that so waighty a cause passed from so simple monthes as began this case to liberties who is so simple that doutes whither A prince that is hed of all the body may not comaund the fete not to stray whan the wold slip. God forbid that youthe should any wais bondage my comandiment. But now whether I some whit you were borne bounde and you haue not no, you were borne bounde and you haue not wyth a gentl prince as your indulges scruph pehannce haue briede your causes blame. And albeit the souting of suche be reprovable in all yet I wold not you fould thinke my simplicite such as I can not make distinctions amonge you as of some

59

Lip-Laboured Orations

Autograph draft of Elizabeth I's speech dissolving parliament,
2 January 1567, delivered by the Lord Keeper, Sir Nicholas Bacon.

British Library, Cotton Ch. IV. 38 (2).

In the November 1566 parliament, MPs – fiercely divided between the supporters of Mary, Queen of Scots and Lady Katherine Grey – debated the issue of the succession again. Elizabeth was furious and tried unsuccessfully to silence the members on what she considered to be a private matter for the queen's prerogative and no business of theirs. Shown here is her speech or 'admonition' drafted for the dissolution of parliament the following January and delivered by Lord Keeper Sir Nicholas Bacon. A remarkable survival, it is one of only two of Elizabeth's parliamentary speeches that have come down to us in her own hand, the other being her speech of 1563 (cat. 49). This is perhaps due to the fact that neither text was published by the government, after which the corrected drafts would ordinarily have been discarded.

Addressing the question of the succession and parliamentary liberties in turn, the queen's vigorous language and multiple scoring-outs convey the full force of her anger.

She severely rebuked her 'iangling subiectz' (jangling is later crossed out) for their unwelcome 'lippe labored orations' on 'so waightey a cause' and reminded them that 'the princes opinion and good wyll ought in good ordar have bine felt in other sort than in so publik a place be vttered'. Despite their 'lewde indevour to make all my realme suppose that ther care was muche whan myne was none at all', Elizabeth was prepared to forgive 'ther handeling of this', 'for I think this be the first time that so waighty a cause passed from so simple mens mouthes'.

Turning to address complaints that she had infringed the traditional liberties of parliament by ordering members not to debate the succession, Elizabeth warned them never to doubt that as 'a prince that is hed of all the body' she could 'command the fete not to stray when they wold slip'. 'God forbid', she added defiantly, 'that your liberty shuld make my bondage'. Elizabeth concluded with a lofty warning: 'let this my displing stand you in stede of sorar strokes never to tempt to far a princes paciens'. This was the last time that the question of Elizabeth's marriage was discussed in parliament, although the succession was raised again in later sessions. AC.

60

Elizabeth I

Attributed to George Gower, c.1567.

Private collection.

This picture, made when Elizabeth was around the age of 34, shows a purposeful, self-possessed woman who had recently reopened talks with the Holy Roman Emperor Maximilian II for a match with his brother Charles, Archduke of Austria. In 1567 Thomas Radcliffe, third Earl of Sussex, was dispatched to Vienna to resume negotiations. A letter to Elizabeth from Antwerp dated 5 July describes his conversation with the Governor of the Netherlands, Margaret of Parma, who was determined to see the portrait of Elizabeth that Sussex had with him and lamented that she only knew Elizabeth's likeness through pictures of poor quality that showed her wearing outdated black attire. Under duress, Sussex acquiesced. The portrait, he wrote, enraptured the aristocrats in attendance, as they attested to the quality of the picture and exclaimed that it was so lifelike that it lacked only breath.

It seems probable that this painting was acquired from a 'Prince Esterházy' by the collector Alfred Morrison for his home at Fonthill, Wiltshire, prior to 1890, and that it had entered the Esterházy collection after the marriage negotiations between Elizabeth and Archduke Charles collapsed. Last seen by the public in Britain in 1933, this is a painting in a remarkable state of preservation and provides one of the very best likenesses of Elizabeth. ET.

Civil War in Scotland

Mary's marriage soon went sour. Darnley was angry that his wife had not allowed him the crown matrimonial and was jealous of her intimacy with her secretary, David Rizzio. At the same time, many of the Protestant lords also disapproved of Mary's reliance on Rizzio and blamed him for her refusal to pardon the Earl of Moray. To forestall parliament forfeiting the earl, namely declaring him a traitor and confiscating his lands, the lords planned a coup. While Mary was at a private dinner with Rizzio and some friends on 9 March 1566, Darnley entered the queen's chamber followed by about eighty armed men. They first tried to take Rizzio away, but when Mary resisted, he was stabbed to death. After winning her husband over to her side, Mary escaped from the palace where she was being kept under guard. She soon raised an army against Rizzio's murderers and entered Edinburgh.

After the birth of her son in July 1566, Mary wanted to reach an accord with Elizabeth. Progress began to be made in talks with Francis Russell, second Earl of Bedford, the English representative at the baby's baptism. However, Mary's relationship with her husband deteriorated further, and she was suspected of orchestrating his murder after he was found dead at Kirk o' Field in February 1567. Elizabeth was horrified and wrote frankly to Mary, urging her to punish Darnley's murderers and not spare James Hepburn, Earl of Bothwell, if – as was rumoured – he was involved. Mary did not heed this advice and three months later married Bothwell.

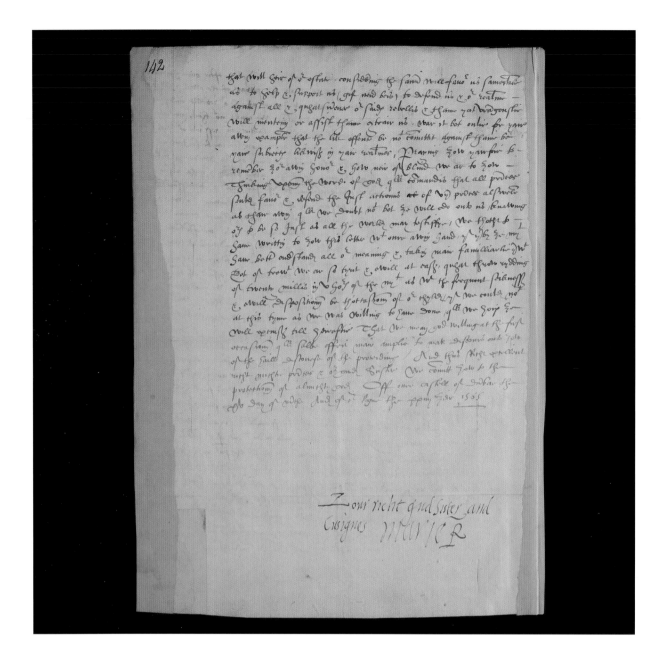

61

The Rizzio Murder

Letter from Mary, Queen of Scots to Elizabeth I,
15 March 1566, Dunbar in East Lothian.

The National Archives, Kew, SP 52/12/38.

The Italian musician David Rizzio arrived in Scotland in autumn 1561, and quickly found favour with Mary on account of his fine singing voice. In December 1564 she appointed him to a position of intimacy and trust as her French Secretary. Rizzio divided opinion at court, where he used his influence with Mary to increase his power. Darnley too resented Rizzio's intimacy with his wife. The exiled Earl of Moray, who was about to be forfeited for treason and have his lands confiscated, and his co-conspirators used Darnley's jealousy of Rizzio to their advantage by persuading him that Rizzio had to be removed. On 9 March Rizzio was murdered in the queen's presence at Holyroodhouse by Darnley and others. He was stabbed fifty-six times, while screaming to her for help, and his body was dumped in the porter's lodge.

Six days later Mary wrote to Elizabeth in anger about the murder. She told Elizabeth that she would not pardon Moray and his co-conspirators, who 'hes takin our houss slane our maist speciall seruand in our awin presence & thaireftir haldin our propper personis captif tressonneblie: quhairby we war constranit to escaipe straitlie about … midnycht … in the grittest danger feir of our lywis & ewill estate'. Mary demanded to know if 'ze be of mynd to help & support thame aganist us as ze boist to do'. 'Remember zowr awin honor & how neir of bluid we ar to zow'. Mary ended by apologising for not writing 'with oure awin hand'; what with morning sickness and riding through the night to escape, she had found herself unable to do so. She was six months pregnant at the time. In fact, the day after Rizzio's death Moray returned from exile, supplied with £1,000 from Elizabeth. AB.

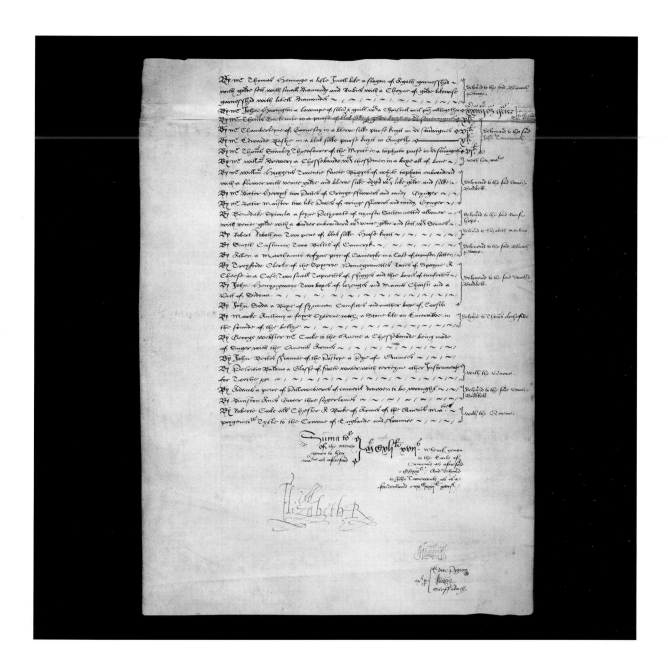

62

The Birth of James VI

New Year's gift-roll of Elizabeth I, 1 January 1567.

British Library, Additional MS 9772.

On 19 June 1566, Mary gave birth to a healthy son.
The birth was greeted with great rejoicing; the guns of
Edinburgh Castle were fired and hundreds of bonfires lit.
The future king of Scotland, England and Ireland was
baptised with lavish ceremony on 17 December in the
Chapel Royal of Stirling Castle according to Catholic
rites. He was given the names Charles James – the first,
although never used, honoured Charles IX of France; the
second was chosen in memory of his grandfather, James V
of Scotland. Darnley, whose relationship with Mary had
by then almost entirely broken down, refused to attend
the ceremony.

Elizabeth agreed to be a godparent but did not attend
personally, choosing instead Jean, Countess of Argyll, as
her proxy and sent Francis Russell, second Earl of Bedford,
who was an experienced Anglo-Scottish diplomat. She did
send Mary a magnificent baptismal gift of a gold font, which
is recorded in the 1567 New Year's gift-roll under 'Sundry
Gifts' as 'Oone ffunte of golde with a couer garnesshid with
sundry curious peces of golde enameled', weighing 333 oz.

Instructed by Elizabeth to avoid participation in any Catholic
rites during the baptism, Bedford, along with the Scottish
Protestant lords, left the chapel during the religious ceremony.
Protestants and Catholics alike fully participated in the three
days of extravagant banquets, masques and firework displays
that followed, which were designed not only to celebrate the
birth of a prince of Scotland but also to convey the promise of
a renewed and more secure Stewart monarchy. AC.

63

Kirk o' Field

Bird's-eye view of the murder scene of Lord Darnley,
February 1567.

The National Archives, Kew, MPF 1/366.

In February 1566 Lord Darnley had made a bond with his
co-conspirators in the Rizzio murder, offering to protect
them from its consequences. He went back on his word once
the act was committed, however, helping Mary escape from
Holyroodhouse. James Douglas, fourth Earl of Morton,
who was forced into exile as a result of this treachery, swore
revenge on him. In the following months Darnley's behaviour
became increasingly unpredictable and difficult, driving
Mary and him further apart. In December he sought safety
with his father, the Earl of Lennox, in Glasgow but became
ill on the way, probably as a result of syphilis. Mary visited
Darnley and persuaded him to return to Edinburgh, where
he was lodged at Kirk o' Field in Midlothian at the beginning
of February 1567. He was murdered there in mysterious
circumstances on the night of 9/10 February.

This bird's-eye view of the murder scene was made for
Sir William Cecil shortly afterwards. It depicts Kirk o' Field
partially destroyed by a gunpowder explosion and the bodies
of Darnley and William Taylor, one of his servants, in a
nearby garden. On realising that the house was surrounded
by conspirators, Darnley and Taylor appear to have lowered
themselves out of a first-floor window (perhaps using the
chair and rope found near their bodies) onto a gallery,
through a door in the town wall and out into Thieves Row,
only to be caught.

Eyewitnesses heard Darnley plead, 'Oh, my brothers,
have pity on me for the love of him who had mercy on all the
world.' He was suffocated along with Taylor. In this image
his infant son, Prince James, is depicted uttering Psalm 43,
'Iudge And Reuenge my caus O lord'. AB.

Heir followis the testament and tragedie of
vmquhile King Henrie Stewart of gude memorie

Imprentit at
Edinburgh be Robert Lekpreuik.
Anno Do. 1567.

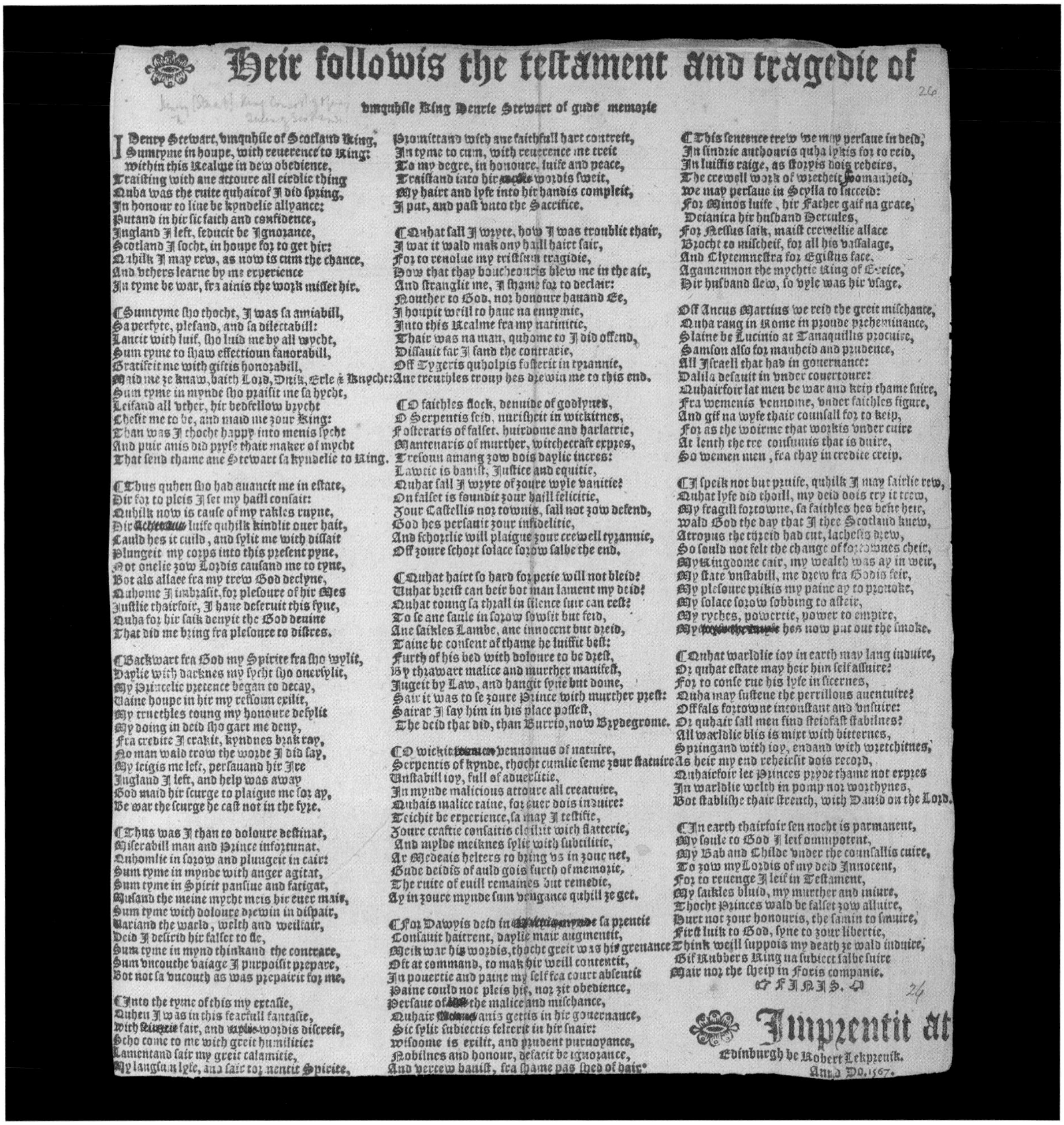

64

The Murder of Darnley

Robert Sempill, *Heir Followis the Testament and Tragedie of Vmquhile King Henrie Stewart of Gude Memorie*, Edinburgh, printed by Robert Lekpreuik, 1567.

British Library, Cotton MS Caligula C i, f. 26r.

Shortly after Darnley's murder, placards began to appear in Edinburgh charging Mary and the Earl of Bothwell with the crime. This unique copy of a ballad, printed in the immediate aftermath of Darnley's murder, found its way into the hands of the English government, ensuring its survival. It takes the form of a prosopopoeia, a figure of speech in which an imagined, absent or dead person is represented as speaking. Here the murdered Darnley recounts his life.

This is a typically Scottish libel because it was printed for distribution to a wide audience and it openly attacked the queen; an early reader has deleted many libellous references to Mary. The government was losing control of public opinion by this time, because it could not effectively censor the printed word.

Ballads were hung up in public places and sold in towns and cities. They were usually sung to familiar tunes and gave up-to-date news to ordinary people. Not much is known about Robert Sempill other than the fact that he was the best-known author of ballads in Scotland, partly due to the fact that they were printed by Robert Lekpreuik, Scotland's dominant printer at the time. Lekpreuik sided with the Confederate Lords (see cat. 66) and was named king's printer in 1568. The Confederate Lords and the Kirk never lost control of Edinburgh and, accordingly, tolerated and perhaps even encouraged the libelling of their opponents. KL-H.

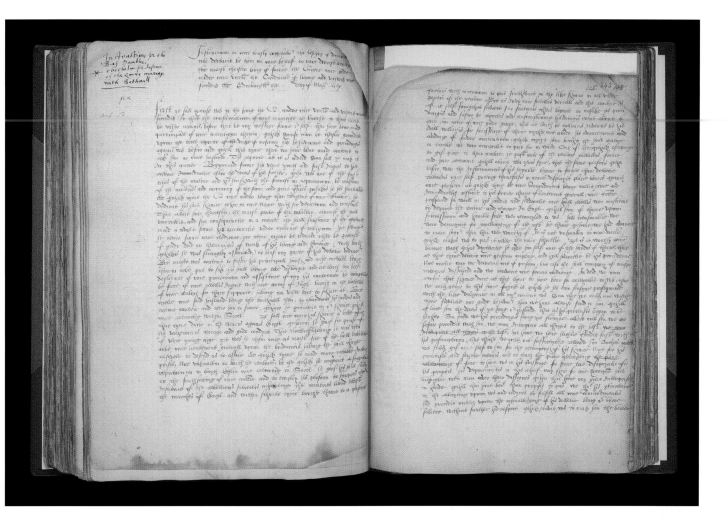

65

Mary's Third Marriage

Instructions for William Chisholm, Bishop of Dunblane,
May 1567, Edinburgh.

British Library, Royal MS 18 B vi, ff. 242v–243r.

Mary's third husband was James Hepburn, fourth Earl
of Bothwell. A strong supporter of Mary of Guise during
her regency in Scotland, he was described by the English
ambassador Sir Nicholas Throckmorton as a 'gloriouse, rash,
and hazardous yonge mann' whose 'aduersaryes shuld both
haue an eye to him'. In 1566, possibly at Mary's suggestion,
he married one of her ladies-in-waiting, Lady Jean Gordon,
which made him one of the most powerful lords in Scotland,
but in the aftermath of Lord Darnley's murder, Bothwell
instructed his wife to request a divorce. He then moved
quickly, abducting the queen and taking her to Dunbar
Castle; he married Mary less than a fortnight after Lady Jean
was granted her divorce.

This document is a contemporary copy of Mary's
instruction to William Chisholm, Bishop of Dunblane,
to communicate her reasons for marrying Bothwell, as
explained in her own words, to Charles IX, Catherine de'
Medici and her uncle, the Cardinal of Lorraine. Another
version was sent to Elizabeth and the English government
with Robert Melville, elder brother of James (see cat. 52).
Mary described how Bothwell had played a key part in

putting down the Chaseabout Raid and, since the murder
of Darnley, she had come to rely on him, notwithstanding
'that as his pretensis began to be hecher Sa fand we his
procedingis somquhat strange'. Mary recounted how 'we
bene heichlie offendit first with his presumptioun, that
thocht we culd not sufficentlie reward him … onles we suld
gif oure self to him for the recompenss of his seruice, Nixt
for his practises and secrete meanes, and at lenth the plane
attempting … of force to haue ws in his pvissance for feare
to be disapoyntit of his purpois'. Mary claimed that Bothwell
had 'cunnyngly' procured the Ainslie Bond, subscribed by
a group of prelates and nobles in support of marriage with
her, and, when she declined his suits, Bothwell kidnapped her
at Almond Bridge, West Lothian. She admitted that, 'albeit
we fand his doingis rude zit wer his answer and wordis bot
gentle'. 'Already wereit and almaist brokin with the frequent
vproaris and rebellionis raisit aganis ws sen we come in
Scotl[and]', Mary could not sustain the burden of ruling
without the 'fortificatioun of a man'. She presumed, based
on Bothwell's assertions, that he had the consent and support
of the estates and, there being nobody else as worthy,
consented at last to take him. He insisted that the marriage
be consummated without delay, fearing his enemies would
overthrow him. Mary concluded 'we can not dissemble that
he hes vsit ws vtherwiss then we wald haue wisched or zit
haue deseruit at his hand'. AC & CB.

Mary's Deposition

Although many nobles had agreed to the Bothwell marriage, old rivalries soon resurfaced. Led by James Douglas, fourth Earl of Morton, Archibald Campbell, fifth Earl of Argyll, and Prince James's guardian, John Erskine, first Earl of Mar, the opposition lords raised an army against Mary and Bothwell. The two armies met at Carberry Hill, a few miles east of Edinburgh, on a very hot day in mid-June 1567. The royal army was on the ridge and the Confederates in the valley below. Evenly matched, neither side was inclined to fight, and after three hours of inaction the French ambassador Philippe du Croc attempted mediation. One way forward was for Bothwell to engage in single combat with one of the Confederate Lords, but Mary intervened to prevent a fight. By then, the royal army – dehydrated from standing without water in the full sun – began to desert, so Mary negotiated with the rebel lords and agreed to a surrender. After one night spent in Edinburgh, she was taken to Lochleven Castle on a tiny island in the middle of a loch. Suffering from a miscarriage and exhaustion, Mary was forced to resign her throne on 24 July in favour of her 13-month-old son. In August the Earl of Moray – who had been absent from Scotland since February 1567 – returned home and was made regent for his young nephew.

Although Elizabeth had reprimanded Mary for marrying Bothwell, she was outraged by these events. But her councillors advised against providing aid to those Scots who opposed Mary's deposition, and they warned that Moray and his allies might kill their captive if Elizabeth interfered. Helpless, Elizabeth could do nothing to stop the coronation of James VI. However, in May the following year Mary escaped her prison. Men flocked to her side, but her army was defeated at the Battle of Langside and she fled to England.

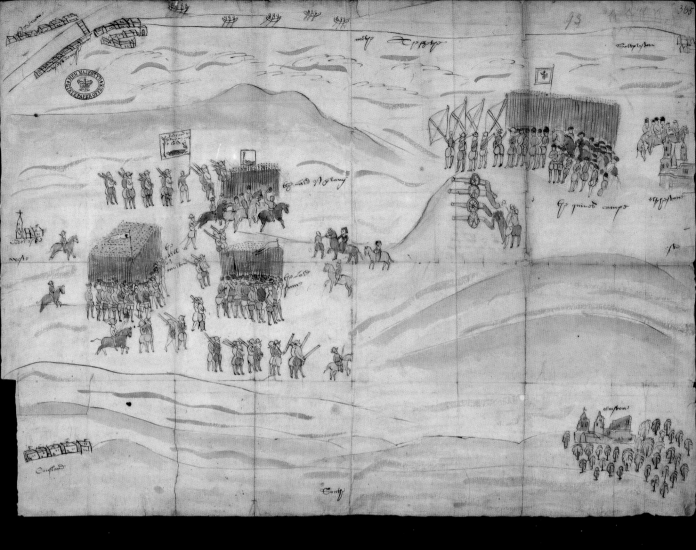

66
Carberry Hill
Bird's-eye view of the Battle of Carberry Hill, 1567.

The National Archives, Kew, MPF 1/366.

After he married Mary at Holyroodhouse on 15 May 1567, Bothwell reneged on his agreement to govern jointly with the nobles who had consented to the marriage in the Ainslie Bond the month before. Opponents of the Bothwell regime began assembling at Stirling and claimed publicly that their purposes were: first, to avenge Darnley's murder, for which Bothwell had been acquitted, after what many believed was a rigged trial in April; second, to liberate the queen from him; and, above all, to safeguard the prince. The Confederate Lords, as they called themselves, took Edinburgh on 11 June, while support ebbed away from Mary and Bothwell, who retreated to first Borthwick Castle in Midlothian, then Dunbar Castle in East Lothian.

This bird's-eye view represents the stand-off on 15 June between Mary and Bothwell and the Confederate Lords at Carberry Hill in East Lothian. The Lords bore two banners, each showing Darnley's corpse; one of them also depicted Prince James uttering Psalm 43 ('Iudg and reueng my caus o lord') before the corpse (p. 88). The rebels probably sang this metrical psalm as a battle cry. Mary is shown twice: on the right, where she is riding side-saddle among the soldiers of 'the quines campe', and also in the centre, where she is on her way to negotiate with the Confederate Lords.

The two sides were evenly matched, and neither would risk open battle. Bothwell challenged James Douglas, fourth Earl of Morton, to single combat but Mary intervened to prevent it. Her army began to desert. She surrendered when the Lords promised to treat her honourably; Bothwell fled, first to Dunbar, then to exile. Mary was led to Edinburgh amid cries from many of her captors of 'burrne the hoore'. She was imprisoned in a burgess's house, fearful and exhausted. AB.

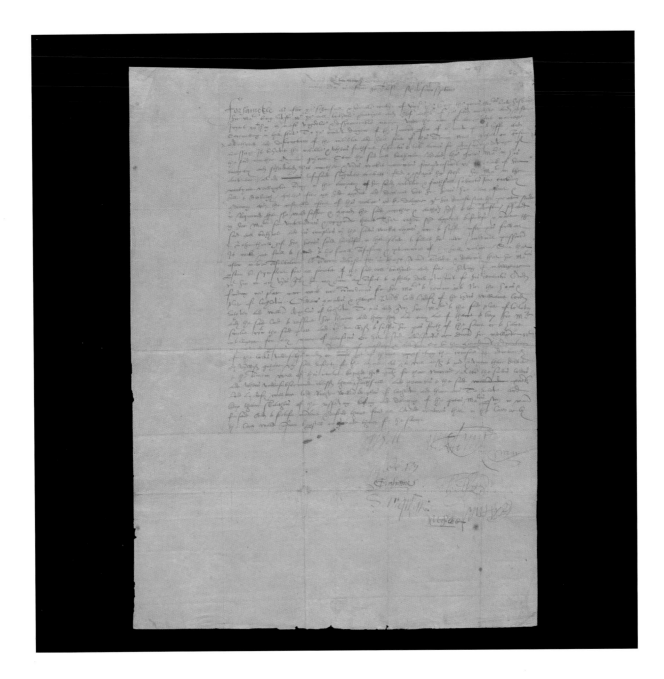

67

Imprisonment and Deposition

Warrant confining Mary, Queen of Scots in Lochleven Castle,
16 June 1567, Edinburgh.

National Library of Scotland, Edinburgh, Morton Cartulary and Papers, MS 76/4, f. 52r.

This legal document begins by recounting recent events
from the viewpoint of Mary's rebels. After the 'schamfull &
horrible murther' of Lord Darnley, Mary 'being revist with
[ravished by]' the Earl of Bothwell, 'therefter Ioynit with
him in maist vngodlie & dishonnorable maner … vnder
the name of ane pretendet mariage'. 'On Iust necessite It
behuvit the nobilitie & vtheris faithfull subiectis to tak armes
for pvnisment & revenge of the said murther', for which
Bothwell was the principal suspect.

The Confederate Lords had confronted the queen at
Carberry Hill on 15 June (cat. 66). After she surrendered
to them, Mary 'apperit to fortefie & mantene the said erll

boithuile … in the saidis wickit crymes, nor to suffer uistice
pas forwart'. In order to prevent her from 'follow[ing] hir
awin Inordinat passioun', the Confederate Lords imprisoned
her at Lochleven Castle in Fife, which was the home of
William Douglas. He was commanded 'to keip hir … suirlie
within the said place and on na wyse to suffer hir pas furth of
the same or to haue intelligence fra ony maner of personis Or
yit to send aduertismentis or direct hir intelligence with ony
levand [living] personis'.

This warrant was issued in order to safeguard Douglas
against future legal action for acting as Mary's keeper.
On 24 July Mary was forced to abdicate in favour of her
son, Prince James. The Earl of Moray, who was Douglas's
half-brother, was named regent on 22 August, exactly one
week after an emotional reunion with Mary in which he
castigated her 'lyke a gostelye father' for the failings of her
reign. AB.

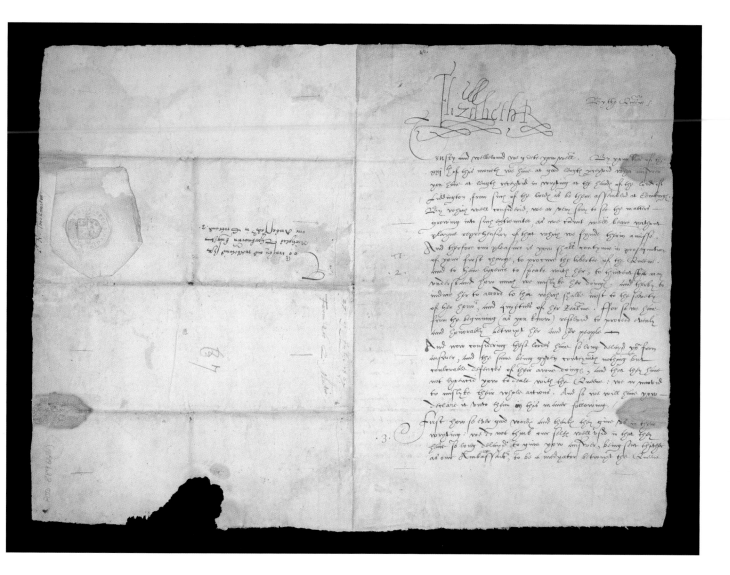

68

The Head Should Not Be Subject to the Foot

Letter from Elizabeth I to Sir Nicholas Throckmorton,
27 July 1567, Windsor Castle.

British Library, Additional MS 88966.

Although Sir William Cecil welcomed the news of Mary's imprisonment, Elizabeth was enraged at the treatment of her cousin. She sent Sir Nicholas Throckmorton to Scotland to mediate on Mary's behalf, but he was denied an interview with the deposed queen. On learning this, Elizabeth went into a fury and sent these instructions to her envoy.

Throckmorton was to continue trying to secure Mary's liberty, and to encourage her to separate from Bothwell, which would be 'most to the savety of her honor, and quyetnes of her Realme'. He was also instructed to remonstrate with the Confederate Lords over their illegal and irreligious conduct, for which they had no 'warrant nor authoritee by the law of God or man'. After all, St Paul had commanded the Romans to 'obey *potestatibus supereminentioribus gladium gestantibus* [higher powers which bear the sword]', whilst there were no examples in Christian or civil law of subjects proceeding against their ruler. The examples which the rebels had found and publicised in 'sedicious balletes' were 'vnlawfull and actes of Rebellion'. Should they depose Mary, Elizabeth and other Christian monarchs would make themselves 'a playne party against theim … for example to all posteritie'. Despite her 'mislyke' of Darnley's murder and the Bothwell marriage, it was not 'lawfull nor tollerable for theim being by Godes ordinunce subiectes, to call her who also by Godes ordinunce is their Superior and prince, to answer to them by way of force, for we do not think it consonant in nature, that the head shuld be subiect to the foote' – a trope favoured by the queen.

Throckmorton was also told to counter the claims of the Confederate Lords that Elizabeth had supported them in the past without enthusiasm or out of self-interest. If the Lords threatened to turn to the French for support, he was to remind them of the unfavourable consequences which had resulted previously. Elizabeth would moreover not be 'inducid to consent to that which we cannot in conscience lyke or allow, but shall remit the consequence therof … to the good will and favour of Almighty God, at whose handes we haue fownd no lack in the doing or omitting of any thinges whervnto our conscience hath inducid vs'. Two days after Elizabeth's letter was written, the 1-year-old James was crowned. Elizabeth, however, refused to recognise him as king. JC.

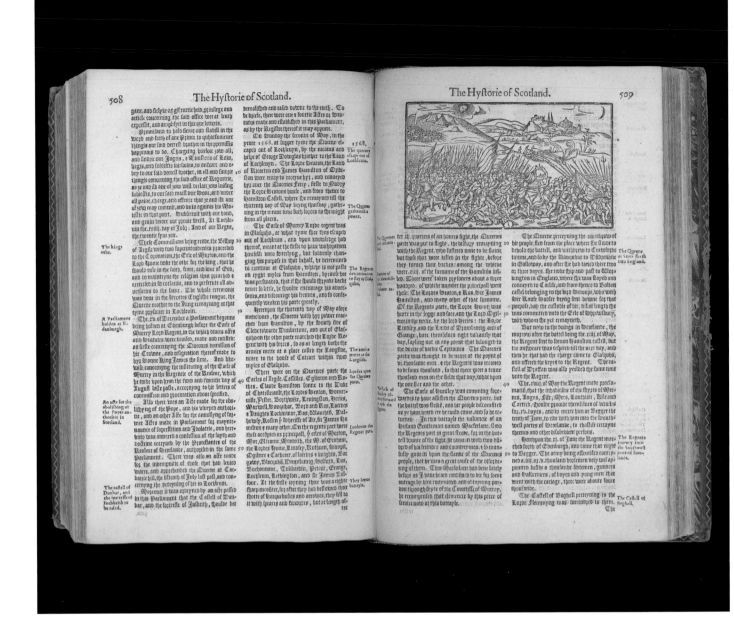

69

Escape from Lochleven

Raphael Holinshed, *The Firste Volume of the Chronicles of England, Scotlande, and Irelande*, London, [printed by Henry Bynneman] for George Bishop, [1577].

British Library, G.6006., pp. 508–9.

Holinshed's *Chronicles* provides a very brief description of Mary's dramatic escape from Lochleven Castle on 2 May 1568 'by the meanes and helpe of George Dowglas', brother to her jailer William. By contrast, the chronicler narrates at length how Mary and the regent Moray raised large armies (about 6,000 men on each side) which met at the Battle of Langside, on 13 May, when 'the Queenes parte was put to flight'. Mary 'perceyuing the ouerthrow of hir people, fled

from the place where she stoode to behold the battell'. After a few days hidden in Scotland 'she tooke ship and past to Workington in England'.

This first edition of Holinshed's *Chronicles* was published in two volumes in 1577. It was primarily a history of England, Scotland and Ireland, and later became one of the most important sources for William Shakespeare and his contemporaries. Although published under the name of Raphael Holinshed, the work was a collaboration between a number of authors of different religious persuasions, ensuring that more than one voice was heard in relation to historical as well as contemporary events. A much expanded and revised second edition of the work was printed in 1587. KL-H.

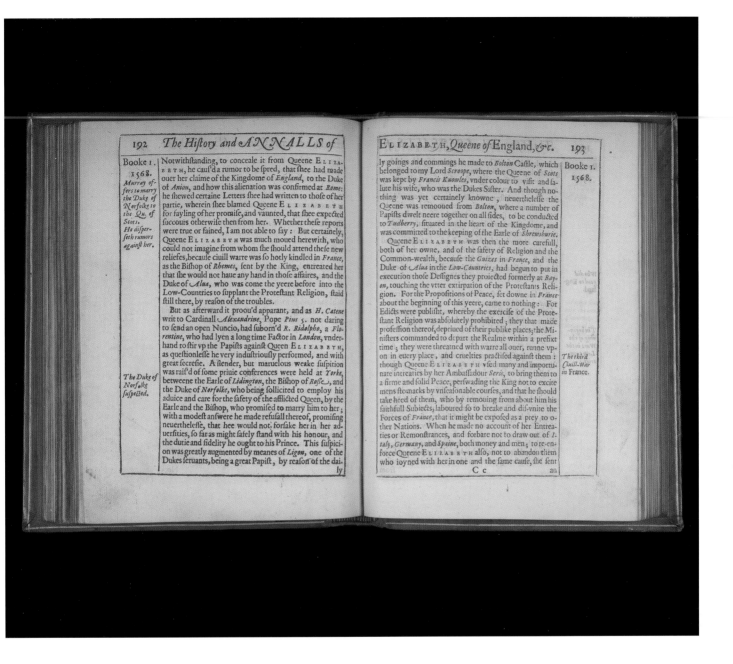

70

The Deterioration of Anglo-Spanish Relations

William Camden, *Annales. The True and Royall History of the famous Empresse Elizabeth Queene of England France and Ireland &c.*, London, [printed by George Purslowe, Humphrey Lownes and Miles Flesher] for Benjamin Fisher, 1625.

British Library, G.4896., pp. 192–3.

The first volume of the *Annales* of William Camden covered Elizabeth's reign to 1589 and was printed in 1615. The second volume, which completes the narrative, was printed posthumously: in 1625 in Leiden and 1627 in London. Both editions appeared in Latin, making this comprehensive survey of recent English history accessible to an international audience and showing the international dimensions of events in England and Scotland. The first English editions, translated by Abraham Darcie from a French translation, were published in 1625 and 1629. Since its publication Camden's *Annales* has been used as the basis for most later accounts of Elizabeth's reign. In this section of his account, Camden focuses on the increasingly tense relationship between England and Spain and highlights some of the events that led to its further deterioration. He describes the meeting between the Guises and the Duke of Alva: 'Queene Elizabeth was then the more carefull, both of her owne, and of the safety of Religion and the Common-wealth, because the Guizes in France, and the Duke of Alua in the Low-Countries, had begun to put in execution those Dissignes they proiected formerly at Bayon, touching the vtter extirpation of the Protestants Religion.' This is followed by a description of the seizure of the Spanish treasure ships by the English crown in December 1568 after Elizabeth had discovered that the money they were carrying did not belong to Philip II of Spain but to a number of Genoese merchants and was intended to be used against the Dutch Revolt. Anglo-Spanish relations deteriorated quickly thereafter. KL-H.

rpellit and the stait of Religioun and libertie of the coūtr
and lyfis of hir pepill wer spairit. The lyke cair weill app
neth of Maij, the zeir of God ane thousand fyue hundzeth
depositioun from our Royall Crowne and to erect ane vth
gow than assegit be thame succourit and releuit. Our said
ground in Scotland, bot that quhilk scho hes bene alway
ing thair returning to our obedience and suretie foz conti
uellis and cair scho hes takin be hir Ambassadouris letter
Quhairin hir laubouris and mediatioun hes at Goddis p
to the acknawledgeing of our Authozitie, and in the place
countrie: our Castell of Edinburgh only exceptit. Quhilk
of Grange knicht to our vse and behufe be vmquhyle our
worthy memozie, the said Williame vnmyndfull of his t
the mair now bypast be the meanis of the same Castell
Royall estait & Authozitie. To the disturbance of Christia
Realme, and reiecting the godlie pacificatioun quhilkis th
auit, procedis in contempteous Rebellioun and weir, gr
stice, and doing besydis quhat in him lyis to procure and
our estait, and troubling the quyetnes of this haill Ile.
tionnis ar detenit within our said Castell, and vsit and
bene erniftly requyzit be our richt traist Cousing James
gis, and Nobilitie of this our Realme, foz ayd and succou
and recouerie of our said Castell. Quhilk scho hes fauoura
the persounis being within our said Castell to our obedier
now preparit and causit put hir forces in full reddynes to
and furthsetting of our Authozitie, in assegeing of our said
stait lie be Delyuerit (with the ordinance, munitioun, Royal
teris and recozdis belanging to vs and our Crown) to b
peace restorit to our said Burgh of Edinburgh and our h

Dangerous Times
1569–1582

JACOBVS·DEIGRATIA·REX
SCOTORVM·ETATIS·SVE·8
1574

6

'NOW MURDER AND WAR UPRISES' (1569–82)

Amy Blakeway

Mary's decision to flee to England after the defeat at the Battle of Langside in May 1568 left Scotland in turmoil. The next five years saw a bloody civil war take hold of Scotland between the Queen's Party – supporters of Mary – and the King's Party – supporters of her son, James VI.

The length and difficulties of the campaign alone show how strong support remained for the queen. With Mary now present in England, effectively a prisoner of the English crown (albeit one enjoying a deluxe form of house arrest), the fight for her throne took place far away from her. This war was fought not only with guns and swords, but also with the tools of persuasion – words and pens – in pamphlets that spread far away from Scotland to England, across the Channel to France and beyond.

The international audience was crucial: securing the support of Elizabeth and her privy council became a matter of life or death for Mary. As soon as Mary crossed the border, she had sought English help to regain her throne, requesting that her cousin would 'aid and assist me in my just quarrel' (cat. 71). Mary's half-brother, now regent, James Stewart, Earl of Moray, also saw how important English support would be. To obtain this coveted prize, the half-siblings and their supporters had to engage not only in politics but also in propaganda, and needed to exploit divisions amongst the English political establishment. Elizabeth still hesitated to accept Mary's deposition as legal.

Yet for Cecil and his supporters in the privy council, Mary's arrival in England represented the chance of a lifetime to finally defeat the woman whose blood made her the single greatest threat facing Elizabeth (cats 72, 74). Meanwhile, Mary's presence south of the border, a Catholic monarch, albeit a captive one, provided a focal point for the grumblings, plots and ambitions of discontented English nobles.

These opposing agendas were first aired in October 1568, at York. The city was chosen as a practical location for a conference – the brainchild of Cecil – to determine whether Mary should be restored to her throne or not. Yet as the ancient centre of English government in the North, York also came with baggage for Anglo-Scottish relations. In the middle ages, the Archbishops of York had claimed to have control of the Scottish Church: therefore, the city was a site imbued with English claims of overlordship. It was also the site of broken Anglo-Scottish diplomacy: the place where first James V and Henry VIII, and later their daughters, had failed to meet in person. This past made it apt symbolically, as well as practically, as the location of a summit. At the conference, each side would present their case to English commissioners headed by Thomas Howard, Duke of Norfolk. It is a sign of how desperate both sides must have been that a question relating to the governance of Scotland was being referred to English judges.

At the beginning of the York conference, Mary's commissioners, John Leslie, Bishop of Ross, and John Maxwell, Lord Herries, approached the negotiations as an exercise in securing a restoration; and Norfolk, reflecting his own queen's distaste for rebellion, was swayed by their case. In November, the conference relocated to Westminster. Despite the arrival of Mary's former regent, James Hamilton, Duke of Châtelherault, as a boost to her negotiating team, in London the tone changed from one of compromise and restoration to one of establishing or denying Mary's guilt in the murder of Lord Darnley the previous year. Perhaps perturbed by the earlier move towards compromise, Moray decided to make it clear that Mary's return to Scotland could not be countenanced, and he offered to prove her a murderess. Unable, in their turn, to engage in discussions which presupposed Mary's guilt, her commissioners withdrew from the conference. Moray then played his masterstroke and presented the 'Casket Letters'. These letters and sonnets, he alleged, had been found amongst Mary's papers and proved her adultery with James Hepburn, Earl of Bothwell, and her foreknowledge of, even complicity in, Darnley's murder. The originals disappeared shortly afterwards, but it is almost certain that the Casket Letters were at best tampered with and, at worst, forged to give a damning impression of Mary's guilt. Regardless, they became a key plank of the propaganda produced against Mary, appearing, for example, in George Buchanan's *Detection of the Doings of Mary Queen of Scots* (cat. 76). Whilst Mary's commissioners had departed with nothing, when

Thomas Howard, fourth Duke of Norfolk, was one of the three English commissioners at York to hear evidence at the 'first trial' of Mary, Queen of Scots in 1568. Soon afterwards, he entered secret talks to marry her.

Unknown artist, c.1565.
National Portrait Gallery, London.

the conference closed Moray left with a loan of £5,000 – but still no formal acknowledgement of his regency by Elizabeth.

Outside the main sessions at the York Conference, however, other discussions had unfolded. Hawking with Norfolk in the countryside, Moray's co-commissioner, William Maitland of Lethington, decided to revive a scheme first floated in the early years of the decade: what if Norfolk married Mary? Separated from Bothwell, with a more suitable English husband than Darnley at her side, Mary could be restored to the Scottish throne. With her return to power Anglo-Scottish peace would be secured and Norfolk himself would be not only king of Scots but, perhaps, in due course, king of England and Ireland. Quizzed by Elizabeth in late 1568, Norfolk denied these rumours. However, by 1569 the prospect of marrying Mary was too much for his ambition and he became deeply committed to the plan. Elizabeth's anger, following the discovery of the plot in August that year, terrified Norfolk. Fearing arrest for treason, he fled the court, refusing to return when summoned by his livid monarch.

NORFOLK'S WITHDRAWAL FROM COURT worried his fellow English Catholics and was the final prompt for Thomas Percy, Earl of Northumberland, and Charles Neville, Earl of Westmorland, to rebel against Elizabeth in November 1569. Seeking to restore Catholicism, they celebrated Mass in Durham Cathedral, and demanded Catholics should assume positions of influence at court. As for Mary, she should be restored to her throne and nominated as Elizabeth's successor. Although the Northern Rebellion, as it is now known, was quickly crushed, as the Protestant polemicist Thomas Norton explained in his *A Warning against the Dangerous Practises of Papists, and Specially the Partners of the Late Rebellion* (cat. 81), it constituted proof that all Catholics were dangerous. Elizabeth too may have been inspired to dip her quill in ink – her verse 'The Doubt of Future Foes' is reputed to have been penned during the Rebellion. Elizabeth's famous allusion to 'the daughter of debate' in that verse perfectly evokes her own mixed feelings about Mary (cat. 79).

Tail between his legs, Northumberland fled to Scotland, where, on Christmas Eve 1569, he was seized by Moray. Capturing Northumberland gave Moray, for the first time, a trump card against Mary: Elizabeth's distaste for subjects who had rebelled against another monarch was only outstripped by her abhorrence for her own subjects who had rebelled against her. If Elizabeth wanted her rebels back, she would have to acknowledge Moray's rule on behalf of James VI as legitimate. Moray's letter to Elizabeth informing her that he had captured Northumberland was the first to his English cousin in which he used his title of regent. Elizabeth's reply was drafted twice. The second draft included a suggestion that Moray's regency would be acknowledged: his instinct was obviously sound.

Moray's new-found security did not last long. On 23 January 1570 he was shot, and slowly, excruciatingly, he bled to death over the following twelve hours. This was the first time a head of state was assassinated by a handgun, and it sparked a propaganda campaign that overtook even the outpouring of cheap print that followed Mary's deposition three years earlier. The title for this chapter is taken from *The Poisoned Shot*, one of the ballads Robert Sempill wrote bewailing Moray's assassination. Yet even as John Knox preached Moray's funeral sermon at St Giles' in Edinburgh, the careful ties that had bound Moray's regime together were loosening. As his discussions with Norfolk had shown, Maitland was not entirely opposed to Mary's restoration to power; meanwhile Sir William Kirkcaldy of Grange, who had led Mary away from Bothwell in the aftermath of the Battle of Carberry Hill in 1567, felt his doubts about the legitimacy of her deposition grow until he too joined the Queen's Party. The King's Party was leaderless and haemorrhaging support. Worse still, their opponents, including the powerful Hamilton family, who had orchestrated Moray's murder, were growing in strength and confidence. With Moray dead, Mary's supporters argued, the form of government laid out in Mary's letters of 'abdication' was shattered and the way was open for her restoration.

In these circumstances, securing a new regent swiftly was key. Yet it took six months – until July 1570 – for the King's Party to name Matthew Stewart, Earl of Lennox, as regent. He seemed to offer the perfect solution; as Darnley's father and James VI's grandfather, he would be loyal to the king. Why, then, was there a delay? Lennox had renounced his Scottish nationality in favour of becoming English during the 1540s. Technically he was Elizabeth's subject and needed her permission to leave England. Elizabeth, for her part, saw disadvantages in the choice. Lennox's mind was set firmly on vengeance for his dead son, an attitude which – combined with the clarion calls to revenge Moray already circulating in Scotland – would not calm the volatile situation.

When Elizabeth gave Lennox's candidacy her blessing she also clearly accepted that if James needed a regent he must, therefore, be king. This was public proof that Elizabeth accepted the King's Party narrative that Mary had been legally deposed and replaced by her infant son. It had been worth the wait for the King's Party, but Mary's supporters were on the defensive and on 10 August 1570 they formally rejected Lennox as regent at a parliament held in Linlithgow.

Lennox's desire for revenge helped to drive the escalation of violence. In April 1571 one of Mary's most prominent supporters, John Hamilton, the Catholic Archbishop of St Andrews, was captured, subjected to a show trial in which he admitted complicity in Moray's murder, and hanged in the marketplace at Stirling. The Queen's Party soon sought their revenge. In September 1571 the King's Party summoned a parliament to meet at Stirling. Under cover of night, Mary's supporters stormed the town. Stirling was only retaken thanks to the decisive intervention of John Erskine, Earl of Mar, who, as Keeper of the King's Person, was responsible for James's safety and upbringing as well as the defence of Stirling Castle. This came too late for Lennox, who had been stabbed. He died in the early hours of 4 September. The fact that the attack came in the very place where Archbishop Hamilton had been hanged neatly encapsulates the character which the Marian civil war was rapidly assuming – ancient noble rivalries were coalescing around lines of loyalty to Mary or to James and making divisions still more bitter.

> AS HIS DISCUSSIONS WITH NORFOLK HAD SHOWN, MAITLAND WAS NOT ENTIRELY OPPOSED TO MARY'S RESTORATION TO POWER

Perhaps surprisingly, however, the two sides were not divided by religion. The Catholic Robert, Lord Sempill, for example, remained a loyal king's man throughout the war, and Archibald Campbell, fifth Earl of Argyll was both a committed Protestant and one of the most prominent Marians. As the war drew on, however, religious divisions also began to sharpen, and this spilt over in increasingly bitter personal propaganda. In England too the line against Catholics had begun to harden in the wake of the Northern Rebellion, and especially following the publication of a papal bull of excommunication against Elizabeth, *Regnans in Excelsis* (cat. 80). This was issued in early 1570 – too late to help the northern rebels, but not too late to cause grave consternation in the English court. However, it was events in France which served to marginalise Catholics in both England and Scotland still further.

On 18 August 1572 Margaret, the sister of Charles IX of France, married Henry of Navarre (the future Henry IV of France). This should have marked a moment of cross-confessional understanding, since Henry was a Huguenot (Protestant). On the night of 23 August, however, Admiral Gaspard de Coligny, a leading Huguenot, was assassinated. This set off an orgy of violence against the Huguenots in Paris, now known as the St Bartholomew's Day Massacre, which spread like wildfire throughout France. The English and Scottish Protestants who were able to seek shelter in the house of Sir Francis Walsingham, then the English ambassador to Paris, were among the lucky few who survived (cat. 92).

THE FACT THAT THE term 'massacre' first entered the English language in reports describing events in Paris shows how shocked English and Scottish Protestants were – a new word was needed to express this level of atrocity. Taking up his pen again, the poet Robert Sempill decried the treatment of his co-religionists, and from this date onwards propaganda produced in Scotland for and against Mary adopted a more clearly confessional (Catholic versus Protestant) tone. This also paved the way for Sempill to express ever more enthusiastically his desire for English help, exhorting his readers to pray for both James VI and 'the Queen of England's majesty'. This was a canny plea: English military help was certainly needed, and given that the English parliament had called for Mary's execution in 1572, it was unlikely to fall on deaf ears.

After Lennox's assassination at Stirling in September 1571, the King's Party had elected Mar as regent. Mar had initially resisted his election – complaining, amongst other things, that he was too old. Elizabeth welcomed Mar's appointment, but acknowledged his dilemma, sympathetically confiding to him that 'we think none could have been named in that Realm more plausible to that nation, nor more meeter [suitable] for the charge, although we know well yourself of good wisdom would have forborne it'. These words were soothing, although what Elizabeth went on to say was still more pleasing. She explained that the veil had finally been ripped from her eyes, and she now saw that Mary's intention was to destroy both England and Scotland by 'the setting on fire both the Realms with wars by bringing into the same of power of strangers' (cat. 87). September 1571 had also been a dramatic month in England: the Duke of Norfolk was arrested for his part in the Ridolfi Plot. Norfolk and Mary had both become entangled with the schemes of Roberto di Ridolfi, a Florentine merchant resident in London who secretly communicated with Guerau de Spes, the Spanish ambassador to England. Together the group plotted for a Spanish invasion of England and an uprising of Catholics, which would secure Mary's release from prison, her marriage to Norfolk and their joint rule over England and Scotland alike (cat. 83). Coming at the same time as Lennox's assassination, it suggested that Mary's supporters seriously threatened Protestant stability on both sides of the border.

Facing such a threat, Elizabeth would, finally, commit money and men to James VI's cause. Mar began his regency with a new siege of Edinburgh Castle, followed by military raids throughout Scotland. However, even given English support, Mar was unable to crush Mary's supporters. By July 1572 he had negotiated a truce. This was still in force when he died on 28 October. Faced with the third regency election in as many years, the King's Party chose James Douglas, fourth Earl of Morton, on 24 November. Having been amongst the leaders of the King's Party since Mary's deposition, Morton was a realist, committed to preventing Mary's return by constructing a viable regime in Scotland. He spent the first few months of his regency negotiating with leading Marians, and in February 1573 the Hamiltons and Gordons signed the Pacification of Perth, recognising James VI as king.

Having picked off most of Mary's supporters, only Edinburgh Castle, held by Kirkcaldy and Maitland, remained to resist Morton's regime. To defeat them Morton used English military assistance. James's proclamation (cat. 90) explaining why so many English soldiers had entered Scotland might have emphasised the amity between the two kingdoms, but the commentary that circulated alongside the map of the siege appearing in Raphael Holinshed's *Chronicles* shows that the English had not abandoned older ideas of conquest. Regardless, in May 1573 the castle fell after a heavy bombardment under the command of the English captain Sir William Drury. Kirkcaldy was executed and Maitland died before he reached the gallows – rumours abounded he had

The Siege of Edinburgh Castle,
as depicted in Holinshed's
Chronicles. On 28 May 1573
the castle was 'delivered up into
the hands' of Sir William Drury
after a two-year siege.
British Library, G.6006.

Wingfield Manor, Derbyshire, the Earl of Shrewsbury's house, where Mary, Queen of Scots was imprisoned in 1569, 1584 and 1585.

Photograph c.1905. Library of Congress Prints & Photographs Division.

taken his own life. The last military support for Mary in Scotland had been eradicated.

This news must have been crushing for the woman who still regarded herself as queen of Scots, although she may have drawn cold comfort from the fact that, despite the braying of her privy council and parliament, Elizabeth remained reluctant to harm her cousin. In February 1569 Mary had been placed in the custody of George Talbot, sixth Earl of Shrewsbury, and his wife, Bess of Hardwick, where she remained until 1584. The large volume of technically accomplished embroideries produced by Mary and Bess in this period shows that Mary had access to a range of continental books, from which she drew inspiration (cat. 96). The gifts prepared for Elizabeth and symbolic pieces such as a phoenix, a symbol of being able to rise again, also show how embroidery allowed Mary to participate in the loaded culture of gift-giving and express her political hopes. Nevertheless, she was closely watched. Shrewsbury reported, for example, the tensions within her household between her French and Scottish servants and Mary's continued diplomatic activity, including her contact with Spain (cat. 94). In turn, he was commanded to keep Mary under ever closer guard since rumours that she was planning her escape were rife (cat. 97).

For all this time James VI had remained in Stirling Castle, developing his ferocious intellect under the guidance of his tutors George Buchanan and Peter Young (cat. 89). In 1578 James declared that he was capable of ruling in his own right and Morton, who had gradually lost support through his mishandling of patronage, relinquished the regency. Although Morton subsequently regained power, in December 1580 he was accused of complicity in Darnley's murder and a show trial swiftly followed. Morton was executed in June 1581, abandoned by his English allies, who had been too preoccupied by Elizabeth's final round of marriage negotiations with the French to send support. This was short-sighted, because with Morton's removal from power, the anglophile foreign policy he had pursued was in tatters.

Increasingly confident and active as king, James relied on Esmé Stuart, a distant cousin who had arrived from France in 1578 to whom he gave the earldom of Lennox. Esmé's favour with James threw Scottish Protestants and English observers alike into fits of anxiety – exacerbated on the English side of the border by the broader religious challenge posed by Jesuits such as Edmund Campion (cat. 93). For Mary, however, her son's assertion of power and friendship with a French Catholic kinsman seemed to offer a glimmer of hope. In October 1581 she proposed a new scheme. Known as the 'Association', it effectively amounted to a power-sharing arrangement between Mary and James VI. Its failure over the following years would push Mary away from diplomacy towards more desperate measures.

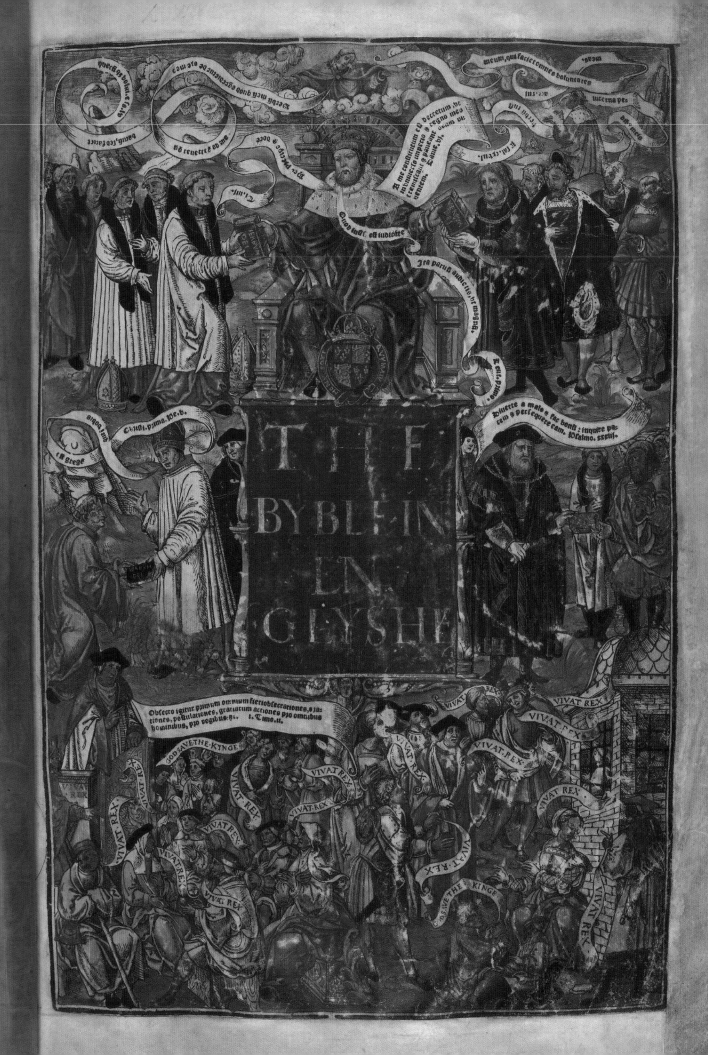

7 | RELIGION AND REFORMATIONS

Alec Ryrie

Amongst the many layers of causes that brought Mary, Queen of Scots to the block – dynastic entanglements, the insoluble dilemmas of female monarchy, her own fatal misjudgements – none was more fundamental than the twin Reformations which overtook England and Scotland in the middle years of the sixteenth century.

Mary and her cousin's story could not have played out remotely as it did without the religious conflict that infused every minor political dispute with an air of existential crisis. Without Scotland's sudden, scrappy and tumultuous Reformation, Mary would have sat far more securely on her throne. And without England's slow, implacable rewriting of its own ancient religious rules, Mary would not have posed so mortal a threat to her hosts that the only solution was to kill her.

Neither Reformation was, in itself, a particularly likely event. The two kingdoms of Great Britain were ancient rivals in religion as in much else, and had taken opposite sides during the great schism of 1378–1417, when Christendom was divided between rival popes. But in the early sixteenth century their rivalry took the form of vying to be faithful, orthodox and Catholic. When Martin Luther triggered a series of schisms in Germany and Scandinavia after 1517, the logical course for both England and Scotland's monarchs was clear: loudly to protest their faithfulness to Rome, while using that ostentatious loyalty to prise fresh legal and financial privileges out of the papacy. It was a protection racket: would it not be a shame if this splendid Church suffered a heretical accident? Taking this approach in the 1530s, James V of Scotland extracted over £10,000 Scots per annum in taxes from the Church and placed four of his own illegitimate infant sons as heads of some of Scotland's wealthiest abbeys, all the while assuring Rome that this would help him defend orthodoxy. And to keep his side of the bargain, he cracked down on incipient Protestantism, with at least fourteen Scots burned for heresy during his reign.

England should have gone the same way. Cardinal Wolsey had been awarded unprecedented powers as a papal legate in 1518 and was bringing the English Church ever more firmly under the crown's control; meanwhile Henry VIII trumpeted his Catholic loyalty, writing against Luther and burning both books and heretics. If Henry had not bumped up against one of the papacy's few truly non-negotiable powers – matrimonial law – and if the legal and political stars had not aligned in just such a way that his sudden, desperate wish legitimately to remarry could not be granted, the English Reformation would have been over before it had properly begun. But as it turned out, the king managed to convince himself not only that his first marriage was an offence in God's eyes, but also that the papacy, which had connived at that offence and then refused to release him from it, was if anything worse. By 1530 Henry had arrived at the momentous conviction that God had made him Supreme Head of the English Church (under Christ, he grudgingly admitted), and that the pope was a usurper, who was no more than the bishop of Rome. That conviction allowed him to throw off both pope and wife, and in 1533 to anoint the newborn Princess Elizabeth as his heir.

It would take several more lurches of England's murderous politics before, improbably, Elizabeth came into that inheritance in 1558, but there could be no doubt she did so both as a Protestant and as head of the English Church. Had she embraced Catholicism, she would have had to admit that she herself was illegitimate. She had no choice but to be her father's daughter. She changed the title from Supreme Head to Supreme Governor, which sounded slightly more modest, but nevertheless, like her father, she left the title undefined, accepting no limits on what she might potentially do. The power of this title was such that she and her ministers succeeded in slowly turning Catholic England into a Protestant nation – indeed, a nation whose defining fear was, increasingly, that Catholicism would return. The memories of the brief but intense persecution of Protestants under Mary Tudor were burnished and taken to be exemplars of Catholicism's inherent cruelty (cat. 26). Elizabeth's comparably bloody persecution of Catholics, and her far more brutal reprisals against the northern regions that had rebelled against her in 1569–70, were framed

Martin Luther (1483–1546), the German theologian whose attacks on the papacy and doctrine of salvation by God's grace alone inspired Protestant Reformations in parts of Europe.

Martin Luther's *On the Captivity of the Babylonian Church* [*De Captivitate Babylonica Ecclesiæ præludium Martini Lutheri*], 1520. British Library, 697.h.21.

Numina cœlestem nobis peperere Lutherum,
Nostra diu maius secla videre nihil.
Quem si Pontificum crudelis deprimit error,
Non feret iratos impia terra Deos.

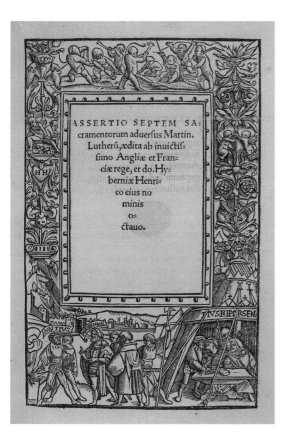

Henry VIII's *Assertio* answering
Martin Luther's assertion that
only two sacraments were
scriptural. In gratitude for this
defence of the Catholic Church,
Pope Leo X granted Henry the
title 'Defender of the Faith'.

*Assertio septem sacramentorum
adversus Martinum Lutherum*, 1521.
British Library, 9.a.9.

as just punishments for traitors, mere policing rather
than any kind of forcing of conscience.

Even as Elizabeth's Reformation bedded down, one
fact made it fragile: the royal supremacy on which it
depended. With virtually unlimited religious power
invested in the crown, the prospect of the crown falling
into the wrong hands became intolerable to the new
Protestant establishment. Meanwhile, the Catholics who
had been shut out of power understood that the royal
supremacy offered a tantalisingly quick, simple way to
reverse England's schism. England's dynastic wars of the
fifteenth century, the so-called Wars of the Roses, looked
inconsequential by comparison: for most practical
purposes, it had made little real difference whether
Lancaster or York reigned. Now, a change of ruler could
push the whole nation towards salvation or damnation.

So the royal succession became a game whose stakes
were too high to be left to chance, or even to the normal
laws of politics. The royal supremacy would, in the
next century, consume Kings Charles I and James II,
whose subjects ultimately decided they could not trust
them with it. In the sixteenth century, it turned Mary,
Queen of Scots – a dynastic queen who had shown
herself perfectly willing to trim to the religious winds
– into an improbable beacon of Catholic hope, and a focus of plots and
conspiracies. And it was the royal supremacy which, in the end, cut off her
head, for ultimately there was no other way to stop another Catholic from
sitting on England's throne.

Scotland's version of this story could hardly have been more different,
but it, too, was decisive in bringing about the crisis of 1587. James V's
sudden death in 1542 meant that his throne was left to a 6-day-old
daughter, who immediately became the most marriageable infant in
Christendom. Henry VIII soon enough launched a war for the young Queen
Mary's hand, and made some attempt to turn that war into a religious
conflict, mobilising Scotland's Protestant sympathisers on his behalf; but
the effort was too half-hearted, English policy was too nakedly aggressive,
Scottish Protestantism was too weak and the old patterns of Anglo-Scottish
conflict too deeply entrenched. The military campaigns of 1542–50 played
out as such struggles always had: the English won the battles and lost the
war, chiefly because they drove the Scots more firmly into the arms of their
old allies, the French.

And so France won the great prize, with the young Scots queen pledged
to the future French king. Their children, it seemed, would inherit a united
Franco-Scottish realm, a pincer which would crack heretical England like
a nut. Throughout the 1550s, the queen herself was in France, and her
regent in Edinburgh – her mother Mary of Guise, in effect the French king's
viceroy in his Scottish province – did her best to draw the religious poison
from Scottish politics. Persecution ceased; leading churchmen pursued
conciliatory, reforming policies; war with England held out the hope of

recovering the lost border town of Berwick.
There was even a kind of religious peace
process, with the prospect in 1557–9 of some
toleration for Protestants being negotiated.

But Mary of Guise was swimming
against a tide of sharpening division. The
negotiations were sabotaged by the hard men
on both sides, and Elizabeth's accession to the
English throne in late 1558 gave the rivalry
with England a religious flavour once again.
A Protestant revolt broke out in May 1559,
and this time it was the French intervention
that was heavy-handed and the English one
that was shrewdly judged. France's own
burgeoning religious conflicts, combined with
the catastrophic shipwreck of a troop ship
in the North Sea, left the French garrison in
Leith isolated. And so, improbably, in the
summer of 1560, Scottish Protestants did
not secure merely the toleration they had
been fighting for. Instead, they transformed

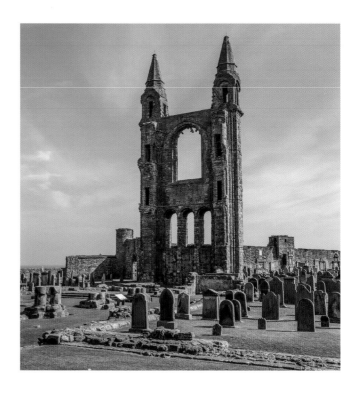

Scotland, the pope's 'special daughter', almost overnight into a Protestant
realm where the Catholic Mass was illegal and where the old enemy, England,
was an ally. When Mary returned warily to Scotland in 1561, the 18-year-old
widow was not only a foreigner in her own realm; she was the Catholic queen
of a Protestant nation.

St Andrews Cathedral, Fife, built
in 1158 and now in ruins. A
crowd incited by the preaching of
John Knox looted and vandalised
its interior in June 1559, and it
was abandoned soon afterwards.

LIKE HER MOTHER, MARY tried valiantly to square that circle, with
some success. She worked within the new reality, to the dismay of her more
ardently Catholic supporters, and managed to drive a wedge between the
Protestant moderates and extremists. But even if she had not made the
disastrous choices she did make in 1565–6 – to adopt a more confrontational
policy with England and to marry Henry, Lord Darnley – she was always
living on borrowed time. The Scots, unlike the English, had no taste for
dynastic civil wars, but it is no accident that within a year of having a
son, Mary was ejected from her throne. She could now be replaced with
an impeccably legitimate successor and, if it helped that he was male, the
decisive advantage was that he could be (indeed, must be) raised a Protestant.
The last person who could be entrusted with his upbringing, and thus with
Protestant Scotland's still fragile future, was his Catholic mother.

Not everyone, yet, accepted the relentless, grinding logic of religious
partisanship. Mary had Protestant supporters, allowing her to mount a
credible bid for a comeback after her escape in 1568, and providing enough
backers to tip Scotland into five more years of civil war. If she had been there,
they could perfectly plausibly have won – at least for a time. But in her most
catastrophic mistake, she failed to recognise that her English cousin, too, was
caught up in the same doomsday machine of religious division. Crossing into
England, she appealed to Elizabeth as an 'escaped prisoner', not realising that
her imprisonment was only beginning (cat. 71).

It was little comfort to know that Elizabeth, too, was trapped, for no-one tried harder or longer to resist the divisive spirit of the age than Elizabeth herself. She had only intervened in Scotland's Reformation war in 1559–60 – late, and reluctantly. Now her Protestant subjects insisted relentlessly that the only safe way to defuse the unexploded Scottish bomb they were holding was execution. They provided ample evidence and legal procedures, and warned against the 'foolish pity' that stayed the queen's hand. Perhaps it was less pity than caution, respect for the monarchical principle, distaste for taking orders and a refusal to let herself be defined by religious conflict. Either way, Elizabeth fought doggedly against the inevitable. Plots and rebellions centred on the imprisoned queen cost plenty of heads, but not Mary's own. Elizabeth tried to stay back from the religious wars spreading across Europe, providing only covert aid to France's Protestants, and seriously pursuing a quixotic plan to marry a moderate French Catholic prince in order to revive the vanishing centre ground.

SHE AND HER COUSIN WERE BOTH CAUGHT UP IN AN ENGINE OF WAR WHICH WAS FORCING ALL EUROPE INTO CONFLICT

But the vice she was caught in was inexorable. Her increasingly agitated Protestant subjects pared away her legal and political room for manoeuvre. In 1585 she was finally drawn into open war with Catholic Spain. Mary, too, was caught by the same logic, compelled at last to accept the role as a Catholic plotter that her zealous supporters had scripted for her. Elizabeth's refusal to take responsibility for the death warrant that she finally signed was both cowardly and politically astute, but it also reflected a deeper truth: her hand had, indeed, been forced. She and her cousin were both caught up in an engine of war which was forcing all Europe into conflict. We may doubt if either of them ever truly wished to be 'milkmaids with pails upon [their] arms', but the option was not open to them (cat. 119). Instead, one of them became a traitor and a martyr, the other a murderer and Gloriana. And there is no reason to think that, had their situations been reversed in 1587, the outcome would have been any different.

Mary's Flight into England

The arrival of Mary, Queen of Scots in England created
a dilemma for Elizabeth I. Her first instinct was to
bring the fugitive to her court and give her aid against
the Scottish rebels. But Sir William Cecil and his fellow
privy councillors advised her against such actions. They
persuaded her not to meet Mary, at least not until her
name had been cleared. In the meantime, Mary was
to remain in custody in the north under the guard of
Sir Francis Knollys and Henry, ninth Lord Scrope. In the
long term, Cecil and most of his colleagues judged that it
was in England's interests for Moray and the Protestant
lords to govern Scotland in the name of the young king.

71

Mary, Queen of Scots Arrives in England
Letter from Mary, Queen of Scots to Elizabeth I, 17 May 1568,
Workington, Cumberland.

British Library, Cotton MS Caligula C i, f. 94v.

On 16 May 1568, Mary crossed the Solway Firth in a
fishing boat and landed at Workington in Cumberland.
The next day, she wrote to Elizabeth in French, announcing
her arrival and describing the treasonable actions of her
enemies. Mary fully expected that her English cousin and
fellow sovereign would help her to regain the Scottish
throne and expressed 'the confidence I have in you, not only
for the safety of my life, but also to aid and assist me in my
just quarrel'. Mary petitioned Elizabeth for an audience;
'I am', she bemoaned, 'in a pitiable condition, not only
for a queen, but for a gentlewoman, for I have nothing in

the world but what I had on my person when I made my
escape, travelling sixty miles across the country the first day,
and not having since ever ventured to proceed except by
night, as I hope to declare before you.' She signed herself,
'your very faithful and affectionate good sister, cousin and
escaped prisoner, Marie R'.

The Scottish queen's unexpected arrival on English soil
plunged Elizabeth and her government into a political
predicament that would last for twenty years. As her
blood relative and fellow anointed queen, Elizabeth was
sympathetic to Mary's situation, but she was also acutely
aware of the threat she posed with her claim to the English
throne. As strongly advised by Cecil, Elizabeth declined to
meet her unwelcome guest and decided to hold her under
temporary guard in the north while she considered her
options. AC.

Sil vous plest auoir pitie comme iespere demoi
extresme infortune de laquelle ie taysseray a me
lamanter pour ne vous inportuner et pour prier
dieu quil vous doint en sante tres heureuse
et longue vie et amoy pasiance et la consolation
que ienfands reseuoir devous a quize presante
mes humbles recommandations de Wiriunton
ce xvii de mey

Votre tres fidelle et affectionnee bonne
sœur et cousine et eschapprisoniere
MARER

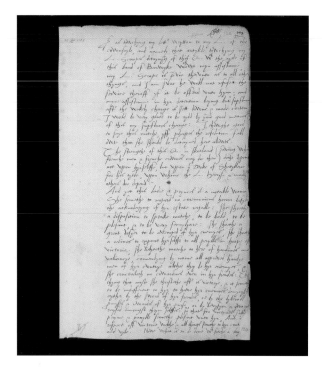

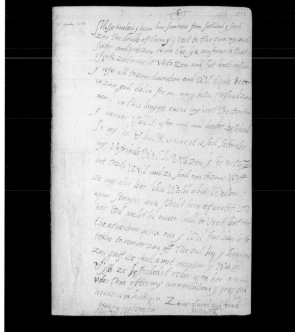

72
What Is to Be Done with Such a Lady?
Letter from Sir Francis Knollys to an unknown addressee,
probably Sir William Cecil, 11 June 1568, Carlisle.

British Library, Cotton MS Caligula C i, f. 124r.

73
Excuse My Evil Writing
Letter from Mary, Queen of Scots to Sir Francis Knollys,
1 September 1568, Bolton.

British Library, Cotton MS Caligula C i, f. 218r.

Instead of being invited to court, as she hoped, Mary, Queen of Scots and her retinue were escorted under armed guard to Carlisle Castle and placed under the temporary custodianship of Henry, Lord Scrope, Elizabeth I's Lord Warden of the Western March, and Sir Francis Knollys, her loyal privy councillor who was also married to her first cousin on the Boleyn side.

Knollys was expected to keep Elizabeth and her government informed of Mary's demeanour and conversations, and this letter was almost certainly intended for Cecil. Despite his fervent anti-Catholicism, Knollys described Mary as 'a notable woman' and recognised her personal charm: 'this ladie & prynces', he declared, 'semethe to regard no ceremonious honor besyde the acknolegyng of hyr estate regalle: she shoethe a disposition to speake motche, to be bold, to be plesant, & to be very famylyare'. He spoke too of her bravery, explaining that she 'shoethe a great desyer to be avenged of hyr enemyes, she shoethe a redines to expone hyr selffe to all perylls in hoope off victorie; she delytethe motche to here of hardines and valiancye'. He also cautioned that 'the thyng that moste she thirstethe after is victorye, & it semeth to be indifferent to hyr to have hyr enemies demynyssh[ed] eyther by the sword of hyr frendes, or by the lyberall promyses & rewardes of hyr purse, or by devysyon & qwaryll[s] raysed amongst theym selffes: so that for victories sake payne & parylle semethe plesant vnto hyr'.

Knollys, who confessed to be eager 'to be rydd … of this my superfluous charge', asked for clarity about Mary's status. Was she 'to be norysshed in ones bosome' or should they 'halte and dissembyll' with her? AC.

In mid-July, Mary was moved from Carlisle Castle to the more secure location of Bolton Castle in Yorkshire, the seat of Lord Scrope. Mary found her new accommodation much more agreeable and she enjoyed the companionship of Scrope's wife Margaret, sister of Thomas, fourth Duke of Norfolk, but still continued to press for a personal audience with Elizabeth I.

On 1 September 1568, Mary wrote this friendly note to Sir Francis Knollys in her child-like, downward sloping hand. She had been learning English – related to Scots, but a different language – under the tuition of her keeper, and this is the first letter that Mary penned in English rather than her native French tongue. She entreated Knollys to intercede with Elizabeth on her behalf and promised to follow his counsel, although she struggled to express her understanding 'in this langasg [language]' and asked him to 'excus my iuel Vreitin for y neuuer Vsed it afor and am hestet [excuse my evil writing for I never used it before and am hasted]'.

Mary made every effort to maintain good relations with Knollys and asked him to assure his wife, Lady Katherine Knollys, of her friendship: 'schu wald a bin weilcom to a pur strenger, hua Nocht bien aquentet vth her wil nocht bi ouuer bald to vreit bot for the aquentans betuix ous [she would have been welcome to a poor stranger, who not being acquainted with her would not be over bold to write but for the acquaintance between us]'. Mary informed Knollys of her intention to send a 'letle tekne [little token]' – described in another letter as a chain with pomander beads – for his wife, 'to rember zou off the gud hop y hevv in zou [to remember you of the good hope I have in you]'. She ended with a final apology for her writing: 'excus my iuel vreitin thes furst tym [excuse my evil writing this first time]'. AC.

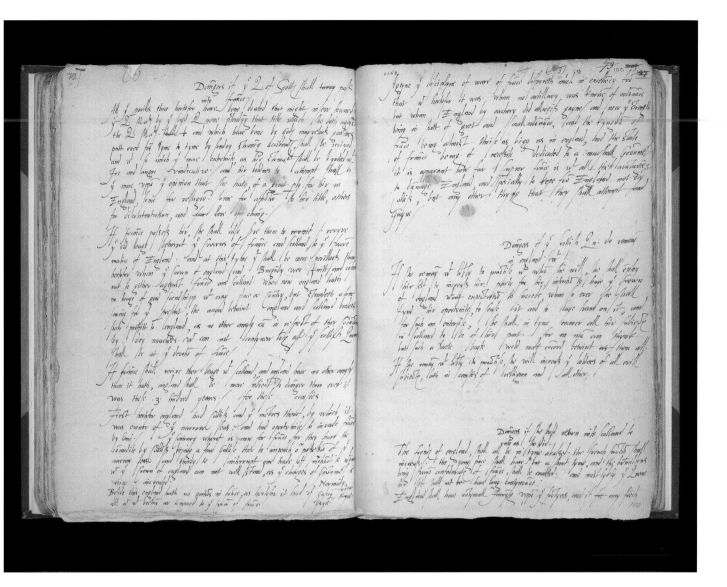

74

Responses to Mary's Asylum

Memorandum by Sir William Cecil, May 1568.

British Library, Cotton MS Caligula C i, ff. 99v–100r.

In this memorandum Cecil debated 'vppon the Scottish Queen comming into England'. He first considered the immediate response to Mary, Queen of Scots, including whether it was best for her to remain 'nere the frontars, or to be brought to the Middell partes of England'. She was to be 'savely and honorably preserved' but watched closely. Charles IX of France should be warned not to intervene in Scotland on her behalf because Elizabeth I 'can nott endure it'.

Cecil then turned to 'Thynges to be well Considered herafter'. He was already thinking in terms of a tribunal to determine whether or not Mary should be restored to her throne. Cecil envisaged Elizabeth presiding over this tribunal because of the 'auncient right' of suzerainty of England over Scotland. First, 'the certenty and truth' of Mary's part in Darnley's murder should be discovered. Even if she were complicit, a way might be found to 'cover the dishonor of the Cryme, and also to satle hir in hir realme with such kynd of Government there as maye preserve the same from the tyrannye of the french, and contynew the good accord betwixt these twoo realmes'. If Mary were exonerated, Cecil argued that she should reign jointly with her son James VI, closely monitored by the Scottish privy council. In all this must be weighed up how Mary had pressed her claim to the English throne, 'not as a second person after the Queen's Maiesty, but afor hir'. Having considered the dangers of permitting Mary to retire to France or returning her to Scotland, Cecil's preferred option was to keep her prisoner in England, even if she were innocent of Darnley's murder. AB.

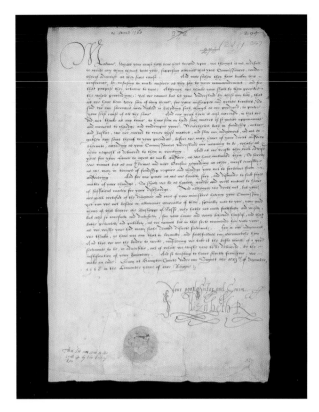

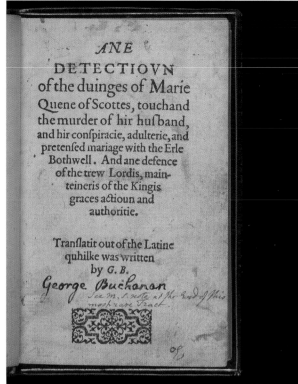

75

Mary's First Trial

Letter from Elizabeth I to Mary, Queen of Scots,
21 December 1568, Hampton Court.

British Library, Cotton MS Caligula C i, f. 367r.

76

The 'Casket Letters'

George Buchanan, *Ane Detectioun of the Duinges of Marie Quene of Scottes*, [London, printed by John Day, 1571].

British Library, G.1724.(1), title page.

On the advice of Sir William Cecil, Elizabeth declined to meet or release Mary. Instead, she offered to mediate between the Scottish queen and the Confederate Lords by setting up a 'conference' to inquire into the reasons behind the lords' rebellion and to consider the validity of their accusations against their queen. Elizabeth hoped that Mary would be found innocent and permitted to return to Scotland, albeit under strict conditions. The tribunal opened in York on 4 October 1568, with the Duke of Norfolk, Thomas Radcliffe, third Earl of Sussex and Sir Ralph Sadler sitting as judges. In November the tribunal relocated to Westminster and on 6 December, the notorious 'Casket Letters' – eight love-letters and twelve love-sonnets allegedly written by Mary in French to Bothwell early in 1567 (cat. 76) – were produced as evidence of Mary's adultery and complicity in the plot to murder Darnley. Mary insisted the letters were forgeries and demanded to be allowed to attend the trial and plead her case in person. Elizabeth refused and Mary withdrew her representatives in protest.

On 21 December 1568, Elizabeth wrote to assure Mary that the sorrows she had long felt for her 'mishappes and greate troubles' were now doubled by the appearance of the letters. Unable, however, to reach a final judgement without hearing Mary's version of events, Elizabeth urged and required her 'as one Prince and nere Cousine regarding an other, moost earnestlye as we may in termes of frendship … not to forbeare from answering'. In January 1569 the case against Mary was declared to be 'not proven'. AC.

The Scottish scholar George Buchanan, once loyal to Mary, Queen of Scots, became closely associated with the Earl of Moray from 1566, and was appointed secretary to the conference at York summoned by Elizabeth I in 1568 to investigate Darnley's murder. Convinced of Mary's guilt, in 1571 Buchanan published *De Maria Scotorum Regina*, a Latin text designed for an international readership that narrated Mary's crimes and branded her an adulterous tyrant.

In late 1571, Buchanan's work was translated into Scots by a non-native speaker in an attempt to make it sound like the authentic voice of the Scottish author. Appended to this translated text were all eight of the 'Casket Letters', which until then were unknown to the English public. Although he is not acknowledged on the title page, there is strong evidence that the translator was the militant Protestant Dr Thomas Wilson and the printer was John Day, who had published Foxe's 'Book of Martyrs' (cat. 26). That William Cecil, now Lord Burghley, was behind the publication seems most probable from a letter sent to him on 8 November 1571 in which Wilson wrote that he was sending 'so moche as is translated into handsome Skottyshe to you' and requesting more material that had not appeared in Buchanan's account. The English edition was followed by a Scottish and a French one in 1572. KL-H.

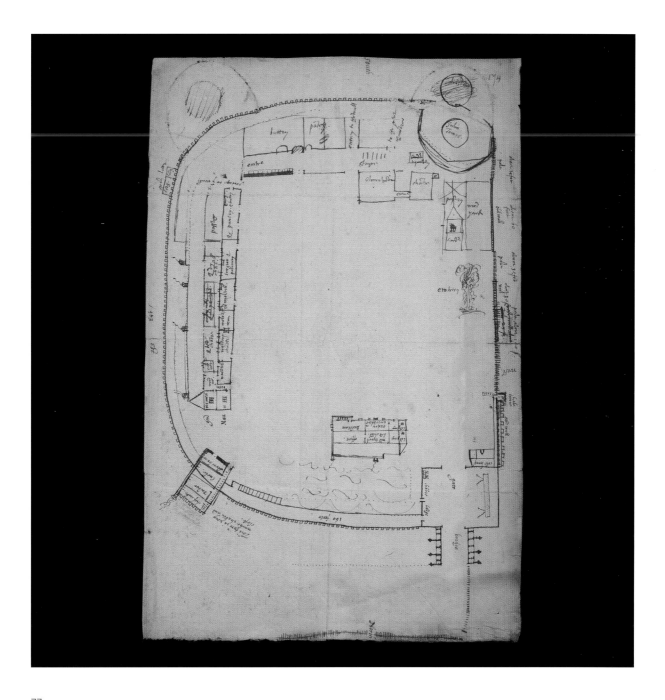

77

Tutbury Castle

Plan of Tutbury Castle, dated 21 December 1584.

British Library, Additional MS 33594, f. 174r.

The tribunal's inconclusive verdict was used to justify Mary's continued captivity in England, and in late January 1569 she was removed to Tutbury Castle in Staffordshire, far from potential sympathisers in the Catholic-inclined north and some distance from any seaport. Mary's new residence was a damp and bleak half-ruined motte-and-bailey castle, and far less comfortable than Bolton Castle. George Talbot, the sixth Earl of Shrewsbury, and his wife Elizabeth Talbot – better known today as Bess of Hardwick – were appointed Mary's new custodians. On 21 January the countess wrote to the Earl of Leicester, explaining that having only received Elizabeth's command to prepare the castle the day before, it was 'unredye yn manye respecctes for the receavyng of the Scottytysh queyne cominge at sodayne', but that she had 'caused workmen to make furwth yn redynes all such thynges as ys moust needfull to be downe before her cominge'.

Despite the Countess of Shrewsbury's best efforts, Mary loathed Tutbury and complained, 'I am in a walled enclosure, on the top of a hill exposed to all the winds and inclemencies of heaven' and that her own apartments were 'two little miserable rooms, so excessively cold, especially at night'. This plan of Tutbury Castle was sketched during a later period of Mary's confinement. The bridge and gatehouse are visible at bottom right, and on the left the queen's presence chamber and bedchamber have been identified, as well as rooms for her gentlewomen of the chamber, surgeon, 'poticary' and her secretary, Claude Nau de la Boisselière. AC.

Reaction in England and Scotland

The arrival of Mary, Queen of Scots unsettled politics in England. Several of Elizabeth I's councillors and nobles thought a sound course would be to marry Mary to a 'safe' Protestant, just as had been attempted in 1564 with the offer of Leicester to the Scottish queen. During 1568 the Duke of Norfolk presented himself to Mary as a potential husband but without the sanction or knowledge of Elizabeth. When Elizabeth learned of the intrigue in September 1569, her rage was so intense that Norfolk withdrew without permission to his estates. He was then arrested and placed in the Tower.

Norfolk's imprisonment set off a rebellion in the north led by the Earls of Northumberland and Westmorland. For a time, the rising of some 7,000 armed Catholics looked serious, but it was suppressed by a royal army before the New Year. The political crisis, however, was not over. Norfolk continued his undercover intrigues with Mary and, still worse, foreign powers became involved. Pope Pius V issued a bull excommunicating Elizabeth in February 1570; and in 1571 Elizabeth's government discovered that Roberto di Ridolfi, a Florentine merchant resident in London, was acting as a point of contact between the Spanish government, Norfolk and Mary.

From now on, most Protestants believed that Mary was at the heart of an international conspiracy to dethrone Elizabeth. MPs in the 1572 parliament pressed for Mary's execution, but Elizabeth ignored their demand. Indeed, the English queen was to act as Mary's protector until the discovery of the Babington Plot in 1586.

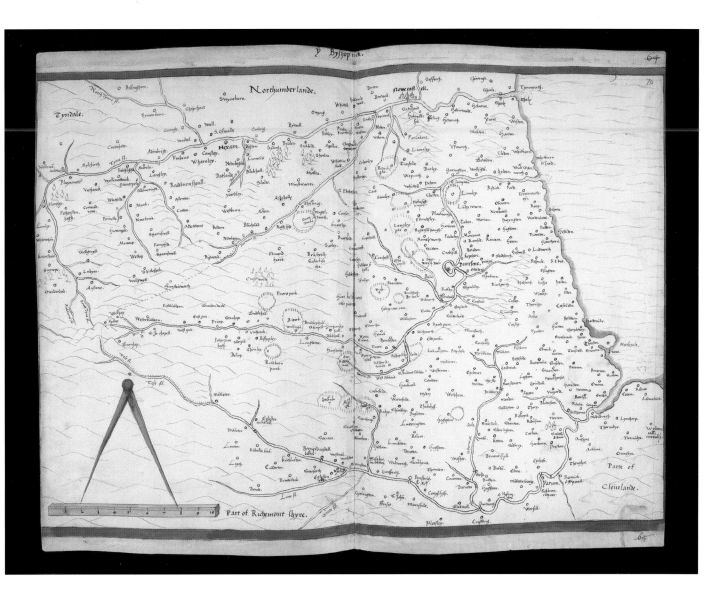

78

The Northern Rebellion

John Rudd, the Burghley-Saxton Atlas, 1576.

British Library, Royal MS 18 D iii, ff. 69v–70r.

In October 1569 Thomas Howard, fourth Duke of Norfolk, was sent to the Tower of London for plotting to marry Mary, Queen of Scots. While on his way there, he urged his co-conspirators, Thomas Percy, seventh Earl of Northumberland, and Charles Neville, sixth Earl of Westmorland, not to rebel, 'for if they did, it shuld cost hym his heade'. Fearing their own arrests, they did not heed Norfolk's plea.

On 14 November Northumberland and Westmorland set up the Mass again at Durham Cathedral, as well as elsewhere in the north. The rebel aims were to depose Elizabeth I in favour of Mary and to restore Catholicism throughout the realm. Although it was quickly crushed, the government regarded the Northern Rebellion as a considerable threat and about 600 rebels were executed as a warning. Northumberland and Westmorland fled to Scotland, where Northumberland was captured on Christmas Eve. In June 1572, in return for £2,000, he was delivered to the English.

His fate seemed uncertain at first. However, he was beheaded for treason at York on 22 August. Westmorland was more fortunate and escaped overseas.

This pen and ink map of County Durham dates from shortly after the Rebellion. It may have been drawn by John Rudd, a prebendary of Durham, who had been commissioned to undertake a survey of the counties of England and Wales, before his servant, Christopher Saxton, took over the task. A number of places associated with the Northern Rebellion are marked on the Durham map, including Brancepeth – where Northumberland and Westmorland first gathered their supporters – and the city of Durham itself.

With William Cecil, Lord Burghley's support, Saxton mapped the counties of England and Wales between 1573 and 1579, and published them in his Atlas in 1579. Burghley received copies of the uncorrected printed proofs of Saxton's county maps, supplementing them with manuscript maps, which he had bound into a volume for his own use in governing the realm. His notes and annotations are found throughout the Atlas (cat. 101). On the Durham map, for example, he has marked Brancepeth as once having belonged to Westmorland. AB.

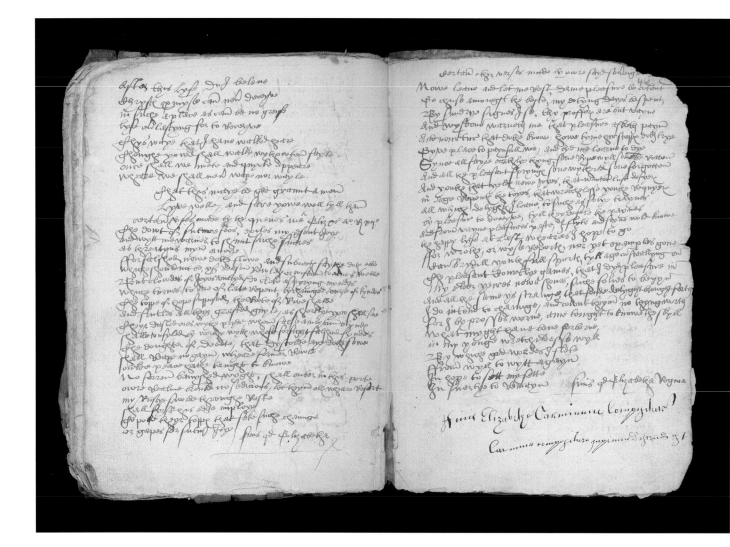

79

The Doubt of Future Foes

Verses composed by Elizabeth I in response to the Northern Rebellion, *c.*1569–70, [copied late 1580s].

British Library, Additional MS 82370, ff. 45v–46r.

Attributed to Elizabeth, this poem, which begins 'The dowt of future foos [foes], exiles my present Joye', was originally composed in the winter of 1569–70, as a defiant admonition to Mary, Queen of Scots and her followers during the Northern Rebellion. Referring to the Scottish queen as 'the doughter of Debate', the poem ends with a vow to defend the country: 'No forren banyshed wyght, shall enter in this porte / owre Realme brouke no sedicions, let theym elleswheare Resort / my Rustye sworde throughe Reste / shall fyrst his edge imploye / To pole [lop off] theyr toppes that seke suche chaunge / or gapes for future Joye.'

The poem is found in the household book of John Hanson, a Yorkshire yeoman who worked as a scrivener and notary. In this provincial anthology the queen's verses are placed alongside legal documents, ballads, calendars and recipes. The manuscript paints a picture of how the monarch's poetry was read and circulated amongst her subjects, as the country responded to the changing political landscape following the Northern Rebellion.

By the time Hanson copied this poem into his anthology in the late 1580s, these verses had taken on a new life following the execution of Mary, Queen of Scots in 1587. As a reminder of the threat posed by the Northern Rebellion, the poem defends Elizabeth's actions and serves as testimony to the English queen's strong rule. AGB.

80

Excommunication of Elizabeth

S.D.N. Pii Papæ V. Sententia declaratoria contra Elisabeth prætensam Angliæ Reginam, & ei adhærentes Hereticos, [Rome?, 1570].

British Library, C.18.e.2.(114*).

This is a printed copy of the papal bull known as *Regnans in Excelsis* which was issued in Latin on 25 February 1570 announcing Elizabeth I's excommunication on grounds of heresy. In translation, Elizabeth is described as 'the pretended Queen of England and the servant of crime' who 'has followed and embraced the errors of the heretics'. The bull also absolved Elizabeth's Catholic subjects from any allegiance to the queen and threatened those who did not obey the pope's instructions with the same punishment: 'Those who shall act to the contrary we include in the like sentence of excommunication.' The promulgation of *Regnans in Excelsis* therefore created a conflict of loyalty for English Catholics between Elizabeth and the pope.

The bull was issued in support of the Northern Rebellion but arrived in England too late to affect its outcome. On 25 May 1570 John Felton published it in England by nailing a copy to the gate of the Bishop of London's palace adjacent to St Paul's Cathedral; he was executed in August for treason. How far the bull was circulated in England is unclear, but it is possible that Mary saw it. In reaction, parliament in 1571 introduced three new statutes: one made it treason to bring in or publish any documents or materials from Rome; the second was a new Treasons Act; the third dealt with Catholics overseas. However, a bill to introduce tough new laws against Catholics was vetoed by the queen. SD.

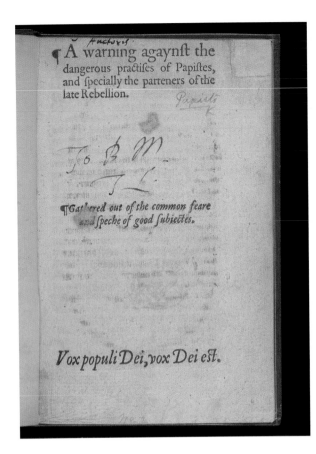

81

Warning against Mary and the English Papists

Thomas Norton, *A Warning agaynst the Dangerous Practises of Papistes, and Specially the Parteners of the Late Rebellion*, [London, printed by John Day, 1569?].

British Library, C.38.c.39., title page.

The Protestant ideologue Thomas Norton wrote a series of anti-Catholic texts in a sustained campaign against Mary, Queen of Scots. All but one of the tracts were printed by John Day, who had close ties with William Cecil. Writing in the aftermath of the Northern Rebellion, Norton used *A Warning* to attack Catholics who were in thrall to the pope. In his view, it was not possible for someone to be a papist and loyal to the queen, especially after the arrival of the bull of excommunication. He argued that, although the Rebellion had been put down, papist treachery had to be rooted out to prevent similar rebellions. Norton offered a series of 'Conclusions' to deal with the papists whom he characterised as enemies of both monarchs and states.

Comparing Catholics to conjurors and astrologers, he argued against dangerous prophecies which predicted that Mary, Queen of Scots and the Duke of Norfolk would marry: 'I speake nothing of the prognosticating toy of a mariage sent vp to be printed.' Norton then discussed how English papists were traitors who were trying to convey the crown to a foreigner (Mary) and concluded that it was necessary to keep Elizabeth and the privy council safe, to purge papists from all offices and to pass penal laws against them. He also criticised 'neuters', by which he meant those Protestant moderates who were not zealous in rooting out papistry or wanted accommodation with Mary. KL-H.

82

Thomas Howard, Fourth Duke of Norfolk

Unknown artist, 1565.

National Portrait Gallery, London, 6676.

Norfolk was the premier nobleman in England and Elizabeth I's cousin through her mother Anne Boleyn. As Earl Marshal he supervised Elizabeth's coronation and later that year was appointed lieutenant general of the north, signing the military treaty with the Lords of the Congregation. An ambitious man, he competed with Cecil and Leicester for influence and was particularly opposed to the latter's ambition to marry the queen.

Norfolk's family life was marked by tragedy: his father, Henry Howard, Earl of Surrey, was executed when he was a child and he was widowed three times. The fragmentary inscription dates this portrait to 1565 and it is possible that his sombre and simple clothing is a mark of his mourning for his second wife, Margaret Audley, who died in 1564. His authority remains clearly signalled in the Howard coat of arms that adorns his ring and the insignia of the Order of the Garter that hangs around his neck.

Following the death of his third wife, Elizabeth Leybourne, in 1567, Norfolk considered marriage to Mary, Queen of Scots. Although he had been one of the potential suitors suggested by Elizabeth a few years earlier, by this point Mary was a deposed queen suspected of involvement in the murder of her second husband. The match did not have Elizabeth's support and, as he pursued it, Norfolk found himself drawn into conspiracy against the queen. He was indicted for treason for his involvement in the Ridolfi Plot and executed in 1572. CB.

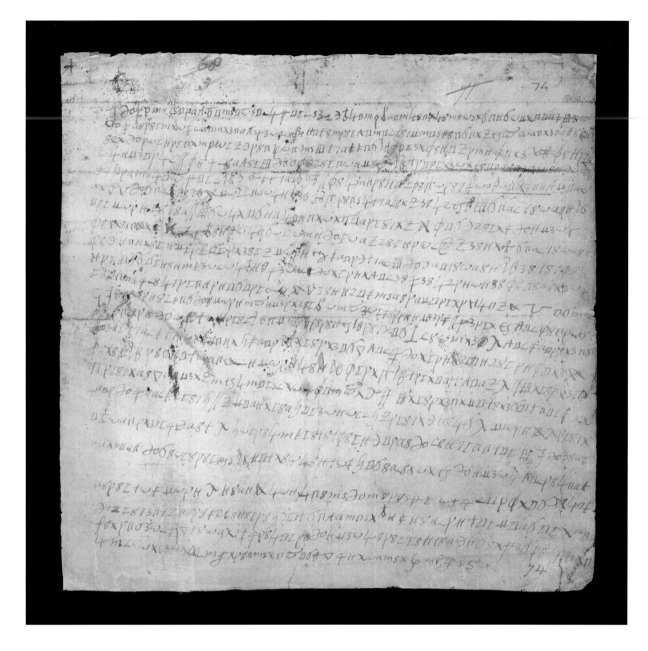

83

The Norfolk–Mary Marriage Proposal

Ciphered letter from Mary, Queen of Scots to Thomas Howard, fourth Duke of Norfolk, 31 January 1570.

British Library, Cotton MS Caligula C ii, f. 74r.

The idea of Mary marrying a Protestant English nobleman was revived during the York–Westminster conference as a convenient way of neutralising the threat she posed to the security of the realm and also resolving the problem of the English succession. The recently widowed Duke of Norfolk was dazzled by the prospect of marrying Mary and had the backing of leading councillors and noblemen, including the Earl of Leicester. Mary responded enthusiastically, believing that the marriage would restore her to freedom. When Elizabeth discovered that her leading nobleman was secretly planning to marry her greatest rival, she was furious. After fleeing the court to escape the queen's wrath and triggering the Northern Rebellion in the process, Norfolk was sent to

the Tower. Mary was moved from her comfortable lodgings at Wingfield back to the inhospitable but more secure Tutbury Castle.

Mary and Norfolk continued to correspond during his confinement. In this remarkable letter, written in cipher, Mary hints at her reckless plan for a double-escape attempt, urging Norfolk to let her know his 'pleasure if I showlde seeke to make any enterpryse'. She assures him 'I care not for my danger' and wishes that Norfolk 'woulde seeke to be the like, for if yow and I cowld escape both too ... beeinge free and honorablie bownde toguether, yow myght make soche good offers for the contreys, and the Queene of England, as they showlde not refuse. Our faulte wer not shameful, yow have promysed to bee myne, and I yours. I beleve the Queene of Englande and Cowntre showlde like of it'. 'Faithful to deathe', Mary pledges to follow Norfolk's direction, 'for I wyl euer bee for your sake perpetual prysoner, or putte my life in peril, for your weale & myne'. AC.

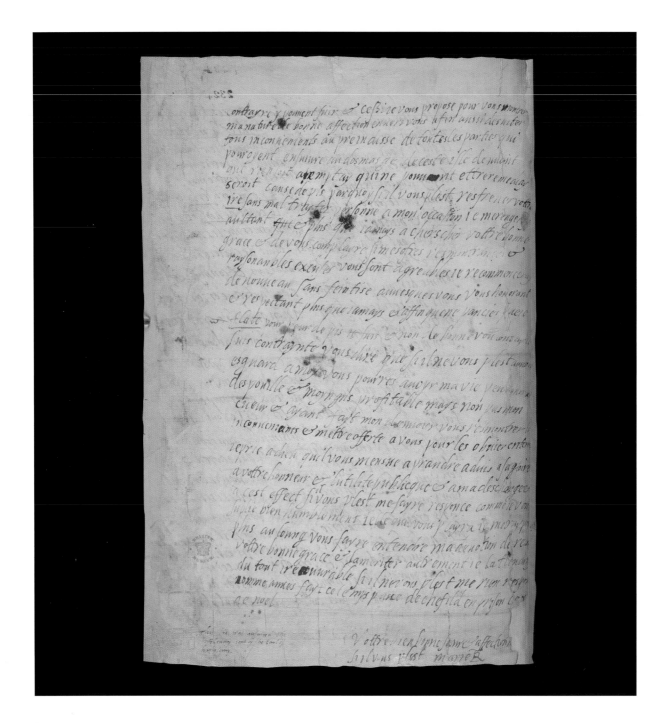

84

The Ridolfi Plot

Letter from Mary, Queen of Scots to Elizabeth I,
25 December 1571, Sheffield.

British Library, Cotton MS Caligula C iii, f. 246v.

After the discovery of the Ridolfi Plot, Mary wrote in
her own hand to Elizabeth, expressing despair at her
imprisonment. She began by complaining that Elizabeth
'disdain[ed] to ... answer' her petitions, instead 'treating
me worse and worse'. She decided she would stop
'break[ing] my head in vain' after one more offer of
reconciliation on Christmas Day 1571. Mary reminded
Elizabeth that 'I am your cousin the closest you have in
the world'. She had given the English queen no cause to
imprison her and asked, 'what you would do in my place?'
Mary had petitioned in the past for a personal audience
with Elizabeth in order to 'unburden my heart to you,
rendering myself all yours'. But her offers were refused. All
Mary had done since her arrival in England in May 1568,
she claimed, was to complain that the queen had given her
no support. Consequently, she had been constrained to
seek help elsewhere. Mary proposed to 'commence again
anew, without pretence with you, honouring and respecting
you more than ever'. If this offer was rejected, 'you can
have my life ... but not my heart'. She signed the letter,
'in prison at Christmas, your very good sister and loving
[cousin], if you please, Queen Mary'. Her letter went
unanswered. AB.

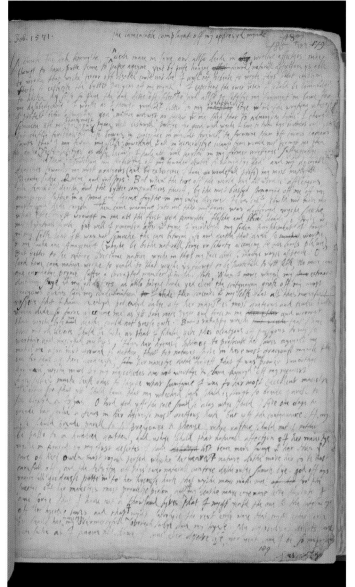

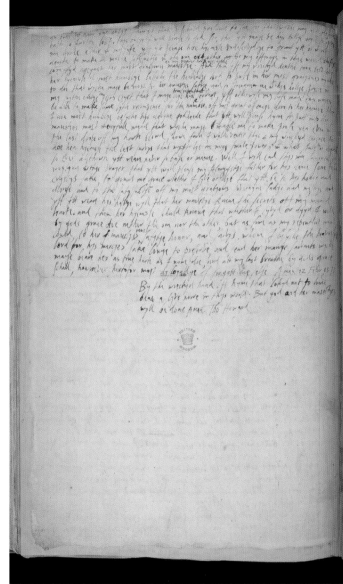

85

Norfolk's 'Complaint'

Petition of Thomas Howard, fourth Duke of Norfolk,
to Elizabeth I, 12 February 1572, Tower of London.

British Library, Cotton MS Caligula C iii, f. 189r–v.

On 16 January 1572 the Duke of Norfolk was convicted of
treason for his part in the Ridolfi Plot. On 12 February he
wrote a 'lamentable complaynt off my oppressyd mynde' to
Elizabeth from his cell in the Tower of London, beginning
'allthowh the lord knowythe, I a dede mane in lawe, and allso
deade in … worldlye affecyons, never thowght to haue putte
penne to paper agayne'. Norfolk had written what he believed
was 'my last letter to my … vnlukkye boye', when he learned
that the queen had granted a stay of execution. 'O lord …

whye schuld I lyve one daye to breade but suche a feare in her
hyenesse most gracyous hart, but yff the contynuaunce off
my lyfe schuld breade parell [peril] to so presyoues a phenyx,
whye rather schuld not I … be putte to a hundred deathes?'
Elizabeth had been associated with the phoenix, symbolising
rebirth, since the beginning of the reign. If he were spared,
Norfolk promised in his 'Complaynt' that he would 'doe her
hyenesse the lest sarvys that mygte lye in my smale power,
in what state or degree so ever allthowh ytt weare never so
base or meane'. He ended, 'by the wrectyd hand off hyme
that lokyd not to haue bene a lyve nowe in thys world. But
God and her maiestyes wyll be done.' Elizabeth hesitated over
executing her cousin Norfolk, but parliament demanded it,
and he was sent to the block on 2 June. AB.

86
'Unica Semper Avis'
'Phoenix jewel' of Elizabeth I, *c*.1570–80.
British Museum, London, SLMisc.1778.

Medals associating Elizabeth with the phoenix date from
the beginning of her reign. Because in ancient mythology it
was reborn from its own ashes, this fabulous bird came to
symbolise the rebirth and renewal of Elizabeth's dynasty. The

claims of Mary, Queen of Scots to the succession represented a
challenge to that renewal, which is why – after his complicity
with Mary in the Ridolfi Plot – the Duke of Norfolk told
Elizabeth that he would gladly accept his own death sentence
'yff the contynuaunce off my lyfe schuld breade parell [peril] to
so presyoues a phenyx' (cat. 85).

On the reverse of this pendant jewel, which shows the bust
of Elizabeth in silhouette, is the device of the phoenix in flames

under the royal monogram, with the crown and heavenly rays above. The enamelled red and white roses encircling the jewel symbolise the Tudor dynasty. This is one of two very similar jewels featuring symbolic birds which Elizabeth is shown wearing in contemporary royal portraits by Nicholas Hilliard. Of these the 'Phoenix Portrait' (National Portrait Gallery) shows the phoenix just as it appears on the reverse of this gold pendant, rising with outspread wings above the flames.

The phoenix features in religious iconography from an early date, symbolising Christ's Resurrection. In Renaissance emblem books it was above all the bird's uniqueness that was significant, as highlighted by the motto to Claude Paradin's phoenix emblem, 'Unica semper avis' ['Only ever one bird']. Paradin's woodcut (*Devises Heroïques*, 1551) shows the bird rising up from the flames just as it does in this jewel, and was almost certainly the artist's source for this image. MB.

Civil War in Scotland

On 23 January 1570, Regent Moray was assassinated.
His successor, Mary's father-in-law, the Earl of Lennox,
was a divisive choice, and Scotland descended once more
into a civil war between the King's Party, led by the regent for
James VI, and the Queen's Party, which attempted to govern
in Mary's name from Edinburgh Castle. When the Queen's
Party raided Stirling, Lennox was fatally wounded and died
on 4 September 1571. The following day, the Earl of Mar
was elected the new regent, but he died in October 1572
with Edinburgh Castle still in the hands of the Queen's Party.
The next regent was the Earl of Morton, who persuaded
Elizabeth to lend him military assistance to capture the castle.
By the end of May 1573, the castle had surrendered after
heavy bombardment. The civil war came to an end and the
anglophile and anti-Marian Morton governed Scotland
until James VI ended his minority in 1579.

87
James VI and Regency Government
Letter from Elizabeth I to John Erskine, Earl of Mar,
2 October 1571, Richmond.

National Records of Scotland, Edinburgh, Mar and Kellie Muniments
GD124/10/30.

Elizabeth wrote to the Earl of Mar in support of his
appointment in September 1571 as regent to James VI, 'for
that surely we think none coulde haue bene namyd in that
Realm, more plausible to that nation, nor more meeter for
the charge; althoughe we know well your selfe of good
wisdom wolde haue forborn it'. Mar succeeded the Earl of
Lennox, who had been killed at Stirling at a time when the
civil war between the supporters of Mary, Queen of Scots and
those of James VI was escalating.

Widely respected for his integrity, Mar had been
appointed by Mary as Keeper of Stirling Castle and guardian
to her son in March 1567, a few months before he played

a key role in overthrowing her. In February 1572 Elizabeth
wrote to Mar's wife, Annabella Murray, saying James would
be thankful one day to Mar 'for the hazardouse service done
in the charge ... and also to yow for his education'. A year or
two later James began one of his own letters to the Countess
of Mar, 'lady minny [Mother]'.

In this letter, with four slits down each side still clearly
visible from when it was folded and sealed shut, Elizabeth
also informed Mar of how 'we haue very lately by Goddes
goodnes discouered suche pernicious practises of the said
Queene [Mary] against vs our person and state; as we are
necessarily occasionid ... not to deale any furder by treatie or
otherwyse in her fauour to haue any Rule by our meanes to
the preiudice of her sonnes estate'. It had only been by God's
providence that the Ridolfi Plot to usurp Elizabeth had been
uncovered, the queen explained. In a postscript, she asked
Mar to look favourably on petitions from Lennox's widow,
who was Elizabeth's nearest living relative. AB.

treated for her, being as we now see them abused by, her and
her ministers, you may be assured that herein we meant not to
giue you cause to doubte of our intention to the trouble of that
estate; And for furder dealing in your fauoure to help you to
an vniuersall quyetnes by a generall obedience to the king, according as
we vnderstand that all the three estate of that Realm (a few only
excepted) haue now in the last parlement accorded, we meane that you
shall be made priuie therof presently from o[ur] said Marshall of Barwik
and as soone after as may be, by our cousin the Lord of Rimsden, o[ur]
gouerno[ur] there, who is appointed presently to repaire thither, and shall
haue powre to treate & conclude w[ith] you and the rest of the
nobilitie, of suche thing as may tend to the common repose of both the
Realmes. And where this bearer m[aster] Cunigam hath
abydden long there since the receipte of yo[ur] l[ett]re, we require you
not to impute the same to him, but to the occasion that we haue
had to be occupied in other matters w[ith] o[ur] counsell, as we could not
sooner expedite him to our l[ett]re.

Your lovinge frende

Elizabeth R

Postscr.

Although we doubte not but you will haue good regarde to all suche causes
as may concerne the State of o[ur] dere cousin y[e] Lady Margaret late wyfe to y[e]
Earle of Lennox; aswell for her own p[ar]ticuler intreste, as for y[e] bene fitt and
aduancement of the house of Lennox, Yet we can not but hope for the
naturall affection we beare to her, & our good will to the house of Lennox &
continuance of the same; most hartely require you to shew to all suche as
shall sollicite her cause there both for her selfe and for the weale of the
house suche fauorable hearing of them, and suche expedition in the effectuall
answearing therof to their contentac[i]on, as we may hereby y[e] rather y[e]
recommendac[i]on hath in some y[e] pleasured her. And furdermore we thinke
very reasonable to kepe you in good remembrance y[t] all suche as haue already
bene found partie contrary[us] to the deathe of o[ur] said Cousin y[e] Earle of Lennox the
late Regent, or that heerafter shall be founde any wise p[ar]ticipant thereof being
not already punished, may be w[ith] all seueritie punished to the example, terror of any
suche like mischefe to be deuysed and attempted. And in this behalfe we trust the rest
of the nobilitie joynig w[ith] you in the obedience of the king, will joyne w[ith] you as in
honor & Justice they ought to doe. Geven vnder o[ur] Signet at o[ur] Mannor of Richmond
the second of October 1571 the xiij[th] yeere of o[ur] Raigne

88

James VI of Scotland

Rowland Lockey, inscribed 1574.

National Trust, Hardwick Hall, NT 1129115.

Inscribed: JACOBVS. DEI GRATIA. REX. / SCOTORVM. ETATIS. SVE. 8 / 1574.

The only son of Mary, Queen of Scots and her second husband Lord Darnley, James became king of Scotland at only 13 months old, after his mother's forced abdication in 1567. He was raised apart from his mother, becoming an able scholar under the instruction of his tutors. Mary evidently wished to hold James's image close to her: she commissioned a portrait of him as an infant in 1566 to accompany portraits of herself and her husband by the French artist Jean de Court, which were all to be inserted into a 'book of gold'; this was probably the similarly described item that was listed among her possessions at her death.

The painting is a copy of a portrait of James made in 1574 when he was 8 years old; it was commissioned by the Countess of Shrewsbury and is listed in the 1601 inventory of Hardwick Hall. James's easy control of the hawk on his hand signals his authority but is also a mark of his genuine enthusiasm for hunting. A number of contemporary versions of the portrait survive, including a small oil painting in the Rijksmuseum in Amsterdam, and it is tempting to speculate as to whether one of these might have been intended for Mary. CB.

89

James VI's Schoolboy Exercises

Inventory of the library of James VI, containing two
of his written exercises.

British Library, Additional MS 34275, ff. 3r and 19r.

Brought up mainly at Stirling Castle, James VI received a
thorough classical education under the guidance of his two
tutors, George Buchanan and Peter Young. This manuscript
contains an inventory of the king's library, beginning in
1573 when he was just 7 years old.

According to his tutor, the young king's morning
routine began with prayers followed by the study of
the Greek New Testament and Greek grammar. In the
afternoon he read Latin from Livy, Justin or Cicero, or
Scottish or foreign history and, when time allowed, he
studied arithmetic, geography, astronomy and rhetoric. The
flyleaves of this volume became an impromptu copy-book

for the young student: on one page the king has copied out
the letters of the alphabet. Beneath, he has experimented
with writing his signature in Latin, French and Scots. In
a slightly later hand, James has made several copies of a
Latin maxim, translated from the Greek of Musonius, a
Roman Stoic philosopher. The saying can be translated
as: 'If you take labour and pain to do a virtuous thing,
the labour disappears and the virtue remains; if through
pleasure you do something ill, the pleasure disappears and
the vice remains.'

The king's library included books formerly belonging
to Mary, Queen of Scots, which had been seized following
her deposition. James's collection was supplemented by
educational works and gifts, such as a present of a pen,
inkhorn and 'tua [two] faire globes'. The manuscript also
notes several more recreational gifts received by the young
king, including bows, arrows and two 'golf cloubbis'. AGB.

The Kingis Maiesteis Proclamatioun beiring the

verie occasioun of the present incuming of the Inglis forces, with his hienes commandement
for thair gude Intreatment and freindly vsage.

AMES be the grace of God king of Scottis, To our Louittis william Bryson Masar, Messingeris our Schireffis in that part coniunctly and seuerallie speciallie constitute greting. Forsamekle as it is not vnknawin to all the gude subiectis of this our Realme, quhat greit gude will and freindschip our dearest sister the Quene of Ingland (being Princesse in the warld neirest to vs baith be blude and habitatioun) hes declarit not onlie towartis vs and the preseruatioun of our Innocent persoun euer sen our birth. Bot als quhat cair, trauellis, and charges our said dearest sister hes takin, borne, and sustenit for the saiftie and preseruatioun of this our Realme in the auld ancient libertie, far aboue the custome of ony hir predecessouris. For it is not to be forgottin bot thankfullie to be rememberit how euin with the beginning of hir Regne (were than standing betuix thir twa Realmes) first of all a godlie peace was maid and concludit, quhilk to this tyme hes happely continewit to the pleasure of God and greit commoditie of this countrie. As alswa how schortlie thairefter this our Realme being in danger of the Frenche conqueist, and Christiane Religioun thairin likly to haue bene vtterly suppressit, be our said dearest sisteris forces and ayd send to the assege of Leyth, the strangeris wer expellit and the stait of Religioun and libertie of the coutrie preseruit, in the quhilk actioun neither hir treasure nor the blude and lyfis of hir pepill wer spairit. The lyke cair weill appeirit in hir quhen he hir forces direct in this our Realme in the Moneth of Maij, the zeir of God ane thousand fyue hundreth thre scoir and ten zeiris, the conspiratouris quhilkis pretendit our depositioun from our Royall Crowne and to erect ane vther authoritie, wer profligat and disapointit, and our Castell of Glasgow than assegit be thame succourit and releuit. Our said dearest sister neuer taking or occupying ony strenth, hald, or fute of ground in Scotland, bot that quhilk scho hes bene alwayis willing to rander to the awneris, vpon na vther conditioun saulfing thair returning to our obedience and suretie for continewance thairat. And sen that tyme it is weill knawin quhat trauellis and cair scho hes takin be hir Ambassadouris letteris and Messages to haue our haill Realme quyetit to our obediëce. Quhairin hir labouris and mediatioun hes at Goddis pleasure takin gude successe, our haill Realme in effect being reducit to the acknawledgeing of our Authoritie, and in the place of the lang ciuile and intestine weir, gude peace restorit ouer all the countrie: our Castell of Edinburgh only exceptit. Quhilk being put in the trust and custodie of williame Kirkcaldy sumtyme of Grange knicht to our vse and behufe be vmquhyle our dearest Cousing James Erle of Murray our Regent for the tyme of worthy memorie, the said williame vnmyndfull of his treuth and promysit allegeance, hes be the space of twa zeiris with the mair now bypast be the meanis of the same Castell raisit and continewit the said ciuile and Intestine weir aganis our Royall estait & Authoritie. To the disturbance of Christiane Religioun, the Lawis, policie, and haill commoun weill of our Realme, and reiecting the godlie pacificatioun quhilkis the cheif Nobill men and vtheris returning to our obedience hes ressauit, procedis in contempteous Rebellioun and weir, greitly annoying our Burgh of Edinburgh being the cheif sait of Justice, and doing besydis quhat in him lyis to procure and draw strangeris in this our Realme for suppressing of Religioun, our estait, and troubling the quyetnes of this haill Ile. And seing our principall Ordinance, Powder, Bullettis, and munitionnis ar detenit within our said Castell, and vsit and spent aganis vs and our gude subiectis, our said dearest sister hes bene ernistly requyrit be our richt traist Cousing James Erle of Mortoun Lord Dalkeith Regent to vs our Realme and liegis, and Nobilitie of this our Realme, for ayd and succouris of men, ordinance, and munitioun, to the expugnatioun, assege, and recouerie of our said Castell. Quhilk scho hes fauourabillie and liberallie grätit, efter all gude meanis vsit to haue brocht the persounis being within our said Castell to our obedience be treatie. Bot the same contempnit be thame and reiectit, hes now preparit and causit put hir forces in full reddynes to enter in this our Realme, to be fully employed for the mantenance and furthsetting of our Authoritie, in assegeing of our said Castell, that the same being recouerit, may Immediatlie and indilaitlie be delyuerit (with the ordinance, munitioun, Royall place, Jowellis, Wardrop, and houshald stuf, and with the Registeris and recordis belanging to vs and our Crown) to vs and our said Regent in our name & to our behufe. And swa thairby peace restorit to our said Burgh of Edinburgh and our haill Realme in our obedience, without ony vther pretense, meaning, or Intentioun in our said dearest sister, or in Schir williame Drurie knicht, Generall of hir saidis forces. OVR will is heirfoir, and we charge zow straitlie and commandis, that Incontinent thir our letteris sene ze pas and in our Name and Authoritie mak publicatioun heirof at the mercat Croce of our Burgh of Edinburgh, and all vther placess neidfull, that nane pretend Ignorance of the same, or sinisterlie depraue and misreport of our said dearest sisteris freindly and fauourabill Intentioun. And that ze command and charge all and sindrie our liegis, that thay and euerie ane of thame thankfully ressaue the Generall of hir forces, and haill persounis being vnder his charge, and to schaw and gif to thame all fauour and gude intreatment in ludgeing, meit, drink, and vtheris thair necessaris vpon thair ressonabill charges, vnrasand the present prices in ony thing. And that nane tak vpon hand to do to thame or ony of thame harme, greif, Iniurie, or vncurtesie in bodyis or gudis be word, deid, or countenance, vnder the pane of deid. Certifying thame that failzeis, thay salbe repute and estemit as seditious and wickit Instrumentis, hinderaris of our seruice and obedience, fauouraris and pertakaris with the declarit Tratouris and Rebellis being within our said Castell, and the pane of deid salbe execute vpon thame with all Rigour in exempill of vtheris. The quhilk to do we commit to zow coniunctlie and seuerallie our full power, be thir our letteris delyuering thame be zow dewlie execute and Indorsat agane to the berare. Geuin vnder our Signet at Halyruidhous the riij. day of Apryle, and of our Regne the sext zeir. 1573.

Per Actum Secreti Consilij.

Imprentit at Edinburgh be Thomas Bassandyne.   CVM PRIVILEGIO REGIS.

90

The Siege of Edinburgh Castle

*The Kingis Maiesteis Proclamatioun Beiring the Verie
Occasioun of the Present Incūming of the Inglis Forces,*
Edinburgh, printed by Thomas Bassandyne, [1573].

British Library, Cotton MS Caligula C iv, f. 73r.

In 1571 Edinburgh Castle was occupied by Mary's supporters
and became the focus of the military conflict in Scotland.
The resulting siege of the castle lasted two years and was
known as the 'Lang Siege'. In 1573, the King's Party asked
for English military support in order to take the castle; and
in April a thousand men arrived under the command of Sir
William Drury, marshal of the English garrison at Berwick-
upon-Tweed.

In this proclamation, issued at Edinburgh in the name of
the boy James VI on 13 April 1573, the English army was
welcomed into Scotland as friends, reminding the Scots of
Elizabeth I's decisive support during the Siege of Leith in
1560 (cat. 35). James's subjects are urged 'that nane pretend
Ignorance of the same, or sinisterlie depraue and misreport of
our said dearest sisteris freindly and fauourabill Intentioun'.
Those who do not follow the king's orders are seen as
traitors siding with the Queen's Party barricaded in the castle:
'Certifying thame that failzis [fails], thay salbe repute and
estemit as seditious and wickit Instrumentis hinderaris of our
seruice and obedience, fauouraris and pertakaris with the
declarit Tratour is and Rebellis within our said Castell.'

While a number of English proclamations from this
period survive, Scottish examples are rare. The broadsheet
or broadside format was relatively new in Scotland in the
sixteenth century, but it had been used in other countries, for
example in Germany in the late fifteenth century. Since the
murder of Darnley in 1567, however, proclamations became
a key part of the propaganda campaign against Mary in
Scotland.

Broadsides like this one were printed in large numbers to
be as widely distributed throughout the country as possible.
They were put up in public places and also read aloud, but,
much like campaign posters today, their ephemeral nature
meant that most of them were discarded once they had lost
their currency. This particular proclamation, printed in black
letter, survives in three slightly different states, suggesting that
minor corrections to the text and imprint were made while
the proclamation went through the press. All three versions
today survive in one or two copies only.

Copies of this proclamation would have been issued
throughout Scotland. The castle surrendered at the end of
May, bringing the civil war to a close. KL-H.

Imprisonment

The mid-1570s were a quiet time for Mary. For a while she seemed reconciled to a restricted life under house arrest, since her hopes of restoration had waned with the defeat of her allies in the civil war and the regency of her long-time enemy, the Earl of Morton. However, when her kinsman Esmé Stuart, Sieur d'Aubigny, arrived in Scotland in 1579 and won the affections of James VI, her hopes began to revive. The fall of Morton in 1579 and his execution in 1581 offered her a new opportunity to negotiate a return to Scotland.

In England, the Catholic threat abroad and at home seemed ever greater. After 1574 Catholic missionaries drifted in from the English seminary established at Douai in the Netherlands, and in 1580 a three-man Jesuit mission arrived from Rome. Abroad, the Catholic powers seemed close to crushing their Protestant rebels. In France, leaders of the Huguenots (French Protestants) had been brutally murdered alongside thousands of their co-religionists during the St Bartholomew's Day Massacre in 1572. In the Netherlands the rising led by Protestants against Spain had escalated after 1572, but Philip was determined to extirpate heresy and his army was strong enough to crush the rebels. Elizabeth's ministers feared that once the two Catholic monarchs were successful in restoring order in their territories, they would mount a crusade against her.

91

Sir Francis Walsingham
Unknown artist after John de Critz the elder, dated 1589.
Private collection.

Little is known about the career of Francis Walsingham
before he rose to prominence in the 1570s; however, he was
a protégé of Sir Nicholas Throckmorton, and it is possible
that he worked with the ambassador on one of his Scottish
embassies in the late 1560s. During this period, he came to
believe that Mary, Queen of Scots posed the greatest threat to
Elizabeth I's rule in England, and he later spoke of his regret
that she was not executed in 1572 following the Ridolfi Plot.
His distrust of Mary continued and in 1586 he was finally
able to engineer her downfall through the discovery of the
Babington Plot.

    After participating in the commission that found Mary
guilty of plotting Elizabeth's assassination, Walsingham was
absent from court through illness when Elizabeth signed
Mary's death warrant – with the English queen darkly joking
that he should be informed because 'the grief thereof will go
near to kill him outright'. Elizabeth called Walsingham 'her
Moor', and whilst the reason for this epithet is not known
(as is the case with so many of Elizabeth's nicknames), it
signifies Walsingham's position among the queen's most
intimate advisors.

    John de Critz was responsible for this portrait type
of Walsingham and a number of contemporary versions
survive (Yale Center for British Art; National Portrait
Gallery). The artist acted as one of Walsingham's many
informal agents in the 1580s during visits to Paris to
purchase art and visit collections. As often occurs with
sixteenth-century portraits, an incorrect inscription has
been added to the painting at a much later date, in this case
identifying the sitter as Sir William Brown. CB.

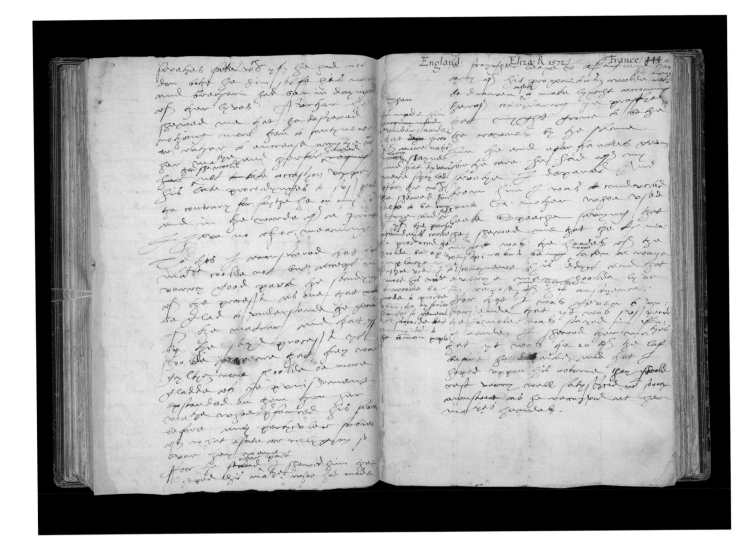

Walsingham and the St Bartholomew's Day Massacre

Letter from Francis Walsingham to Sir Thomas Smith,
2 September 1572, Paris.

British Library, Cotton MS Vespasian F vi, ff. 163v–164r

This is the draft of the letter which Francis Walsingham, then ambassador to France, wrote to Sir Thomas Smith, Principal Secretary, reporting his first audience with Charles IX after the massacre of Huguenots in Paris, which began on St Bartholomew's Day, 24 August 1572. The massacre had two components. First a panicky king ordered the killing of some seventy Huguenot leaders. Then the presence of the king's death squads triggered a wider massacre, as the Catholic militants of Paris turned against the Huguenots in their midst. Perhaps 3,000 were murdered in Paris, despite royal orders to stop the killing; many more died in the provinces.

When Walsingham attended the king on 1 September, the killing had only wound down two days earlier; for his own safety he was guarded on his way to the palace. The king justified the execution of the Huguenot leaders, 'he being constrayned to his greate greafe to doe that which he dyd for his savetyes sake'. The passage in the margin of this letter talks of the broader massacre: when the king offered to do justice against those who had plundered and – in three cases – murdered English people, Walsingham replied that this would be hard to do, 'the dysorder beinge so generall, the swoorde being commytted to the common people'.

The state of the draft conveys something of Walsingham's shock. The massacre left a deep scar on him and the fear of Catholic violence informed his actions against Mary, Queen of Scots. It had a similarly profound impact on English Protestant opinion, as is graphically embodied in Christopher Marlowe's play *The Massacre at Paris* (1592). TW.

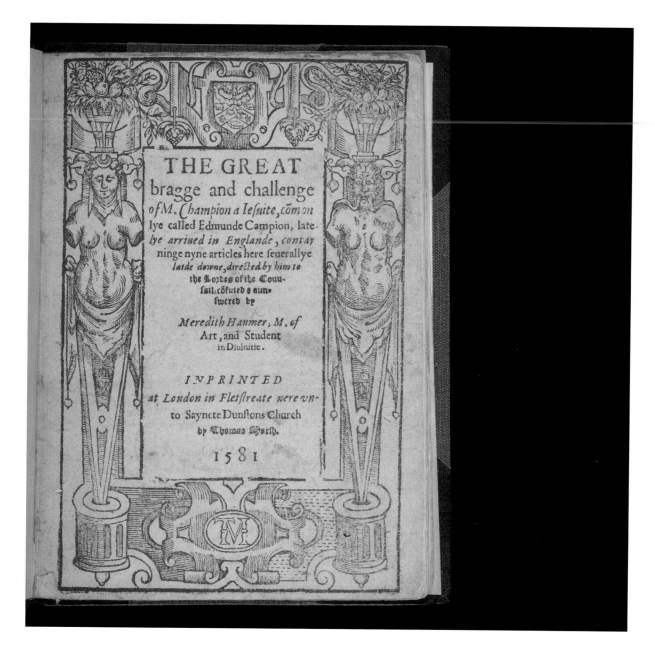

THE GREAT
bragge and challenge
of M. Champion a Iesuite, comonlye called Edmunde Campion, latelye arriued in Englande, contayninge nyne articles here seuerallye laide downe, directed by him to the Lordes of the Counsail, confuted & aunswered by

Meredith Hanmer, M. of Art, and Student in Diuinitie.

INPRINTED
at London in Fletstreate nere vnto Sayncte Dunstons Church by Thomas Marsh.

1581

93

The Jesuit Mission to England

Edmund Campion, *The Great Bragge and Challenge of M. Champion a Iesuite*, London, printed by Thomas Marsh, 1581. British Library, C.135.a.14., title page.

When Elizabeth visited Oxford in 1566, Edmund Campion welcomed her on the university's behalf and gained the patronage of the queen's favourite, the Earl of Leicester. However, Campion, who was already a Catholic, left Oxford for Dublin in 1570 for reasons of conscience. There he wrote a history of Ireland which was revised and incorporated into Holinshed's *Chronicles*. After briefly returning to England, Campion left to study at the English College at Douai before travelling on foot to Rome where he became a Jesuit.

In April 1580 Campion, Robert Persons and a lay brother were the first Jesuits to embark on the dangerous mission to England. Soon after arriving in London, Campion challenged Protestants to debate religion with him, arguing that they could not 'maintayn their doctrine in disputation'. Addressed to the privy council, the challenge, which became known as Campion's *Bragge*, was circulated and published against his intentions, provoking replies from Protestants and leading to a hunt for the Jesuit.

Campion was arrested in 1581 and interrogated under torture, by Thomas Norton among others. The Jesuit was allowed to defend himself in a disputation, as requested in his *Bragge*, but it was rigged against him. At his trial in November, the indictment was changed from the religious offence of reconciling a subject to Rome (under a new law of 1581) to the secular crime of imagining the queen's death (under the 1351 treason statute). Campion defended himself by saying that adhering to his faith was not treason because he had always remained Elizabeth's loyal subject. Inevitably found guilty, he was hanged, drawn and quartered on 1 December 1581. The Jesuit was canonised in 1970 and is also known as Saint Edmund Campion. KL-H.

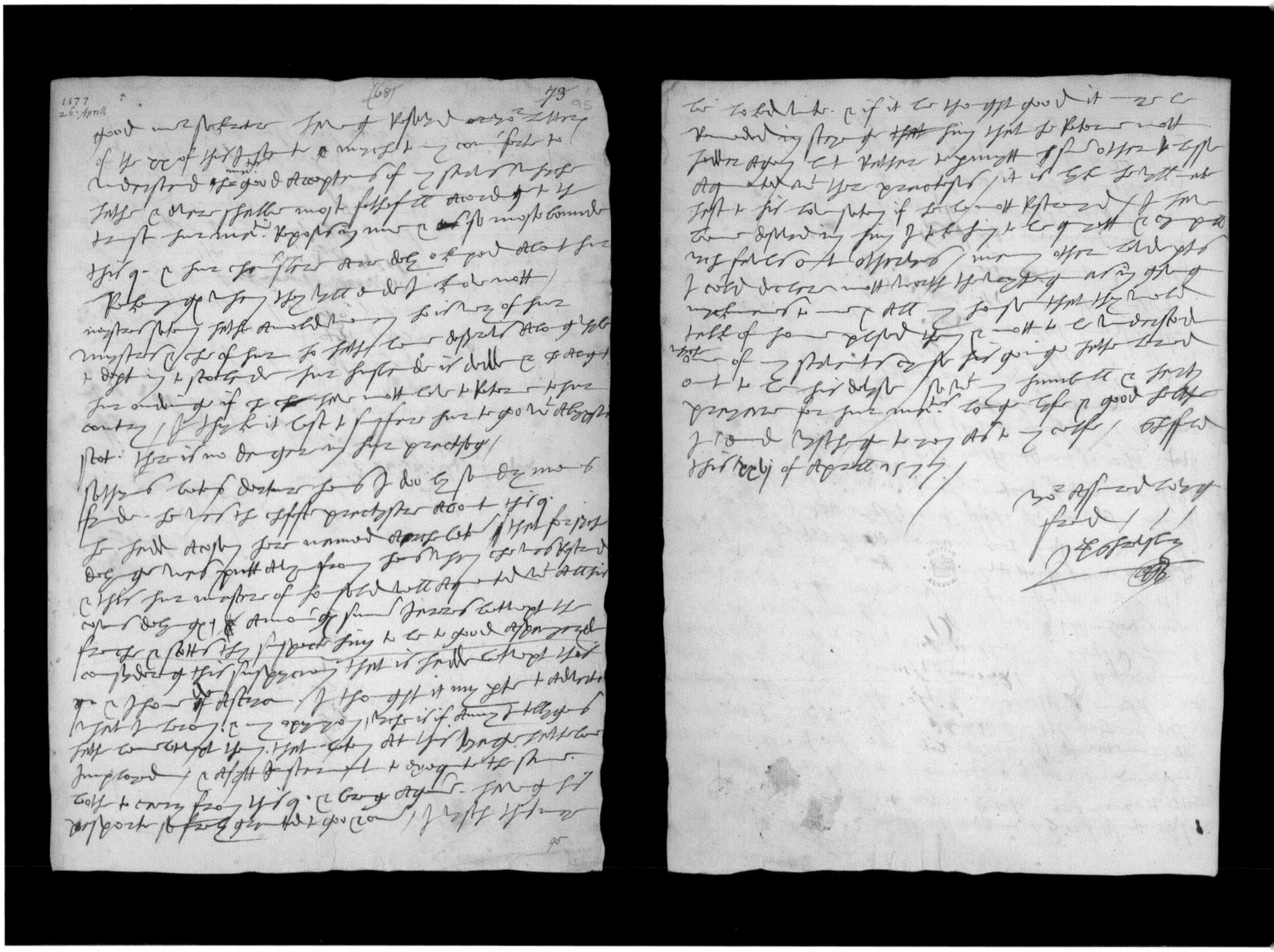

94

Mary 'A Poor Prisoner'

Letter from George Talbot, sixth Earl of Shrewsbury,
to Sir Francis Walsingham, 26 April 1577, Sheffield.

British Library, Cotton MS Caligula C v, f. 95r–v.

In February 1569, the Earl of Shrewsbury was appointed Mary, Queen of Scots' keeper and she remained in his custody for most of the next sixteen years, dwelling mainly at Sheffield Castle and Sheffield Lodge in Yorkshire and occasionally at Wingfield or Chatsworth in Derbyshire. At first he allowed Mary a substantial degree of freedom, though he always watched her closely.

Shrewsbury wrote to the government regularly concerning his charge. In this letter of April 1577 he thanked the Principal Secretary, Sir Francis Walsingham, in his almost illegible hand for informing him of 'hur maiesties good aceptans of my sarvis'. He then told

Walsingham what passed in Mary's household, beginning with the visit of her *chancelier*, Gilles du Verger, with whom she was occupied accounting for her revenues as dowager queen of France. Mary lived off this revenue, but Shrewsbury wanted to know if du Verger and she were discussing anything other than her finances. He described how the usher of Mary's chamber, Archie Beaton, had been behind 'sume Iarres [discord] betwext the frenche & scottes [who] suspecte him to be to good a spanyarde'. Both his cousin, the Master of the Household, Andrew Beaton, and he had left Mary's service, but Shrewsbury believed the latter man to be acting as her secret messenger. Aware that Andrew Beaton was in love with Mary Seton, one of the Four Marys who had been the Scottish queen's closest companions since childhood, Shrewsbury commented that 'it is lyke he wyll make haste to his love seten if he be nott Restoryd'. AB.

95

George Talbot, Sixth Earl of Shrewsbury
Unknown artist, inscribed 1582.
National Portrait Gallery, London, 6343.

Shrewsbury was one of the wealthiest men in England, and in 1567 he was able to consolidate his power through marriage to one of the wealthiest women in the country, Bess of Hardwick. Shrewsbury was appointed Lord High Steward for the trial of Thomas Howard, Duke of Norfolk, and created Earl Marshal following Norfolk's execution. With a large estate in northern England, and properties including Sheffield Castle and Lodge, Shrewsbury was ideally placed to act as the keeper of Mary, Queen of Scots; however, the personal and financial strain of responsibility for guarding Mary took its toll on his marriage, and he and the countess separated in 1583.

The French inscription on this portrait records that Shrewsbury's likeness was taken at Sheffield Castle during Mary's captivity. The inscribed date of 1582 is a later addition that may be incorrect, as the drawing relates to a painted portrait of Shrewsbury that is dated 1580 (Hardwick Hall, National Trust). As he was Mary's gaoler, Shrewsbury's portrait was of interest to the French court; in 1586, François de Civille, an agent of Walsingham, wrote to the earl asking for his portrait so that it could be sent to Henri de la Tour, Duke of Bouillon.

Portrait drawings of English sitters are very unusual for this period. It is possible that this work was a specific commission that would have allowed the earl's portrait to be sent to France more inconspicuously, alongside other correspondence. CB.

96

Virescit Vvlnere Virtvs: Virtue Grows from its Wounds
The Marian Hanging, 1570–85.
Victoria & Victoria & Albert Museum, London, T.29-1955.

This magnificent 'Marian Hanging' is one of three great hangings decorated with Mary's hand-sewn embroideries. The smaller panels on these depict particular types of subject, all in distinctive shapes: cruciform panels showing animals and birds; octagonal ones showing either monograms or named plants; and the larger square centrepieces using emblems with symbolic devices and Latin mottoes. Such use of distinctive shapes for different types of subject is unique to these embroideries, most of which were sewn during the Scottish queen's nineteen years of exile as Elizabeth's unwelcome visitor in England. The creatures depicted here include a tiger, unicorn, lynx, gannet, phoenix, pelican, monkfish, swordfish, bees, caterpillars and snails, many copied from Conrad Gessner's great sixteenth-century *Historia Animalium* (1553).

The 'she-dolphin' here is visibly giving birth and is undoubtedly also heraldic, for as a young princess betrothed to the future king of France Mary herself had the French title of 'Dauphine de France', so by showing it in the act of parturition on this embroidery Mary must surely have been alluding to her own success (unlike her cousin Elizabeth) in producing a male heir to the throne. The 'Byrd of America' is a toucan, which Mary had seen illustrated in André Thevet's description in *La France Antarctique* (1558).

The great centrepiece is an original Renaissance emblem, combining a symbolic image and a sententious Latin motto, and expressing the moral that virtue will recover (literally 'flourish') from its wounds: a hand is shown pruning a vine to make it more fruitful. Undoubtedly Mary's own invention, this emblem was used in several other artefacts at this time: it was carved into her silver handbell, and as early as 1557 appeared on a medal. In 1572 it played a notable role as evidence in the most important state trial of Elizabeth's reign, when Mary's supporter, John Leslie, testified that he had witnessed one of Mary's servants delivering an embroidered cushion as a love token to the Duke of Norfolk (her intended bridegroom) 'with this Sentence, VIRESCIT VVLNERE VIRTVS [virtue grows from its wound], and a Hand with a Knyfe cuttynge downe the Vynes, as they use in the Sprynge Tyme; al which Work was made by the Scots Quene's own Hand'. This evidence helped secure the duke's execution and it is interesting to note that when, forty years later, his younger brother Henry Howard, Earl of Northampton, was composing the Latin verses that are inscribed on the tomb of Mary, Queen of Scots in Westminster Abbey, he alluded to this very emblem (*Sic vitis succisa gemit fecundior uvis*, 'Thus does the pruned vine groan with a greater abundance of grapes'). MB.

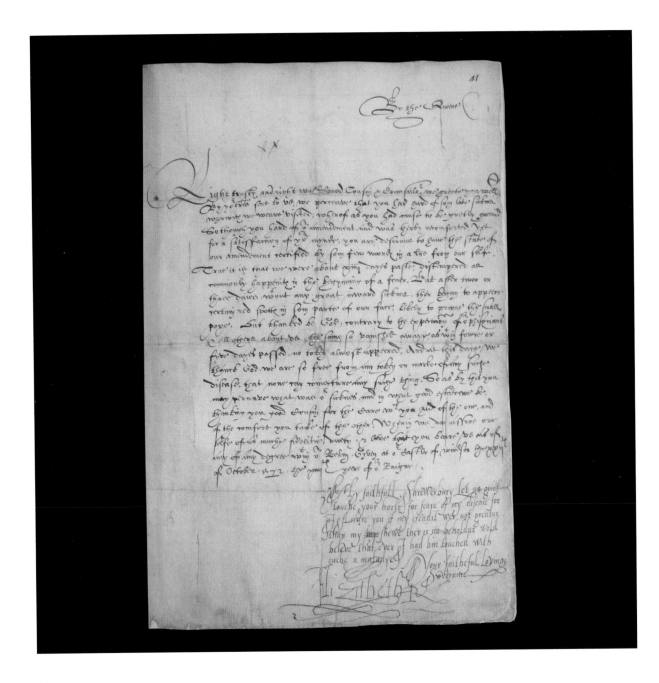

97

'The Dearest Jewel'

Letter from Elizabeth I to George Talbot, sixth Earl
of Shrewsbury, and Elizabeth Talbot, Countess of
Shrewsbury, 25 June 1577, Greenwich.

Lambeth Palace Library, London, MS 3206, p. 819

Elizabeth wrote to thank the Earl and Countess of
Shrewsbury for entertaining her favourite Robert Dudley,
Earl of Leicester, at Chatsworth and the spa at Buxton
in Derbyshire, 'houlding him in that place of fauor we
do [and] reputing him as annother our self'. 'In this
acknowledgement of new debtes we maie not forgett our
ould debte, the same being as great as a Soueraigne can owe
to a subiect, when thorough your loyall & most carefull
looking to the chardge [Mary, Queen of Scots] committed
to you both we and our realme enioy a reasonable
gouernement, the best good happe that any prince on

earthe can befaule'. Yet a few months later the queen was
'perplexed' by rumours that Mary was planning her escape.
Shrewsbury was cautioned, 'the dowbt that hir Maiesty
hath of secret hydden practises, to be wrovght rather by
corruption of some of yours whom yow shall trust, than by
oppen force, moveth hir ... to warn ... that yow contynew
or rather increass your vigilancy ... that yow be not
circvmvented herin'. In response to such criticisms, which
often originated from uninformed courtiers, Shrewsbury's
son, Lord Gilbert Talbot, once claimed Mary was so closely
guarded that, 'vnles she could transforme hir selfe to a
flee or a mouse it was vnpossible that she should scape'.
Leicester supported Shrewsbury by using his influence
with Elizabeth to further his suits and reassuring him of
her continued favour. Shrewsbury treasured this letter of
affirmation from her, endorsing it in his own hand as 'to be
... kept as the dereste Iuell [jewel]'. AB

98

Mary's 'Perpetual Testimony'

Letter from Mary, Queen of Scots to Elizabeth I,
8 November 1582, Sheffield Castle.

British Library, Cotton MS Caligula C vii, ff. 77r and 81v.

This is Mary's longest written communication and is sometimes called her 'De Profundis' letter after Oscar Wilde's 50,000-word letter of the same name (meaning 'from the depths'), which he penned in 1897 during his incarceration in Reading Gaol. Consisting of ten pages of densely written French text, it was sent to Elizabeth in November 1582, following news of the seizure of her son, King James VI. The 15-year-old had recently taken up direct rule after ending the regency of the pro-English, Protestant Earl of Morton, only to fall under the sway of his half-French, Catholic cousin, Esmé Stuart, created Duke of Lennox in 1581. To remove James from the powerful influence of Lennox – an ally of the Guise and a supporter of Mary – a group of anglophile Scottish Protestant lords took him by force to Ruthven Castle in Perthshire. This turn of events temporarily dashed Mary's growing hopes that she might be allowed to return to Scotland to rule jointly with her son. Comparing James's situation to hers, Mary complained that his authority has been 'ravished from him, and assigned over to two or three traitors, who ... will take from him, as they have from me, both the name and title of it'.

Believing that she was dying, Mary penned her letter to 'serve you [Elizabeth] as long as you live after me for a perpetual testimony and engraving upon your conscience'. Her 'just and melancholy complaints' included the 'ill treatment' she had suffered for ten years, 'not as a prisoner ... but as some slave', 'the cruelties, calumnies, and traitorous designs' of her enemies, and that 'the sincerity of [her] actions' had been 'neglected and calumniated'. Somewhat optimistically, Mary called for 'the establishment of a good amity between us, and a sure understanding between these two realms in future'. Protesting that 'I look this day for no kingdom, but that of my God', Mary begged Elizabeth to permit her 'to draw myself out of your realm, into some place of repose, to seek some comfort for my poor body, worn out as it is with continual sorrows, that, with liberty of conscience, I may prepare my soul for God, who is daily calling for it'. Mary wished to be remembered as a martyr for the Catholic faith and requested an 'honest churchman, to remind me daily of the course which I have to finish, and to teach me how to complete it conformably with my religion, in which I am firmly resolved to live and die'. She subscribed herself 'Your very disconsolate nearest kinswoman, and affectionate cousin, Marie R.' AC.

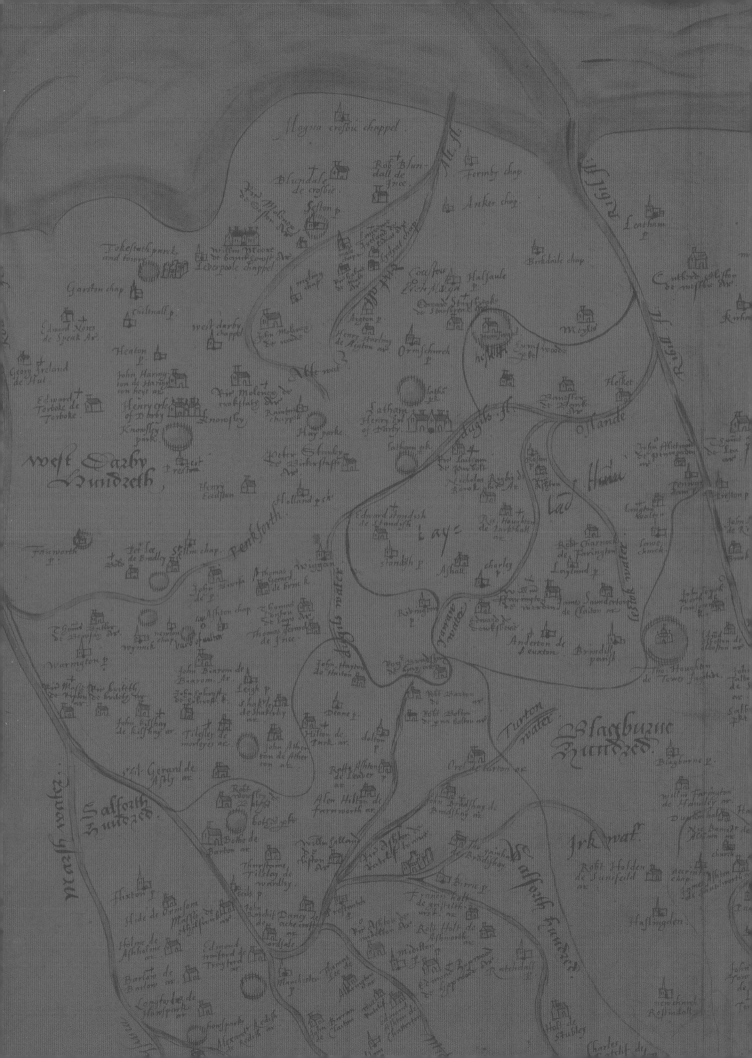

'Use But Old Trust and New Diligence'

1583–1588

8

'USE BUT OLD TRUST AND NEW DILIGENCE' (1583–7)

Stephen Alford

The years between 1583 and 1587 were for Elizabeth's government a time of emergency. The queen's advisers wrestled with plots and invasion plans both real and imagined. They monitored the co-ordinated infiltration into England of missionary Catholic priests whose intent, so far as the government was concerned, was to stir up treason and rebellion.

Propaganda and bitter polemic came from printing presses on both sides of the English Channel, as hardline English Catholic émigrés and Elizabeth's ministers sought to claim God and the truth for their respective causes. And it was clear that the problem of Mary, Queen of Scots was reaching its crisis. What would or could be done with the royal prisoner? Was there an acceptable treaty to be negotiated between her, Elizabeth and James VI? Or was it preferable simply to isolate her and so neutralise the dangers she presented to Elizabeth? The options were in reality few. 'For there must be an end of this matter, either by the death of this Lady, or by some honourable composition.' So wrote Sir Ralph Sadler, then Mary's keeper, in October 1584.

One of the neatest illustrations of just how febrile and anxious the times were is the case of John Somerville, a Warwickshire gentleman, who in October 1583 set out from his home to murder Elizabeth. In Oxfordshire he was heard by witnesses to say that 'he was in hope to see the queen's majesty and he meant to shoot her through with his dag [pistol] and hoped to see her head to be set upon a pole, for that she was a serpent and a viper'. His treason spoke to something more than anxieties over security. A Catholic supposedly under the powerful influence of both his wife and a priest living secretly with the family, Somerville was arrested in possession of an *Agnus Dei*, a small wax tablet stamped with the image of the Lamb of God notionally consecrated by the pope. He was, to Elizabeth's government, a soldier in a spiritual war, where loyal subjects were (in the words of William Cecil, Lord Burghley) 'stirred up by the Devil the father of rebels'. From the beginning Somerville had shown signs of psychological disturbance and he hanged himself in prison. In Burghley's pamphlet defending Elizabeth's government, *The Execution of Justice* (published in December 1583, reprinted in January 1584), Somerville's suicide was a providential illustration 'of God's severity against such as presume to offer violence to His anointed'.

God's anointed, as her advisers knew only too well, was never entirely safe. Nor were her kingdoms of England and Ireland, both of which were vulnerable to attack. In 1583 Henry, Duke of Guise sponsored an ambitious plan for invading England, known from an English perspective as the 'Throckmorton Plot' because of the modest part played in it by yet another young Catholic gentleman, Francis Throckmorton. Throckmorton's interrogations in the Tower of London revealed the negotiations that had taken place with Philip II's ambassador in Paris for support and money, as well as secret meetings in England with disaffected Catholic noblemen. Implicated too was Philip's ambassador to Elizabeth, Don Bernardino de Mendoza, who was promptly expelled from the kingdom. And Mary was never far away from centre stage. The official account of Throckmorton's trial for treason in July 1584 made public the evidence of the 'resolute determination agreed on by the Scottish queen and her confederates in France and in other foreign parts, and also in England, for the invading of the realm'. The ultimate aim of the Guise plan was clear: 'the intention (the bottom whereof should not at the first be made known to all men) should be upon the queen's majesty's resistance, to remove her majesty from her crown and state' (cat. 104).

1584 was in many ways a critical year. In early July (in fact in the week of Throckmorton's execution) Elizabeth's ministers absorbed the news of the assassination of William of Nassau, Prince of Orange, in Delft. William, the leader of the Dutch Revolt against Spanish rule, was a hero of Protestant Europe, and his murder made the independence of the liberated provinces of Holland and Zeeland look more fragile than ever. Walsingham commented bleakly that the Dutch 'being left to themselves they shall be forced ere Christmas next to become Spanish'. Already in June the death of Francis, Duke of Anjou, heir to his brother King Henry III, had left the Dutch without French aid, although admittedly the duke's intervention on behalf of the rebels had been less than helpful. His death also promised (as one experienced English diplomat put it) 'some notable alteration' in France. It

SOMERVILLE'S SUICIDE WAS A PROVIDENTIAL ILLUSTRATION 'OF GOD'S SEVERITY AGAINST SUCH AS PRESUME TO OFFER VIOLENCE TO HIS ANOINTED' left the Protestant Henry of Navarre heir to the throne, though his claim was strenuously resisted by the Catholic nobility. Anjou was an ally of England and Elizabeth's last suitor, and the queen took the news badly. The politics of Western Europe were once again shifting, with who knew what consequences.

In early September 1584 Mary indicated to Elizabeth her wish to enter into talks. On the day she was moved from Sheffield Castle in Yorkshire to Wingfield Manor in Derbyshire she expressed 'such good will and love towards the queen's majesty' and offered to send her secretary, Claude Nau, as a personal emissary to 'utter her whole mind and to procure Her Highness's resolution'. Mary believed that she had a workable proposal for a treaty as well as a controlling influence over her son in Scotland, whose loyalty to England Elizabeth's government had long found impossible to fix with certainty. Mary emphasised that Elizabeth 'should find good cause to think better of me than she hath done'.

In an ambitious play for the diplomatic initiative, Mary cast herself as the facilitator of Anglo-Scottish friendship: after all, she was – as she rather daringly told Sadler – 'come of the blood and noble progeny of England'. Sadler reported Mary's self-confidence at being able to guide James VI 'in all things he may honourably do for the preservation and continuance of peace and good amity between these two realms'. Sadler also testified to Mary's show 'of an inward affection and zeal to perform that she promiseth'.

ELIZABETH WAS CHARACTERISTICALLY SLOW to commit herself, but in October it was decided to allow Nau to come to court. This was another key month for political decision-making. First, on 10 October her privy council debated the situation in the Netherlands and examined whether the time had come for the queen to intervene militarily in the Dutch Revolt. So began the process that led ten months later to the Treaties of Nonsuch and the sending of an English army to aid the Dutch (cat. 102). Second, on 19 October, Elizabeth's councillors put their signatures and seals to the 'Instrument of an Association' that bound its signatories by an oath to revenge to the death any attack on the person of the queen or any invasion of her kingdoms (cat. 108). With the assassination of William of Orange very much on their minds, the Instrument was the brainchild of Burghley and Walsingham, who co-ordinated its circulation throughout England. Over the following months there were mass oath-takings across the kingdom. A new parliament, summoned to sit in November, would complete the task of preserving the queen's safety, cracking down on Jesuits and other missionary Catholic priests covertly at work in England.

Elizabeth's government was also fighting back in the war of words. An effort was made in October 1584 to suppress the 'divers false, slanderous, wicked, seditious, and traitorous books and libels' that were being smuggled into England. One of these books, which had appeared over the summer, was the scurrilous *Copy of a Letter written by a Master of Art of Cambridge*, or 'Leicester's Commonwealth', attributed to the Jesuit Robert Persons. This was a vicious assault on the Earl of Leicester, 'his ambition, his tyranny, his crimes and treasons against the country and the queen, his whole manner of life and utter knavery'. Just as subversive were those works which challenged

Elizabeth's title to the English throne. In late summer Sir Edward Stafford, Elizabeth's ambassador at the court of Henry III, had picked up some pages of *A Treatise Touching the Right, Title, and Interest of the Most Excellent Princess Mary, Queen of Scotland, and of the Noble King James, Her Grace's Son, to the Succession of the Crown of England* (Rouen, 1584; cat. 103). Alleged also to have been discovered among Throckmorton's papers, here was a dangerous book indeed.

About Mary, Queen of Scots as the principal enemy of Elizabeth's state there was, by November 1584, a resounding and deliberate silence. The Association did not mention her by name, and in parliament she was not referred to by those privy councillors leading the effort to put the Instrument into the form of a 'safety' or 'surety' statute. The reason was that Nau was busy negotiating for Mary with Elizabeth in conditions of absolute confidentiality. In the last week of November he presented the privy council with the text of a treaty which received a guarded response. The tenth clause of Nau's treaty stated that in return for her liberty Mary would 'enter into' the Association, though she wanted its terms to be explained more clearly to her. The official observation on this article – perhaps it was Elizabeth's own – was as laconic as it was important: 'Left to her own free choice to subscribe or not unto it.'

Sadler believed, as he wrote to Elizabeth, that prison life and grief had 'wrought some good effect' on Mary. His view was that in trying to reach a settlement with her there was nothing to lose: if she meant not 'so sincerely as she protesteth, the lack thereof may return and fall upon herself'. By early December Mary was deeply anxious over the progress of Nau's mission, and her relief was obvious when he at last returned to her on 29 December. Nau's account to Mary of his negotiations was, so far as Sadler could tell, wholly positive:

> She seemeth to be very well satisfied in all things. And promiseth to deserve all the favour which it may please her majesty to bestow upon her, when it shall please God to grant her the means to show it here, and in all places where with Her Highness's good liking she may be, and end the rest of her years.

On 5 January 1585 Mary gave her oath of assurance to the Association, authenticated by sign manual (signature) and seal. The paper was soon in Burghley's safekeeping, and he wrote on the back of it: 'The Queen of Scots' bond in association to be an enemy to all that shall attempt anything against her majesty's life.' It was against this that all her future actions would be judged.

The treaty came to nothing. James VI and those who advised him had no intention of being guided or instructed by his mother. Instead, in 1586

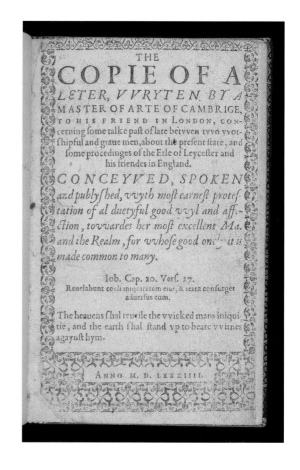

'Leicester's Commonwealth' (1584), a scurrilous Catholic libel attacking Robert Dudley, Earl of Leicester. Known as 'Leicester's Commonwealth' (although the phrase is only used once in the text and not on the title page), the tract circulated widely in manuscript.

The copie of a leter, wryten by a Master of Arte of Cambrige, 1584. British Library, G.1999.

he signed a defensive treaty with Elizabeth. Meanwhile, Mary remained in England under close guard, as isolated as ever. Her earnest professions of loyalty to Elizabeth began to sound increasingly hollow, for what became clearer than ever to Elizabeth's ministers over the months of 1585 and 1586 was an extensive and secret correspondence between Mary and her supporters across Europe. A key figure here was Thomas Morgan, Mary's loyal agent and spy in Paris, whose role as a chief conspirator against Elizabeth was exposed in the Parry Plot. Parry was supposedly recruited by Morgan to assassinate Elizabeth – yet another murder plot, revealed in February 1585, and this time one that was uncomfortably close to the Cecil family. Parry, long a seeker of Cecil patronage and Burghley's volunteer spy in France, tripped over his own duplicities after trying and failing to play both sides for his own advantage. He was hanged, drawn and quartered (cat. 110). Burghley made sure that in *A True and Plain Declaration* (1585) only a carefully redacted official account of Parry's treason appeared in print.

MORGAN'S DIFFICULTY WAS GETTING letters to Mary, and he relied on willing couriers. One of these was Anthony Babington, a rich gentleman from Derbyshire, who in London in the early summer of 1586 made contact with a priest named John Ballard, also one of Morgan's recruits. By late summer Babington and a small group of other sympathetic English Catholic gentlemen were beginning to formulate a plan to liberate Mary. Another of Morgan's couriers was Gilbert Gifford, a kinsman of Throckmorton, who in autumn 1585 was briefed by Morgan and instructed in the art of secret writing. When Gifford arrived in England in late December 1585 he was arrested. Persuaded by Walsingham to work as a double agent, Gifford, supposedly Morgan's man but really now Walsingham's, became the key to unlocking the secret correspondence that Mary was conducting through and with Babington.

The Babington Plot broke in August 1586 when Mary was being held at Chartley in Staffordshire. Gifford was a key player in its unravelling, as was Thomas Phelippes, Walsingham's servant, who, positioned near Chartley, was able to copy, decipher and read Mary's letters thanks to his careful management of an often unpredictable Gifford and his own superlative skills as a cryptanalyst. In a letter posted from Chartley from 18 July, Mary seemed to indicate that she endorsed a proposal Babington himself made by letter for 'the dispatch of the usurper' – the murder of Elizabeth (cat. 115). Phelippes and Walsingham pounced on Mary's reply to Babington, which seemed enough to demonstrate her complicity in a murder plot. Or almost: when sending on the 'bloody letter' to Babington, they took care to amplify Mary's response by adding a postscript to the original in order to demonstrate beyond reasonable doubt her 'privity' to the conspiracy (cat. 116). The entrapment of Mary was real enough, but we should not underestimate her careful responsiveness to the plots and plans that were being made on her behalf against Elizabeth. Neither queen was simply a victim.

What followed was the endgame for Mary. Tried by special commission in person at Fotheringhay Castle and in absentia at Westminster in October 1586, Mary strenuously defended her innocence. Every aspect of the trial was planned to the last detail, down to the precise measurements of the hall and

its seating arrangements (cat. 118). Before the hearing began Burghley briefed his fellow commissioners on 'the indignities and wrongs done and offered by the Queen of Scots to the queen's majesty', going all the way back to 1559. When at last Mary agreed, with considerable reluctance, to appear before the commission she maintained her innocence: 'It is no small grief for me to think how hardly the queen doth use me after my long misery of imprisonment and indisposition of body.' She was, she said, the victim of private enemies. And there was no evidence in her own hand of her complicity in Babington's plot, as she – and Burghley and Walsingham – well knew. Mary had always been scrupulous to communicate only through her private secretaries.

THE COMMISSION'S VERDICT WAS never in doubt. Its final sentence was given in Star Chamber in late November. Only a few days earlier Elizabeth, pressed by parliament to execute justice against Mary, had spoken to her Lords and Commons. Two separate speeches were in essence meditations by the queen on the burdens of power (cat. 119). 'I am not so void of judgement as not to see mine own peril,' she said in her second address, 'nor yet so ignorant as not to know it were in nature a foolish course to cherish a sword to cut mine own throat.' She refused to say precisely what she would do, giving her parliament what she called 'my answer answerless'. But really she had no choice but to make public Mary's guilt, and on 6 December 1586 the necessary proclamation was read out across Westminster and London (cat. 120). Elizabeth, it emphasised, was 'greatly and deeply grieved' to think that such unnatural and monstrous acts had been 'either devised or willingly assented to' by a princess of the queen's own sex and blood 'and one whose life and honour we had many times before saved and preserved'.

The Funeral of Mary, Queen of Scots, 1587. Mary's corpse was conveyed by night in a 'chariot' from Fotheringhay to the Bishop's Palace in Peterborough, more than five months after her execution. On 5 August, she was buried in the cathedral.

British Library, Additional MS 35324, f. 16r.

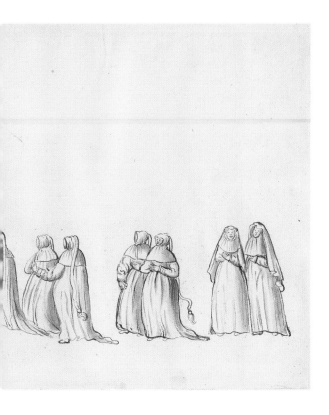

For six weeks Elizabeth resisted her ministers' persuasions to sign the warrant for Mary's execution. It was on the eve of Candlemas, 1 February 1587, that the queen instructed the more junior of her two secretaries, William Davison, to bring it to her. She signed it and told Davison to take the paper to the Lord Chancellor, Sir Christopher Hatton, for the Great Seal, as well as to Walsingham, who was sick and away from court. Elizabeth is supposed to have told Davison to 'communicate the matter with him [Walsingham], because the grief thereof would grow near (as she merrily said) to kill him outright'. Elizabeth maintained that she quickly countermanded her instruction. But Davison had already told Hatton about the signed warrant, and Hatton told Burghley, who saw his opportunity for action. With the assent of the privy council convened in private session, Burghley and Walsingham contrived to dispatch the death warrant secretly to Fotheringhay. That was on 2 February. Six days later Bull the executioner removed Mary Stewart's head from her shoulders (cat. 125).

Uppermost in Elizabeth's mind was the impossible position that Mary's treason had put her in. She knew the reality of what had to be done but wanted to bear no personal responsibility for it, and she took refuge in self-justification. As she wrote to James VI: 'Be not carried away, my dear brother, with the lewd persuasions of such as instead of informing you of my too, too needful and helpless cause of defending the breath that God hath given me ... may perhaps make you believe that ... the offence was not great.'

On the day Elizabeth signed Mary's death warrant she also instructed her secretaries to communicate to Mary's custodians at Fotheringhay, Sir Amias Paulet and Sir Dru Drury, her wish that they take appropriate action under the Association they had both sworn, for she herself was indisposed to shed blood. The queen wanted Mary secretly to be killed. Paulet's response was clear: 'God forbid that I should make so foul a shipwreck of conscience ... to shed blood without law or warrant.' For Elizabeth, who had taken so long to put her sign manual to the death warrant, Paulet and Drury might have spared her the pain. Davison, whom Elizabeth accused of mishandling the warrant, was likewise on the sharp end of the queen's recriminations. He found himself in the Tower and on trial in Star Chamber. It was his word against Elizabeth's.

If Mary's death was not inevitable, by 1586, after those brief glimmers of hope in 1584, its logic was unquestionable. And so the end was not, as Sadler had put it, by an honourable composition, but by the death of the lady.

9

SURVEILLANCE

J. P. D. Cooper

The heraldic arms of the Security Service of the UK, otherwise known as MI5, include red roses in honour of Sir Francis Walsingham, the Elizabethan statesman and spymaster who used the rose on his seal. Also featuring a crowned portcullis – the Tudor royal symbol that has become a ubiquitous emblem of British government – the insignia adopted by MI5 imply a clear connection between the modern forces of state surveillance and their sixteenth-century antecedents.

The two contexts are obviously different: an Elizabethan secret service that was rudimentary in its methods, diffuse in its organisation and ideologically inflected to the highest degree, versus the technologically sophisticated and politically accountable agency of today. And yet the similarities are there, from the strategies of infiltration practised by both sixteenth- and twenty-first-century surveillance, to the prevailing fear of conspiracy and existential threat. At the court of Elizabeth I, the authorities responsible for state security justified their power and their funding with reference to a flood of assassins foiled and plots averted: a scenario that remains all too recognisable.

The idea of a 'spy' as a secret agent or military scout long pre-dated the Tudors. But the Elizabethans also coined new words, 'intelligencer' and 'discovery' (in the sense of detecting someone who wanted to remain hidden), reflecting the state of enhanced watchfulness that was a by-product of the Reformation. Modern notions of privacy barely existed in the sixteenth century: people expected to watch, and be watched by, their neighbours for any deviance from the norm, whether in terms of religious observance, sexual morality or signs of witchcraft. But the religious reforms of Henry VIII and Edward VI, followed by the Catholic Reformation of Mary I, put a premium on conformity to the faith defined by the state. Anyone absent from church, or complaining about government policy, risked being reported and disciplined. Surveillance extended its reach from open opposition to the regime – traditionally the definition of treason – to private acts of defiance. The Elizabethan religious settlement initially focused on behaviour more than belief, binding the nation together within one round of common prayer. But by the later 1560s a harsher religious climate was setting in, with the arrival of Mary, Queen of Scots on English soil and the gathering hope (and fear) that Catholicism might yet be restored. The Northern Rebellion, the papal bull deposing Elizabeth, and the Duke of Norfolk's confession that he had conspired to marry Mary raised the spectre of ideological resistance to the regime, and led to calls in parliament and the privy council to enforce conformity more strictly (cats 80, 85). Surveillance became an urgent priority of the state.

There was no single Elizabethan secret service: multiple voices competed for the queen's ear, employing agents within their own households and keeping their counsel close. The control of information was a powerful motive force in the politics swirling around the sovereign. Two men, however, came close to establishing a monopoly over the gathering of intelligence at home and abroad, and it was no accident that they served in turn as Principal Secretary to the queen. William Cecil and Francis Walsingham have each been compared to 'M', the head of the Secret Intelligence Service as imagined by Ian Fleming. Though not always in agreement on government policy, they shared a belief that Mary, Queen of Scots threatened the Elizabethan regime to its core. Within months of Mary's flight to England in May 1568, Cecil was studying copies of the 'Casket Letters' that appeared to incriminate her in the death of Lord Darnley. The case raised questions about the forgery of documents that would later resurface during the Babington Plot of 1586, but it was the official line – the letters were genuine – that was printed in George Buchanan's *Detection of the Doings of Mary Queen of Scots* (cat. 76). With her political reputation in ruins, Mary's best chance of escape now lay with the plotters who saw her as the rightful Catholic queen of England.

In 1568 Cecil recruited the Protestant former exile and MP Francis Walsingham to help him track the activities of Mary's supporters in Paris. So began the political career of the man who, more than any other, has been credited with the creation of an Elizabethan secret service. Dressed in shadowy black, a cameo jewel of the queen his only adornment, Walsingham seems the very image of a spymaster. Though he never achieved the political intimacy with Elizabeth that sustained Cecil throughout his long career, his use of the principal secretaryship to construct a network of informers in the British Isles, across Europe and as far afield as Muscovy and

The Insignia of MI5. Amidst its many symbols, the five-petalled rose alludes to the '5' in MI5 and to the state intelligence work of Sir Francis Walsingham, who used the rose on his seal.

Constantinople enabled Walsingham to influence policy at the highest level. The combined subtlety and brutality of his campaign against Catholicism proved devastatingly effective, and in some circles he is reviled to this day. Surveillance operations mounted by Walsingham revealed hundreds of seminary priests and their protectors, driving recusant Catholics into a hunted existence and putting unprecedented power into the hands of searchers and interrogators. The highest-profile victims faced terrible deaths at Tyburn; imprisonment and crippling fines were prescribed for the rest. Many are now venerated as martyrs. And yet there is no avoiding the fact that a minority of the targets of Walsingham's secret service were actively conspiring against the state: whether to remove heretic councillors at court and replace them with Catholics, or to strike harder and deeper against Elizabeth herself. Propaganda condemning the 1583 Throckmorton Plot was effective precisely because Francis Throckmorton had been working for a Catholic invasion of England, as reported by Walsingham's mole working within the French embassy in London (cat. 104).

HOW CLOSE DID QUEEN Elizabeth come to being assassinated? The sequence of plots 'discovered' before they were mobilised – Ridolfi, Throckmorton, Parry, Babington – appears to argue for the effectiveness of government surveillance, right down to the Gunpowder Plot of 1605. A stream of intelligence was sent from the heart of the enemy camp in Rome, where agents such as Charles Sledd (dubbed 'Judas' by Cardinal William Allen, spiritual leader of the English Catholic exiles) and Anthony Munday posed as priests in training in order to report on their fellow students. Walsingham's astonishing ability to penetrate the Catholic underground has led to claims that he fabricated plots himself, in order to uncover them and sustain himself in power. Characters like Thomas Phelippes, who devised a method of frequency analysis to decipher encrypted documents, or Arthur Gregory, supplying Walsingham with recipes for secret ink, seem to have stepped out of a John le Carré novel (cat. 114). But the Elizabethan secret service had its failures as well as its successes. Arriving in England in 1580, the Jesuit Edmund Campion convinced the mayor of Dover that he was a jewellery salesman from Dublin; his defence of the Catholic faith was printed on a secret press and distributed at St Mary's Church in Oxford before Campion was arrested, having preached widely across the north of England (cat. 93). Campion's fellow Jesuit Robert Persons evaded capture, slipping away to the continent to petition the Catholic powers for military support.

THE ELIZABETHAN SECRET SERVICE HAD ITS FAILURES AS WELL AS ITS SUCCESSES

Priests could be executed, but the flow of ordinands could not be staunched. Walsingham's own papers reveal that, far from being the Machiavellian manipulator depicted on film and television, he was deeply fearful that the battle against Catholicism was being lost.

Double agents and ciphered letters, dead drops and secret ink: all these elements came together in the most famous surveillance operation of them all, the ensnaring of Mary, Queen of Scots in the Babington Plot. Whether Walsingham happened upon the Catholic cleric Gilbert Gifford by chance,

or had been running him as an agent from the start, can only be guessed. Whatever Gifford's motivation, his willingness to betray Mary and cooperate in an elaborate deception, whereby letters were smuggled out of her prison at Chartley concealed in barrels of beer, provided Walsingham and Cecil with the evidence of treason for which they had waited so long. Gifford's good faith was attested by Thomas Morgan, Mary's key agent in Paris; his security clearance could hardly have been higher. In truth the entire set-up was a sting: Mary's letters were deciphered by Thomas Phelippes and reported to Walsingham, before being resealed and allowed to reach their destination. Over a period of months, the conspiracy to liberate Mary and deal with Elizabeth (stabbing her in the chapel royal or shooting her as she walked in the palace gardens were both discussed) spread from the community of Catholic exiles in Paris to the idealistic young Anthony Babington and his friends. Remarkably, Babington made contact with Walsingham when the Plot was close to ignition, perhaps to turn queen's evidence. What Babington didn't know was that his companion Robert Poley – 'sweet Robyn' – was Walsingham's spy. Supervising the stakeout at Chartley, Phelippes sketched a gallows on his decrypt of the letter from Mary to Babington that would finally legitimise her execution (cat. 115).

With the death of the most credible Catholic claimant to the throne, the focus of surveillance shifted from internal to external threats. That Philip II intended to send an armada against England was hardly a secret; the trick was to know when it would launch, and where it would be heading. Walsingham was able to eavesdrop on Spanish plans via his agent in Florence, and he had reports from merchants and sea-captains of ships assembling in Lisbon and Cádiz. From another source, the ambassador Sir Edward Stafford, he heard that the invasion fleet had been stood down: a story that made Walsingham suspicious, and indeed we now know that

The Rainbow Portrait of Elizabeth I, the eyes and ears embroidered into her dress symbolising the fact that she – or, more likely, the Cecils through their spy network – see and hear everything. The rainbow is a symbol of peace.

Attributed to either Marcus Gheeraerts the Younger or Isaac Oliver, *c*.1600. Marquess of Salisbury, Hatfield House.

Stafford was a double agent receiving a Spanish pension. When the invasion armada finally sailed in 1588, Walsingham alone seems to have known their intended destination: 'their whole plot and design is against the City of London'. How he gathered this vital piece of intelligence is not known, but it was on that basis that Elizabeth's army was mustered at Tilbury rather than Kent. In the event the weather settled the matter, so the reliability of Walsingham's source was never put to the test.

Following Walsingham's death in 1590, the 'secret cabinet' in his house was cleared of its contents, perhaps by Robert Devereux, second Earl of Essex, his son-in-law and in some sense his political legatee. The subsequent loss of those papers means that the identity of many operatives, the intelligence they supplied and payments that were made will probably never be recovered. What we can discern is that agents whose job it was to create false identities in order to embed themselves among opponents of the regime were left dangerously exposed during the 1590s. Rival operations cut across each other, with fatal consequences. The playwright Christopher Marlowe, who had done some intelligence work for the government, got a knife in the eye during a quarrel in Deptford; Robert Poley was in the room when it happened.

MULTIPLE VOICES COMPETED FOR THE QUEEN'S EAR

Essex fashioned himself as a spymaster in opposition to his rival Robert Cecil, but a Catholic assassin identified by one of his agents turned out to be a spy in the service of Lord Buckhurst. Unlike Walsingham, Essex was not too concerned whether a plot was genuine; the perception that the queen was in danger was still useful to him. The execution in 1594 of Walsingham's former physician and sometime agent Roderigo Lopez, slandered as a 'vile Jew' (he was actually a Christian convert) intent on killing the queen, was contrived by Essex to revive his faltering reputation as an intelligencer. Although a measure of stability returned when Cecil inherited his father's former role of Principal Secretary in 1596, surveillance was not what it had been under Walsingham. A report on the follow-up Spanish armada of 1596 was accurate but arrived in London ten days after the fleet had been dispersed by a storm: had it not been for the weather (again), the Elizabethan regime might yet have been taken by surprise.

The Crisis Years of the 1580s

During the 1580s the international situation grew ever more perilous for Elizabeth. In 1580 Philip II augmented his power by assuming the crown of Portugal through conquest. On 31 December 1584, he signed the Treaty of Joinville with the leaders of the Catholic League in France – Mary's cousins Henry, Duke of Guise, and his brother Charles, Duke of Mayenne – in which both sides committed themselves to preventing the Huguenot leader, Henry of Navarre, from succeeding to the French throne. Navarre was heir presumptive, since Henry III's brother Francis, Duke of Anjou, had died in June that year.

In the Netherlands Philip II's governor, Alexander Farnese, Duke of Parma, had by the beginning of 1584 recaptured most of the towns in the southern provinces, and in July he began the siege of the great seaport Antwerp. That same month the Protestant leader, William the Silent, Prince of Orange, was assassinated, leaving the rebels in disarray. In August 1585 Elizabeth was persuaded that, without her military aid, the northern provinces would also succumb to Parma. And once the Revolt was crushed, Philip would be free to mount a crusade against England.

In 1580 Philip II had already shown his hostility to Elizabeth by helping a small papal army leave Spain to aid her rebels in Ireland. These soldiers surrendered at Smerwick and were afterwards massacred by the English army. Meanwhile in Scotland, James VI had ended Morton's regency in 1579 and come under the sway of James's French cousin Esmé Stuart, Sieur d'Aubigny, who was believed in England to be an agent of the Guise family. Seizing the opportunity, Mary opened up negotiations with her son to share rule in Scotland in a scheme known as the 'Association'. Even after Esmé Stuart (now Duke of Lennox) had been expelled from Scotland in 1582, Elizabeth had reason to suspect that James was secretly collaborating with his mother to renew the 'Auld Alliance' between France and Scotland and thereby endangering her position in England. However, James rejected the scheme and the 'Association' became a dead letter. Nonetheless, Sir Francis Walsingham and others remained unsure as to where the Scottish king's loyalties really lay.

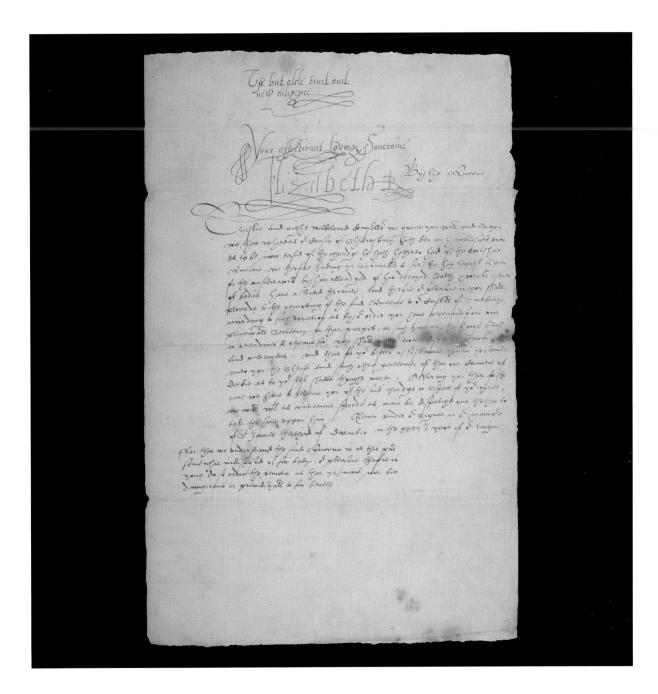

99

'Olde Trust and New Diligence'

Letter from Elizabeth I to Sir Ralph Sadler, 3 December 1584,
St James's Palace.

British Library, Loan MS 128 [4].

In the summer of 1584, against the backdrop of an
increasingly dangerous international situation, the collapse
of the Earl of Shrewsbury's marriage made it necessary to
find a new keeper for the Scottish queen. In December 1584,
Elizabeth wrote to Sir Ralph Sadler to confirm his relief
of Shrewsbury and order Mary's removal from Wingfield
Manor in Derbyshire to the more secure location of Tutbury
Castle in Staffordshire. In a postscript, Elizabeth advises that,
in view of Mary's declining physical condition, Sadler was
to 'order the remove as that yt maie not be daingerous or
preiudityall to her healthe'. The letter carries a warning in the

queen's own hand that Sadler should 'Use but olde trust and
new diligence'.

Elizabeth provided strict security instructions in a separate
communication; Mary was, for example, 'not permitted to
ride farre abroad but onely suffered on foot or in a Coche
to take the ayre and vse some such exercise neere the howse
where she shall lye'. The number of watchmen posted in
local towns and villages was to be increased and 'kept and
continewed as well in the day as in the night'. Local justices
of the peace were also to ensure that no 'roages or other
masterles or wandering persons be suffered to resort to the
Townes, villages or places next adioyning to the place where
the said Queen shall lye'. The freedom that Mary's servants
had enjoyed under Shrewsbury was to be curtailed and special
care taken for the 'restraint of Laundresses and such as haue
been permitted to resort into the Town of Sheffield'. AC.

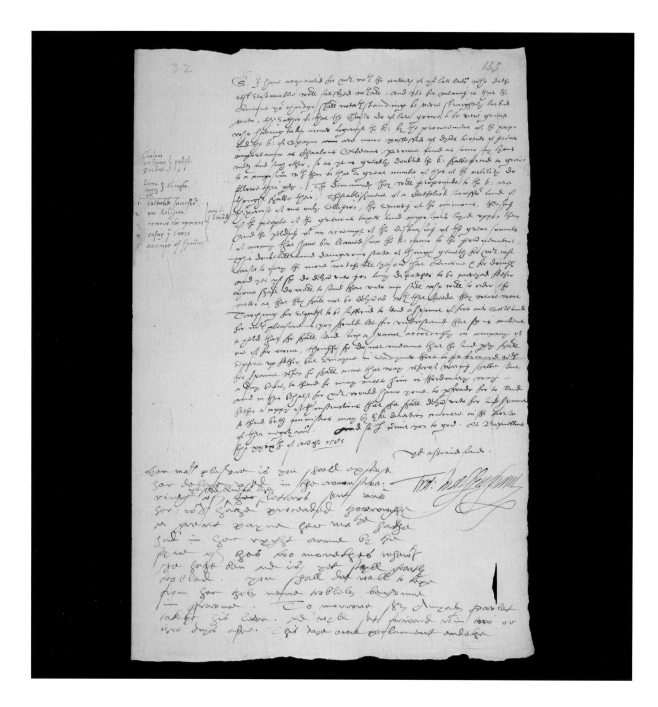

100

The 'Doubtful and Dangerous State' of France

Letter from Sir Francis Walsingham to Sir Ralph Sadler,
29 March 1585, Barn Elms.

British Library, Loan MS 128 [37].

In March 1585 Sir Francis Walsingham reported to Mary's new keeper, Sir Ralph Sadler, that the Catholic League 'do of late growe to be verie great who having taken armes' against Henry III had seized a number of important towns. The League, funded since the Treaty of Joinville by Philip II, now forced Henry III to make a 'composicon' excluding Henry of Navarre (the Huguenot leader) from the throne, accepting a Catholic succession and revoking all edicts of toleration for his Huguenot subjects. Both Guise and Navarre prepared for civil war. Philip's intervention in France was one of the considerations that spurred Elizabeth to side openly in the Dutch Revolt against him, leading to war between England and Spain.

'This doubtfull and daingerous state of thinges geueth hir maiesty iust cause to cary the more watchfull eye ouer that Queene & hir doinges.' Mary's correspondence was to be vetted by Walsingham, for example, who instructed Sadler to 'exscvse' Elizabeth's delay in replying to her, 'which hathe proceeded thorowghe a great payne her maiestye hathe had in her ryght arme by the space of thes two monethes wherwith she hathe ben and is yet styll greatly trobled'. Sadler was to keep from Mary 'these newe trobles begvnne in ffravnce' and was informed that Sir Amias Paulet would join him as her keeper in two or three days. AB.

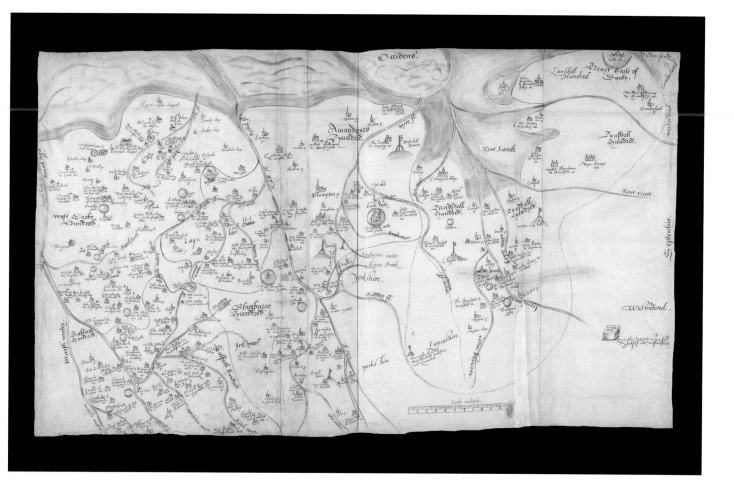

101

Burghley's Saxton Atlas

Map of Lancashire, c.1577–9.

British Library, Royal MS, 18 D iii, ff. 81v–82r.

This map of Lancashire was copied around 1577–9, possibly by the cryptographer Thomas Phelippes, for Lord Burghley, who kept it with his proof copies of Saxton's county maps in the Burghley-Saxton Atlas – a jewel in his extensive cartographical collection (cat. 78). Oriented with west at the top, the map shows the area between the River Mersey on the left and the Furness Peninsula on the right. A cube labelled 'Countie Stone' in the bottom right corner marks the county boundaries between Lancashire, Yorkshire and Westmorland. Red lines denote the division of Lancashire into hundreds for administrative purposes; townships or parishes, which played a key role in local government, are identified. Leading gentry, many of whom served as Justices of the Peace, are named alongside their estates. Most prominent of all is Henry Stanley, fourth Earl of Derby, whose residences at Knowsley and Lathom are marked. Derby was actively involved in local government and sent regular reports to the privy council on the state of security in the county. It is therefore possible that he commissioned the original vellum map from which Lord Burghley's copy was produced.

Burghley's annotations on this and other maps demonstrate his appreciation of their value as a tool of government and for understanding the state of the realm. They supplied essential information about the composition and topography of the country and the geography of civil and ecclesiastical administration. They also served as aids to national defence, providing vital knowledge about borders and borderlands. The map of Lancashire and others like it facilitated the surveillance of the national population. Recording the precise location of leading gentry families, the crosses that he added (or had added) enabled Burghley to pinpoint troublesome individuals and monitor potential areas of internal unrest. Several indicate Puritans but during the period in question, Lancashire had the largest Catholic community in England and in 1578 had 304 convicted recusants. No doubt Burghley would have consulted the map alongside records of recusants to locate leading Catholic gentry such as John Rigmaiden of Woodacre near Garstang, John Townley of Townley, Sir Edward Norris of Speke and John Allen of Rossall, a relative of Dr William Allen, leader of the English Catholics. Thomas Hoghton, who fled overseas to join William Allen in exile in the early 1570s, was added to the map twice, alongside his properties at Hoghton Tower and Lea, and recorded as a 'fugitive'. AC.

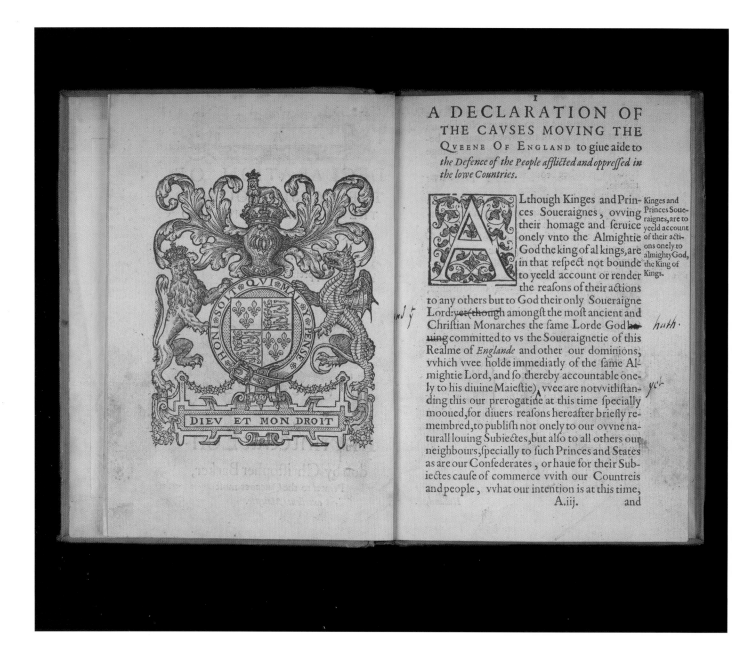

I

A DECLARATION OF
THE CAVSES MOVING THE
QVEENE OF ENGLAND to giue aide to
*the Defence of the People afflicted and oppressed in
the lowe Countries.*

Lthough Kinges and Prin_ Kinges and
ces Soueraignes, ovving _Princes Soue-
their homage and seruice _raignes, are to
onely vnto the Almightie _of their acti-
God the king of al kings, are _ons onely to
in that respect not bounde _almighty God,
to yeeld account or render _Kings.
the reasons of their actions
to any others but to God their only Soueraigne
Lord: yet (though amongst the most ancient and
Christian Monarches the same Lorde God ha-
uing committed to vs the Soueraignetie of this
Realme of *Englande* and other our dominions,
vvhich vvee holde immediatly of the same Almightie Lord, and so thereby accountable onely to his diuine Maiestie), vvee are notvvithstan-
ding this our prerogatiue at this time specially
mooued, for diuers reasons hereafter briefly re-
membred, to publish not onely to our ovvne naturall louing Subiectes, but also to all others our
neighbours, specially to such Princes and States
as are our Confederates, or haue for their Subiectes cause of commerce vvith our Countreis
and people, vvhat our intention is at this time,
A.iij.   and

102

War Against Spain

*A Declaration of the Cavses Mooving the Qveene of England
to Giue Aide to the Defence of the People Afflicted and
Oppressed in the Lowe Countries,* London, printed by
Christopher Barker, [1585].

British Library, C.194.a.851., sig. A2v–A3r.

Following the assassination of William of Orange in July
1584 and the fall of Antwerp to the Spanish forces of the
Duke of Parma in August 1585, Elizabeth was persuaded
by her councillors, against all her natural caution, to go
to war and formally come to the aid of the leaderless and
beleaguered Dutch Protestants. On 12 and 20 August 1585
the Treaties of Nonsuch were signed with the Dutch, and it
was agreed that Elizabeth would send some 7,000 soldiers to
the Netherlands under the command of the Earl of Leicester.

Although it was not a formal declaration of war, the
anonymous *Declaration*, printed by the royal printer in
October 1585, provides a justification for going to war. With
its simultaneous publication in Latin, Dutch, French and
Italian, it was a concerted attempt to organise government
propaganda on an international scale. The *Declaration*
explained that Spanish aggression in the Netherlands and
the planting of Spanish troops 'so neere to our countries'
endangered England's security, especially because of the
'many troublesome attemptes against our Realme'.

This piece of state propaganda has long been attributed to
Elizabeth's two chief councillors, Lord Burghley and Sir Francis
Walsingham, but it is likely that the queen herself had some
input into the text. This copy is a rare surviving working proof
with manuscript corrections in Burghley's hand and was used
by the royal printer for the second printing. KL-H.

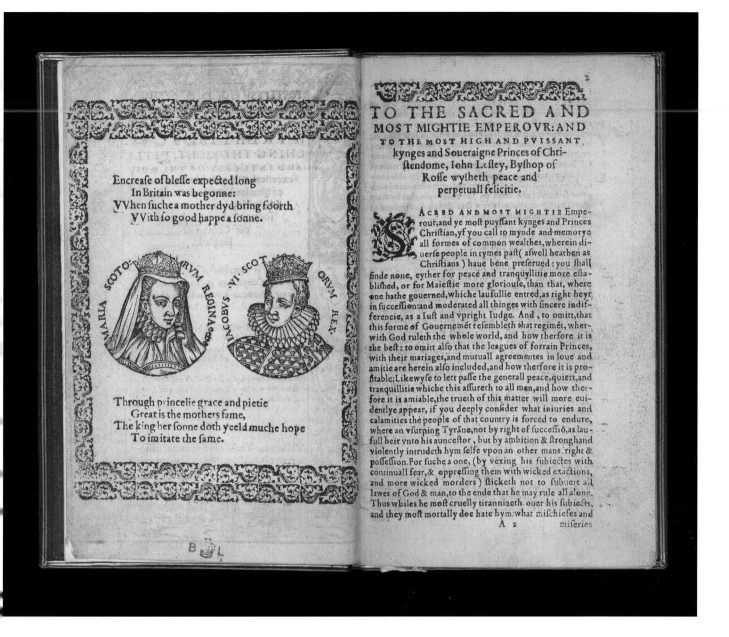

103

The 'Association'

John Leslie, *A Treatise Tovvching the Right, Title, and Interest of the Most Excellent Princesse Marie, Queene of Scotland, and of the Most Noble King Iames, Her Graces Sonne, to the Succession of the Croune of England*, [Rouen, printed by Georges L'Oyselet], 1584.

British Library, G.1734., ff. 1v–2r.

In 1584 Mary's long-term supporter and polemicist John Leslie, Bishop of Ross, issued an English edition of his defence of her title and indefeasible hereditary right. It was a revised fourth edition of an earlier work and a translation of the Latin edition of 1580. In this pamphlet Leslie not only continued to dismiss the arguments used to exclude Mary from the succession but also supported the 'Association'. He had in fact been the first to advocate the project for Mary to be released and share sovereignty with James VI in Scotland.

The title page looked forward to a united Britain under the Stewarts with the lines: 'All Britaine Yle (dissentions ouer past) / In peace & faith, will growe to one at last'. The next page (illustrated here) visually embodies the 'Association' scheme with its picture of Mary and the inscription 'Maria, Scotarvm Regina' alongside that of James, 'Jacobvs VI Scotorvm Rex'.

The book has two dedicatory epistles. The first one – to the kings and princes of 'Christendome' – lauded 'all forms of common wealthes' that were governed by the 'right heyr in succession' and entreated foreign rulers to take the part of Mary and 'ioyne with her against her enemies'. The second epistle was to Mary and James, 'Quene and Kyng of Scotland'. There Leslie spoke of the love and care Mary had always shown her son and urged James to show like care for her. So, while the second epistle implicitly advocated the 'Association', the first explicitly appealed for a continental Catholic league led by the pope to intervene in England on behalf of the Scottish queen. SD.

Plots and Espionage

By 1583 Mary, Queen of Scots had been imprisoned for fifteen years and was ready to participate again in plots backed by Philip II and the Guise party. In the early 1580s Mary's cousin, Henry, Duke of Guise, devised an 'enterprise' in which he would raise an army in the Low Countries, financed by the pope and Philip II, for an invasion of England with the purpose of deposing Elizabeth in favour of Mary. One of the conspirators with knowledge of the Plot was the Catholic gentleman Francis Throckmorton. He had conferred with Mary's agents while travelling in the Low Countries, Spain and France, and on his return to England he acted as a courier between Mary and the Spanish ambassador in London, presumably passing on information about the projected invasion. However, the highly efficient intelligence network developed by Sir Francis Walsingham and Lord Burghley soon discovered that Throckmorton was engaged in treason. He was arrested in November 1583 and revealed all when put on the rack.

The discovery of the Throckmorton Plot increased Protestant fears of Catholic treason at home or an invasion from abroad. The assassination of William of Orange in July 1584 added to the sense of urgency. To deter potential assassins, in October that year Burghley and Walsingham circulated a 'Bond of Association', which bound its signatories to pursue to the death anyone who might benefit from the queen's murder, whether the attempt was successful or not. When parliament met in November 1584, its members introduced a bill based on the Bond. One voice against the bill came from William Parry. Within two months he was arrested for devising another plot to assassinate the queen.

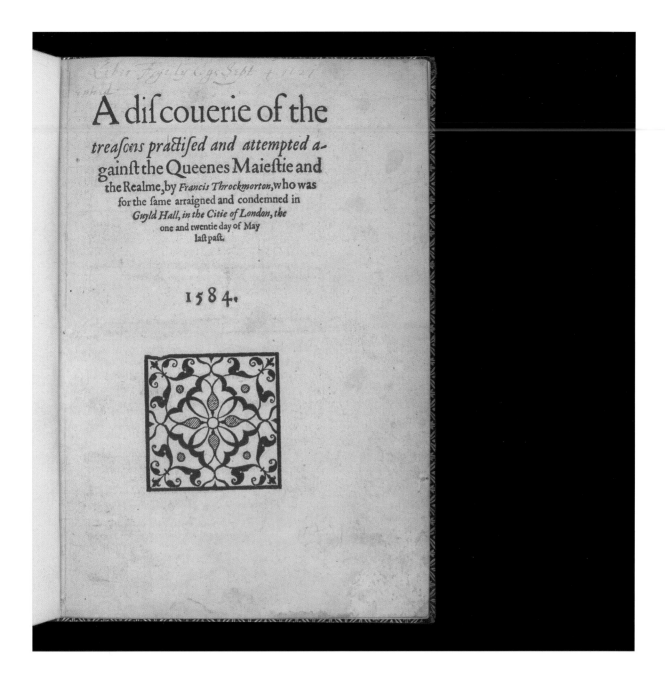

A diſcouerie of the treaſons practiſed and attempted a-gainſt the Queenes Maieſtie and the Realme, by *Francis Throckmorton,* who was for the ſame arraigned and condemned in *Guyld Hall, in the Citie of London, the* one and twentie day of May laſt paſt.

1584.

104

The Throckmorton Plot

A Discouerie of the Treasons Practised and Attempted against the Queenes Maiestie and the Realme, by Francis Throckmorton, [London, printed by Christopher Barker], 1584.

British Library, G.6142., title page.

Named after one of its participants, Francis Throckmorton, the Plot of 1583 was perhaps the most serious conspiracy against Elizabeth by English and foreign Catholics. It aimed to depose the queen, replace her with Mary, Queen of Scots, and restore Catholicism to England by means of a Spanish-backed invasion led by Henry, Duke of Guise, and supported by an uprising of English Catholics.

This anonymous pamphlet purported to be 'a verie perfect declaration of the whole proceedings' composed by a personal acquaintance of Throckmorton, who had 'by the meanes of a secret friend' obtained the relevant information.

In fact, the pamphlet was a government publication designed to expose the danger of the Catholic threat and further discredit Mary before a wide audience.

Describing the Plot in full, the account mentions papers seized by the government, such as the description of the 'Hauens for the commodious landing of forces' during an invasion of England and the 'Names of Noblemen and Gentlemen in euery Countie fitt to bee dealt withall in this matter'. The Spanish ambassador, Bernardino de Mendoza, was implicated in the account; more importantly, so was Mary. In Throckmorton's confession, which was obtained under torture, the conspirator allegedly said: 'Nowe I haue disclosed the secrets of her who was the dearest thing vnto me in the worlde (meaning the Scottish Queene) … I see no cause why I shoulde spare any one, if I could say ought against him: & sith I haue failed of my faith towards her, I care not if I were hanged.' SD.

105

The Cost of Treason

Inquisition into the land held by Francis Throckmorton in Warwickshire, 15 June 1584, Westminster.

British Library, Additional Ch 72091.

On 15 June 1584 an inquisition was appointed under the great seal to enquire into all property held in Warwickshire by the conspirator Francis Throckmorton. He had been arrested at his London house in November 1583, was found guilty of treason in May 1584, and hanged, drawn and quartered on 10 July. As a further punishment, most of his property was forfeit to the crown.

Throckmorton was a member of one of the most important Warwickshire families, with many of his kin prominent in local government, despite several among them being Catholic like his brother Thomas and himself. He had succeeded his father, Sir John Throckmorton of Feckenham in Worcestershire, in May 1580. The commissioners appointed in 1584 to enquire into his Warwickshire property included several of Throckmorton's gentry neighbours: Sir Fulke Greville, Sir Thomas Lucy, Sir John Harrington, Thomas Babington and Clement Fisher. Babington played the leading role and was instructed with the rest to survey 'all and each separate deed to [Throckmorton's] lands and holdings in detail'. Throckmorton held manors in Warwickshire at Packhurst and Winderton. Similar surveys of his property were carried out in Herefordshire, Shropshire and, presumably, Worcestershire, where the bulk of his estate lay. Lord Burghley took an interest in these surveys, asking the Remembrancer of the Exchequer, Thomas Fanshawe, in April 1585 to see them all. Feckenham itself was granted in August to Sir Thomas Leighton, a Gentleman of the Privy Chamber. AB.

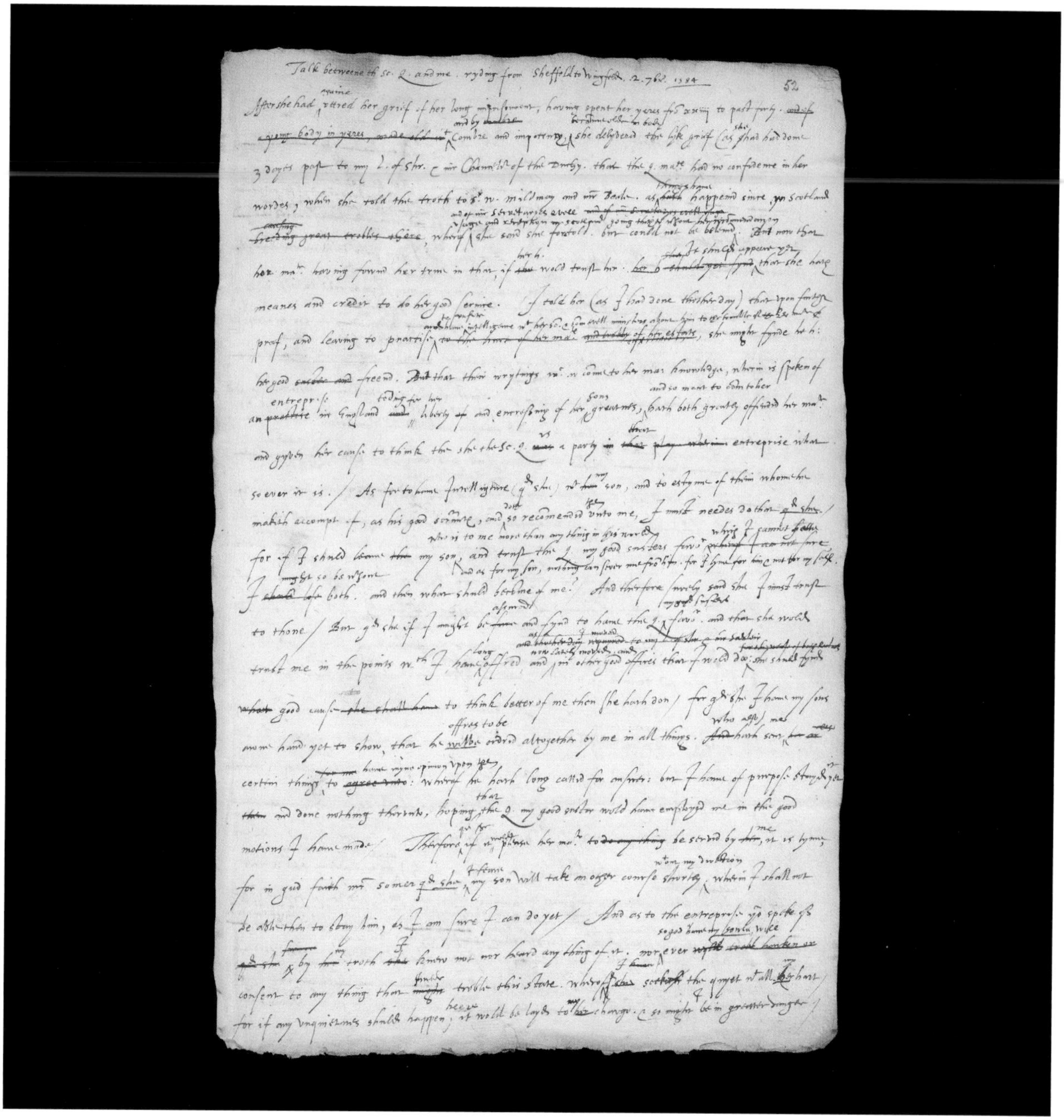

106

Mary and James

John Somer's report, 2 September 1584.

British Library, Additional MS 33594, f. 52r.

In a conversation with Sir Ralph Sadler's son-in-law, John Somer, during their journey from Sheffield to South Wingfield in Derbyshire on 2 September 1584, Mary appeared to reveal her views about her captivity, her relationship with her son James VI and political affairs. We cannot, however, take her words at face value, as she was still attempting to get Elizabeth to agree to the 'Association' and her release.

Lamenting her 'long imprisonment' and Elizabeth's mistrust, she insisted that she would never escape as she would 'rather dye in this sort with honor then run away with shame'. If Elizabeth granted her freedom, she would visit James briefly, then retire to France, 'and never troble herself with the goverment agayn … nor never dispose my selfe to marry agayne any more'. She would not stay in Scotland, where she had had 'so many Indignities & evell tretmentes'. If she could live in honour in England, she would remain there.

Mary refused to cease communicating with her son, James VI, 'who is to me more than any thing in this world … nothing can sever me from him, for I lyue for him & not for my self'. When Somer questioned her about how she would promote good relations between Elizabeth and James, she advised Elizabeth to offer him a pension. She promised that although she was a 'Catholick Queene', both James and she would jointly rule and oppose the 1570 papal bull *Regnans in Excelsis* so that no-one would 'dare tooche thone Realme for religion without offending both'. Though Mary claimed that James had promised to be 'ordrid altogether' by her 'in all things', one year later he declined to rule jointly with her. JC.

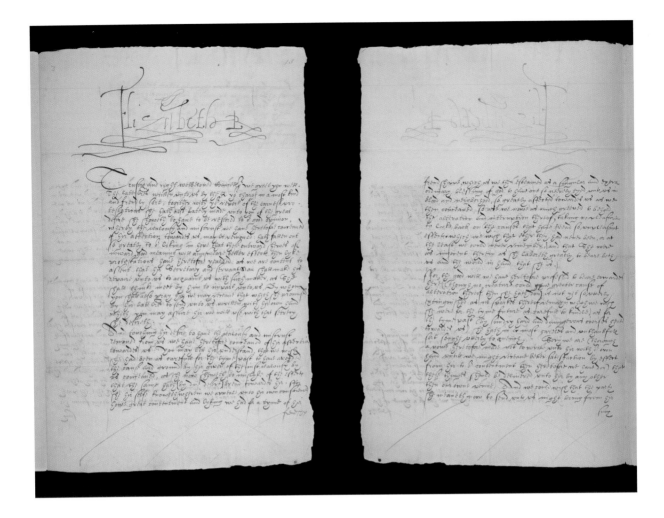

107

Attempts at Reconciliation

Letter from Elizabeth I to Sir Ralph Sadler, 31 October 1584,
Hampton Court.

British Library, Loan MS 128 [3].

In this letter written barely a fortnight after the privy council
signed the Bond of Association, Elizabeth – speaking with
rare candour – gives an extraordinary insight into the current
state of her relationship with Mary. Although addressed to
Sadler, who had recently replaced the Earl of Shrewsbury as
Mary's gaoler, it was intended to be read or shown to Mary.
This oblique method of communication was made necessary,
Elizabeth explains, 'thorough a vowe heretofore made not to
writte vnto hir with our own hand vntill we might receave
better satisfaction by effect from hir to our contentment then
heretofore we have don'.

The letter is the only known instance when Mary's direct
appeals as Elizabeth's prisoner provoked such a detailed
response. Besides 'earnest protestations' made verbally
through Sadler, as the English queen begins, Mary had also
written to her 'in a most kind and frendly sort'. Elizabeth
informs Sadler that those requests 'hath fallen out so greatly
to our liking' that she was 'content to assent' that Claude
Nau, one of Mary's secretaries, should ride south 'to acquaint
vs with such matter as she shall thinke meet by him to impart
vnto vs'. He was to bring with him proposals 'as might
worke vppon good ground a thorough reconciliation between

vs, which as she seameth greatly to desire, so should we also
be most glad thereof'.

Nau did have at least one audience with Elizabeth. But
no progress was made. The stumbling block had very likely
come at the outset after Mary expressed her wish to Sadler
that the 'iealousy and mistrust' she believed Elizabeth had
conceived of her should be removed. As the English queen
responds icily:

> we wish she had been as carefull for the tyme past to have
> avoyded the cause and ground by hir given of the iust
> iealousy by vs conceaved, as she now sheweth to mislyke
> of the effectes that the same hath (by due desert) bread
> towardes hir. Ffor she hir selfe knoweth (wherein we
> appeale vnto hir own conscience) howe great contentment
> and lyking we had for a tyme of hir frendshippe, which as
> we then esteamed as a singular and extraordinary blessing
> of god to have one so neerely tyed vnto vs in blood and
> neigborhood, so greatly affected towardes vs as we then
> conceaved, so are we nowe as much greeved to behold the
> alteration and interuption thereof.

Despite Mary's 'sundry hard and daungerous coorses heald
towardes vs', Elizabeth was genuinely torn. As she puts
it: 'the good will we have heretofore professed to beare
towardes here [sic] … is not yet so vtterly extinguished as no
sparkes thereof remayn.' JG.

108

The Bond of Association

Instrument of an association for the preservation of the
queen's majesty's royal person, signed by Mary, Queen of Scots,
5 January 1585, Wingfield Manor.

British Library, Additional MS 48027, f. 249r.

Burghley and Walsingham responded to the discovery of the
Throckmorton Plot and assassination of William of Orange
by devising the Bond of Association, a call to arms for the
protection of Elizabeth I, whose life, 'for the furtherance &
advancement of some pretended titles to the crowne of this
realme ... hathe bene most traiterously & develis[h]ly sought
& the same foll[o]wed most dangerously to the perill of
her persone'. The Bond was signed by the privy council on
19 October 1584. Copies were distributed throughout the
country and signed by tens of thousands of loyal subjects,
who pledged to defend their queen from pretended successors

'to the uttermost extermination of them, their consellors,
aiders and abettors'. On 5 January 1585 Mary also subscribed
to the Bond of Association, even though it was clearly aimed
at her and her supporters, 'to give proof of her entire and
sincere affection' towards her 'good sister'. This is a copy, but,
curiously, Mary signed it also. Beneath her signature, a note
by Robert Beale, clerk of the privy council, certifies that he
had seen the original Bond 'under the hand and seale of the
Scotishe Queene remayning with Mr Secretary Walsingham'.

In March 1585, Elizabeth gave royal assent to an Act for
the Surety of the Queen, which established a legal process
for trying any claimant to the throne implicated in plots
against Elizabeth. On her insistence, it did not exclude
Mary's son, James VI, from the succession unless he was
directly involved in treason. After thirty years of refusing
to name a successor, this was the first clear signal Elizabeth
gave of her likely heir. AC.

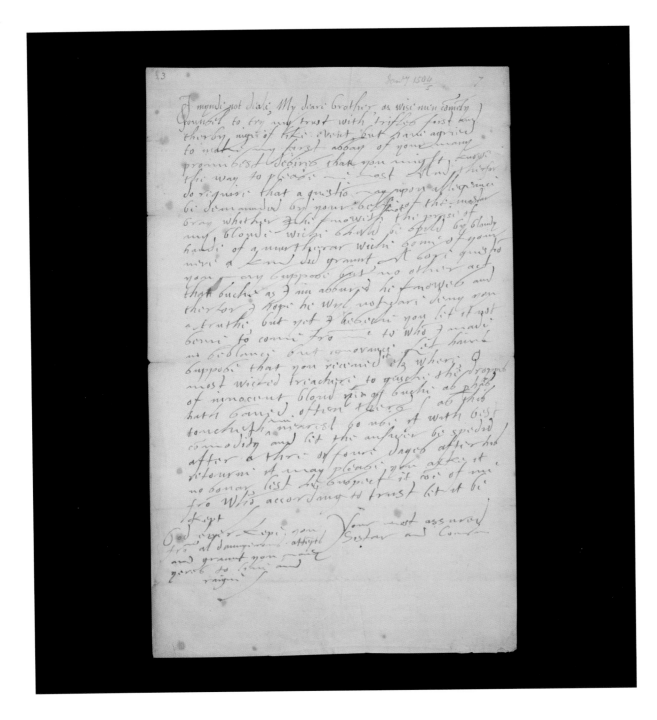

109

Elizabeth I and James VI

Letter from Elizabeth I to James VI, January 1585.

British Library, Additional MS 23240, f. 7r.

Although she never explicitly recognised him as her heir apparent, Elizabeth I favoured and protected James VI, making it clear that he had great expectations if he would but follow her counsel. Their correspondence was by turns friendly and acrimonious, reflecting the changing fortunes of Anglo-Scottish relations. In January 1585, when this letter was written, the two monarchs were not on good terms, but Elizabeth was hoping to encourage James to enter into an offensive and defensive league with England. The letter is one of her earliest to James, written quickly in a much looser italic hand than her childhood one. She wrote 'I mynde not [to] deale, My deare brother, as wise men commenly counsel to try my trust with trifles first and therby iuge of like event, but haue agried to make my first assay of your many promises & desires that you might knowe the way to please me most.' Therefore, she demanded he question his ambassador to England, Patrick, Master of Gray, about 'whether he knoweth not the prise of my bloude wiche shuld be spild by bloudy hande of a murtherar wiche some of your nere a kin did graunt'. Gray seems to have known about plots which Elizabeth said 'toucheth me nearest', although William Parry's treason had yet to come to light. Like all her letters and speeches, this one is a rhetorical tour de force. AB.

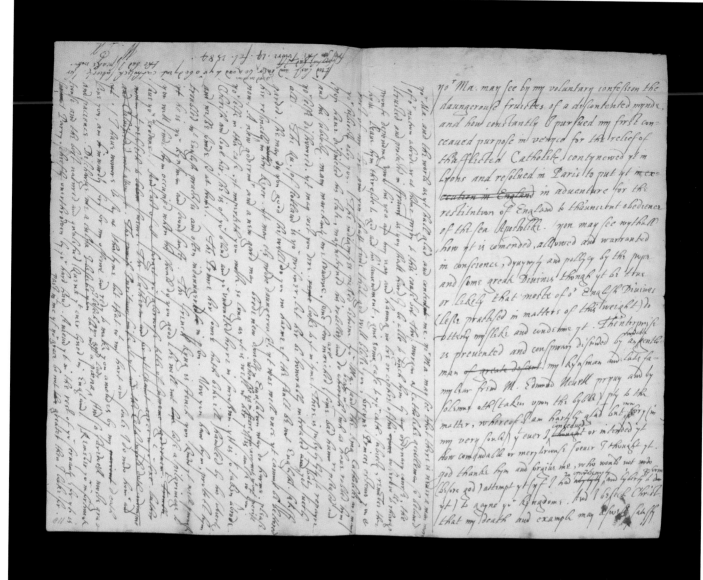

110

The Parry Plot

Letter from William Parry to Elizabeth I, 14 February 1585,
Tower of London.

British Library, Lansdowne MS 43, ff. 117v–118r.

William Parry, who had been reconciled to the Catholic
Church in 1582, operated as a double agent. In early 1584
he had returned to England from Italy, where he had received
encouragement from the papacy for some plot against
Elizabeth. He confessed this to the queen, in order to win
her trust by demonstrating his skill as a spy. Disgruntled
with what reward he received, Parry began conspiring her
death. 'Th'enterprise' was 'preuented' when one of the co-
conspirators, Edmund Neville, denounced him as a traitor on
8 February 1585. Parry was arrested. 'Whereof I am hartyly
glad but now sory … that euer I … conceaued or intended
that [act]', he told the queen in his letter written from the
Tower of London on 14 February. 'Your Maieste may see

by my voluntary confession the daungerouse fruictes of a
discontented mynde, and how constantly I pursued my first
conceaued purpose … for the relief of th'afflicted Catholikes
[and] the restitution of England to th'auncient obedience of
the sea Apostolike.' A week later he was tried for treason.

In this letter Parry offered Elizabeth some counsel,
providing an extraordinary insight into English Catholic
opposition to her government. He warned her that Philip
II would not tolerate how she had 'disquieted his state,
[and] mayneteyned his rebelles'. It was possible to repair
the damage, though, if Mary was 'honorably intreated
… but yet suerly garded'. 'Cherish and loue her, she is of
your bloud and your vndoubted heyre in succession.' Parry
urged Elizabeth to 'forget your gloriouse title of supreme
gouernour' and offer toleration to her Catholic subjects. He
was hanged on 2 March. 'When his bowelles were taken out
he gaue a great groane,' according to one eyewitness account,
before he was beheaded and quartered. AB.

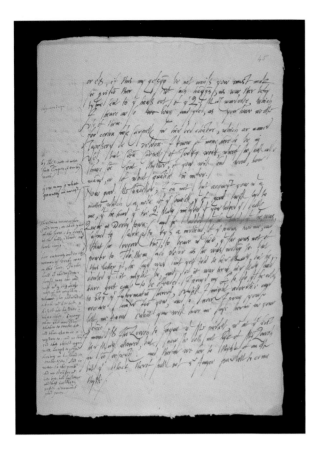

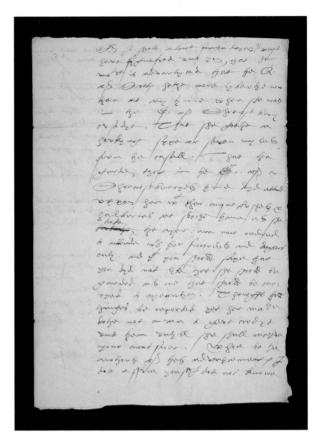

111

Mary's Entertainment at Derby

Letter from William Cecil, Lord Burghley, to Sir Ralph Sadler,
1 February 1585, Greenwich.

British Library, Loan MS 128 [22].

Burghley wrote to Sir Ralph Sadler to report that Sir Amias
Paulet had been appointed to replace him as Mary's keeper.
One reason Paulet had been chosen was for his excellent
French, which would make it easier to converse with Mary.

Mary's secretary, Claude Nau de la Boisselière, had
petitioned the government for certain concessions for her.
The most important – to hear a Mass – 'was vtterly to be
reiected for hir to committ idolatry by the Queen's Maiesties
assent, thovgh she may percase commit it in hir own
thoughts'. Burghley told Sadler how he had heard 'that
yow lodged [Mary] in Derby town. And … that she was
suffred to salvte & to kyss a mvltitud, of the towns women,
and that she regard them, to beare with hir, that she was
not of power to do them such plesvr as she was willing to'.
Sadler's son-in-law, John Somer, added a marginal note that
'her enterteynment to the wemen of Derby was in this sort.
In the hall of the wydowes house, was the good wife with 3
or 4 at the most of her neighbors. Whome she saluted with
a beck with her hed & kissed her hostesse & none other,
sayeng that she was come thither to troble her. And that she
was a wydow to, and so trusted they shuld agree well inough
to gether having no husband to troble them.' Burghley
asked Sadler to explain himself, but warned him that, if the
account were true, Elizabeth 'shuld have gret cause to be
offended'. AB.

112

Hawking

Letter from Sir Francis Walsingham to Sir Ralph Sadler,
19 March 1585, the Court [at Greenwich].

British Library, Loan MS 128 [32].

Sadler was a sympathetic custodian and allowed Mary,
Queen of Scots to accompany him when he went hawking,
a favourite pastime for both of them, which broke the
monotony of being enclosed in Tutbury Castle. However,
his role as Mary's keeper meant that he was constantly
under intense scrutiny, and on 19 March 1585 Sir Francis
Walsingham wrote to Sadler to report Elizabeth I's displeasure
at learning that Mary 'hathe more lybertye now then at any
tyme when she was in the E[arl] of Shrewsebury cvstodye'.
Fearful of rescue attempts, the queen was dismayed to
understand that Mary 'goethe a hawkyng syxe or seven
myles from the castell. That the garde that in the E[arl]
of Shrewseburyes hire dyd attend vppon her with their
arquebvshes & halbertes at soche hand as she tooke the
ayre: are now ordered to attende with ther swoordes and
dagers only.' Elizabeth also expressed concern that Sadler had
reportedly said that he 'dyd not lyke that she shoold be garded
as one that shoold be carryed to execvtyon'. Walsingham
assured Sadler that he did not know 'whoe be the awthore of
thes advertysementes', but that it was necessary to be 'ovar
readye here to geve care to sooche raporteres'.

In his reply to Walsingham, Sadler defended himself,
explaining that he had used his discretion and 'thought I did
well, but syns it is not so well taken, I wolde to God som
other had the charrge, that wolde use it with more discression
then I can; for I assure you I am so wery of it'. AC.

113

Letter in Cipher

Letter from Mary, Queen of Scots to Patrick, Master of Gray, [October–November] 1584.

The National Archives, Kew, SP 53/14/30.

James VI had appointed his favourite Patrick, Master of Gray, as Scottish ambassador to England in October 1584, with instructions to open secret negotiations with Elizabeth for a pension, in return for which he offered to repudiate plans to restore his mother to joint sovereignty in Scotland. Mary was kept ignorant of this and believed that the Master of Gray was acting in her best interests. She wrote to him in nomenclator cipher, with a command to petition Elizabeth to free her, either to return to Scotland or to remain in England, saying that there was no just reason to keep her imprisoned. While her release was negotiated Mary wanted to be returned to 'the keeping' of the Earl of Shrewsbury. This was in order to protect her reputation against the 'inventors and sowers of the bruit' that Shrewsbury and she were lovers. She accused the earl's estranged wife, Elizabeth, Countess of Shrewsbury, and her sons, William and Charles Cavendish, of slander and demanded 'justice in the name of my son'.

Mary's letter was intercepted by Sir Francis Walsingham's spies and deciphered by his cryptographer, Thomas Phelippes. Phelippes was fluent in six languages and 'of a stayd and secrett nature, good judgment for his bringing vppe and studious'. By 1578 he was spying for Walsingham, employed in particular as a cryptographer, ciphering and deciphering codes. Nomenclators use elements of substitution ciphers and of codes. They generally combine a small codebook with large homophonic substitution tables and were a common form of cryptography. AB.

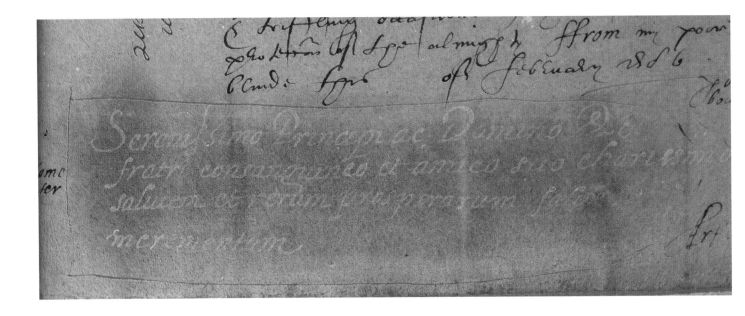

114

Secret Ink

Letter from Arthur Gregory to Sir Francis Walsingham, 1586,
'ffrom my poore house'.

British Library, Harley MS 286, f. 78r.

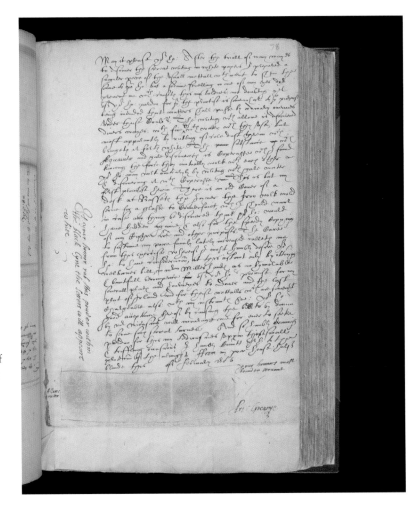

Dating from February 1586, this letter sheds light on the
secretive intelligence practices developed under Elizabeth's
Principal Secretary and spymaster, Sir Francis Walsingham.
Sent by Arthur Gregory, a skilled counterfeiter, the letter
relates his experiments with innovative techniques for using
and reading invisible ink, in order to uncover the secret
writing of Mary, Queen of Scots.

Gregory describes his observations of copperas and gall,
which was used as a common and reversible invisible ink
during the period. He reports that, despite his experiments
being prevented by a swelling in his eye, he had discovered
a technique using alum to create secret writing: 'The writing
with allome is discovered divers ways; with fire and with
water, which they use; but most apparantly by rubbing of
cole dust thereon which bringeth it forth white.'

The master forger used the letter's postscript to
demonstrate his secret writing technology to Walsingham.
Enclosing a packet of coal dust, Gregory tells Walsingham, 'If
your honnor rub this pouder within the black lyne the letters
will appeare white.' As the letter demonstrates, Walsingham
followed these instructions, using the black coal dust to
reveal white letters. Although Gregory's secret writing is no
longer visible with the naked eye, multispectral imaging has
enabled it to be recovered. Translated from Latin, Gregory's
message addressed his 'excellent master' Walsingham, and
wished 'health and many successes' for his 'brother, cousin
and dear friend'. AGB.

Trial and Execution

The Babington Plot brought Mary, Queen of Scots to trial and execution. The government knew about it from the outset, since Walsingham had set up a system to read all of Mary's correspondence when she was moved to Chartley Hall in December 1585. Double agents were intercepting the packets of ciphered letters hidden by her couriers in beer barrels and handing them over to Walsingham's cryptographer. Thomas Phelippes then copied and deciphered them before the originals were sent on to their intended addressee. Mary was entrapped. When her complicity in the plot to assassinate Elizabeth was evident from a letter, Walsingham pounced.

With the revelation of the Babington Plot, Elizabeth too was caught in a trap. The queen had no choice but to put Mary on trial, and once the inevitable guilty verdict was pronounced, she really could do no other than carry out the sentence. For six weeks she resisted the pressure. Then on 1 February 1587 she signed the death warrant and told her junior Secretary William Davison to take it to be sealed. Elizabeth later maintained that she quickly revoked her order. If so, it was too late. On 2 February the sealed warrant went to Fotheringhay Castle and on 8 February Mary, Queen of Scots met her death.

Mary's execution caused a storm in Scotland and France. France, however, was again descending into civil war and James VI was too weak to act alone. Besides, he had too much to lose in breaking the alliance which he had signed with Elizabeth in the summer of 1586, including the loss of a substantial English pension. So, despite the furore, Mary's death went unavenged.

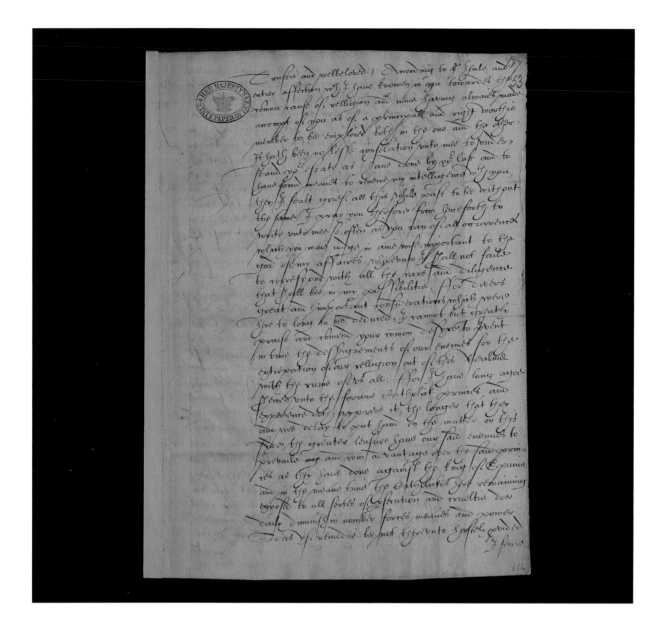

115

The 'Gallows Letter'

Letter from Mary, Queen of Scots to Anthony Babington,
17 July 1586, Chartley in Staffordshire.

The National Archives, Kew, SP 53/18/53.

The 'Gallows Letter' is the key document in the 1586
Babington Plot. It was intercepted by Walsingham's spies
and passed on to his cryptographer Thomas Phelippes to be
deciphered. Upon decoding it, Phelippes drew a gallows on
the address leaf of his deciphered copy indicating that its
content would condemn Mary to death for treason against
Elizabeth. The original letter was then resealed and sent to its
intended addressee, Anthony Babington.

In May–June 1586 Babington began plotting a Catholic
uprising against Elizabeth supported by a Spanish invasion.
The queen would be assassinated and Mary freed from prison
and crowned in her place. Babington opened the Plot to
Mary on 6 July, proposing the 'dispatch of the vsurper [by]
six noble gentlemen … who for the zeale they beare to the
Catholick cause and your maiesties service will vndertake

that tragicall execution'. In the 'Gallows Letter' written by
her secretaries Claude Nau and Gilbert Curle on 17 July,
Mary authorised the Plot and made recommendations.
The time to act was now, she said, because the English
Catholics, 'exposed to all sortes of persecution and crueltie
doe daily diminish in number forces meanes and power'.
The conspirators were to prepare support for a Spanish
invasion. Then Elizabeth was to be assassinated ('sett the six
gentlemen to woork') and Mary rescued from prison and
crowned queen. Mary also wanted the Protestant regime
in Scotland overthrown and 'some sturring in Ireland'. She
warned Babington that, if the Plot failed, Elizabeth would,
'catching mee againe … enclose mee for ever in some hole,
forth of the which I should never escape yf shee did vse mee
no worse'. She also cautioned that Henry III of France was
not to be trusted: he 'enterteineth with [Elizabeth] a course
farr contrarie to our desseignementes'. Mary, though, left
the detail of the Plot to Babington, who burned the original
'Gallows Letter' after reading it. This is the closest surviving
copy. AB.

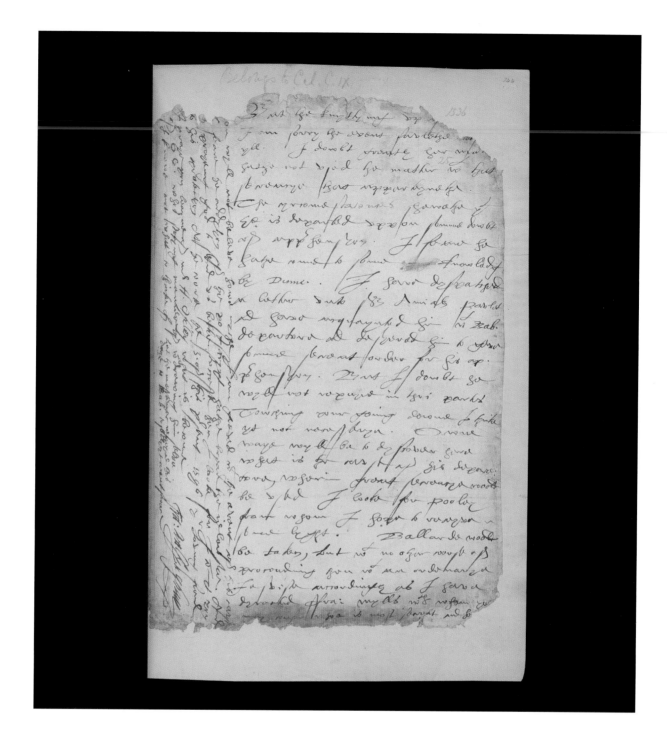

116

The Postscript

Letter from Sir Francis Walsingham to Thomas Phelippes,
3 August 1586, the Court [at Richmond].

British Library, Cotton MS Appendix L, f. 144r.

Walsingham amended several passages in the 'Gallows Letter' and forged a postscript asking Babington to name the six assassins and to say 'how you proceed and as soon as you may'. On 3 August he ordered the arrest of Babington and his co-conspirators. In this letter Walsingham confessed to Phelippes, 'you wyll not beleve howe mych I am greved with the event of this cavse and feare the addytyon of the postscrypt hathe bread the iealousie [suspicion]'. At least one suspect, Gilbert Gifford, had fled before arrest. 'And … prayeng god to send vs better svccesse then I looke for.'

It seems that the postscript did not tip Babington off. He only realised his arrest was imminent over the course of dinner with one of Walsingham's double agents on 5 August, and made his escape. Babington hid in St John's Wood, Middlesex, for a time but was caught on 14 August. Mary's secretaries, Nau and Curle, were apprehended on 11 August and her papers seized. They were interrogated and confessed on 5 September that they had written the 'Gallows Letter' at Mary's command. Babington confessed the same. The evidence of Mary's complicity could not be suppressed, as it was needed to convict Babington and his co-conspirators. AB.

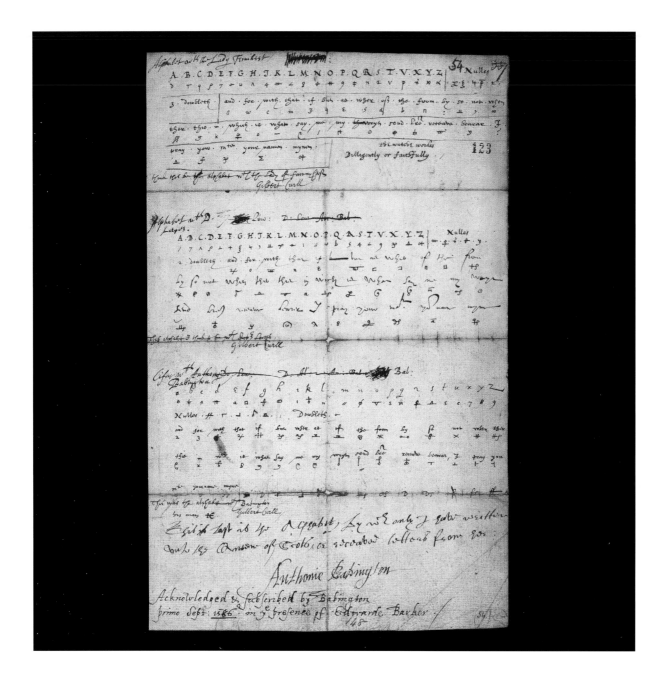

117

The Babington Cipher

Cipher used by Mary, Queen of Scots to communicate
with Anthony Babington, 1586, Chartley.

The National Archives, Kew, SP 12/193/54, f. 123r.

Following Mary's arrest for treasonous communications
with Anthony Babington, her rooms at Chartley Hall in
Staffordshire were searched and all of her papers seized.
Among them were more than 100 different ciphers, which
the deposed queen had used to secretly correspond with her
supporters and co-conspirators during her captivity. The
cipher set out by Phelippes on the lower half of this page is
the one used by Mary in her correspondence with Babington.
It consists of twenty-three symbols which could be substituted
for letters of the alphabet (with the exception of 'j', 'v' and
'w') and thirty-five symbols that represented individual words
or phrases, such as 'letter' and 'bearer', 'send' and 'receive',

'from' and 'by', 'majesty' and 'pray'. The difficulty of the
cipher was increased by the addition of four 'nulls' or blanks
that had no meaning, and another symbol that signalled that
the next symbol represented a double letter.

During his interrogation on 1 September, Babington was
shown the cipher and, in the presence of Edward Barker,
a public notary, testified with his own signature that 'this
last is the alphabet by which only I have written vnto the
Queene of Scotes or receaved letteres from her'. Mary's
cipher secretary, Gilbert Curle, who had encrypted the
queen's communications to Babington, also affirmed that
this was the alphabet used by Babington and 'his man'
Chidiock Tichborne, who assisted him in deciphering
letters. Babington and thirteen co-conspirators, including
Tichborne, were found guilty of treason between 13 and
15 September. Babington was hanged, drawn and quartered
on 20 September. AC.

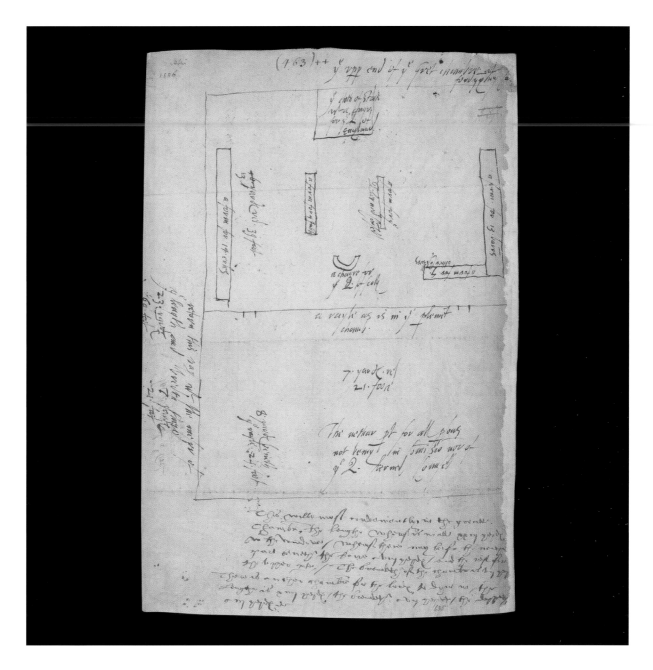

118

Mary's Second Trial
Lord Burghley's seating plan for the trial in the Great Chamber
at Fotheringhay Castle, 11 October 1586.

British Library, Cotton MS Caligula C ix, f. 635r.

Plans were made for Mary, Queen of Scots to be tried
by a special judicial commission under the terms of the
1585 Act for the Surety of the Queen. Unwilling to leave
anything to chance, Burghley oversaw all of the practical
arrangements, setting out the timetable for the trial and
personally writing to his fellow commissioners with
instructions for their attendance.

This is Burghley's sketch of the Great Chamber at
Fotheringhay Castle in Northamptonshire, chosen by
Elizabeth as the place for Mary's trial. Roughly executed
yet extremely detailed, it provides a precise layout of the

hall, which measured 23 yards by 7. At the top, 'ye cloth
of state with a chayr for the Q[ueen] of England' represents
Elizabeth, who did not attend the trial, and in the centre, 'a
chayre for ye Q. of Scotts' is positioned before a dividing rail,
behind which local gentry were permitted to stand. 'Forms' or
benches are arranged on both sides of the hall for peers of the
realm, including the Earls of Shrewsbury and Kent and Lord
Burghley, who presided over the trial.

The trial began on 14 October 1586. Mary, a skilled orator,
delivered a strong defence, questioning the commission's
jurisdiction and declaring 'I will neuer make shipwrack of my
soule, by conspiring my dearest sisters death and ruine.' The
commission adjourned the following day and reconvened on
25 October in the Star Chamber in Westminster Palace. The
thirty-six peers, privy councillors and judges found Mary
guilty of plotting to assassinate Elizabeth. AC.

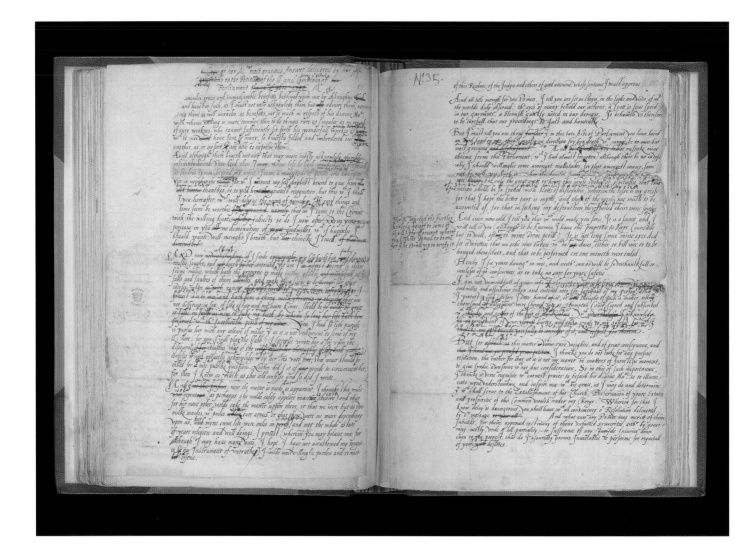

119

Two Milk Maids

Elizabeth I's response to parliamentary petitions
calling for the execution of Mary, Queen of Scots,
12 November 1586.

British Library, Lansdowne MS 94, ff. 84v–85r.

This is Elizabeth's own working copy of the speech she
delivered to parliament in response to its call for Mary's
immediate execution. It is written in a scribal hand and
revised in several places by the queen herself for publication.

Elizabeth began by expressing grief that 'one not
different in sex, of like estate and my neare kinne, shold be
fallen into so greate a Crime'. She lamented the fact that she
and Mary were not 'but as two milke maides, with pailes
vpon oure armes, or that there were no more dependency
vpon us, but myne owne life were onlie in danger and

not the whole estate of youre religion and well doings'.
Reluctant to authorise the execution of a kinswoman and
anointed queen, Elizabeth told parliament 'you haue laied
an hard hand on mee, that I must giue direction for her
death, which cannot be but most greiuous and an yrksom
burdon to me'. Fully aware that her honour was as much
at stake as Mary's life, Elizabeth declared 'wee Princes …
are set on stages, in the sight and veiw, of all the worlde
duly obserued, th'eyes of many behold our actions, a spott
is sone spied in our garments, a blemish quickly noted in
our doinges. It behoueth vs therefore to be carefull that
our proceedings be Iust and honorable.' Elizabeth was
unable to give a 'speedie awnswere' on a matter of such
great consequence. A few days later she asked parliament
whether another solution could be found to avoid Mary's
death. AC.

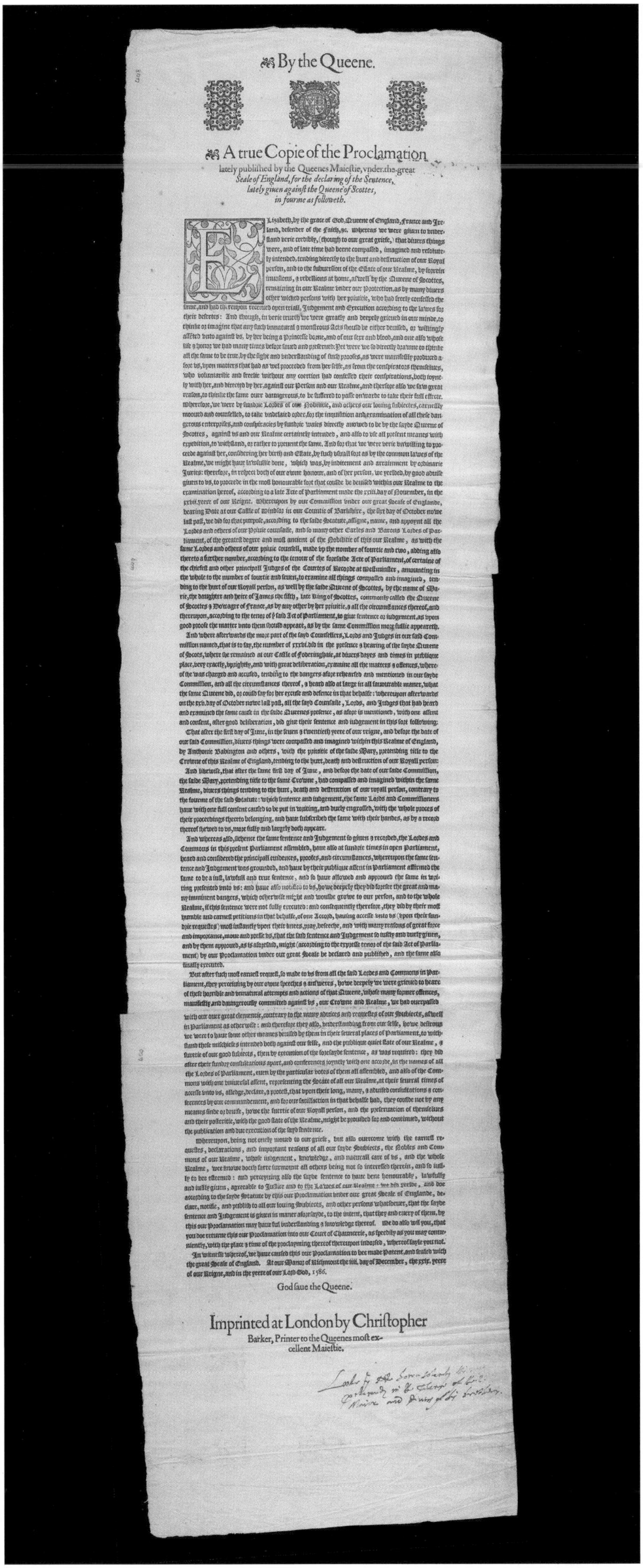

The left portion of the page contains a full-length photographic reproduction of a printed sixteenth-century proclamation broadside, headed "By the Queene" and titled "A true Copie of the Proclamation lately published by the Queenes Maiestie, vnder the great Seale of England, for the declaring of the Sentence, lately giuen against the Queene of Scottes, in fourme as followeth." The lengthy body text is too small and faded to transcribe reliably, ending with "God saue the Queene." and the imprint "Imprinted at London by Christopher Barker, Printer to the Queenes most excellent Maiestie."

120

Proclaiming Mary's Conviction in London

A True Copie of the Proclamation Lately Published by the Queenes Maiestie, vnder the Great Seale of England, for the Declaring of the Sentence, Lately Giuen against the Queene of Scottes, in Fourme as Followeth, London, printed by Christopher Barker, [1586].

British Library, Additional MS 48027, ff. 448r–450r.

Proclamations were printed royal directives, publicly read. Robert Beale, clerk of the privy council, preserved this important proclamation in his papers, noting its formal reading in London: 'Looke ye howe solemnly this was proclaymed in the presence of the Lord Mayor and divers of his brethern.' A contemporary account expands on the occasion: the City officers, nobility and gentry present, as well as 'eighty of the most gravest and worshipfullest cittizens, in coates of velvet and chaines of gould', all on horseback; the trumpeters; and the reading of the proclamation in four places. That account also records the 'greate and wonderfull rejoyceing of the people of all sorts': the ringing of bells, making of bonfires and singing of psalms in the streets of London.

The proclamation laid out the legal basis for Mary's trial and conviction; it also declared Elizabeth's reluctance and preference for an alternative to Mary's execution, and her final acquiescence to the loving judgement and care of her subjects in parliament. Its measured terms downplayed the anger in parliament and the queen's resistance.

Under the Act for the Surety of the Queen (1585), the proclamation was an essential stage in the process of bringing Mary to execution. It also, under a proviso of the Act inserted by Elizabeth, enabled anyone to kill Mary, without the queen's execution warrant. The significance of the proclamation was recognised by Beale, who had been involved in negotiations with Mary and would carry her execution warrant to Fotheringhay in February 1587. TW.

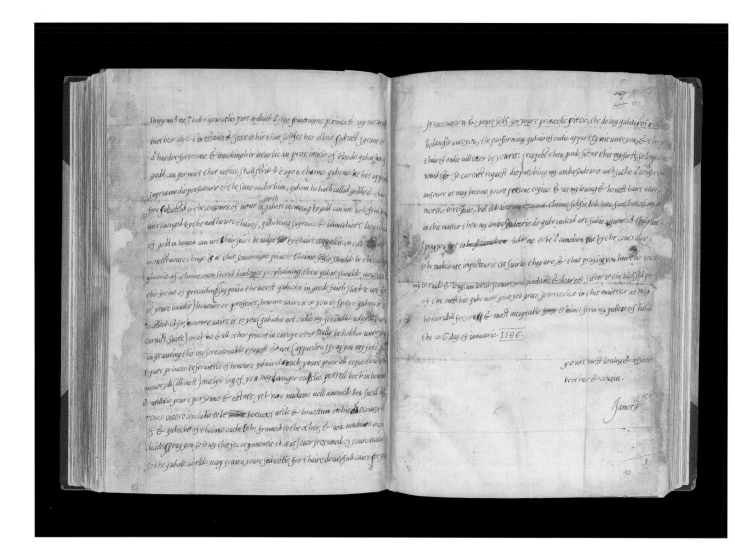

121

Pleading for his Mother's Life

Letter from James VI to Elizabeth I, 26 January 1587,
Holyroodhouse, Midlothian.

British Library, Cotton MS Caligula C ix, ff. 192v–193r.

This personal letter was sent by James VI of Scotland to his 'dearest sister [monarch]' on 26 January 1587, in a final attempt to save the life of Mary, Queen of Scots, the mother he barely knew. 'Quhat thing', he asked Elizabeth, 'can greatlier touche me in honoure that [being] a King & a sonne than that my nearest neihboure, being in straittest [friend]shipp with me shall rigourslie putt to death a free souueraigne prince & my naturall mother, alyke in estaite & sexe to hir … & touching hir nearlie in proximitie of bloode?'

Ambitious and pragmatic, James was motivated to write out of concern for his own reputation and status rather than any overwhelming sense of emotional attachment to his mother or concern for her plight. He urged Elizabeth to consider 'quhat number of straitis I uolde [be] dreuin unto & amongst the rest hou it micht perrell my reputation amongst my subiectis'. James further argued that as an anointed monarch, Mary 'being supreme & immediatt lieutenant of godd in heauen can not thair foire be iudgit by thaire equallis in earth'.

With one eye already fixed on the English throne, James was not prepared to go as far as to threaten to break the Anglo-Scottish alliance to save his mother. Instead, he warned Elizabeth not 'to putt princes to straittis of honoure quhair through youre generall reputatione & the uniuersall (allmost) mislyking of you may daingerouslie perrell both in honoure & utillitie youre personne & estate'. AC.

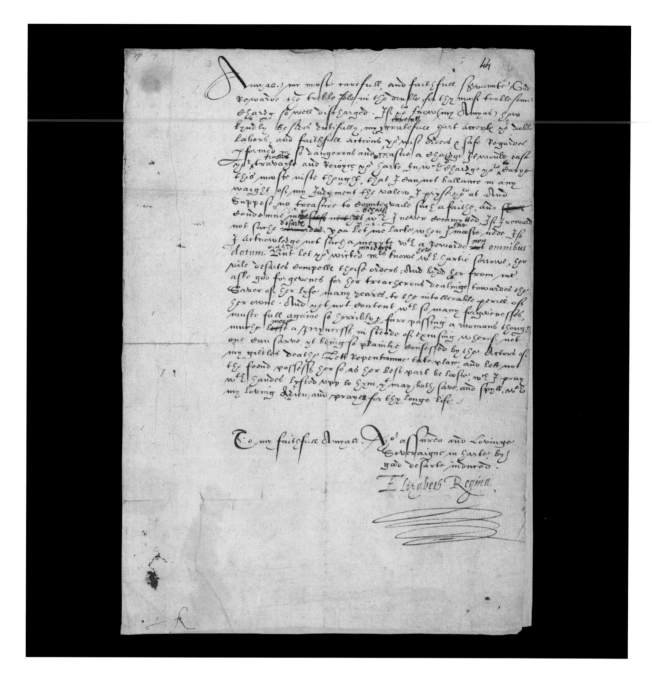

122

'My Most Careful and Faithful Servant'

Letter from Elizabeth I to Sir Amias Paulet, [25 October 1586–
8 February 1587].

British Library, Lansdowne MS 1236, f. 44r.

This is a draft of the letter Elizabeth wrote to Sir Amias
Paulet after Mary, Queen of Scots had been convicted of
treason on 25 October 1586, the final copy of which does not
survive. It begins: 'Amyas, my mooste carefull, and faithfull
servaunte, God Rewarde the treble fold in the double, for
thy moost troble some Charg so well discharged. If yow
knew (my Amyas) how kyndly be sides dutifully, my gratefull
carefull hart acceptes your dooble labors, and faithfull
actions, your wise orders & safe Regardes performed in so
dangerous and craftie a Chardge, it would ease your trobles
travayle & Reioyce your harte'.

As her custodian, Paulet had been immune to Mary's
blandishments, kept her more closely guarded, restricted her
correspondence and curtailed her household servants and
magnificence. He even once admitted to her that he would
kill her himself rather than permit her escape. Elizabeth told
him to 'let your wicked murderes Mistress [Mary] knowe
how with hartie sorrowe, her vile desartes Compelles theise
orders: and bydd her from me aske god forgevenes for the
treacherous dealinge towardes the Saver of her lyfe many
yeares, to the intollerable perill of her owne'. Elizabeth
ended, 'lett Repentaunce take place, and lett not the feend
possess her so, as her best part be looste', praying God be
merciful on Mary. Elizabeth was never told that Walsingham
had known about the Babington Plot from the start, giving
it the means to grow in order to entrap Mary and force the
queen into executing her. AB.

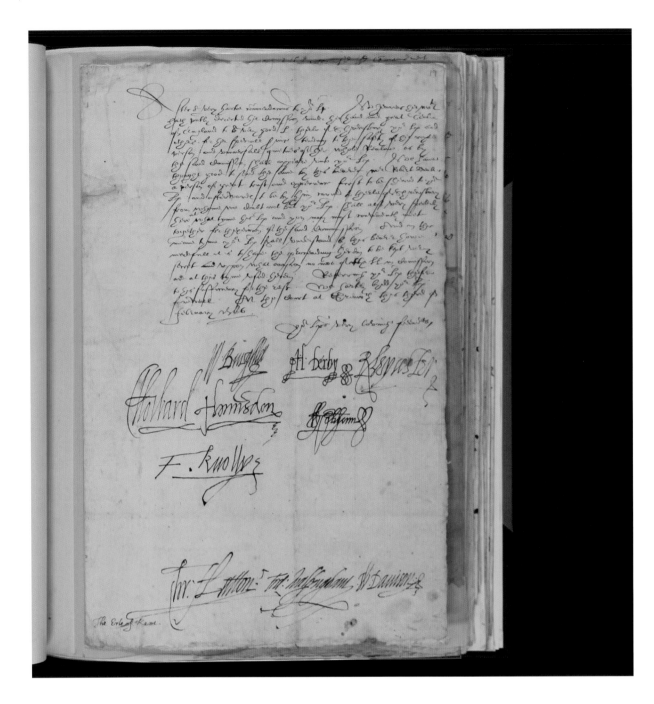

123

The Warrant for Mary's Execution

Letter from the privy council to Henry Grey, sixth Earl of Kent,
3 February 1587, the Court [at Greenwich].

Lambeth Palace Library MS 4267, f. 19r.

Mary was executed in the Great Hall at Fotheringhay Castle
around 8 am on the morning of Wednesday 8 February 1587.
Cecil had drafted the warrant in which he called for speedy
justice against a woman who was an 'undoubted danger' to
Elizabeth and the 'publyke state of this realme, aswell for
the cause of the gospell and the trewe religion of Christ'.
Elizabeth signed it with extreme reluctance on 1 February,
ordering her Secretary, William Davison, to bring it to her
only after Cecil had confirmed a false rumour that Spanish
troops had landed in Wales. She backtracked the next day,
complaining of Davison's unseemly haste in getting it sealed,
with the result that Cecil intervened, directing Davison to
give it to him and summoning selected privy councillors to
his chamber at the court in Greenwich. There, on 3 February,
they agreed to proceed with the execution and not tell
Elizabeth 'until it were done'. The Earls of Shrewsbury and
Kent were commissioned to preside at Fotheringhay. Letters
to them, of which this is Kent's copy, justified this as for the
queen's 'speciall seruice tending to the safety of her royall
person and vniuersall quietnes of her whole Realme' and
warned that 'the proceading herein [was] to be kept very
secret'. Since Shrewsbury's copy of the letter is lost and
Elizabeth almost certainly destroyed the original signed
warrant after Mary's death, this document is one of the most
authentic relics of a momentous event. JG.

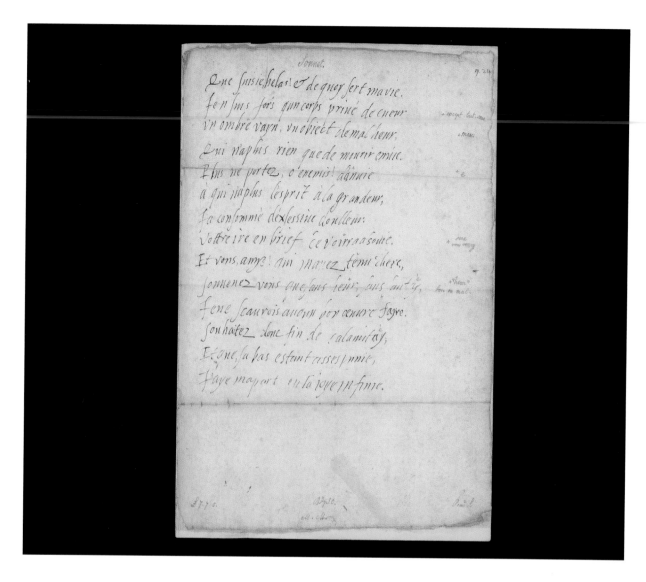

124

Mary's Last Night

Poem by Mary, Queen of Scots, 7/8 February 1587,
Fotheringhay Castle, Northamptonshire.

The Bodleian Libraries, University of Oxford, MS. Add. C. 92, f. 24r.

On 7 February 1587 Mary was informed by the Earls
of Shrewsbury and Kent that she was to be executed
the following morning. Under the terms of the Bond of
Association, Elizabeth had wanted her killed secretly but
her keepers, Sir Amias Paulet and Sir Dru Drury, refused.
Burghley and Walsingham stood firm too. This forced
Elizabeth's hand and she accepted that Mary must be
executed instead.

Mary took the news, which she received at dinner, calmly,
despite the fact that Paulet and Drury pulled down the cloth
of state above and behind her seat. She told the assembled
company that she was 'not useful and cannot be useful to
anyone', before recounting her past efforts at reconciliation
with Elizabeth and again denying complicity in the Babington
Plot. She petitioned to be buried in France and to reward her
loyal servants. Shrewsbury doubted that Elizabeth would
permit the first request, but allowed the second. After this –
her final – audience, Mary ate little, prayed for an hour, then
composed her last will and testament and distributed her
possessions among her servants.

At 2 am Mary wrote her final letter, to her childhood
friend and brother-in-law, King Henry III of France. In it her
overriding tone was one of injured innocence, expressing regret
for 'throw[ing] myself into the power of the queen my cousin,
at whose hands I have suffered much for almost twenty years'.
She told Henry how she was to be 'executed like a criminal at
eight in the morning', despite her innocence. Mary insisted that
she had been condemned only for her Catholic faith and for
'the assertion of [her] God-given right to the English crown'.

Accompanying Mary's letter to Henry was a sonnet, written
in her own hand in French and beginning 'What am I, alas,
and what use is my life?' It may, in fact, have been the last
thing she ever wrote. The poem expresses Mary's sorrow and
resignation at her fate; she describes herself as 'a vain shadow,
an object of misfortune, / Who no longer has anything in life,
but to die'. She forgoes her royal dignity and implores her
enemies to 'no longer … be envious'. But she also articulates
her determination to have a good, Catholic death, anticipating
her 'share in everlasting joy'. Her sonnet was intended for both
Henry and 'you, friends, who have been so dear to me'. Mary,
Queen of Scots was, at heart, French. AB.

125

'In The End Is My Beginning'

Ink and pencil drawing of the execution of Mary, Queen of Scots at Fotheringhay Castle, 8 February 1587.

British Library, Additional MS 48027, f. 650*r.

This eyewitness drawing of Mary's execution is from the papers of Robert Beale, who was in attendance at Fotheringhay Castle on the morning of 8 February 1587. Mary is depicted three times: entering the hall; being attended by her gentlewomen on the scaffold; and kneeling at the block with the executioner's axe raised ready to strike. The Earls of Shrewsbury (1) and Kent (2) are shown seated to the left of the scaffold, and Sir Amias Paulet (3) behind it.

Mary was determined to die a Catholic martyr's death and conducted herself accordingly. She entered the hall, dressed in black with a white veil, carrying her ivory crucifix and Latin prayer book, with an *Agnus Dei* (p. 190) around her neck and a rosary on her girdle. Refusing the Protestant prayers offered by Richard Fletcher, Dean of Peterborough Cathedral (6), Mary recited her own Latin prayers before affirming that she was fixed in the ancient Roman Catholic religion and ready to die for it. Her ladies then disrobed her to reveal her satin petticoat and bodice of deep crimson – the liturgical colour of Catholic martyrdom.

Mary's final moments were witnessed by Sir Robert Wingfield of Upton, who reported to Lord Burghley that 'lying upon the blocke most quietly and stretching out her armes [she] cryed "In manus tuas domine [Into your hands, O Lord]" three or fowre tymes'. With two strokes of the axe, 'the executioner cutt of her head saving one little grisle which being cutt a sunder he lift up her head to the view of all the assembly, and bad[e] God save the Queene'. According to some accounts she also spoke the words of her motto, 'In the end is my beginning', at her death. AC.

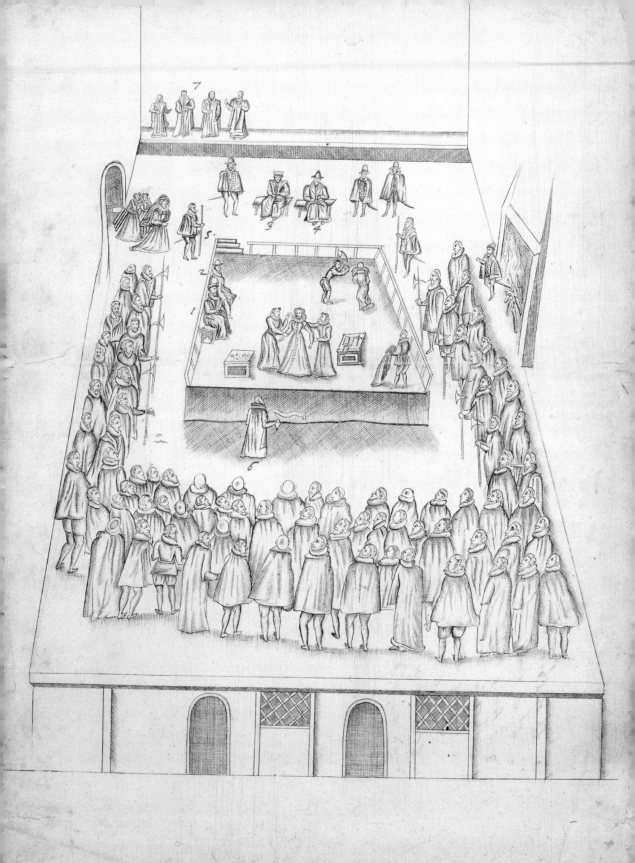

126

The 'Penicuik Jewels'
A gold necklace, and a gold and enamelled pendant locket
associated with Mary, Queen of Scots, late sixteenth century.

National Museums Scotland, Edinburgh, H.NA 421, H.NA 422.

The oval locket, framed by threaded seed pearls, contains
two miniature painted portraits said to be of Mary and her
son, James VI. The necklace comprises fourteen large gold
oval beads of filigree work, divided by smaller circular beads.
These larger filigree beads would have originally held scent,
and are properly known as paternoster beads, because they
usually formed a rosary. Alternatively, they could be termed
pomander beads. They were made with plain and beaded
wires, and soldered together. During scientific analysis, some
odorous black material was recovered from the central large
bead of the necklace and is thought to be ambergris.

The 'Penicuik Jewels' have among the best provenance
of jewellery associated with Mary, Queen of Scots. It is
possible that the necklace was made from the beads of
bracelets given by the queen to Giles Mowbray, one of
her attendants during her English imprisonment, shortly
before her execution. A member of the Clerk of Penicuik
family married a granddaughter of Giles, and the locket
and necklace were preserved by the Clerks as a relic of
Mary. Elizabeth's ministers were keen to suppress such
memorialisation of Mary and ordered her clothing to be
burnt in a fireplace at Fotheringhay, immediately after
her execution, to prevent any mementoes being taken.
However, in the tradition of royal gift-giving to seal
personal loyalties, Mary was also being careful to preserve
her memory. She may have commissioned the locket with
this in mind. AG.

127

The Blairs Reliquary

Unknown artist, 1586; framed 1610–22.

The Scottish Catholic Heritage Collections Trust (Blairs Museum), Aberdeen, T9109BLRBM.

On the morning of her execution, Mary, Queen of Scots gave a small portrait of herself in a gold case to her lady-in-waiting, Elizabeth Curle. This extraordinary act of self-commemoration has long been associated with the portrait contained within this reliquary, which was probably assembled in the Scots College in Douai in the early seventeenth century for Hugh Curle, Elizabeth Curle's son. The reliquary presents Mary as a martyr, with the Marian monogram 'MRA' on the reverse combined with the names of Catholic saints, and by the association of her image with relics from Margaret of Scotland and contemporary Jesuit martyrs. In creating this devotional portrait, Hugh was following the example of his mother, who had commissioned the large-scale painting known as the 'Blairs Memorial Portrait' a decade after Mary's execution (Blairs Museum).

The artist responsible for the portrait miniature contained within the reliquary has not been identified; however, it appears to have been produced in multiples, as a related miniature survives in the Rijksmuseum in Amsterdam. Mary's attempts to commission small portraits that could be sent to her supporters in France are recorded in her correspondence; in August 1577 her secretary, Claude Nau, noted in a letter to the Archbishop of Glasgow in France that he had hoped to be able to send a portrait of the queen, but that the artist had not completed it in time. CB.

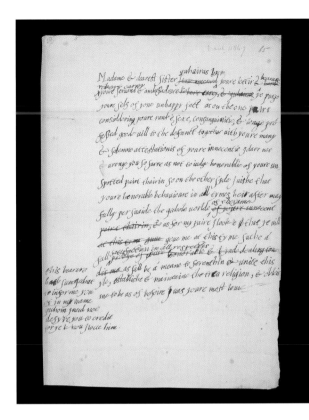

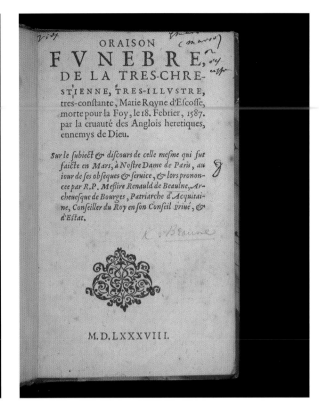

128

'Satisfaction' for His Mother's Death
Letter from James VI to Elizabeth I, late February 1587.
British Library, Additional MS 23240, f. 65r.

Four days after the execution of Mary, Queen of Scots,
Elizabeth wrote a letter to James VI which expressed her
'extreme dolor' at the 'miserable' turn of events and protested
her innocence in them. Elizabeth was attempting to prevent
the development of a rift with the Scottish king, who had
been pleading for his mother's life. James, however, was
not appeased. He refused to admit Elizabeth's messenger,
Sir Robert Carey, into his presence and was heard muttering
revenge. In a flurry of letters to Scotland, both Burghley and
Walsingham made plain to James that he had far more to
lose than gain by breaking off the Anglo-Scottish league. Not
only would he lose his pension, but also a revival of the two
realms' ancient enmity would make his accession impossible.
Recognising this political reality, James let it be known that
he required compensation for the unjust treatment of his
mother. In this draft letter to Elizabeth, he hinted that the
'satisfaction' he sought was to be named Elizabeth's heir.

James started by accepting Elizabeth's innocence: 'youre
many & solemne attestationis of youre innocentie I darr
not wronge you so farre as not to judge honorablie of youre
unspotted pairt thairin'. But he then added: 'I looke that
ye will geve me at this tyme suche a full satisfaction in all
respectis as sall be a meane to strenthin & unite this yle,
establishe & maintaine the trew religion.' He would not be
more specific but waited for Elizabeth to make an offer. The
queen, however, declined to designate him her heir or to offer
him the title of Prince of Wales. Relations between the two
monarchs remained tense, but the league between the two
realms held. SD.

129

Obsequies for Mary
Renaud de Beaune, *Oraison Fvnebre de la Tres-chrestienne,
Tres-illustre, Tres-constante, Marie Royne d'Escosse*,
[Paris], 1588.
British Library, 1359.b.13., title page.

After Mary's execution at Fotheringhay Castle on 8 February
1587, she was buried in Peterborough Cathedral. As she
had been queen of France as well as of Scotland, Mary had
requested an elaborate funeral to be held for her in France,
but there is no evidence that any took place.

The reactions to Mary's execution and the religious
ceremonies in which she was remembered in Catholic
countries around Europe were not uniform but were instead
driven by each country's own political agenda and used for
propaganda purposes. In France the obsequies were used by
members of the Guise family to score political points. Philip II
of Spain had been reluctant to mourn for Mary until the pope
had privately declared her a martyr. James VI of Scotland
and his court mourned his mother for a year in order to
demonstrate to Elizabeth how she had slighted his honour.

This sermon was preached at Notre Dame in Paris
by Renaud de Beaune. The title page dates Mary's
execution as 18 February, following the new Gregorian
calendar (introduced in 1582) which was ten days ahead
of the Julian one still used in England. In addition to the
text of the sermon, which makes up the greatest part
of the volume, it also contains epitaphs and sonnets
commemorating Mary, Queen of Scots and France.
According to de Beaune, Mary was an innocent martyr
and should be a role model for English Catholics. Other
publications expressing views on Mary and her execution
were published widely in Europe. KL-H.

The Spanish Armada

The death of Mary, Queen of Scots did not bring security
to Elizabeth I. Philip II of Spain had already made plans to
invade England in reaction to her military intervention in
the Netherlands and the heavy raids of Sir Francis Drake
in 1585 on Spanish ports and shipping in the Caribbean.
Mary's execution prompted Philip to speed up the launch
of 'the Enterprise of England'. However, Drake's lightning
assault on Cadiz in April 1587, which destroyed some
twenty-four Spanish ships, together with his temporary
occupation of Sagres caused a postponement of the armada
until the summer of 1588. In the meantime, Elizabeth and
her council made preparations for the anticipated invasion.
All merchant shipping was stayed in their home ports;
most of the Earl of Leicester's troops were brought back
to England; trained bands of English were at the ready;
the navy was brought up to strength; and attention was
paid to England's coastal defences.

Simultaneously Elizabeth re-opened contacts with the
Duke of Parma to discuss a negotiated peace. While
Parma's representatives were stringing the queen along, he
made ready the barges for the invasion. Even as talks were
underway, the armada set off from Corunna in May 1588
under the command of the Duke of Medina Sidonia, and
on 19 July it was sighted off the Lizard.

130

'The Enterprise of England'

Letter from Philip II, King of Spain, to Enrique de Guzmán y
Ribera, Count of Olivares, Spanish ambassador in Rome, 21/31
March 1587 (NS), San Lorenzo, El Escorial, Madrid.

Archivo General de Simancas, Secretaría de Estado, MS 949, 35.

The execution of Mary, Queen of Scots in 1587 hardened
Philip's resolve to invade England and overthrow its
heretical queen and Protestant establishment. This is a
draft of the letter he sent to his ambassador in Rome, the
Count of Olivares, after receiving news of Mary's death.
He was, he told Olivares, 'extremely grieved at the death
of the Queen of Scotland, which is to be much regretted
for, being such a devout Catholic, she would have been
the most suitable instrument for restoring those countries
[England and Scotland] to our Holy Catholic faith'.
Correctly anticipating that Pope Sixtus V would now urge
him to accelerate plans for holy war and keen to secure
papal funding, Philip instructed Olivares to inform Sixtus
'how much I have been pained, and that I am desirous of
pushing the enterprise on as quickly as the circumstances
will allow'. For the avoidance of doubt, the king added one
of his characteristic scrawled marginal notes, instructing his
clerk to change 'my' circumstances to 'the' circumstances,
'so that it may not appear that it is *my* affairs which cause a
delay'. AC.

E 949, 35

E 949/237

Estoy aguardando con desseo respuesta
de lo que se os escriuio a los xj de
Hebrero en la materia principal, y
hasta ver lo q' viene sobre aquello
no se offrece q' dezir a lo q' estos
dias me haueys escrito a aquel proposito,
solo se offrece auisar q' me tiene muy
lastimado la muerte de la Reyna
de Escocia q' es mucho q' sentir por
hauer sido tan Catholica, y por q' pudiera
ser tan apropiado instrumento por
reduzir aquellos reynos a nra santa
fe Catholica viuiendo al tiempo de la
empressa, Mas pues Dios lo ha
ordenado assi (cuyos juizios son
secretos) el se siruira de acudir y por
otras vias a causa tan de su seruj°
como esta, y a todo lo q' se puede juz-
gar conforme a razon este malo sucesso
haze doblado mas necess° lo que en
aquel desp° se os ordeno q' propusiessedes
assi de mi parte, agora lo podreys
dezir la pena q' esto me ha dado,
y q' me ha auiuado el desseo de apressurar

la execucion todo lo mas q' el estado
de las cosas permitiere, tocando le
a buelta desto como el vsar en ello
de mas o menos breuedad os persuadis
q' depende de q' aya abundancia de
dinero, y assi de las ayudas de
su S°, y procurad enterar le de
mi buena voluntad para en hauiendo
forma y manera a ello, Preuini-
endo con este officio para q' si quando
el supiere la muerte de la dicha Reyna
quisiere amonestar me a abreuiar
entienda q' no he menester ser persuadi-
do pues lo estoy, sino mas ayudado
para ello, pero esto se haga de
manera q' nunca parezca sobrar
ni q' se tiene en poco lo q' el ha offre
çido y aca se ha acceptado para
quando las cosas den lugar, que
esto antes se ha de afirmar, sino q'
si su S° quisiere q' se salga deste
passo entienda q' el medio seria
auisarme sobre aquello con el tiempo
q' tengo apuntado, Agora que sabeys
mi intento podreys hazer el officio
como vieredes mas conuenir no

apartando os deste fin, y vsando
del medio de Alano y Roberto en
lo q' vieredes q' ha de ser mejor
recebido proponiendo lo a ellos q' vos,
y de lo q' se hiziere y se os offre-
çiere auisareys

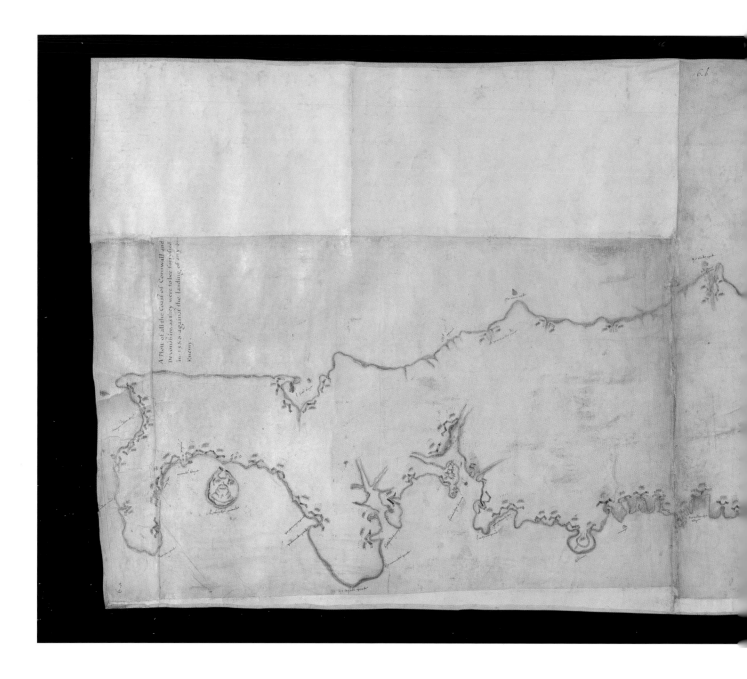

131

Coastal Fortifications

'A Plott [Map] of all the Coast of Cornwall and Devonshire as they were to bee fortyfied in 1588, against the landing of any Enemy'.

British Library, Cotton MS Augustus I.i.6.

As part of the preparations to withstand a Spanish invasion, detailed surveys of coastal defences in England and Wales were produced. These revealed that decades of neglect had left many land defences and fortifications in a state of disrepair and of little use against an experienced and mighty enemy. In March 1588, a report considering 'such meanes as are fittest to putt the forces of the Realme in order to withstand any Invasion' identified Milford Haven, Helford, Falmouth, Plymouth, Torbay, Portland, Portsmouth and the Isle of Wight as 'aptest for the Army of Spaine to land in' and therefore particularly vulnerable.

This surviving map, measuring 1.5 metres in length, charts the coastline from Land's End to Combe Martin in the north and to Sidmouth in the south. Unlike the highly decorative coastal fortification maps produced for Henry VIII in the 1540s, this survey was hastily created at a time of imminent invasion. Highly functional, it does not include a scale bar or show any topographical detail beyond the coastlines. The surveyor's sole focus was to identify all potential landing places and record the vast defensive preparations required to face the Spanish threat. The map shows that the main means of defence employed was a system of trenches and earthworks, built along the most likely invasion beaches. These temporary fortifications were known as breastworks for they were rapidly constructed up to breast height to protect the local parties of militia who were trained and, as shown on the map, armed with pikes to resist a landing. AC.

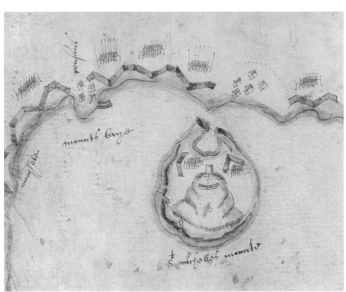

239

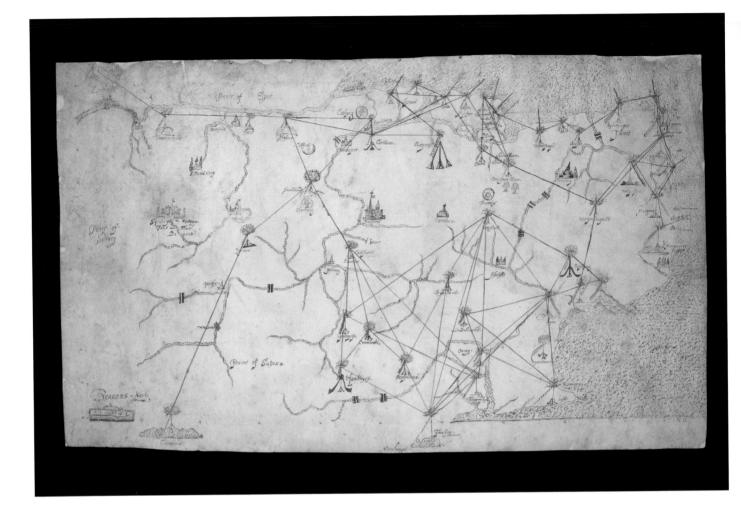

132

Warning Beacons

Map of the beacon system in Kent by William Lambarde, August 1585.

British Library, Additional MS 62935.

In the summer of 1588, the network of warning beacons located throughout southern England was overhauled. In use since at least the early fourteenth century, the beacon system remained the most effective way of alerting authorities and local militia to the threat of invasion. It consisted of a series of iron pitch-pots mounted on tall timber structures and sited on hilltops about 15 miles apart. Watchers were posted at beacons from March to October, when the threat of invasion was highest due to the more favourable weather.

This remarkable map of the Kent beacon system was produced in 1585 by the antiquarian William Lambarde,

who in 1576 had written *Perambulations of Kent*, the first history of any English county, and also served as a justice of the peace and commissioner for musters. The map shows Kent's forty-three beacon sites as well as connecting beacons in the neighbouring counties of Essex, Surrey and Sussex. The complex network of sight lines reveals that the key beacon for alerting Kent was that at Fairlight (Farley) in Sussex, and that warning signals were conveyed to the capital via a beacon on Shooter's Hill, now in south-east London.

Like Kent, Devon had forty-three beacon sites, Essex twenty-six, Sussex twenty-four and Norfolk sixteen. Hampshire had twenty-four beacons, positioned so that they were also visible in Somerset, Oxfordshire and Berkshire. On 19 July 1588 the Spanish fleet was spotted off the Lizard in Cornwall and beacon fires were lit along the coast to give warning of the enemy. AC.

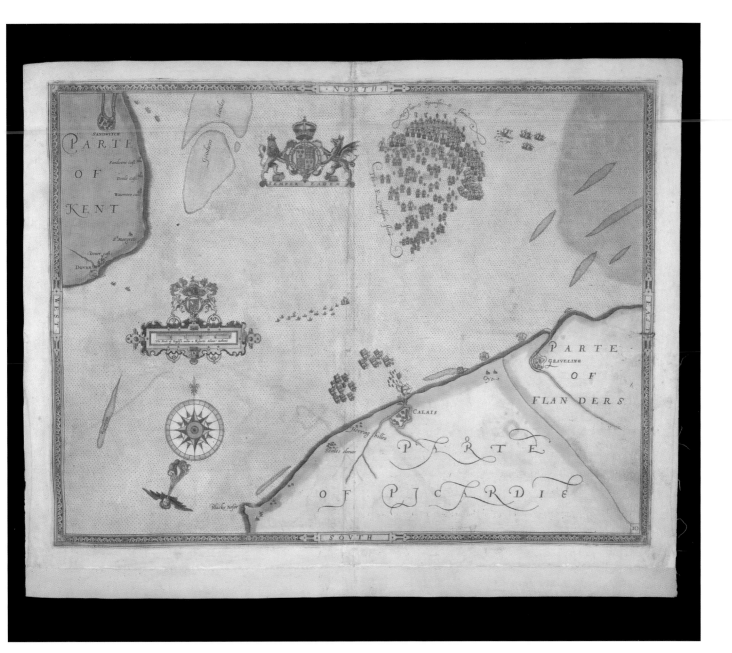

133

Defeat of the Spanish Armada

An atlas of England and Wales, drawn by Christopher Saxton and engraved by Augustine Ryther, Remigius Hogenberg, Cornelius de Hooghe, Nicholas Reynolds, Lenaert Terwoort and Francis Scatter, [London, 1574–9], with Augustine Ryther's engraved charts of the course of the armada illustrating Petruccio Ubaldini's *Discourse concerning the Spanish Fleet inuadinge Englande in the yeare 1588* [London: A. Hatfield and A. Rither, 1590].

British Library, Maps C.3.bb.5, item 2, plate 10.

This is James I's copy of Christopher Saxton's atlas, coupled with Augustine Ryther's engravings of the armada, copied from manuscript charts by Robert Adams. They constitute a magnificent image of Elizabeth's achievements, her arms on each map associating her with every county in England and Wales while the charts illustrate her successful and near-miraculous defence of her realm. This map shows parts of

Kent, France and Flanders, with the English defeating the Spanish fleet during the armada action of 1588.

On 29 July 1588 the English dispatched eight fireships to attack the Spanish fleet, which was at anchor off Gravelines under the command of the Duke of Medina Sidonia. While the fireships did not cause any significant damage to the Spanish fleet, they created panic and broke up the battle formation as ships sailed away in flight. The next day the English fleet fought the Spanish, making use of its lighter and better-armed ships. When ammunition had been used up and the wind had turned, the Spanish fleet escaped to the north-east but got trapped in the North Sea. The armada was forced to return to Spain by sailing around the north of Scotland and down the west coast of Ireland, but they lost many of the ships and thousands of men in the process. While this battle was decisive for the English, the war had not yet been won. KL-H.

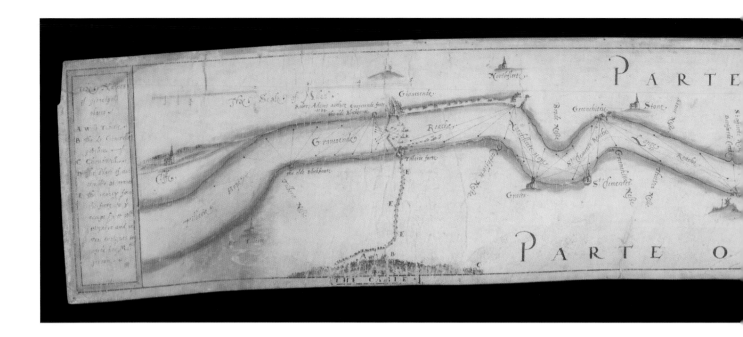

134

Defending London

Chart of the Thames estuary showing existing and proposed
defences on the Thames, Robert Adams, 1588.

British Library, Additional MS 44839.

This pictorial chart of the Thames estuary was drawn in
1588 by Robert Adams, Surveyor of the Queen's Works,
and shows the preparations undertaken to defend London
against the Spanish armada. Oriented to the south with
Kent marked uppermost and Essex below, the chart runs
from Westminster on the right to Tilbury Hope at the mouth
of the Thames on the left, passing Lambeth, Southwark,
Deptford, Limehouse, Greenwich, the Isle of Dogs,
Woolwich, Northfleet and Gravesend.

Lines radiating across the Thames indicate the position
and reach of cannon that could be fired from nine batteries
located between 'the olde Blockhouse' on Coalhouse Point
and Woolwich. Also shown are two defence booms (chains
of ship masts across the river), the first between Gravesend
and Tilbury and the second at Lee Ness, just before
Blackwall Reach. A force of about 25,000 men was gathered
at West Tilbury (marked as A) under the leadership of the
Earl of Leicester, whom Elizabeth had created Lieutenant
and Captain General of the Queen's Armies and Companies.
It was envisaged that these men would defend the realm by
engaging the Spaniards in battle should they attempt to sail
up the Thames and land.

For a while after the Battle of Gravelines (cat. 133), it
was feared that the Spanish armada might regroup and
attempt another invasion. On 8 August, therefore, Elizabeth
journeyed down the Thames to Tilbury Camp to join the
Earl of Leicester and review the assembled troops. Robert
Adams added a 'Pricked Line' to 'sheweth her Maiesties
progresse to the Campe'. AC.

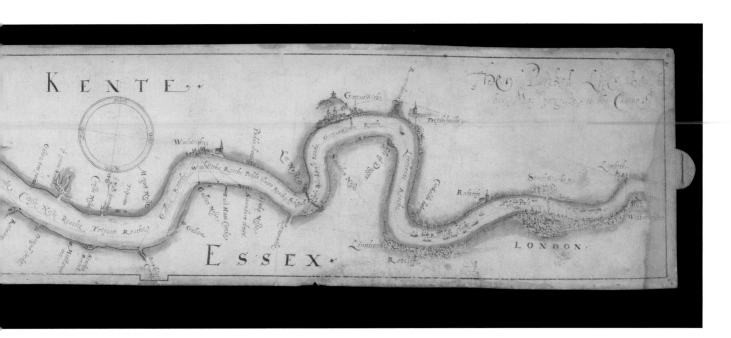

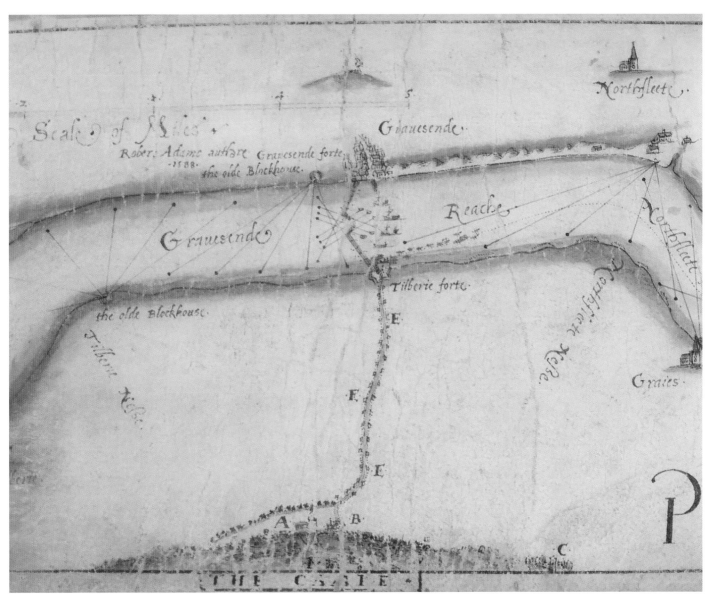

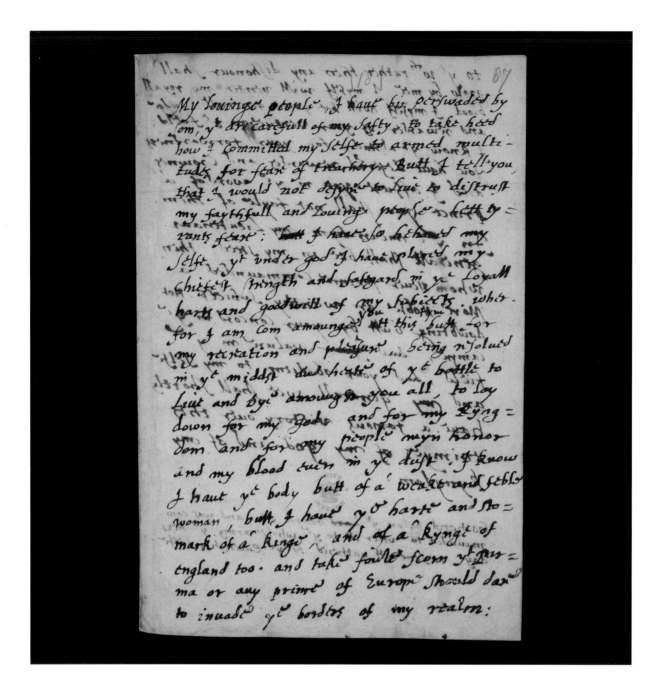

135

'Heart and Stomach of a King'

Elizabeth I's 'Tilbury Speech', undated.

British Library, Harley MS 6798, f. 87r.

This is a contemporary copy of Elizabeth's most famous speech, her address on 9 August 1588 to the troops mustered at Tilbury to defend England against a possible Spanish invasion. The manuscript is in the handwriting of Dr Leonell Sharpe, the Earl of Leicester's chaplain, who was in attendance when Elizabeth visited her army. He wrote down the speech so that it could be redelivered to the troops after her departure. A masterpiece of succinct rhetoric, it would have taken only about two and a half minutes to speak.

Elizabeth's address follows themes present in her other orations. First she emphasises the reciprocity of love between herself and her subjects: she has come before the 'armed multitudes' of men against the advice of her councillors because of her trust in her 'faythfull and loving people' and has placed her 'chefest strength and safegard' in her people's 'loyall harts and goodwill'. In return for their love, she is ready 'in ye middst and heate of ye battle to live and bye [dye] amoungst you all'. Second, Elizabeth deals with the issue of her gender by conflating her natural and political bodies: 'I know I have the body butt of a weak and feble woman butt I have the harte and stomack of a kinge and of a kynge of England too.' The heart was the source of courage, while the stomach was the organ for carrying out violent acts.

Elizabeth ends her short speech with the promise of 'a famous victory over thes enimyes of my god and of my kyngdom'. However, there was to be no future 'famous victory', for the armada had already been scattered and the invasion attempt forestalled. SD.

136

Elizabeth I

Unknown artist, late sixteenth century.

Private collection.

This imposing portrait from the late 1580s stresses Elizabeth's sovereignty. The thick, ermine-lined parliament robes in heavy crimson velvet create an exaggerated silhouette, subsuming the woman as an individual into an icon of queenship. The play between bejewelled femininity and regal authority is resonant of her famous rallying cry to her troops at Tilbury (cat. 135).

Shown with the literal symbols of her power, in the form of the crown and sceptre, this portrait draws on the iconography of the illuminations that decorated legal documents. It may have been commissioned for a civic space, in a similar manner to another portrait of Elizabeth in her parliament robes, which was commissioned by the Corporation of Dover for display in the Town Hall in 1598 (Dover Museum). CB.

Dennis Let 302.

ADD 16738   59

The Final Years
1589–1603

10

THE FINAL YEARS: ENGLAND, SCOTLAND AND THE SUCCESSION (1588–1603)

Paulina Kewes

Elizabeth's final years were fraught with anxiety about the future. The eternally youthful Gloriana of the official portraits was a far cry from the ageing and increasingly isolated monarch whose subjects pined, if not for change, at least for certainty about who would succeed her.

Mary's execution in 1587, and the following year's victory over the Spanish armada, have often been seen as a watershed. Yet that is not how these events were perceived at the time. Admittedly, the main Catholic pretender had been eliminated, and the gravest threat of invasion since the Norman Conquest had been repelled. But the issue of succession remained unresolved and fears persisted of conspiracy and regicide. The Catholic fifth column appeared to be growing in strength even as Puritan dissent intensified. Meanwhile, the war against Spain dragged on, and the outbreak of rebellion in Ireland in 1594 compounded the drain on men and resources. With English troops engaged in the Netherlands, in France, in Ireland and elsewhere, there was no guarantee that a second armada would not triumph.

This dangerous prospect was rendered all the more likely by the rapid deterioration of Anglo-Scottish relations. James VI considered himself to be the undisputed hereditary successor to England's crown and hoped that Elizabeth would officially recognise him as such. During the armada scare,

Queen Elizabeth I ('The Ditchley portrait').

Marcus Gheeraerts the younger, c.1592. National Portrait Gallery, London.

he had loyally stood by England despite feeling humiliated by Elizabeth's rejection of his plea that she should pardon his mother. But he was to be disappointed again, for the queen flatly refused to name James as her heir apparent. This was not because she opposed his candidacy. On the contrary, Elizabeth seemed to favour James and never put any real obstacles in his way. Nonetheless, she chose to withhold public confirmation of his title in order to manage and control his conduct and, just as significant, prevent her subjects from turning to the 'rising sun'.

The personal correspondence between the two monarchs at this time reveals their mutual distrust and mounting exasperation. James felt that his patience and recent good offices went unremarked and unrewarded. Elizabeth, for her part, was incensed by the Scottish king harbouring fugitive English Puritans. She was equally angered and alarmed by James countenancing the influx of Jesuits and secular priests into Scotland, and by his cordial relationship with hispanophile Catholic lords, such as the Earl of Huntly, who were engineering a Spanish-papal invasion of England via Scotland. The English suspected James of complicity, for he made but a half-hearted attempt to punish the lords and soon restored them to his favour. Elizabeth vented her ire in a sharp letter rebuking James as a 'seduced king'. He pointedly reversed the charge in a rude reply calling the woman he aspired to succeed a 'seduced queen'. By the start of 1594, as their relations reached a nadir, James was obsessed that he might lose out on England's crown.

Although the two reconciled later in the year, with Elizabeth agreeing to act as godmother to James's first-born son Prince Henry, the Scottish king had reason to be worried. His claim was far from unassailable; there were numerous other competitors; and many across the confessional divide found him unacceptable on various counts. The objections to the Stewart title which had been repeatedly raised against Mary applied with equal force to her son. First, James's foreign birth was alleged to preclude him from inheriting in common law; and second, according to Henry VIII's will, which had been authorised by statute, the descendants of his younger sister – the so-called Suffolk line – were assumed to have priority over the Stewarts, descended from Margaret, his elder sister (cat. 10).

James thus had to reckon with both English and foreign dynastic rivals. Key among them were Edward Seymour, Lord Beauchamp, of the Suffolk line, who, however, had been declared illegitimate in his infancy at Elizabeth's behest; James's cousin Arbella, the English Stuart from a cadet line who was rumoured to have the backing of Burghley; and the Infanta Isabella Clara Eugenia of Spain whose title harked back to the fourteenth century and whom radical hispanophile Catholics were beginning to promote as a propitious alternative to the heretical James. There was also Henry Hastings, Earl of Huntingdon, a distant descendant of Edward III who commanded considerable Puritan support on account of his religious fervour and uncompromising campaign against Catholics in the north.

THE PERSONAL CORRESPONDENCE BETWEEN THE TWO MONARCHS AT THIS TIME REVEALS THEIR MUTUAL DISTRUST AND MOUNTING EXASPERATION

Quite apart from what the law did or did not say about the rights of succession – and the situation was murky in the extreme – Elizabethans were guided in their preferences by their confessional loyalties and national sentiment. Militant Protestants who had clamoured for the exclusion and then trial and beheading of James's Catholic mother were unlikely to embrace James overnight once she was gone. For might he not seek to avenge her death? Or prove as treacherous as she had been? So, too, the staunchest of Mary's Catholic champions were loath to transfer their allegiance to the son who had betrayed both her and her faith. Even so, some Catholics, heartened by his lenient treatment of their co-religionists in Scotland, were beginning to hope that he might convert or at least grant them toleration. Meanwhile, middle-of-the-road Protestants eyed with dismay the mighty Scottish Kirk, while James's ambivalent stance towards it fuelled their misgivings that he might overturn the episcopacy and remake the English Church in the image of its Scottish counterpart. It also raised the broader question of whether in his heart of hearts James adhered to any faith at all or whether he was guided solely by self-interest.

RELIGION ASIDE, JAMES'S CANDIDACY was rendered acutely problematic by pervasive anti-Scottish prejudice, which memories of bloody wars between England and Scotland kept alive. Given England's historic claim of suzerainty over the northern kingdom, and abiding contempt for its supposedly uncouth, perfidious inhabitants, the English struggled to accept that they might be ruled by a Scot. They fretted that the union of the crowns would diminish the English nation's stature, and that on his arrival James's grasping countrymen would hold sway at court.

Moreover, despite the statutory ban on discussing the succession, a good deal of controversial material was finding its way into the public domain. And, initially, much of it appeared either ambivalent about or downright hostile towards the Scottish king. The first author to address the issue head-on after Mary's execution was the Puritan MP Peter Wentworth. In *A Pithy Exhortation to her Majesty for Establishing her Successor to the Crown* (*c.*1587), a tract circulating in manuscript, Wentworth urged the queen to let parliament determine the succession. Barely concealing his antipathy to the Stewart title, he envisaged that MPs would in essence elect the claimant whom they judged the most likely to protect the public good and the Protestant Church. In a brief sequel of 1591, allegedly written in prison at the behest of the privy council, Wentworth bluntly called for the Scottish king to plead his case in parliament alongside the other contenders.

Having failed to win the backing for his proposal of either Burghley or the rising royal favourite Robert Devereux, Earl of Essex, Wentworth tried to co-ordinate a wider campaign in favour of raising the succession in the parliament of 1593. But the queen would have none of that. As soon as the government got wind of Wentworth's plans, both he and his few associates were sent to the Tower. Their imprisonment created a public furore. It painfully underscored that, with Elizabeth nearing 60, the future of England's crown was as uncertain as ever.

Pro-Spanish Catholic polemicists hurried to exploit the Wentworth imbroglio. Ever since the armada defeat, they had used continental presses to attack the Elizabethan regime in a series of searing libels. Rife with increasingly derogatory comments about the Scottish king, their pamphlets now mockingly prophesied imminent catastrophe of the regime's own making. Without a clear successor, they argued, the English commonwealth would die with the queen. Cleverly mimicking both earlier Protestant polemic and Wentworth's recent missives, these 'Spanish Elizabethans' sought to foment unrest and division. Meanwhile, their leaders Cardinal William Allen and the Jesuit Robert Persons worked behind the scenes to coax Philip II of Spain into launching another assault on England.

Allen and Persons thought Philip might be amenable to the plan given that his attempt to profit from the French Wars of Religion lay in ruins. This tense conjuncture in British and continental affairs gave rise to the most incendiary and influential Elizabethan succession tract: *A Conference about the Next Succession to the Crown of England*, attributed to Persons. Written in 1593, printed in 1594 and published in

Robert Devereux, second Earl of Essex, Elizabeth's last favourite who in February 1601 led a rising on the streets of London, purportedly to defend James VI of Scotland's right to the succession.

Portrait from the studio of Marcus Gheeraerts the younger, 1596–1601. National Gallery of Art, Washington, Gift of Mrs Henry R. Rea.

autumn 1595, it masqueraded as the work of Robert Doleman. Replete with historical precedents and a fold-out genealogical tree, the tract purported to give an impartial review of the sundry dynastic claims. In reality, it sowed nothing but confusion. Persons declared the matter doubtful and the field still wide open, all the while subtly promoting the title of the Spanish infanta and discrediting that of King James. The honeyed dedication to the Earl of Essex, who was cast as kingmaker, exploited the growing rift between Essex and the Cecils. Could Persons have guessed that Essex had been secretly corresponding with the Scottish king?

Persons portrayed the English as hopelessly divided in both their politics and religion. Assuming the pose of scholarly detachment, he mounted a lethal attack on the hereditary principle and the pre-eminence of monarchy itself. *A Conference* provocatively upheld each individual's right to oppose the accession of a candidate of a contrary faith. Worse yet, it blithely justified resistance to kingly authority in the name of the common good. Surveying England's confessional landscape, Persons magnified the number and likely influence of the Catholics. He did so to prepare the ground for another Spanish invasion and, simultaneously, to intimidate James into granting concessions to English Catholics, perhaps even converting to the Roman faith.

Ironically, *A Conference* proved detrimental to Persons's cause. As well as riling both the English and the Scottish regimes, and causing ripples in Rome and Madrid, it induced people of various confessions at home to rally around James. Take Wentworth's sudden change of heart. Living out his days in prison, he wrote a passionate refutation of 'the Spanish-hearted papist'. In it, he abandoned his prior commitment to a parliamentary settlement of the crown and instead powerfully endorsed James's indefeasible hereditary right. Smuggled into Scotland, Wentworth's trio of tracts chronicling his conversion to the Jacobean succession were printed in 1598/9 with the tacit connivance of the king.

In addition to sponsoring this and other rejoinders to *A Conference*, James made a public bid for recognition as the right man to succeed Elizabeth. He issued two major works of political theory to advertise his princely wisdom and experience. *A True Law of Free Monarchies* (1598) contrasted hereditary kingdoms such as England and Scotland with elective ones. It argued that resistance was utterly illegitimate, and royal authority subject to the judgement of none but God; conversely, elected princes entered into a contractual relationship with their subjects, who could therefore call them to account. *Basilikon Doron* (1599) was a manual of kingship (cats 142, 143). It distilled James's understanding of royal duties for the benefit of his heir, Prince Henry, to whom it was addressed. Both *A True Law* and *Basilikon Doron* implicitly countered the subversive political theories of the Jesuit Persons and the Calvinist George Buchanan, James's one-time tutor. Neither, however, identified its target by name. Sophisticated appeals to the literate classes, the king's books were a potent reminder that his elevation would bring peace and dynastic stability to the British Isles.

By the turn of the century, James's chances seemed on the rise: Huntingdon had died in 1595; the 1596 armada had failed; and neither Philip III of Spain, who had succeeded his father Philip II in 1598, nor his sister the infanta and her consort Archduke Albert, both of them now joint rulers of the Spanish Netherlands, had any appetite for another invasion on the infanta's behalf. The lack of an agreed Catholic candidate, whether English or foreign, prevented continental powers from heeding Catholic exiles' recurrent appeals for action. Besides, Pope Clement VIII welcomed James's diplomatic overtures hinting that he might convert, and he would be unlikely to authorise any such attempt.

Faithful to her motto, *Semper eadem* (always the same), Elizabeth, now approaching 70, stubbornly refused to acknowledge James as her heir. The queen's intransigence rankled more than ever before. For, unnervingly, Essex, who had been the Scottish king's secret ally since 1589, fanned his suspicions that he had powerful enemies at the English court, notably Sir Walter Raleigh and the Cecils (cat. 137). According to Essex, they were poisoning the queen's mind against James, perhaps even hatching a pro-Spanish plot. They must be stopped at all costs. Indeed, among the aims of Essex's ill-fated rising in February 1601 was the summoning of parliament and proclamation of James's rightful title.

However patriotic or high-minded their motives, the rebels' plan to compel Elizabeth to settle the crown on James was an action that was understandably seen by the government as tantamount to resistance and forcible deposition. Comparisons

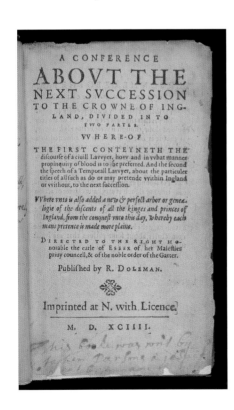

A Conference About the Next Succession to the Crowne of Ingland, Divided into Two Partes, attributed to the Jesuit Robert Persons under the pseudonym R. Doleman. The first part argued for elective monarchy, and the second part examined the titles of possible successors to Elizabeth I.

British Library, G.15425.

to the removal of Richard II by Henry IV abounded; the public was well schooled in the Machiavellian politics of regime change by a plethora of popular history plays, Shakespeare's *Richard II* chief among them. From the Wars of the Roses and French Wars of Religion to the Spanish takeover of Portugal in 1580, native and foreign dynastic crises were daily staged in London's commercial theatres and productions were also taken to the provinces. Contemporaries, however humble, knew to interpret their own predicament in this wider historical and transnational context, and it was no coincidence that the Essexians had commissioned a revival of a play about Richard II, perhaps Shakespeare's, on the eve of the earl's rising.

Essex's fall could have spelled disaster for James if the earl had not burnt the papers that would have surely incriminated the Scottish king and alienated Elizabeth. Fortunately for James, moreover, the Scottish envoys arriving in London shortly after Essex's execution managed to forge a close rapport with Sir Robert Cecil, now the most powerful figure at Elizabeth's court. Hitherto seen as hostile to James, Cecil now enthusiastically embraced his cause, no doubt to secure his own position under a new regime. He engaged in a technically treasonable correspondence with the Scottish king, albeit professing scrupulous loyalty to his royal mistress.

IN HIS LETTERS, CECIL counselled James to cease pressing Elizabeth for official recognition of his claim and by no means to court her subjects (cat. 138). Instead, the king should patiently await his turn, secure in the knowledge that Cecil and a handful of others would smooth his way to the throne, for 'a choice election of a few in the present, will be of more use than any general acclamation of many'. Cecil did his best to allay James's fears that the queen might decide to exclude him, soothing the king's sensibilities as one 'whom God hath instituted to sit (in his due time) in the chair of state'. James, for his part, never tired of rehearsing his royal credentials. 'My claim is both just and honourable', he told Cecil; 'God', he impressed on the Earl of Northumberland, 'hath by lineal descent cleede [clothed] me with an undoubted right to your crown'.

True to his word, Cecil discreetly worked to advance his prospective master's interests. Crucially, moreover, he lit on an inspired stratagem to bypass the official embargo on succession disputes without leaving so much as a trace. Cecil took advantage of a vicious quarrel between the Jesuits and secular priests (those not members of a religious order) that developed in 1598 over the pope's appointment of a supreme leader, an archpriest, over all English Catholic clergy. Cecil quietly assisted the secular priests and gave them surreptitious access to London presses. The beauty of this enterprise was that intra-Catholic divisions were being exposed to the world even as James's title received the much-needed oxygen of publicity, for the disputes between English Catholics also centred on the succession. In their pamphlets the secular priests tore into the Jesuits as traitorous subversives, vowed loyalty to the crown and warmly defended the Jacobean claim. Most Catholics, Cecil soon cheerfully reported to James, 'do declare their affection absolutely to your title, and some of them have learnedly written of the validity of the same'. Such public expressions of allegiance boosted the growing sense that the Protestant son of the 'Scottish Jezebel' would be

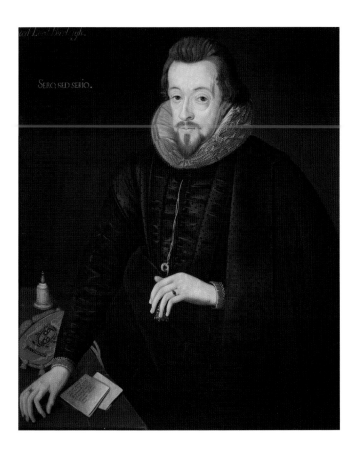

SERO SED SERIO.

Sir Robert Cecil, the younger son of Lord Burghley who became Principal Secretary in 1596. He entered into a secret correspondence with James VI in 1601 and managed his accession on Elizabeth I's death.

By or after John de Critz the elder, 1589.
Private collection.

accepted by all, save perhaps a few viperous Jesuits such as Persons.

When Elizabeth's final illness came, Cecil and his allies were ready. They promptly dispatched a draft proclamation of his accession for James's approval. Its text, enthused one of the king's Scottish intimates, 'is set of music that soundeth so sweetly in the ears of [the king] that he can alter no notes in so agreeable a harmony'. On 24 March 1603, within hours of the old queen's death, James VI of Scotland was duly proclaimed James I, King of England, France and Ireland, 'by Law, by Lineal succession, and undoubted Right'. Although by then there was no plausible alternative, his accession arguably violated both common law and statute. Indeed, as many realised, even the body of privy councillors, noblemen and other prominent figures whom Cecil had quickly assembled to issue the proclamation had no shred of constitutional validity.

We have been accustomed to thinking of the Jacobean succession, and more generally of the transition from the Tudors to the Stuarts, as natural and inevitable. It was anything but. Despite palpable relief that civil war had been averted, and that for the first time in over half a century the country had a royal family, doubts remained about why exactly this foreigner should be king. The outpouring of celebratory print supplied conflicting definitions of James's title: assertions of his hereditary right competed with reports of Elizabeth's deathbed nomination and intimations that he had been elected by the people.

In his pursuit of England's throne, James had raised countless mutually contradictory hopes and expectations, whether to do with religion or patronage or the relative standing of the English and the Scots, or foreign policy. Many of those were bound to be frustrated. The queen was dead but it would not be long before her idealised alter ego, Good Queen Bess, returned to haunt her successor.

Rolas Regna Iacobus.

QVÆ DEVS CONIVNXIT NEMO SEPARET

The Imperiall Lyne. of Great Britaine.

HONI · SOIT · QVI · MAL · Y · PENSE

JAMES King of great Britaine France and Ireland, the first of y.e Surname of Stewart that held dominion in England, became sole Monarche of both Kingdoms the 24 day of March 1602 as next & imediat heir to Henry y.e 7 and Elizabeth his Queene descended from their Lady Margaret their eldest daught maried to Iames y.e 4 K. of Scots whereby he descended on...

TO THE HIGH AND MIGHTY AND MOST RENOW
NED MONARCH IAMES BY Y.e GRACE OF GOD K
of great Britaine. France and Ireland. defender of the faith &c.

EPITAPHIVM HENRICI OCTAVI

Henricus princeps prope lustra peregerat octo,
Et populum magna prudens cum laude regebat,
Ex quo magnatos tractauit sceptra Britanni:
Cum Deus omnipotens morbo obrepente moneret
Hinc emigrandum de vita Proh dolor ingens!
Quot pia plebs lachrymis quam festibus ora rigauit?
Quam grauiter regem pretereat placuere cubantem?
Anglia tota iacet moerens lugubris & amens,
Nil opis apportant medici, nil profuit herba,
Qua solet humana membris asserere salutem:
Pharmaca nil profuit prebetur potio frustra:
Heu nulla tristis mors est medicabilis arte.

MOST Gracious Soueraigne seeing it hath pleased God in the person of your sacred Maiestie to vnite the two mightie Kingdomes of England & Scotland in ane entyre Monarchye...

EPITAPHIVM HENRICI SEPTIMI

Septimus hic situs est Henricus gloria regum
Cunctorum illius qui temperate fuerunt
Ingenio atq; clarus gestarum nomine rerum
Accellere silubus natura dona beniigna,
Frontis honos facies augusta, heroica forma
Iunstaq; et suauis coniunx perpulchra, pudica
Et secunda fuit foelices prole parentes,
Henricum quibus octauum terra Anglia debet.

Your Highnes
most loyall Subiect
THOMAS LYTE in all
humility consecratith this
BRITTANS MONAR-
CHIE

DAUGHTER OF EDWARD THE FOVRTH THE GOOD QVEENE ELIZABETH THE ELDEST

FRANCE LORD OF IRELAND N.o 1485 HENRY

Henry
the 7 & first of y.e surname of Tudir
began his raigne 22. of August 1485. he
was y.e son of Edmund E of Richmond y.e son of
Owen Tudir lineally descended from the Britishe
Kings & Princes of Wales & Margaret daughter & sole
heir to Iohn D of Somerset y.e son of Iohn E of Somerset
second son to Iohn of Gaunt, wherby y.e saide Henry for
want of succession in y.e right lyne from Hen: y.e 6 became
y.e aparent heir of y.e house of Lancaster who by that
royall match w. Elizabeth y.e eldest daughter of Edward y.e 4 conioyned y.e tow Princely Famelyes:
which from Richard y.e 2 had continued
in ciuell discention aboue 80 yeeres
during y.e seuerall raignes of 6
Kings.

NON · DORMIT · QVI · CVSTODIT
Emblema. Henrici Septimi.

HONI · SOIT · QVI · MAL · Y · PENSE

NEC · SPE · NEC · TIMERE
Symbolum Edwardi quinti.

The Saxons arriue out of Germanye in
the ayde of Hengest against the Britaynes

ETERNA QVÆ MVNDO

11   ANGLO-SCOTTISH UNION: THE NEW BRITAIN

Arthur Williamson

Anglo-Scottish union, and in many respects modern Britain, find their origins in the late 1540s. Under Edward Seymour, Duke of Somerset and Lord Protector for the child king Edward VI, the conflicting claims of English suzerainty and Scottish autonomy partially relaxed, and in their stead emerged a sense of Protestant solidarity, founded on an idea of a primordial British state that had embraced the entire archipelago.

In the autumn of 1547 England invaded Scotland, intending to enforce adherence to the Treaty of Greenwich (1543), whereby the young Mary, Queen of Scots and Prince Edward were betrothed. The Scots had agreed to it, ratified it in parliament, then thought better of it and backed off. England had invaded Scotland with some regularity over the centuries (often enough with Scotland reciprocating), but this occasion was very different, for the marriage was seen as realising a Protestant British order, at once altogether new and yet anchored in the ancient British past. In unprecedented language, the invasion was portrayed as a war for liberation, rather than conquest, whose outcome would underwrite wide-ranging reform in both countries. A surprising number of Scots and English at various points embraced the idea with visible enthusiasm.

The idealism and expectations of this moment can prove simply astonishing. As Somerset's Scottish advisor, the Edinburgh merchant James Henrisoun, put it: 'we shall do no less therefore than Romulus did at the first Inhabiting of Rome'. Both realms would arise on new foundations, for the religious reform achieved through the creation of Britain inherently entailed legal, economic and social reform. Henrisoun envisioned a commission of 'certain of the most godly & prudent men of both realms' that would restore the primitive Church of Christ. The commission, dominated by laymen, would then proceed to reform the law, to codify it and make it accessible – 'as was the civil law in [the] time of Justinian', language widely characteristic of the Edwardian reformers. Even so, Somerset was emphatic that Britain did not entail the imposition of English common law onto Scotland, and the status of specifically British law remained unclear.

Law reform served only as a prelude to a much further-reaching transformation. Henrisoun proposed that the Protector's government would sponsor the training of Scots in the latest techniques of mining, salt production and handicrafts, and for three years Dutch ships would be engaged to teach the Scots how to exploit their fisheries. Appropriate ports would be constructed, and there would even be a grand canal to link western resources to eastern markets. At the same time the aristocracy would become engaged in administration, while the peasantry obtained secure land tenures. Henrisoun is explicit and passionate that all classes of society would find themselves uplifted in the new era.

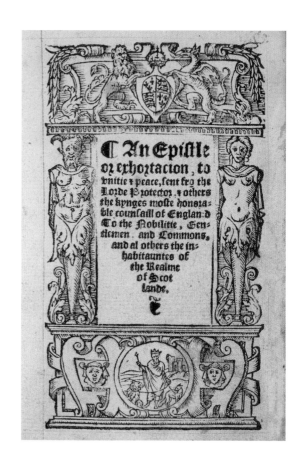

An 'Epistle' to the Scots, sent from Lord Protector Somerset in 1548 offering union with England.

An epistle or exhortacion, to unitie and peace, sent from the Lorde Protector, 1548.
British Library, G.5912.

Yet arguably the most radical dimension of the great reform lay in the supplanting of English and Scottish identities altogether by a shared sense of being British. Henrisoun went so far as to argue that a core British ethnicity survived the coming of both the Scots and the English. Scots and English, whatever their differences, were drawn together through a shared lineage that made the prospective Britain the realisation of their true selves. The Edward–Mary marriage remained essential, but the heart of the matter lay elsewhere, in profoundly political, popular, even civic engagement. Popular commitment became decisive rather more than dynastic authority, public sentiment more than juridical niceties. For as Henrisoun at one point put it: 'We seek no lands, but the hearts of men.' His phrase will have carried a freshness and energy in the sixteenth century that it no longer does in the twenty-first. The reform of the Church and the restructured society that emerged from it formed part of the prophesied historical redemption and occurred within an apocalyptic frame in what were perceived to be the 'latter days' of the world.

All sorts of English found themselves powerfully attracted to Somerset's British vision. John Cheke, the young king's tutor and a leading Edwardian intellectual, was visibly anguished that it might not be realised. John Mardeley, Edwardian poet and

Christopher Goodman and John Knox blowing their trumpets at the two queens.

Woodcut in *An Oration against the Vnlawfull Insurrections of the Protestantes of our Time, under pretence to Refourme Religion,* 1566.
British Library, C.37.d.47.

pamphleteer, warned Scots not to let themselves be absorbed into imperial France, ruled like the Rome of Tiberius and Augustus, and instead to choose the common realm of Israelite Britain, that redeemed Old Testament promise and fulfilled Judaic mission. But the most effective and enduring statement came from the Protector himself, in his 'Epistle' to the Scots of February 1548. With soaring rhetoric, the letter reached out: 'We offer love, we offer equalities & amity, we overcome in war and offer peace, we win [strong] holds and offer no conquest, we get in your land and offer England.' In terms at once pungent and compelling, the Protector laid out the contrast between French empire and British fellowship. Translated into Latin and German on the continent, the 'Epistle' became a template for much unionist literature, especially Scottish writing, well into the seventeenth century.

Of course Somerset's Britain did not emerge. Instead of liberating Scotland, English forces increasingly brutalised it; a great many Scots including Scottish Protestants remained resolutely unpersuaded and looked to France for security, while the Protector's government itself was overthrown in 1549, in part because of its social radicalism. Yet the idealism of the moment persisted throughout the Edwardian years. It is surely no accident that an English rendering of More's *Utopia* should appear in this time of high expectation.

Perhaps unexpectedly, something of the Somerset spirit greeted the opening of the Elizabethan regime, with John Knox's *First Blast of the Trumpet against the Monstrous Regiment of Women* (1558). The tract is far more than a (commonplace) critique of female governance; its central concern is Anglo-Scottish union. This question also informed the early policies of the revolutionary government in Edinburgh that had seized power in 1560 (with crucial English aid; see p. 33).

Nor was this simply a Scottish phenomenon. In 1562 an anonymous English author denounced at length the horrific persecution of the French Huguenots. His solidarity with the French Reformation extended to the Reformations in Germany, Switzerland, Denmark and 'far-off' Sweden, each of which had made a notable contribution to the great common cause. So too did the Scottish Reformation, but, unlike the others, it

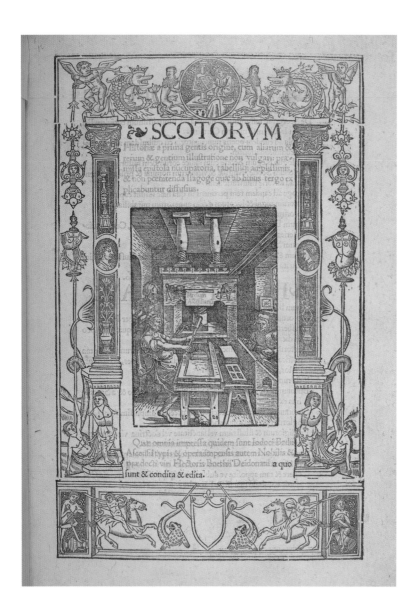

Scotorvm Historiae a Prima Gentis Origine by Hector Boece explored Scotland's past from its origin myth until the murder of James I in 1437.
Paris, 1526.
British Library, G.5674.

involved 'our own flesh and blood, knit to us afore by nature' and who were now joined by the gospel as well.

Broadly similar attitudes informed the English government at the highest levels. Throughout his career William Cecil had a British orientation (he had been, after all, a colleague of James Henrisoun), though it would be an outlook Queen Elizabeth did not share and never quite managed to acquire. A pattern emerged that characterised Elizabeth's England: the more reformist an individual, the more likely he would be to find himself sympathetic to Scotland and union; the more conservative, traditional, and suspicious of reform, the more likely it was that union held no appeal and might loom as a threat.

Irrespective of this deepening divide, other cultural factors worked in favour of union. Nothing furthered the Anglo-Scottish connection more deeply than the Bible in English, especially the Geneva Bible (1560). Scots and English might speak quite differently, but they read from the same page. This circumstance ensured that Scots and English did not evolve into separate and, potentially, mutually unintelligible languages, as they seemed likely to do in the 1530s. The entire trajectory of Anglo-Scottish relations shifted as a result.

To be sure, leading figures within the earlier Scottish Renaissance did not necessarily find a problem with Anglo-Scottish union. Even Hector Boece, whose *Scotorum Historiae a Prima Gentis Origine* (1527) firmly proclaimed Scottish autonomy to a European audience, nevertheless did express sympathy for political union among the 'Albionis'. John Mair actively urged Anglo-Scottish union in his *Historia Maioris Britanniae, tam Anglie quam Scotiae* (1521). Yet a genuinely Catholic British vision would not surface until the 1570s, when John Leslie, Bishop of Ross, fought for Mary Stewart's restoration to the Scottish crown and for her claim to the English one as well. Legitimist and traditional, Leslie came late to the idea, writing when the British vocabulary had long established itself as carrying a reforming agenda. Worse still, leading Counter-Reformers from England, such as the Jesuit Robert Persons, utterly foreclosed union as they struggled to subvert James VI's succession (see pp. 252–3). In the end Britain emerged a Protestant idea.

We do encounter a notable exception with one of the great minds of the sixteenth century, George Buchanan. The Calvinist Buchanan wholeheartedly supported a close amity with England, one that might even extend to France. Yet we never encounter him endorsing political union. His vehement anti-imperialism as well as his republican sensibilities made such a meta-state unpalatable. Yet he did contribute to the British project in one way: in Book II of his *Rerum Scoticarum Historia* (1582), Buchanan developed a remarkably precocious historical linguistics that identified and connected the various tongues that formed the Celtic language grouping. Their linguistic unity and coherence appeared to underwrite a unified and coherent British past. Thereby Buchanan seemed to validate not only familiar British and Scottish narratives but, crucially, a once and future Britain.

A SPECIES OF PRACTICAL unionism occurred during the great push for Church reform in 1584. This was a pan-British struggle: the reforming elites of both kingdoms saw themselves participating in a common cause, and activists could become engaged in either country. The funeral in London late that year for the Scottish minister James Lawson brought forth a huge and striking physical statement of Anglo-Scottish solidarity. If in the end reform eventually succeeded in Scotland and not in England, the enduring sense of shared purpose and common objectives remains unmistakable. The Scottish intellectual David Hume of Godscroft would write poetry celebrating and thanking the English Secretary Sir Francis Walsingham that spoke to a deep connection.

The end of the 1580s and the early 1590s saw a growing number of apocalyptic writings that projected an increasingly articulated prophetic future – a development in which James VI directly participated. Almost without exception, that future proved British and unionist. At moments, however, such unionist projections could trigger serious tensions, as happened at the baptism of James's son and heir, Prince Henry, in 1594. For this occasion the preacher, professor and poet Andrew Melville provided poetry (the *Principis Scoti-Britannorum Natalia*; 'On the birth of the Scoto-Britannic Prince') with specific apocalyptic themes: not only would King James create a 'Scoto-Britannic commonwealth', but Prince Henry would subsequently also lead its 'Scoto-Britannic Champions' and the Protestant world in a climactic struggle against 'the legions of Antichrist'. For Melville and other reformers the Roman Church in league with imperial Spain – both committed to a messianic drive for universal empire – were simply a continuation of the Roman Empire. 'Spanish Rome' continued its grasping spirit, its conquering oppression and its deep corruption, all inspired by false faith. The emerging 'Scoto-Britannic' kingdom would now confront this expanding global empire in a cosmic struggle for liberation that would determine the destiny of mankind, the prophetic culmination of human experience.

Melville's verses would see publication in Edinburgh in 1594. Yet they were more than a statement for local consumption. For, centrally important, Melville's colleague at St Andrews, the legal scholar William Welwod, also secured their publication in the Hague in the same year. The *Natalia* and its claims thereby became a statement to Europe, announcing Scottish and British purpose.

Much in Melville's language would unsettle English sensibilities. The phrase 'Scoto-Britannic commonwealth' rather than 'Britain' unequivocally affirmed Anglo-Scottish parity. Worse still, the poem totally sidelined Elizabeth and implied that the world would become a better place after her departure. The English ambassador, Robert Bowes, found this unacceptable and lodged a complaint, and King James characteristically ran for cover.

Bowes's complaint forms part of a deepening reaction in the 1590s against both reform and the Scots. Conservatives in England found their voice, their theology and their poets during the decade. We now encounter the stage Scot, often associated with the stage Jew. Far more than that, King James and his queen became increasingly conservative through the course of the decade. James of course continued to seek passionately, even desperately the succession to the southern crown. But if he sought Anglo-Scottish union, he had also acquired a visceral distaste for reform. In its place, he proclaimed in his signature works – the *Daemonologie* (1597), *The True Law of Free Monarchies* (1598) and most prominently the *Basilikon Doron* (1599) – the natural, scriptural and legal foundations of headship and hierarchy as principles suffusing the structure of the cosmos (cat. 143).

At the end of Elizabeth's reign two competing projections of the prospective Britain had emerged. One was King James's monarchical incorporation of both realms, focused on the person of the king and hierarchical authority. Against it appeared Hume of Godscroft's *De Unione Insulae Britannicae* (1605) which marks the culmination of the British reform movement and is clearly a riposte to the *Basilikon Doron* and the unionism it prescribed. The *De Unione* breathes the spirit of the Somerset project and, in some respects, forms its culmination as well. Where James's union looked to the dynastic, Hume's looked to the civic. Where James's outlook remained

JAMES CONTINUED TO SEEK PASSIONATELY THE SUCCESSION TO THE SOUTHERN CROWN, BUT IF HE SOUGHT ANGLO-SCOTTISH UNION, HE HAD ALSO ACQUIRED A VISCERAL DISTASTE FOR REFORM

fundamentally (and vigorously) traditional, Hume's involved high levels of participation and, like the Edwardians, was preoccupied with 'the hearts of men'. To an astonishing extent, prospective Britons themselves would create the new Britain.

Hume's commitment to participation and to civic life as the highest form of human association suffuses the entire work. Anyone could contribute to the public good. After all, Hume directly asks, what else was he doing – as a private citizen with no authority whatever – in writing his treatise? This outlook looms dramatically with his discussion of Church reform, the largest chapter and integral to the society he hoped to create. Hume firmly believed that most English and Scots wanted reform and that a British Presbyterian Church would prove congenial to both realms. Consistent with the Edwardians and the reform movement, Hume's new Britain promised to play a signal role in the overthrow of the papal Antichrist. Yet Hume did differ from at least some of the Edwardians in one significant way: he did not envision Henrisoun's industrial programme, and he is visibly uncomfortable with mercantile issues and economic vocabularies. Here emerged what would become an enduring tension within the reform movement and, eventually, the Atlantic republican tradition.

Elizabeth's reign ended with various forms of Anglo-Scottish union proposed. Never again would the erasure of Englishness and Scottishness prove more unblinking, and reconstruction of British identity be more boldly imagined. The end of England, the end of Scotland – before a liberated and liberating Britain.

Towards Accession

After the execution of his mother, James VI was
determined to be acknowledged as Elizabeth I's legitimate
heir. Seeking allies at the English court, he turned to
the Earl of Leicester's stepson, the second Earl of Essex,
who had become a war hero and favourite of the queen.
However, Essex fell into disgrace in 1598 and was
executed in 1601 after trying to raise London against his
enemies at court. Needing another influential friend at the
English court, James approached Sir Robert Cecil, who
was the queen's Principal Secretary and a dominant figure
on the privy council. A secret correspondence opened
between them during the first half of 1601; although they
occasionally wrote directly to each other, most of their
communications were carried out through intermediaries.

Elizabeth died after a short illness in the early hours
of 24 March 1603 at Richmond Palace, and James
was immediately proclaimed king. Unlike her father
and grandfather, Elizabeth left no directions about her
burial place. Cecil, who took over the arrangements,
fixed the date of 28 April (the Thursday after Easter)
for the funeral and the site of Westminster Abbey for
her tomb. Two months later, James was crowned in the
Abbey. He inherited a realm exhausted from war, not
only the fighting on the continent against Spain, but also
in Ireland, where Hugh O'Neill, Earl of Tyrone, had
launched a major rebellion in 1594. The Irish war came
to an end just days before Elizabeth's death, and James
signed a peace treaty with Spain in August 1604.

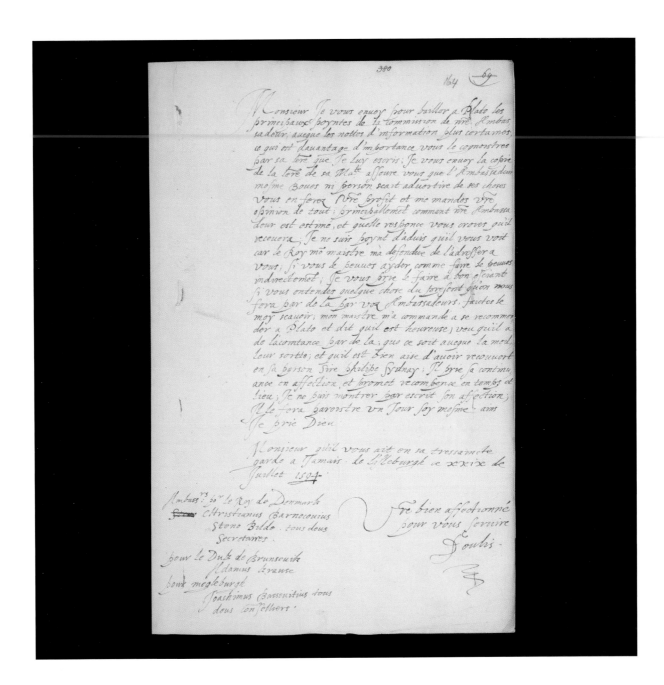

137

James VI and Robert Devereux, Second Earl of Essex

Letter from David Foulis to Anthony Bacon,
29 July 1594, Edinburgh.

British Library, Additional MS 4125, f. 164r.

In 1592 Anthony Bacon became secretary to Elizabeth I's last favourite, Robert Devereux, second Earl of Essex, and was soon managing his foreign correspondence with contacts across Europe, the Scotsman David Foulis among them. Between 1594 and 1602 Foulis was sent as envoy to Elizabeth, principally to receive payment of James VI's English pension. In March 1594 James entered into 'a mutual understanding' with Essex through the correspondence of Foulis and Bacon. James and Essex communicated indirectly and secretly, exchanging news and opening up the subject of the English succession. In this correspondence, which was in French, Foulis and Bacon referred to James as Tacitus or 10 and Essex as Plato or 28.

In April the king sent two envoys to Elizabeth to protest that she was harbouring Francis Stewart, Earl of Bothwell, who had been forced into exile because of his disloyalty, disruptive conduct and alleged witchcraft. In this letter of 29 July Foulis asked Bacon how the Scottish envoys had been received at court, before saying that James had likened Essex to Sir Philip Sidney, the hero of the international Protestant cause, who had died from a battle wound in 1586. James promised he would remember all that Essex had done in supporting his succession, although this could only be expressed in indirect terms, as 'he prays to remain in [Essex's] affection, and promises reward in due time'. James needed an English champion who would advocate his cause in the face of what he perceived as hostility from the queen, William Cecil, Lord Burghley, and his son, Sir Robert Cecil. Keen to safeguard his place in national politics after Elizabeth's death, Essex was ready to take on this role. AB.

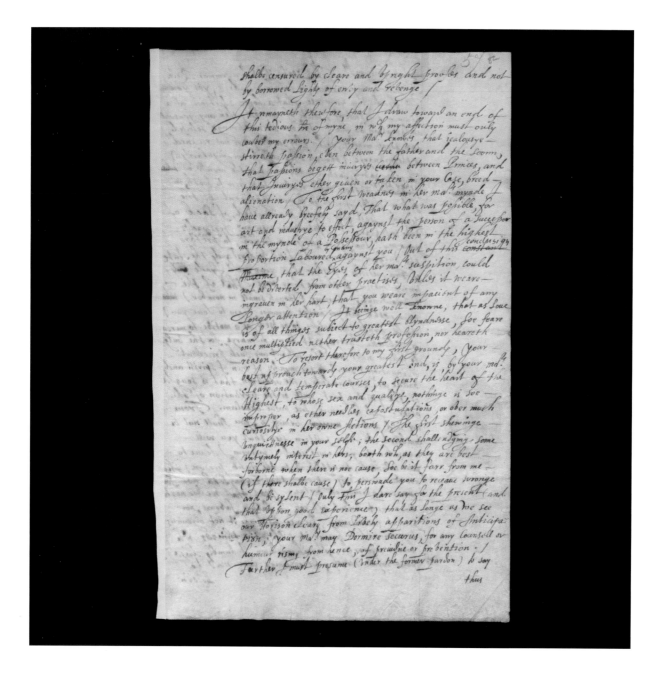

138

Secret Correspondence between James VI and Sir Robert Cecil
Letter from Sir Robert Cecil ('10') to James VI of Scotland ('30'),
March 1601.

By kind permission of the Most Hon. the Marquess of Salisbury,
Hatfield House, Cecil Papers 135/55.

This is the first letter in Cecil's secret correspondence with the Scottish king. Cecil wants to make it plain that writing to the king of a foreign nation should not be construed as an act of disloyalty to his own mistress. His first duty was still to Elizabeth I 'whoese creature I am' and 'insidious spirittes' had no reason to suspect that he 'would varrye from the former compass of a sole dependencye, by which I have only steered my courses'. Cecil then went on to deny that he had favoured the Spanish infanta's claim to the succession over that of James VI, an accusation that had been made by the Earl of Essex. On the contrary, Cecil had an 'affectionate care to your maiesties future happines, whom God hath instituted to sitt (in his dew tyme) in the chayre of state'. For this reason, he gave the king the following advice.

Because of Elizabeth's suspicion of James, Cecil wrote, 'your best approach towardes your greatest end, is by your maiesties cleare and temperate courses, to secure the heart of the Highest, to whose sex and qualitye, nothinge is soe improper, as ether needles expostulations, or over much curiositye in her owne actions'. In other words, James should stop antagonising the queen and pressing her to declare his title. Additionally, he should not busy himself with securing popular support since 'a choyce election of a feaw in the present, wilbe of more vse then any generall acclamation of many'.

It was good advice, and James followed it. Consequently, his relations with Elizabeth generally improved, and her privy council arranged for him to be proclaimed king of England during Elizabeth's last illness. SD.

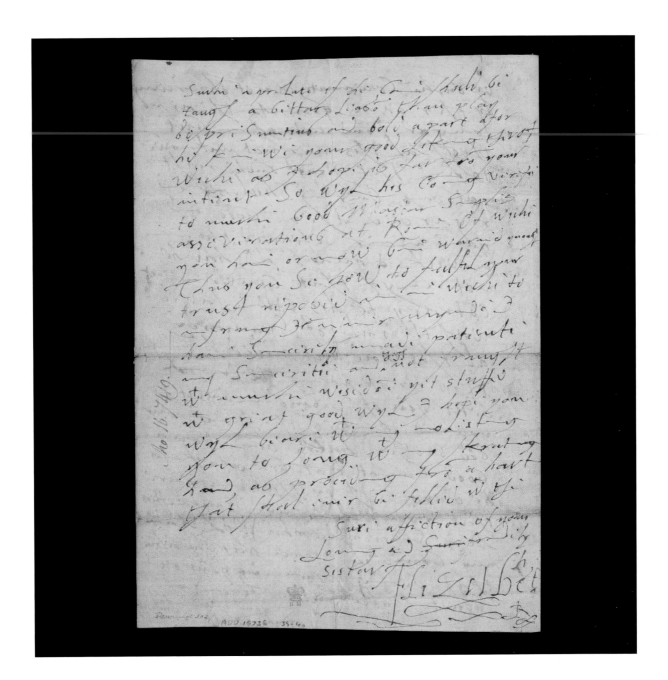

139

Elizabeth I's Last Letter

Letter from Elizabeth I to James VI, 5 January 1603.

British Library, Additional MS 18738, f. 40v.

Elizabeth's letter to James is difficult to read, so it is no wonder that she apologised for her 'skrating hand'. Painful rheumatism in her right arm and fingers made letter-writing difficult as she grew older, but she did not use a secretary in her letters to James VI because it was a sign of esteem and friendship to send a holograph.

Elizabeth's communication begins and ends in a friendly tone. She starts by expressing her pleasure that James understands and takes well her 'true intents'; and she ends with the sentence: 'I hope you wyl beare with my molesting you to long, with my skrating hand, as proceding from a hart, that shoud ever be filled, with the sure affection of your lovinge and frendely sistar.'

The main part of the letter, however, expresses her concern at James's continuing peaceful relations with her enemy the King of Spain and at the possibility that he might 'neglect soe muche yower owne honor to the world, (thogh you had no peculiar Love to me) as to permit his Embassador in your Land'. Elizabeth justifies her conduct towards Spain and military intervention in the Netherlands on behalf of the Dutch rebels and derides Philip for the plots against her: 'Disserved I suche a recompence, as many a Complot, both for my Life and Kingdome?' As she explains, she had not aimed at taking over the Netherlands but on the contrary had turned down the provinces' offer of sovereignty.

Shortly after this letter was sent, the 69-year-old queen fell ill. Sir Robert Cecil and others at her bedside maintained she signified that James was her heir shortly before her death, but this assertion is doubtful. SD.

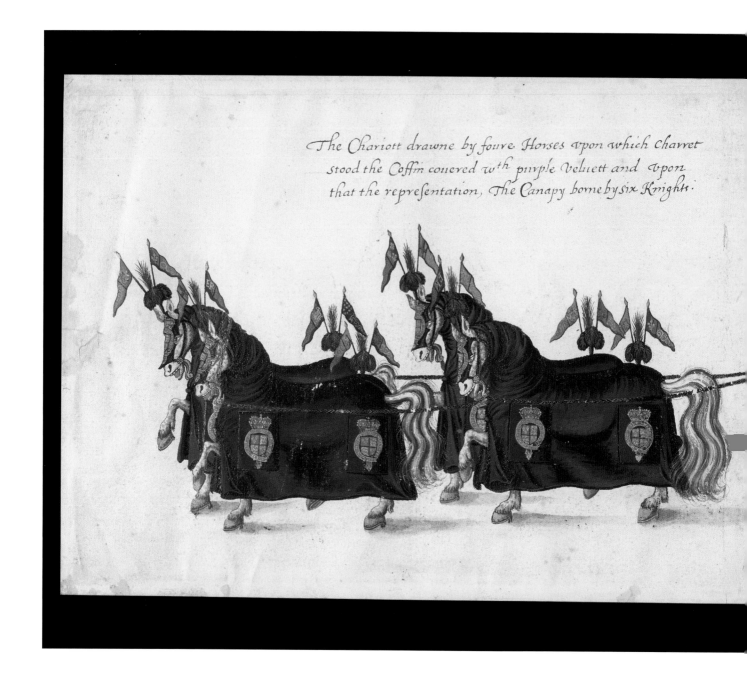

The Chariott drawne by foure Horses vpon which charret stood the Coffin couered wᵗʰ purple Veluett and vpon that the repreſentation, The Canapy borne by six Knights.

140

Elizabeth I's Funeral

The funeral procession of Queen Elizabeth to Westminster Abbey, early seventeenth century.

British Library, Additional MS 35324, f. 37v.

This is one of two drawings of Elizabeth's funeral procession, which made its way from Whitehall Palace, where the queen's body was lying in state, to the Abbey, where she would be buried. Both manuscripts are the first pictorial records of the funeral procession of an English sovereign. Originally a roll, the drawing has been cut into sections and inlaid into paper.

More than 3,000 mourners walking in rows of four or five took part, and there were said to have been some 200,000 spectators lining the route. The centrepiece of the procession was the coffin placed in an open chariot, which was drawn along by four horses draped in black velvet emblazoned with the arms of England and Ireland. The coffin was covered with purple velvet and on its top lay a full-size effigy of the crowned queen, dressed in her golden parliamentary robes and a cloak of red velvet and ermine, and holding an orb and sceptre. Her face, painted from a death mask, was described as lifelike. Six noblemen held aloft the fringed black velvet canopy over the chariot, while twelve barons carrying bannerols (banners about a yard square) walked on each side.

As was customary, the new monarch did not attend the funeral of his predecessor. At the time, James VI and I was still making his way down slowly from Scotland and did not arrive in London until 7 May. SD.

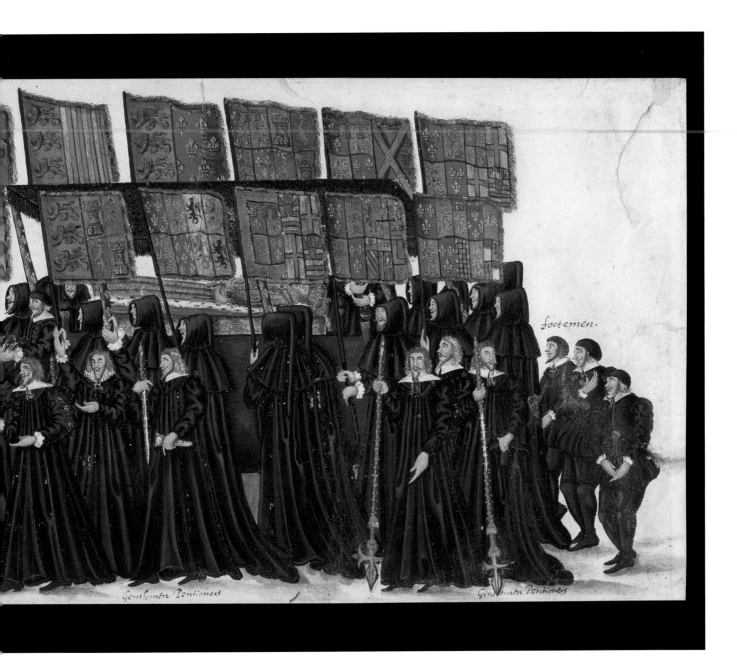

footemen.

Gentlemen Pentioners

Gentlemen Pentioners

141

Peace and Plenty

Gold medal of James I, 1604.

British Museum, London, 1844,0425.24.

One of James's first acts as King of England and Ireland was to negotiate a peace treaty with Spain. The treaty, signed in London in August 1604, put an end to the Anglo-Spanish War. Although it freed the country from the expense of conflict, the treaty was deeply unpopular in England. With this medal James intended both to celebrate the new peace and to allay any fears.

On the front James is shown wearing the type of broad-rimmed plumed hat that appears in miniatures, but here with the rather odd addition of a crown to emphasise his royal status. The legend describes him as King of England,

Scotland, France and Ireland. On the back, image and text amplify each other: a figure of Peace, holding a palm branch and cornucopia, faces Religion, who has a lit beacon and a cross, while the encircling Latin inscription translates as 'From here [flow] peace, plenty and pure religion'.

Although the medal marks a definite shift in foreign policy, the means by which this message is proclaimed closely follow Elizabethan precedent. Medals had long been made to be held in the hand, but the loop indicates that this medal, like some of those of Elizabeth, was intended for wearing in the manner of a miniature. The three-quarter face portrait had also been favoured by the queen, notably in a medal attributed to the miniaturist Nicholas Hilliard. This patronage also continued. In December 1604 Hilliard was paid for twelve gold medals – most likely this peace medal. PA.

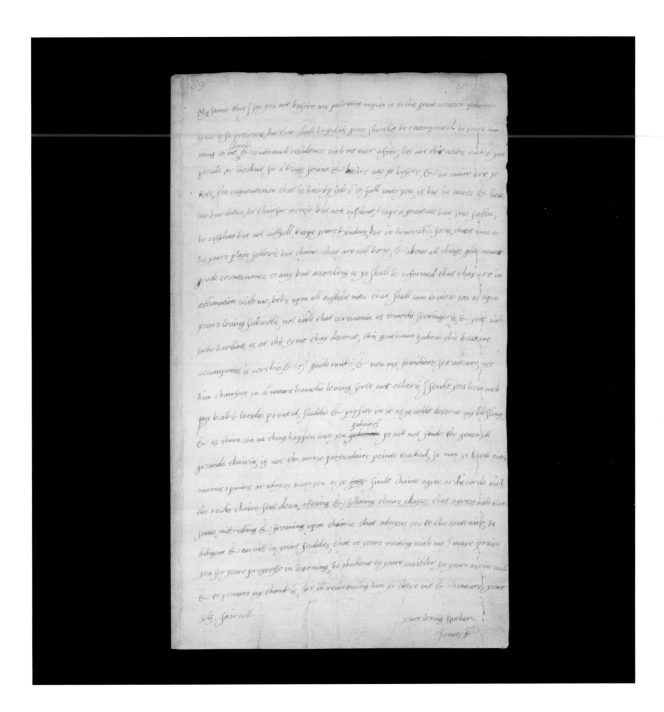

142

Advice from Father to Son

Letter from James VI and I to Prince Henry, April 1603.

British Library, Harley MS 6986, f. 65r.

When James was proclaimed King of England and Ireland, his 9-year-old son and heir Henry was residing in Stirling Castle under the guardianship of the Earl of Mar and his elderly mother. Prince Henry had been placed there – as was customary for Scottish heirs to the throne – when he was a baby and despite the opposition of his mother, Queen Anna. Here James is saying farewell to his son before departing for England, and he explains that it would not be long before 'by Goddis grace' Henry would be in 'continuall residence with me ever after'. As was his wont, James also offered his son advice: 'lett not this newis make you proude or insolent, for a Kings sonne and heire was ye before, and na maire are ye yett'. His new inheritance, warned James, would bring but 'heavie burthens; be thairfor merrie, but not insolent; keepe a greatnes, but *sine fastu* [without ambition]; be resolute, but not willfull; keepe youre kyndnes, but in honorable sorte; choose nane to be youre playe fellowis but thaime that are well borne'. James had given Henry similar counsel in his book *Basilikon Doron* (1599), and now he sent a newly printed copy of the book and urged him to 'studdie and profite in it as ye wolde deserve my blessing, and as thaire can na thing happen unto you quhairof ye will not finde the generall grounde thairin'. James ended the letter with the hope that at their next meeting, he might praise Henry for his 'progresse in learning'. SD.

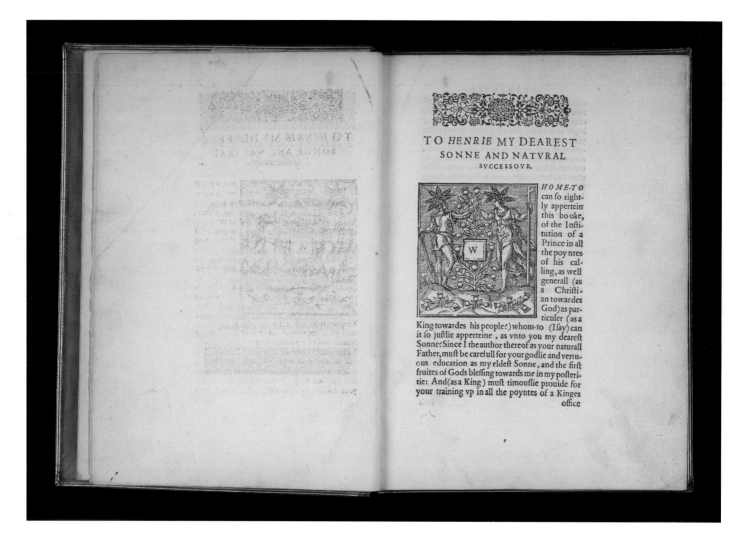

TO *HENRIE* MY DEAREST
SONNE AND NATVRAL
SVCCESSOVR.

HOME-TO can so rightly apperteín this booke, of the Institution of a Prince in all the poyntes of his calling, as well generall (as a Christian towardes God) as particuler (as a King towardes his people?) whom-to (I say) can it so justlie apperteine, as vnto you my dearest Sonne? Since I the author thereof as your naturall Father, must be carefull for your godlie and vertuous education as my eldest Sonne, and the first fruites of Gods blessing towards me in my posteritie: And (as a King) must timouslie prouide for your training vp in all the poyntes of a Kinges office

143

Basilikon Doron

(above) James VI. *Basilikon Doron. Devided into three books,* Edinburgh, printed by Robert Waldegraue printer to the kings maiestie, 1599.

British Library, G.4993., sig. [A]3v–[A]4r.

(opposite) James VI's autograph manuscript, *c.*1598.

British Library, Royal MS 18 B xv, lower cover.

James's large literary output was unusual for a king. He regularly retreated to his study to write, an occupation which for him was integral to being an effective ruler. He was a patron of poets but also a poet himself, and he laid down the rules for Scottish poetry in his *Reulis and Cautelis to be Observit and Eschewit in Scottish Poesie* (1584).

James wrote two books on the nature of kingship. In 1598 he published *The Trew Lawe of Free Monarchies*, in which he reflected on his kingship in Scotland in a European context. This was followed in 1599 by the publication of the *Basilikon Doron* (The King's Gift), a letter to his young son, Henry. Drawing on his own experience as king of Scotland, it offered advice on how to be an effective ruler, including very practical guidance, such as on the choice of his marriage partner or the need for a king to keep fit.

The text is divided into three sections which discuss a monarch's duty to God, his duties of office and advice on his daily conduct. *Basilikon Doron* upholds the theory of the divine right of kings – the idea that a monarch's authority to rule comes directly from God and that the monarch is not subject to any earthly authority. It also warns Henry against the threat of both Catholics and Puritans, and while James advocated peace, he also advised his son to be prepared for unavoidable wars. *Basilikon Doron* emphasises the importance of union and the dangers of the division of a kingdom. From the moment of his accession James intended to bring about a political union of Scotland, England and Ireland by statute. However, he had to admit defeat in 1607 in the face of parliamentary opposition in England.

The binding of purple velvet with the royal initials and the Scottish lion and thistles in gold, illustrated on the right, covers James's own working manuscript of the *Basilikon Doron*, which contains evidence of his writing process such as erasures and insertions. The book was first printed in Edinburgh in 1599 in only seven copies, of which the above is one. A second edition was published in London in 1603 immediately after Elizabeth's death and James's accession to the English and Irish thrones as King James I. While the 1599 edition had been deliberately private, the 1603 edition was equally intentionally public. It was the *Basilikon Doron* to which James himself is said to have referred to more frequently than to any of his other works. KL-H.

144

Sic Transit ...

Tomb effigy of Elizabeth I by Maximilian Colt, 1605–7.

Westminster Abbey, Henry VII Chapel.

When James VI of Scotland ascended the English throne in 1603 he was faced with the problem of legitimising his accession as a Scottish Stewart, whilst also commemorating the status and achievements of his immediate predecessors on that throne, and above all the glorious Elizabeth. Although both bloodlines flowed through his own royal veins, this was a moment of dynastic change: 'Tudor' to 'Stuart'. Mary's descendants changed the Scottish spelling of their name to follow her French spelling of it, and she spelled her name thus because she was brought up in France and French does not use the letter 'w'. The construction of

tombs for Elizabeth and Mary was one of the ways James attempted to unify the two kingdoms.

Elizabeth's tomb was the work of the stonemason Maximilian Colt, who had come to England from the Netherlands in the 1590s; in 1608 he was made master carver to the king. He did other work for the Cecils, including the double-effigy monument at Hatfield House for the Earl of Salisbury, who as Lord Privy Seal had authorised payments and overseen the building of Elizabeth's monument in the Abbey. Elizabeth's effigy is thought to be copied not from existing portraits but from the effigy used on the hearse that carried her to the Abbey; as the Venetian ambassador remarked at the time, Elizabeth's coffin lay under a catafalque with the queen's carved and painted wooden effigy resting on it. MB.

145

Mary as Martyr?

Tomb effigy of Mary, Queen of Scots by Cornelius Cure, 1612.

Westminster Abbey, Henry VII Chapel.

In August 1603, only weeks after his coronation, King James ordered a pall of rich velvet to be placed, with due ceremony, on the tomb of his mother in Peterborough Cathedral, where her beheaded corpse had lain since her execution at nearby Fotheringhay nearly seventeen years earlier. In 1612 her remains were disinterred and transported from Peterborough, under the same velvet pall, for reburial in the magnificent tomb James had commissioned in Westminster Abbey.

This is the work of Cornelius Cure, whose father had been brought from Holland by Henry VIII to work on Nonsuch Palace: Cornelius became royal master mason in 1596. The placing of recumbent effigies under pillared canopies, forming a quasi-classical triumphal arch, was a way of symbolising the soul's triumph over death. Mary's monument is substantially larger than Elizabeth's, with Mary's copying relatively recent portraits of her as a mature woman, whilst Elizabeth's effigy removes the 'mask of youth' fiction that controlled her image in later life to show her, finally, as the elderly woman she actually was. Cure's death in 1608 caused a delay in completing Mary's monument and his son William, who took over the project, completed his work in 1612. MB.

THEY USED
EVERY PASSION IN THEIR INCREDIBLE DUEL
...AND EVERY MAN IN THEIR SAVAGE GAMES OF INTRIGUE!

When in Southern California visit Universal Studios

MARY,
QUEEN OF SCOTS
who ruled with the
heart of a woman!

ELIZABETH, QUEEN
OF ENGLAND,
who reigned with the
power of a man!

A
Hal Wallis
Production

Vanessa Redgrave · Glenda Jackson

Patrick McGoohan · Timothy Dalton · Nigel Davenport
in

Mary, Queen of Scots

Trevor
Co-starring Howard · Daniel Massey · Ian Holm

Music Composed and Conducted by JOHN BARRY · Original Screenplay by JOHN HALE · Directed by CHARLES JARROTT
Produced by HAL B. WALLIS · A UNIVERSAL RELEASE · TECHNICOLOR® · PANAVISION® **GP** PARENTAL GUIDANCE SUGGESTED All Ages Admitted ORIGINAL SOUNDTRACK ALBUM NOW AVAILABLE EXCLUSIVELY ON DECCA RECORDS

12

ELIZABETH I AND MARY, QUEEN OF SCOTS: AFTERLIVES IN FILM

Thomas S. Freeman

The monarchs of early modern Europe may have impressed their contemporaries and preoccupied their subjects, but few of them, even the mightiest, are popularly remembered today. Elizabeth I and her cousin Mary are conspicuous exceptions to this. For centuries the two queens have been major figures in popular culture, with novels, plays, paintings and even an opera retelling their fates.

They have also been prominent figures in film, the most accessible and popular of the arts. Although films are, of course, a product of the twentieth century, those dealing with the relationship between the two queens preserved, and were shaped by, a conception of them which went back to Mary's nemesis John Knox, and also to William Camden, the great early modern historian of Elizabeth's reign (cats 44, 70). In this view, fostered by the patriarchal gender stereotypes that flourished from the sixteenth into the twentieth century, Elizabeth and Mary were linked together not merely as enemies or rivals but as archetypes of 'masculine' and 'feminine' virtues and vices.

A particular combination of circumstances led to the first major film about Mary and Elizabeth, *Mary of Scotland*, in 1936. The first was the astonishing success of *The Private Life of Henry VIII* – the first international

Poster for the 1971 film *Mary, Queen of Scots* starring Vanessa Redgrave as Mary and Glenda Jackson as Elizabeth.

hit produced by the British film industry – in 1933, which initiated a brief flood of films about historical monarchs. At the same time, the increasing censorship in the film industry from the early 1930s onwards, embodied in the United States by the Hays Code, made it more difficult to produce or distribute films in the US which depicted contemporary 'loose women' such as prostitutes, con artists and gun molls. But filmmakers had a somewhat freer hand in historical films and could entice audiences with films about sensational women in the past. And so MGM produced *Queen Christina* (with Greta Garbo as the seventeenth-century Swedish monarch) in 1933 and Paramount produced *The Scarlet Empress* (with Marlene Dietrich as Catherine the Great) in 1934, while British studios released *Nell Gwynn* and *The Rise of Catherine the Great* in the same year. In this climate, it made sense to make a film about Mary, Queen of Scots, especially since Maxwell Anderson had written a play, *Mary of Scotland*, in 1933, which had been a hit on Broadway and provided pre-sold material for a film.

Anderson's play had continued traditional stereotypes about the two queens by contrasting a Mary who epitomised feminine virtue with a cold, hard and Machiavellian Elizabeth. The film exaggerated Anderson's already polarised portrayal of the two monarchs. In the film, as in the play, neither Mary nor Bothwell has any involvement in Darnley's murder. In the film, Bothwell does not abduct Mary; rather, they share a romantic idyll at his castle. (Anderson's play did not deal with the issue of the abduction at all.) Not only Mary's innocence is emphasised, but her gender as well: she is portrayed in the film as being unable to rule without male guidance, particularly that of Bothwell. And the film insistently hammers home the message that Mary is the happier and more successful of the two figures because she has embraced her identity as a woman. An exchange at the end of the film makes the point clearly, if unsubtly:

> Mary: You're not even a woman.
> Elizabeth: I'm a queen. You've been a woman, see where it's brought you.
> Mary: It has brought me happiness you'll never know, Elizabeth. I wouldn't give up the memory of one day with Bothwell for a century of your life.

Mary of Scotland was both a critical and a box office failure and it would be thirty-five years until another film was made in English about Mary Stewart and her relationship with Elizabeth. Obviously the failure of *Mary of Scotland* discouraged further cinematic treatments of this topic, but there were other factors as well. The abdication of Edward VIII in 1936 placed depictions of royal marital scandals off limits and made Mary's chequered marital career problematic for filmmakers. A few years later, Elizabeth would become a patriotic icon in films such as *Fire over England* (1937) and *The Sea Hawk* (1940). The years just before and during World War II were not the time, at least in the English-speaking world, for films that portrayed Elizabeth as the persecutor of a righteous queen of Scots. In fact, the Nazis realised this and made a film, in 1940, about Mary and Elizabeth. *Das Herz der Königin* (The Heart of a Queen) presented Mary as a kind and good person (Mary was played by Zarah Leander, a popular film star

Poster for the 1936 film *Mary of Scotland* starring Katharine Hepburn as Mary, Fredric March as Bothwell and Florence Eldridge as Elizabeth.

and singer in the Third Reich). Elizabeth, on the other hand, is ruthless and devious, bent on overthrowing Mary, so that she can annex Scotland. After World War II, audience tastes changed, and films shifted from portraying monarchs and statesmen to portraying more diverting figures such as athletes and entertainers. Such films as there were about historical figures were usually set in the ancient world, the Middle Ages or the American West.

The surprise financial and critical success of *A Man for All Seasons* (1966) revived the interest of audiences, and thus filmmakers, in early modern British history. And with major implications for the future, for the first, but not the last, time, television of the next few years would enjoy international success with films on sixteenth-century Britain: *The Six Wives of Henry VIII* (1970) and *Elizabeth R* (1971). One of the six episodes in *Elizabeth R* is devoted to Mary and the Babington Plot; it portrays a Mary (Vivian Pickles) who is unabashedly guilty of participating in the Babington Plot and – inaccurately – an Elizabeth (Glenda Jackson) who acts decisively, without hesitation or regret, in ordering Mary's execution.

The success of *Elizabeth R* seems to have inspired Hal B. Wallis to produce *Mary, Queen of Scots* in 1971. Certainly he hired a reluctant Glenda Jackson, at some cost, to reprise her highly praised performance as Elizabeth. Wallis must have been confident in the film's box office potential. He also hired Vanessa Redgrave, an actor who had already received multiple Oscar nominations, to play Mary, and an impressive cast to support the film's two leads. Yet *Mary, Queen of Scots* lost money and received, at best, lukewarm reviews. What went wrong? There seem to have been two basic problems. The first is that while Elizabeth in the film is comprehensible, if not necessarily likeable, Mary's character is difficult to understand. Although *Mary, Queen of Scots* is generally sympathetic to Mary, it also presents Mary as an adulterer and an accessory to murder who conspires in Darnley's assassination. At times, as when confronting John Knox, Mary appears resolute and determined; at other points she is timorous and unsure. It is difficult for an audience to maintain interest in a character they do not understand. Most fundamentally, in key respects, *Mary, Queen of Scots* was out of step with the times in which it was made.

Second-wave feminism was progressing in the UK throughout the late 1960s and early 1970s, winning at least one major triumph with the passing of the Equal Pay Act in 1970. One reason for the success of *Elizabeth R* was that viewers perceived Glenda Jackson's Elizabeth as a woman whose tough-minded pragmatism and self-discipline allowed her to succeed at a traditionally male job. Vanessa Redgrave's queen displays almost diametrically opposite qualities. Throughout the film, Mary follows, almost slavishly, the advice offered by either Moray or Bothwell. *Mary, Queen of Scots* is careful not to depict the Scottish queen engaging in any 'male' activities. Mary's suppression of Moray's rebellion is omitted from *Mary, Queen of Scots* because the actual events, especially the Scottish queen riding with her troops wearing a steel cap and carrying a pistol, showed a decidedly masculine Mary. Similarly, Mary's escape from Lochleven and her fighting the Battle of Langside are not shown in the film.

Mary, Queen of Scots not only repeats the gendered 'masculine' Elizabeth and 'feminine' Mary dichotomy, it goes further and, like its 1936 predecessor, endorses Mary's putative devotion to love and family as superior to Elizabeth's dedication to ruling England. At the conclusion of their first meeting – this film has two meetings of the monarchs – Elizabeth tells Mary she is unfit to be a queen. Mary angrily tells Elizabeth that she will be childless and die 'a solitary old woman'. The endnotes to the film present this as both a prophecy and an indictment by stating that Elizabeth 'died as she had lived, unmarried and childless'. It is likely that the same viewers who applauded *Elizabeth R* would have been uncomfortable with the increasingly dated views on gender relations in *Mary, Queen of Scots*.

The failure of *Mary, Queen of Scots*, coupled with the failure of Ken Hughes's *Cromwell* the year before, brought an all but total end to historical films on early modern Britain for nearly thirty years. Some of this was doubtless due to the disappointing box office performances of *Cromwell* and *Mary, Queen of Scots* and there may well also have been audience fatigue with early modern historical epics. Yet there were other factors at work. Historical films are relatively expensive to make and in the 1970s UK government funding for films dried up. This had a knock-on effect as subsidies to US filmmakers for producing films in England also vanished, bringing a great deal of the American investment in British films to an end. Now the money was not there for British filmmakers to take the costly gamble that a historical film represented. The situation changed somewhat in the 1980s and 1990s as globalisation led to the absorption of English film companies into international conglomerates, thus effectively, albeit a bit circuitously, increasing American and European investments in British films and in filming in Britain.

AT THE SAME TIME, the rise of heritage films in the 1980s, such as *Chariots of Fire* (1981) and *Maurice* (1987), not only demonstrated that there was a market for films about the past, but also eventually led to profitable historical films such as *The Madness of King George* (1994) and *Mrs Brown* (1997). In 1998, a commercially adroit combination of the heritage film with the gangster film made Shekhar Kapur's *Elizabeth* a success. This paved the way for other historical films set in early modern England, such as *Shakespeare in Love* (1998), *To Kill a King* (2003) and *Elizabeth: The Golden Age* (2007). Nor was television far behind: *Henry VIII* (2003), *Elizabeth I: The Virgin Queen* (2005) and *Elizabeth I* (2005) rapidly followed on the heels of *Elizabeth*. But there was relatively little attention paid to Mary in this flurry of films. She appeared in the two 2005 television programmes and in

Elizabeth: The Golden Age, but as only one of numerous characters, friend and foe, circling in Elizabeth's orbit. The one film that focused on Mary was *Gunpowder, Treason and Plot* (2004), a two-part BBC television programme about Mary and James I. What is striking about this film is how harshly it judges Mary. She is shown masterminding Darnley's murder and ordering Bothwell to carry it out. She is also shown confessing this to a priest, who tells her that she will burn in hell, whereupon Mary implacably responds 'So be it.' It would appear that twenty-first-century filmmakers, and presumably audiences, were now unwilling to accept Mary as a passive victim. This would become clear with the next and, so far at least, final film about Mary and Elizabeth.

The new film, *Mary Queen of Scots* (2018), contained some traditional elements, notably a fictitious meeting between Mary and Elizabeth (this is a virtually omnipresent feature of films about the queens). But the 2018 film differed from its predecessors in two crucial respects. The first is in presenting Mary as a strong, forceful ruler who engages in such 'masculine' activities as leading her troops into battle. It also portrays her as an adept ruler whom Elizabeth at one point declares is 'more capable than my privy council'. The other difference is that while Elizabeth is portrayed as an accomplished ruler in her own right, she is not shown spinning plots against Mary or as being bent on the Scottish queen's destruction. In fact, when the two queens meet soon after Mary's arrival in England, Elizabeth is visibly saddened as she tells Mary that she cannot supply her with an army because Mary is a Catholic. With her voice breaking, Elizabeth assures Mary that she will be safe in England, but that that is all that she can offer. The interview breaks down and Elizabeth, insulted by Mary, walks out. Years later, as Mary is being led to her execution, Elizabeth, in her thoughts, says farewell to the 'young fierce queen whom I have always loved and admired'. The traditional depiction of Mary and Elizabeth as being locked in a deadly rivalry is now replaced by a depiction of a sincere, but tragically unsuccessful, attempt at female solidarity.

It is doubtful that depictions of interactions between Mary and Elizabeth will vanish from popular culture, as their lives and personalities offer too much scope for drama and art. But how they will be depicted is more difficult to predict. Will a fierce and independent Mary become an icon for those championing Scottish independence? Will future films go even further in depicting an emotional sisterhood between the two queens? No one can safely say, but what does seem certain is that there will be future films on the two queens and that portrayals of Elizabeth and Mary will continue to be as powerfully affected by social, cultural and political beliefs and prejudices as past portrayals of the two queens have been.

> IT WOULD APPEAR THAT TWENTY-FIRST-CENTURY FILMMAKERS AND AUDIENCES WERE NOW UNWILLING TO ACCEPT MARY AS A PASSIVE VICTIM

ELIZABETH

13

AFTERWORD

Alan Bryson, Andrea Clarke,
Susan Doran and Karen Limper-Herz

In October 1561 Elizabeth's ambassador to France, Sir Nicholas Throckmorton, reported a remarkable conversation he had had with Mary's uncle, Francis, Duke of Guise. Guise told him 'there should be nothing left undone that might occasion good and perfect amity between the Queen your mistress and the Queen of Scotland. They be … both queens in one isle, near kinswomen and in manner of one language. A good accord between them should bring more commodities and felicities to them both, to their realms and subjects, than any other amity between other princes.'

Guise saw the opportunity for a fresh start between England and Scotland – but one to France's advantage – if only Elizabeth recognised Mary as her heir presumptive. Others, like Maitland, backed the scheme enthusiastically, and throughout her personal reign Mary pursued it as the bedrock of her relationship with Elizabeth, offering an alliance in return. Elizabeth always claimed to have supported her fellow monarch, who, like her, had been called by God to reign over her subjects. In their dealings together, she placed Mary's rank and hereditary right over objections to her religion but would not name Mary as her heir, for fear it might encourage plots. Yet, while Elizabeth did her best to protect Mary's

**Plate depicting
Queen Elizabeth I.**

David Hume, *The History of England*, London 1790–1. British Library, 587.g.2.

right to the succession, her government repeatedly undermined Mary's rule in Scotland. This was because William Cecil had persuaded Elizabeth that, for reasons of state, bolstering the Protestant regime in Scotland must take precedence over any fellow feeling the queen had for Mary.

But even without English or French interference, ruling Scotland was not easy. With the exceptions of James IV and James V, all Stewart monarchs before Mary had faced serious and sometimes insurmountable challenges to their authority from their subjects. The Scottish Reformation made matters worse. Although Mary was undogmatic in her religion, her drive for Catholic toleration – perhaps even restoration – jeopardised the fragile consensus she had achieved on her return to Scotland, and her marriages to Darnley and Bothwell destroyed it. However, her deposition from the throne and captivity in England did not make Mary a spent force. The majority of her subjects still supported her. Furthermore, like many others in England, Norfolk and Leicester thought Mary's claim to the English succession unstoppable, which goes some way to explaining the complex reaction towards her. Only when the Norfolk marriage proposal collapsed in the face of Elizabeth's implacable hostility did Mary begin plotting to depose the queen as the only means of escape, a decision that defined the remainder of Mary's life.

In 1598, in his last letter to his son and political heir, Robert Cecil, Burghley told him to 'serve God by serving the Queen for all other service is indeed bondage to the Devil'. Burghley died within weeks, attending to the business of government until the end. But in fact he had served himself as well as the queen, becoming rich from what today we would call corruption as well as monopolising power after the deaths of Leicester, Walsingham and the Lord Chancellor, Sir Christopher Hatton, a factor that contributed to the faction that soured Elizabeth's final years. In March 1603 the queen's robust health failed, in part because of melancholy. Neither eating nor sleeping, she leaned against a pile of cushions, eventually losing the power of speech and dying of a throat infection or bronchitis at Richmond Palace in the early hours of 24 March. Elizabeth was 69 and had reigned for almost forty-five years. It was reported that she acknowledged James VI as her heir at the end, although whether by words or a gesture was disputed.

IN TRUTH, WAR-WEARINESS, HIGH taxation, bad harvests, low wages and plague made many yearn for peace with Spain and look optimistically to the future, when a childless old woman would be succeeded by a married man and father. On his way south James was greeted enthusiastically by his new English subjects, but tensions quickly arose over how to make the union of the crowns work, his lavish generosity and his Scottish household. To ease concerns, James tried to reassure his subjects that nothing significant had changed, and he underlined continuity with the past by using some of Elizabeth's emblems and encouraging his wife, Anna of Denmark, to wear the late queen's dresses, rather than recycling them, which was the more conventional cost-saving exercise. Anna also raided Elizabeth's wardrobe for the court masque of January 1604, Samuel Daniel's *Vision of the Twelve Goddesses*, where she appeared as Pallas, a deity associated closely in people's minds with the late queen. Similarly, Anna commissioned portraits by Marcus Gheeraerts the Younger, one of which depicts her in a farthingale, directly mimicking Elizabeth's pose in the Flemish artist's most famous work, the Ditchley Portrait (p. 248).

Nonetheless, while exploiting Elizabeth's image, both king and consort were determined to eclipse her. They especially drew on their success in procreation to present themselves as a young, fertile and dynamic couple in contrast to the decrepit and barren queen who had recently passed away. Elizabeth's accession day was ignored and instead the new national holidays were James's coronation day (25 July) and two new holy days that marked his providential escape from death: Gowrie Day on 5 August (when James escaped a supposed assassination attempt) and the foiling of the Gunpowder Plot on 5 November. The relocation of Elizabeth's tomb to the north aisle of Henry VII's chapel in Westminster Abbey, placed over that of her barren half-sister Mary, was another deliberate effort to sideline her, for in 1612 James removed his mother's remains from Peterborough Cathedral and had them reburied on the south aisle of the chapel, alongside the other matriarchs of the Stuart dynasty – Margaret Beaufort (Henry VII's mother) and Margaret Douglas, Countess of Lennox (James's grandmother). In death Elizabeth was confined to the Tudor past, whereas Mary represented the Stuart present and future.

Given James's attitude, it is hardly unsurprising that William Camden's *Annales* (1615 and 1625), the first official history of Elizabeth's reign, eulogised Mary rather than Elizabeth. However, Camden wrote in Latin, and his English translators, Abraham Darcie (1625) and Robert Norton (1630), reinterpreted the tone of his text to celebrate Elizabeth's reign and show less sympathy for Mary. Norton's version, telling of the 'halcyon days' of 'our late glorious Sovereign of renowned memory', became for centuries the definitive account of Elizabeth's reign and the relationship between the two queens, which took up a huge amount of the text. Consequently, assessments of Elizabeth remained generally favourable throughout the eighteenth and early nineteenth centuries. Additionally, historians then constructed a narrative of England's rise to imperial greatness founded on the triumph of the Reformation, which embraced rationalism and modernity, and on Anglo-Scottish union. The Victorian historian Thomas Babington Macaulay was but one to treat Elizabeth as a great ruler because she was identified with the nation's manifest destiny as a naval imperial power. By contrast, Mary seemed to run counter to inevitable historical progress. Continuing in this tradition was John Neale's biography of Elizabeth (1934), which despite its age is still an essential read. One discordant note came from the Victorian James Anthony Froude, who argued that the major achievements of Elizabeth's reign had been made despite rather than because of her.

Historians also depicted the two queens in ways that reflected the gender stereotypes and norms of their own societies. In *The History of England* (1759), for example, David Hume wrote of Elizabeth's 'masculine spirit' and 'feminine coquetry', and described Mary as a woman who 'seemed to partake only so much of the male virtues as to render her estimable, without relinquishing those soft graces, which comprise the proper ornament of her

WHILE EXPLOITING ELIZABETH'S IMAGE, BOTH KING AND CONSORT WERE DETERMINED TO ECLIPSE HER

sex'. A century later, in Victorian England, Mary was appreciated for her feminine and maternal qualities, whereas Elizabeth's single status, political power and ruthless conduct made her a far less appealing character to writers and presumably readers. This pattern was also found in imaginative literature, where authors largely treated Mary as a tragic figure of romance and Elizabeth as her nemesis. In Friedrich Schiller's highly influential play *Maria Stuart* (1800), which centres on an imaginary meeting between the two queens, Mary is portrayed as both villain (a murderer) and victim (a prisoner soon to die), while Elizabeth is trapped in the dilemma of managing two irreconcilables, her roles as woman and ruler. Generally speaking, Elizabeth was praised (except by Froude) as a good ruler and bad woman, in contrast with Mary, who was considered a good woman but flawed ruler.

Twentieth-century scholarship took a more critical approach towards Elizabeth's governance, emphasising among other things the fragility of the regime, the exclusion and persecution of Catholics, the uncertainty and instability created by her decision not to marry, and the immediate and long-term consequences of the conquest of Ireland. But she remains a powerful and glorious figure in the popular imagination. Mary's reputation has improved in recent decades, especially since the 1960s, when the anaesthetist-turned-textual critic M. H. Armstrong Davison overturned many long-held assumptions about her by demonstrating that the 'Casket Letters' were at best doctored, at worst forged. The two major modern biographers, Antonia Fraser (1969) and John Guy (2004), offered significant and generally positive reassessments. Mary still has her detractors, though, most notably perhaps the late Jenny Wormald, whose provocative but compelling 1988 book is subtitled *A Study in Failure*.

In a moment of light reverie in 1560, Throckmorton had offered Leicester a novel solution to Elizabeth and Mary's dynastic problem: 'methinks it were to be wished of all wise men, and her Majesty's good subjects, that one of these two queens of the Isle of Britain were transformed into the shape of a man, to make so happy a marriage, as thereby there might be a unity of the whole isle.' Mary had joked as much herself. Fatefully, such a neat resolution was impossible. Elizabeth and Mary found themselves entrapped by dynastic and religious circumstance, unable to live and reign securely because the one was Catholic heir to the other. For many, Elizabeth's only surety lay in the destruction of her cousin, an act of regicide from which she recoiled for two decades before her hand was finally forced by her privy council; while for James VI and Protestant Scotland, the deposed Mary must never be permitted home for fear of renewed civil war to restore her to her throne.

The unprecedented and extraordinary dynastic accident that had placed Elizabeth on the throne and made the Catholic Mary her heir presumptive combined explosively with the politics of the Reformation. In building a magnificent tomb for Mary in Henry VII's Lady Chapel, where Elizabeth herself was also buried, James VI and I finally drew a line under the contention between the two queens in one island.

FOR MANY, ELIZABETH'S ONLY SURETY LAY IN THE DESTRUCTION OF HER COUSIN

Plate depicting Mary, Queen of Scots.

David Hume, *The History of England*, London 1790–1. British Library, 587.g.2.

MARY,
Queen of Scots.

BIBLIOGRAPHY

STC: *A Short-Title Catalogue of Books Printed in England, Scotland, and Ireland and of English Books Printed Abroad, 1475–1640*, compiled by A. W. Pollard and G. R. Redgrave (London, 1926).

STC²: *A Short-Title Catalogue of Books Printed in England, Scotland, and Ireland, and of English Books Printed Abroad, 1475–1640*, compiled by A. W. Pollard and G. R. Redgrave, revised by W. A. Jackson, F. S. Ferguson and K. F. Pantzer (London, 1976–91).

Primary Printed Works

Acts of the Privy Council of England, ed. J. R. Dasent et al., new series, 46 vols (London, 1890–1964).

Allen, W., *The Execution of Justice in England by William Cecil, A True, Sincere, and Modest Defense of English Catholics*, ed. R. Kingdon (Ithaca, NY, 1965).

Anon, *A Treatise of Treasons against Q. Elizabeth, and the Croune of England* ([Louvain], 1572; STC² 7601).

Bain, J. (ed.), *The Hamilton Papers: Letters and Papers Illustrating the Political Relations of England and Scotland in the XVIth century*, vol. 2, 1543–1590 (Edinburgh, 1892).

Berthelet, T., *A Declaration, Conteynyng the Iust Causes and Consyderations, of this Present Warre with the Scottis, wherin alsoo Appereth the Trewe & Right Title, that the Kinges Most Royall Maiesty hath to the Souerayntie of Scotlande* (London, 1542; STC² 9179).

Bindoff, S. T. (ed.), *The History of Parliament: The House of Commons 1509–1558*, 3 vols (London, 1982).

Buchanan, G., *The Tyrannous Reign of Mary Stewart*, ed. W. A. Gatherer (Edinburgh, 1958).

Calendar of the State Papers, Relating to Scotland … The Scottish Series, of the Reigns of Henry VIII, Edward VI, Mary, Elizabeth. 1509–1603, ed. M. J. Thorpe, 2 vols (London, 1858).

Calendar of State Papers, Foreign: Edward VI, Mary, Elizabeth I, ed. J. Stevenson et al., 23 vols (London, 1861–1950).

Calendar of State Papers, Relating to Scotland and Mary, Queen of Scots, 1547–1603, ed. J. Bain et al., 22 vols (Edinburgh, 1898–1952).

Clifford, A. (ed.), *The State Papers and Letters of Sir Ralph Sadler*, 2 vols (Edinburgh, 1809).

Doleman, R. (pseud.), *A Conference about the Next Succession to the Crowne of Ingland, Divided into Two Partes* ([Antwerp], 1594; STC² 19398)

Elizabeth I, *Collected Works*, ed. L. S. Marcus, J. Mueller and M. B. Rose (Chicago, 2000).

Elizabeth I, *Autograph Compositions and Foreign Language Originals*, ed. J. Mueller and L. S. Marcus (Chicago, 2003).

Elizabeth I, *Selected Works*, ed. S. W. May (New York, 2004).

Elizabeth I, *Translations, 1592–1598*, ed. J. Mueller and J. Scodel (Chicago, 2009).

Ellis, H. (ed.), *Original Letters, Illustrative of English History … from Autographs in the British Museum and … Other Collections*, first series, 3 vols (London, 1824).

Harrison, G. B. (ed.), *The Letters of Queen Elizabeth* (London, 1935).

Hartley, T. E. (ed.), *Proceedings of the Parliaments of Elizabeth I*, vol. 1, 1558–1581 (Leicester, 1981).

Hasler, P. W. (ed.), *The History of Parliament: The House of Commons, 1558–1603*, 3 vols (London, 1981).

Haynes, S. (ed.), *A Collection of State Papers … Left by William Cecil, Lord Burghley* (London, 1740).

Henrisoun, J., *An Exhortacion to the Scottes, to Conforme … to the Vnion, betwene Englande and Scotlande* (London, 1547; STC² 12857).

Hughes, P. L., and J. F. Larkin (eds), *Tudor Royal Proclamations*, 3 vols (New Haven and London, 1964–9).

Keith, R., *History of the Affairs of Church and State in Scotland from the Beginning of the Reformation to the Year 1568*, ed. J. P. Lawson, 3 vols (Edinburgh, 1844–50).

Knox, J., *The Works of John Knox*, ed. D. Laing, 6 vols (Edinburgh, 1846–64).

Knox, J., *History of the Reformation in Scotland*, ed. W. C. Dickinson, 2 vols (New York, 1950).

Labanoff, A., *Lettres, Instructions et Mémoires de Marie Stuart, Reine d'Écosse; Publiés sur les Originaux et les Manuscrits du State Paper Office de Londres et des Principales Archives et Bibliothèques de l'Europe*, 7 vols (London, 1844).

Lawson, J. A., (ed.), *The Elizabethan New Year Gift Exchanges 1559–1603* (Oxford, 2013).

Leslie, J., *A Treatise Concerning the Defence of the Honour of the Right High, Mightie and Noble Princesse, Marie Queene of Scotland* (Louvain, 1571; STC² 15506)

Letters and Papers, Foreign and Domestic, of the Reign of Henry VIII, 1509–1547..., ed. J. S. Brewer, J. Gairdner and R. H. Brodie, 23 vols in 38 (London, 1862–1932).

Letters, Despatches, and State Papers, Relating to the Negotiations between England and Spain, Preserved in the Archives at Vienna, Brussels, Simancas and Elsewhere, ed. M. A. S. Hume, R. Tyler et al., 13 vols in 19 (London, 1862–1954).

Lodge, E. (ed.), *Illustrations of British History, Biography, and Manners, in the Reigns of Henry VIII, Edward VI, Mary, Elizabeth, and James I, Exhibited in a Series of Original Papers*, 3 vols (London, 1838).

MacRobert, A. E. (ed.), *Mary Queen of Scots and the Casket Letters* (London and New York, 2002).

Manning, C. R. (ed.), 'State Papers Relating to the Custody of the Princess Elizabeth at Woodstock', *Norfolk Archaeology*, 4 (1855), 133–231.

Mason, R. A. (ed.), *Knox on Rebellion* (Cambridge, 1994).

Melville, J., *Memoirs of His Own Life, by Sir James Melville of Halhill*, ed. T. Thomson (Edinburgh, 1827).

Murray, J. A. H. (ed.), *The Complaynt of Scotlande* (London, 1872).

Neale, J. E. (ed.), 'Sir Nicholas Throckmorton's advice to Queen Elizabeth on her accession to the throne', *English Historical Review*, 65 (1950), 91–8.

Nicolas, N. H. (ed.), *The Life of William Davison, Secretary of State and Privy Councillor to Queen Elizabeth* (London, 1823).

Patten, W., *The Expedicion into Scotlande of the Most Woorthely Fortunate Prince Edward, Duke of Soomerset, Vncle vnto our Most Noble Souereigne Lord ye Kinges Maiestie Edward the VI Goouernour of Hys Hyghnes Persone, and Protectour of Hys Graces Realmes, Dominions & Subiectes* (London, 1548; STC 19479; STC² 19476.5).

Pollen, J. H., *Mary Queen of Scots and the Babington Plot* (Edinburgh, 1922).

Ponet, J., *A Shorte Treatise of Politike Power, and of the True Obedience which Subiectes Owe to Kynges and other Ciuile Gouernours, with an Exhortacion to All True Naturall Englishe Men* (Strasbourg, 1556; STC² 20178).

Robertson, J. (ed.), *Inventaires de la Royne Descosse Douairiere de France: Catalogues of the Jewels, Dresses, Furniture, Books, and Paintings of Mary, Queen of Scots, 1556–1569* (Edinburgh, 1863).

Robinson, H. (ed.), *Original Letters Relative to the English Reformation ... Chiefly from the Archives of Zurich, Parker Society*, 2 vols (Cambridge, 1846–7).

Rodríguez-Salgado, M. J., and S. Adams (eds), 'The count of Feria's dispatch to Philip II of 14 November 1558', *Camden Miscellany*, 28 (1984), 302–44.

State Papers Published under the Authority of His Majesty's Commission: King Henry the Eighth, 11 vols (London, 1830–52).

Statutes of the Realm, ed. A. Luders, T. E. Tomlins, J. France, W. E. Taunton and J. Raithby, 11 vols (London, 1810–28).

Strype, J. (ed.), *Ecclesiastical Memorials, Relating Chiefly to Religion, and the Reformation of it, and the Emergencies of the Church of England under King Henry VIII, King Edward VI, and Queen Mary I*, 3 vols in 6 (London, 1822).

Secondary Works

Adams, S., 'The release of Lord Darnley and the failure of the amity', *Innes Review*, 38 (1987), 123–53.

Adams, S., 'The English military clientele, 1542–1618', in C. Giry-Deloison and R. Mettam (eds), *Patronages et clientélismes, 1550–1750 (France, Angleterre, Espagne, Italie)* (Villeneuve d'Ascq and London, 1990), pp. 217–27.

Adams, S., *Leicester and the Court: Essays on Elizabethan Politics* (Manchester, 2002).

Adams, S., '"The Queenes Majestie ... is now become a great huntress": Elizabeth I and the chase', *Court Historian*, 18 (2013), 141–64.

Alford, S., 'Reassessing William Cecil in the 1560s', in Guy (ed.), *The Tudor Monarchy*, pp. 233–53.

Alford, S., *The Early Elizabethan Polity: William Cecil and the British Succession Crisis, 1558–1569* (Cambridge, 2002).

Alford, S., *Burghley: William Cecil at the Court of Elizabeth I* (New Haven and London, 2008).

Alford, S., 'Some Elizabethan spies in the office of Sir Francis Walsingham', in R. Adams and R. Cox (eds), *Diplomacy and Early Modern Culture* (Basingstoke, 2011), pp. 46–62.

Alford, S., *The Watchers: A Secret History of the Reign of Elizabeth I* (London, 2012).

Allinson, R., *Monarchy of Letters* (Basingstoke, 2012).

Armstrong Davison, M. H., *The Casket Letters* (London, 1965).

Auerbach, E., *Nicholas Hilliard* (London, 1961).

Barber, P., 'Les îles britanniques', in M. Watelet (ed.), *Gerardi Mercatoris: Atlas Europae. Fac-similé des Cartes de Gérard Mercator Contenues dans l'Atlas de l'Europe, vers 1570–1572* (Antwerp, 1994), pp. 43–78.

Barber, P., 'Mapmaking in England *ca.* 1470–1650', in D. Woodward (ed.) *The History of Cartography*, vol. 3, *Cartography in the European Renaissance* (Chicago, 2007), pp. 1589–669.

Barber, P., 'Putting Musselburgh on the map: two recently discovered cartographic documents from the "rough wooing"', in P. van Gestel-van het Schip and P. van der Krogt (eds), *Mappae Antiquae Liber Amicorum Günter Schilder* (Amsterdam, 2007), 327–38.

Basing, P., 'Robert Beale and the Queen of Scots', *British Library Journal*, 20 (1994), 65–81.

Bath, M., *Emblems for a Queen: The Needlework of Mary Queen of Scots* (London, 2008).

Beckett, M. J., 'The political works of John Lesley, Bishop of Ross (1527–96)' (PhD thesis, University of St Andrews, 2002).

Bellamy, J., *The Tudor Law of Treason: An Introduction* (London, 1979).

Bernard, G. W., 'The downfall of Sir Thomas Seymour', in Bernard (ed.), *The Tudor Nobility*, pp. 212–40.

Bernard, G. W. (ed.), *The Tudor Nobility* (Manchester and New York, 1992).

Blakeway, A., 'The response to the Regent Moray's assassination', *Scottish Historical Review*, 88 (2009), 9–33.

Blakeway, A., 'A Scottish anti-Catholic satire crossing the border: "Ane bull of our haly fader the paip, quhairby it is leesum to everie man to haif tua wyffis" and the Redeswyre raid of 1575', *English Historical Review*, 129 (2014), 1346–70.

Blakeway, A., *Regency in Sixteenth-Century Scotland* (Martlesham, 2015).

Blakeway, A., 'James VI and James Douglas, Earl of Morton', in M. Kerr-Peterson and S. J. Reid (eds), *James VI and Noble Power in Scotland 1578–1603* (London, 2017), pp. 12–31.

Bolland, C., *Tudor and Jacobean Portraits* (London, 2018).

Bolland, C., and T. Cooper, *The Real Tudors: Kings and Queens Rediscovered* (London, 2015).

Borman, T., and A. Weir, 'Elizabeth I: what does this forgotten portrait tell us about her?', *BBC History* magazine, June 2008.

Bossy, J., *Under the Molehill: An Elizabethan Spy Story* (New Haven and London, 2001).

Brady, C., *The Chief Governors: The Rise and Fall of Reform Government in Tudor Ireland 1536–1588* (Cambridge, 1994).

Brown, K. M., 'The price of friendship: the "well affected" and English economic clientage in Scotland before 1603', in Mason (ed.), *Scotland and England, 1286–1815*, pp. 139–62.

Bryson, A., and M. Evans, 'Seven rediscovered letters of Princess Elizabeth Tudor', *Historical Research*, 90 (2017), 829–58.

Buisseret, D. (ed.), *Monarchs, Ministers and Maps: The Emergence of Cartography as a Tool of Government in Early Modern Europe* (Chicago and London, 1992).

Bush, M. L., *The Government Policy of Protector Somerset* (London, 1976).

Cameron, J. S., 'Crown–magnate relations in the personal rule of James V, 1528–1542' (PhD thesis, University of St Andrews, 1994).

Cavanagh, S., 'The bad seed: Princess Elizabeth and the Seymour incident', in J. M. Walker (ed.), *Dissing Elizabeth: Negative Representations of Gloriana* (London, 1998), pp. 9–29.

Collinson, P., *The English Captivity of Mary Queen of Scots* (Sheffield, 1987).

Collinson, P., *Elizabethan Essays* (London and Rio Grande, 1994).

Collinson, P., 'The monarchical republic of Queen Elizabeth I', in Guy (ed.), *The Tudor Monarchy*, pp. 110–34.

Cooper, J., *The Queen's Agent: Francis Walsingham at the Court of Elizabeth I* (London, 2011).

Cowan, I. B., 'The Roman connection: prospects for counter-reformation during the personal reign of Mary, Queen of Scots', *Innes Review*, 38 (1987), 105–22.

Cowan, I., 'The Marian Civil War, 1567–1573', in Norman MacDougall (ed.), *Scotland and War AD 79–1918* (Edinburgh, 1991), pp. 95–112.

Cust, L., *Notes on the Authentic Portraits of Mary Queen of Scots* (London, 1903).

Dawson, J. E. A., 'Two kingdoms or three? Ireland in Anglo-Scottish relations in the middle of the sixteenth century', in Mason (ed.), *Scotland and England, 1286–1815*, pp. 113–38.

Dawson, J. E. A., 'William Cecil and the British dimension of early Elizabethan foreign policy', *History*, 74 (1989), 196–216.

Dawson, J. E. A., *The Politics of Religion in the Age of Mary, Queen of Scots: The Earl of Argyll and the Struggle for Britain and Ireland* (Cambridge, 2002).

Dawson, J. E. A., *Scotland Re-formed, 1488–1587* (Edinburgh, 2007).

Dawson, J. E. A., *John Knox* (New Haven, 2015).

Dietz, F. C., *English Public Finance 1485–1641*, 2 vols (London, 1964).

Dobson, M., and N. J. Watson, *England's Elizabeth: An Afterlife in Fame and Fantasy* (Oxford, 2002).

Donaldson, G., *The First Trial of Mary, Queen of Scots* (London, 1969).

Donaldson, G., *All the Queen's Men: Power and Politics in Mary Stewart's Scotland* (London, 1983).

Doran, S., *Monarchy and Matrimony: The Courtships of Elizabeth I* (London, 1996).

Doran, S., 'Revenge her foul and most unnatural murder? The impact of Mary Stewart's execution on Anglo-Scottish relations', *History*, 85 (2000), 589–612.

Doran, S. (ed.), *Elizabeth: The Exhibition at the National Maritime Museum* (London, 2003).

Doran, S., 'Loving and affectionate cousins? The relationship between Elizabeth I and James VI of Scotland', in S. Doran and G. Richardson (eds), *Tudor England and its Neighbours* (Basingstoke, 2005), pp. 203–34.

Doran, S., *Mary Queen of Scots: An Illustrated Life* (London, 2007).

Doran, S., 'From Hatfield to Hollywood: Elizabeth I on Film', in S. Doran and T. S. Freeman (eds), *Tudors and Stuarts on Film* (Basingstoke, 2009), pp. 88–105.

Doran, S., *Elizabeth I and her Circle* (Oxford, 2018).

Doran, S., *Regime Change: From Elizabeth I to James I* (Oxford, forthcoming).

Doran, S., and P. Kewes (eds), *Doubtful and Dangerous: The Question of Succession in Late Elizabethan England* (Manchester, 2014).

Doran, S., and D. R. Starkey, *Henry VIII: Man and Monarch* (London, 2009).

Durkan, J., 'The library of Mary, queen of Scots', *Innes Review*, 38 (1987), 71–104.

Duffy, E., *The Stripping of the Altars: Traditional Religion in England c.1400–c.1580* (New Haven, 1992).

Duffy, E., *Fires of Faith: Catholic England under Mary Tudor* (New Haven, 2010).

Edwards, J., *Mary I: England's Catholic Queen* (London, 2011).

Felch, S. M., 'The rhetoric of biblical authority: John Knox and the question of women', *Sixteenth-Century Journal*, 26 (1995), 805–21.

Ferguson, W., *Scotland's Relations with England: A Survey to 1707* (Edinburgh, 1977).

Fraser, A., *Mary Queen of Scots* (London, 1969).

Freeman, T. S., '"As true a subiect being prysoner": John Foxe's notes on the imprisonment of Princess Elizabeth, 1554–5', *English Historical Review*, 117 (2002), 104–16.

Gajda, A., *The Earl of Essex and Late Elizabethan Political Culture* (Oxford, 2012).

Gilbert, J. M., 'Hunting with Mary Queen of Scots', *Review of Scottish Culture*, 28 (2019), 18–42.

Goldring, E., *Nicholas Hilliard: Life of an Artist* (New Haven and London, 2019).

Goodare, J., 'Queen Mary's Catholic interlude', *Innes Review*, 38 (1987), 154–70.

Goodare, J., 'The first parliament of Mary, queen of Scots', *Sixteenth Century Journal*, 36 (2005), 55–75.

Goy-Blanquet, D., 'Killing the queen: "it lawfully maie be done"', *Law and Humanities*, 7 (2013), 193–203.

Graffius, J., 'Relics and cultures of commemoration in the English Jesuit College of St Omers in the Spanish Netherlands', in J. E. Kelly and H. Thomas (eds), *Jesuit Intellectual and Physical Exchange between England and Mainland Europe, c.1580–1798* (Leiden and Boston, 2018).

Graves, M. A. R., 'Thomas Norton the parliament man: an Elizabethan MP, 1559–1581', *Historical Journal*, 23 (1980), 17–35.

Graves, M. A. R., *The Tudor Parliaments: Crown, Lords and Commons, 1485–1603* (London, 1985).

Greengrass, M., 'Mary, dowager queen of France', *Innes Review*, 38 (1987), 171–94.

Guy, J. A., *Tudor England* (Oxford, 1988).

Guy, J. A., 'Introduction. The 1590s: the second reign of Elizabeth I?', in Guy (ed.), *The Reign of Elizabeth I*, pp. 1–19.

Guy, J. A. (ed.), *The Reign of Elizabeth I: Court and Culture in the Last Decade* (Cambridge, 1995).

Guy, J. A., 'Tudor monarchy and its critiques', in Guy (ed.), *The Tudor Monarchy*, pp. 78–109.

Guy, J. A. (ed.), *The Tudor Monarchy* (London, 1997).

Guy, J., *My Heart is My Own: The Life of Mary Queen of Scots* (London, 2004).

Guy, J. A., *Mary Stuart and the Failure of the Darnley Marriage* (Sevenoaks, 2006).

Guy, J., 'Mary Queen of Scots (1971)', in S. Doran and T. S. Freeman (eds), *Tudors and Stuarts on Film* (Basingstoke, 2009), pp. 136–49.

Guy, J. A., *The Children of Henry VIII* (Oxford, 2013).

Guy, J. A., *Elizabeth: The Forgotten Years* (London, 2016).

Guy, J. A., *Gresham's Law: The Life and World of Queen Elizabeth I's Banker* (London, 2019).

Hackett, H., *Virgin Mother, Maiden Queen: Elizabeth I and the Cult of the Virgin Mary* (Basingstoke, 1995).

Haigh, C., 'The Church of England, the Catholics and the people', in Haigh (ed.), *The Reign of Elizabeth*, pp. 195–219.

Haigh, C. (ed.), *The Reign of Elizabeth* (London, 1984).

Haigh, C., *English Reformations: Religion, Politics, and Society under the Tudors* (Oxford, 1993).

Hammer, P. E. J., 'Patronage at court, faction and the earl of Essex', in Guy (ed.), *The Reign of Elizabeth I*, pp. 65–86.

Hammer, P. E. J., *The Polarisation of Elizabethan Politics: The Political Career of Robert Devereux, 2nd Earl of Essex, 1585–1597* (Cambridge, 1999).

Head, D. M., 'Henry VIII's Scottish policy: a reassessment', *Scottish Historical Review*, 61 (1982), 1–24.

Heard, K., and L. Whittaker, *The Northern Renaissance: Dürer to Holbein* (London, 2011).

Hearn, K. (ed), *Dynasties: Painting in Tudor and Jacobean England 1530–1630* (London, 1995).

Hewitt, G. R., *Scotland Under Morton: 1572–1580* (Edinburgh, 1982).

Hoak, D. E., *The King's Council in the Reign of Edward VI* (Cambridge, 1976).

Hoak, D. E., 'The succession crisis of 1553 and Mary's rise to power', in E. Evenden and V. Westbrook (eds), *Catholic Renewal and Protestant Resistance in Marian England* (Farnham, 2015), pp. 17–42.

Holmes, P. J., 'Mary Stewart in England', *Innes Review*, 38 (1987), 195–218.

Houlbrooke, R. A., 'Henry VIII's wills: a comment', *Historical Journal*, 37 (1994), 891–9.

Ives, E. W., 'Henry VIII's will: a forensic conundrum', *Historical Journal*, 35 (1992), 779–804.

Ives, E. W., *The Life and Death of Anne Boleyn: 'The Most Happy'* (Oxford, 2004).

Jackson, W. A., 'The funeral procession of Queen Elizabeth', *The Library*, 26 (1945), 262–71.

Jones, N. L., *Faith by Statute: Parliament and the Settlement of Religion, 1559* (London, 1982).

Jones, N. L., 'Elizabeth's first year: the conception and birth of the Elizabethan political world', in Haigh (ed.), *The Reign of Elizabeth*, pp. 27–53.

Kaufmann, M., *Black Tudors: The Untold Story* (London, 2017).

Kesselring, K. J., *The Northern Rebellion of 1569: Faith, Politics and Protest in Elizabethan England* (Basingstoke, 2010).

Klarwill, V. von, *Queen Elizabeth and Some Foreigners* (London, 1928).

Lake, P., *Bad Queen Bess? Libels, Secret Histories, and the Politics of Publicity in the Reign of Queen Elizabeth I* (Oxford, 2016).

Lang, A., 'The household of Mary queen of Scots in 1573', *Scottish Historical Review*, 2 (1905), 345–55.

Latham, B., *Elizabeth I in Film and Television* (Jefferson, NC and London, 2011).

Lebel, G., 'British–French artistic relations in the XVI century', *Gazette des Beaux-Arts*, 33 (1948), 267–80.

Levey, S. M., and P. K. Thornton, *Of Houshold Stuff: The 1601 Inventories of Bess of Hardwick* (London, 2001).

Levine, M., *The Early Elizabethan Succession Question, 1558–1568* (Stamford, CT, 1966).

Lewis, J. E., *Mary Queen of Scots: Romance and Nation* (London and New York, 1998).

Lloyd, S., *Portrait Miniatures from the National Galleries of Scotland* (Edinburgh, 2004).

Loades, D., 'Philip II and the government of England', in C. Cross, D. Loades and J. J. Scarisbrick (eds), *Law and Government under the Tudors* (Cambridge, 1988), pp. 177–94.

Loades, D., *Mary Tudor: A Life* (Oxford, 1989).

Lynch, M., 'Queen Mary's triumph: the baptismal celebrations at Stirling in December 1566', *Scottish Historical Review*, 69 (1990), 1–21.

Lynch, M., *Scotland: A New History* (London, 1998).

Macauley, S., 'Matthew Stewart, fourth Earl of Lennox and the politics of Britain, c. 1543–1571' (PhD thesis, University of Cambridge, 2006).

MacCaffrey, W. T., *The Shaping of the Elizabethan Regime* (Princeton, 1968).

MacCaffrey, W. T., *Elizabeth I and the Making of Policy* (Princeton, 1981).

MacCaffrey, W. T., *Elizabeth I: War and Politics, 1588–1603* (Princeton, 1992).

MacCulloch, D. (ed.), *The Reign of Henry VIII: Politics, Policy and Piety* (London, 1995).

MacCulloch, D., *Thomas Cranmer: A Life* (London, 1996).

MacCulloch, D., *Tudor Church Militant: Edward VI and the Protestant Reformation* (London, 1999).

MacLeod, C. (ed.), *Elizabethan Treasures: Miniatures by Hilliard and Oliver* (London, 2019).

Marshall, R. K., *Mary, Queen of Scots* (Edinburgh, 2013).

Mason, R.A., 'Scotching the Brut: politics, history and national myth in sixteenth-century Britain', in Mason (ed.), *Scotland and England, 1286–1815*, pp. 60–84.

Mason, R. A. (ed.), *Scotland and England, 1286–1815* (Edinburgh, 1987).

Mason, R. A. (ed.), *Scots and Britons: Scottish Political Thought and the Union of 1603* (Cambridge, 1994).

May, S., and A. Bryson (eds), *Verse Libel in Renaissance England and Scotland* (Oxford, 2016).

May, S., and A. F. Marotti (eds), *Ink, Stink Bait, Revenge, and Queen Elizabeth: A Yorkshire Yeoman's Household Book* (London, 2014).

McElroy, T. A., 'Politics and performance in Buchanan's *Detectioun*', in R. Mason and C. Erskine (eds), *George Buchanan: Political Thought in Early Modern Europe and the Atlantic World* (Farnham, 2012).

Mears, N., '*Regnum cecilianum*? A Cecilian perspective of the court', in Guy (ed.), *The Reign of Elizabeth I*, pp. 46–64.

Mears, N., *Queenship and Political Discourse in the Elizabethan Realms* (Cambridge, 2006).

Merriman, M. H., 'The struggle for the marriage of Mary queen of Scots: English and French intervention in Scotland, 1543–1550' (PhD thesis, University of London, 1974).

Merriman, M. H., 'Mary, queen of France', *Innes Review*, 38 (1987), 30–52.

Merriman, M. H., 'James Henrisoun and "Great Britain": British union and the Scottish commonweal', in Mason (ed.), *Scotland and England, 1286–1815*, pp. 85–112.

Merriman, M. H., *The Rough Wooings: Mary Queen of Scots, 1542–1551* (East Linton, 2000).

Millar, O., *Pictures in the Royal Collection: Tudor, Stuart and Early Georgian Pictures*, 2 vols (London, 1963).

Murphy, J., 'The illusion of decline: the privy chamber, 1547–1558', in Starkey et al. (eds), *The English Court*, pp. 119–46.

Neale, J. E., *Queen Elizabeth* (London, 1934).

Neale, J. E., 'The Elizabethan political scene', in J. E. Neale, *Essays in Elizabethan History* (London, 1958), pp. 59–84.

Neale, J. E., *Elizabeth I and her Parliaments 1559–1601*, 2 vols (London, 1965).

Parker, G., *The Grand Strategy of Philip II* (New Haven, 1998).

Phillips, J. E., *Images of a Queen: Mary Stuart in Sixteenth-Century Literature* (London, 1964).

Philo, J. M., 'Elizabeth I's translation of Tacitus: Lambeth Palace Library, MS 683', *Review of English Studies*, 71 (2020), 44–73.

Pollitt, R., 'The defeat of the Northern Rebellion and the shaping of Anglo-Scottish relations', *Scottish Historical Review*, 64 (1985), 1–21.

Pollnitz, A., *Princely Education in Early Modern Britain* (Cambridge, 2015).

Probasco, N. J., 'Queen Elizabeth's reaction to the St Bartholomew's Day massacre', in C. Beem (ed.), *The Foreign Relations of Elizabeth I* (New York, 2011), pp. 77–100.

Questier, M. C., *Catholicism and Community in Early Modern England. Politics, Aristocratic Patronage and Religion, c.1550–1640* (Cambridge, 2006).

Ramsay, G. D., 'The foreign policy of Elizabeth I', in Haigh (ed.), *The Reign of Elizabeth*, pp. 147–68.

Read, C., *Mr Secretary Walsingham and the Policy of Queen Elizabeth*, 3 vols (Oxford, 1925).

Read, C., *Mr Secretary Cecil and Queen Elizabeth* (London, 1962).

Redworth, G., '"Matters impertinent to women": male and female monarchy under Philip and Mary', *English Historical Review*, 112 (1997), 597–613.

Reynolds, G., *The Sixteenth and Seventeenth-Century Miniatures in the Collection of Her Majesty the Queen* (London, 1999).

Richards, J. M., 'Mary Tudor as "sole queen"?: gendering Tudor monarchy', *Historical Journal*, 40 (1997), 895–924.

Richards, J. M., *Mary Tudor* (London, 2008).

Richards, J. M., *Elizabeth I* (London, 2012).

Rodríguez-Salgado, M. J. (ed.), *Armada 1588–1988* (London, 1988).

Ryrie, A., *The Origins of the Scottish Reformation* (Manchester, 2006).

Ryrie, A., *The Age of Reformation: The Tudor and Stewart Realms, 1485–1603* (London, 2017).

Rowse, A. L., 'The coronation of Elizabeth I', *History Today*, 3 (1953), 305–7.

Scarisbrick, J. J., *Henry VIII* (London, 1968).

Shannon, W., and M. Winstanley, 'Lord Burghley's map of Lancashire revisited, *c.* 1576–1590', *Imago Mundi*, 59 (2007), 24–42.

Sherlock, P., 'The monuments of Elizabeth Tudor and Mary Stuart: King James and the manipulation of memory', *Journal of British Studies*, 46 (2007), 263–89.

Shrank, C., '"This fatall Medea", "this Clytemnestra": reading and the detection of Mary Queen of Scots', *Huntington Library Quarterly*, 73 (2010), 523–41.

Skelton, R. A., and J. Summerson, *A Description of Maps and Architectural Drawings in the Collection Made by William Cecil, First Baron Burghley, Now at Hatfield House* (London, 1971).

Smailes, H., and D. Thomson, *The Queen's Image: A Celebration of Mary, Queen of Scots* (Edinburgh, 1987).

Starkey, D. R., 'Representation through intimacy: a study of the symbolism of monarchy and court office in early modern England', in Guy (ed.), *The Tudor Monarchy*, pp. 42–78.

Starkey, D. R., *Elizabeth I: Apprenticeship* (London, 2000).

Starkey, D. R., *Six Wives: The Queens of Henry VIII* (London, 2003).

Starkey, D. R., et al. (eds), *The English Court: From the Wars of the Roses to the Civil War* (London and New York, 1987).

Stedell, R., *Mary Queen of Scots' Downfall: The Life and Murder of Henry, Lord Darnley* (Barnsley, 2017).

Stewart, A., *The Cradle King: A Life of James VI and I* (London, 2003).

Strong, R., *Gloriana: The Portraits of Queen Elizabeth I* (London, 1987).

Taviner, M., 'Robert Beale and the Elizabethan polity' (PhD thesis, University of St Andrews, 2000).

Taylor, D. A. H. B., 'A Derbyshire portrait gallery: Bess of Hardwick's picture collection', in D. Adshead and D. A. H. B. Taylor (eds), *Hardwick Hall: A Great Old Castle of Romance* (New Haven and London, 2016), pp. 71–85.

Thiry, S., '"In open shew to the world": Mary Stuart's armorial claim to the English throne and Anglo-French relations (1559–1561)', *English Historical Review*, 132 (2017), 1405–39.

Town, E., *A Biographical Dictionary of London Painters, 1547–1625* (London, 2014).

Tyacke, S., and J. Huddy, *Christopher Saxton and Tudor Map-making* (London, 1980).

Warnicke, R. M., *Mary Queen of Scots* (London, 2006).

Webb, C. L., 'The "gude regent?" A diplomatic perspective upon the earl of Moray, Mary, Queen of Scots and the Scottish Regency, 1567–1570' (PhD thesis, University of St Andrews, 2008).

Wernham, R. B., *The Making of Elizabethan Foreign Policy, 1558–1603* (London, 1980).

White, R., 'The cultural impact of the massacre of St Bartholomew's Day', in J. Richards (ed.), *Early Modern Civil Discourses* (Basingstoke and New York, 2003), pp. 183–99.

Williams, N., *Thomas Howard, Fourth Duke of Norfolk* (London, 1964).

Williams, P., *Philip II* (Basingstoke, 2001).

Wilkinson, A. S., *Mary Queen of Scots and French Public Opinion, 1542–1600* (Basingstoke, 2004).

Wilson, D., *Sweet Robin: A Biography of Robert Dudley, Earl of Leicester, 1533–1588* (London, 1981).

Woodward-Reed, H., 'The context and material techniques of royal portrait production within Jacobean Scotland: the courts of James V and James VI' (PhD thesis, University of Glasgow, 2018).

Wormald, J., *Court, Kirk, and Community: Scotland 1470–1625* (London, 1981).

Wormald, J., *Mary Queen of Scots: A Study in Failure* (London, 1988).

Wormald, J., 'The creation of Britain: multiple kingdoms or core and colonies?', *Transactions of the Royal Historical Society*, sixth series, 2 (1992), 175–94.

Wright, P., 'A change in direction: the ramifications of a female household, 1558–1603', in Starkey et al. (eds), *The English Court*, pp. 147–72.

Yungblut, L. H., *Strangers Settled Here Amongst Us: Policies and the Presence of Aliens in Elizabethan England* (London, 1996).

LIST OF EXHIBITS

Cotton MS Vespasian F v, ff. 163v–164r
Cotton MS Vitellius C xi, f. 225r
Egerton MS 3320, ff. 4v–5r
G.1724.(1).
G.1734.
G.4896.
G.4993.
G.6006.
G.6142.
G.11837.
G.12101.
G.12188.
Harley MS 283, f. 75r
Harley MS 286, f 78r
Harley MS 336, ff. 69v–70r
Harley MS 6798, f. 87r
Harley MS 6986, f. 23r
Harley MS 6986, f. 65r
Lansdowne MS 4, f. 26r
Lansdowne MS 43, ff. 117v–118r
Lansdowne MS 94, f. 29v
Lansdowne MS 94, f. 30r
Lansdowne MS 94, ff. 84v–85r
Lansdowne MS 1236, f. 16r
Lansdowne MS 1236, f. 44r
Loan MS 128 [3]
Loan MS 128 [4]
Loan MS 128 [22]
Loan MS 128 [32]
Loan MS 128 [37]
Maps C.3.bb.5.
Royal MS 7 D x, ff. 5v–6r
Royal MS 18 B vi, ff. 242v–243r
Royal MS 18 B xv, lower cover

Royal MS 18 D iii, ff. 69v–70r
Royal MS 18 D iii, ff. 81v–82r
Sloane MS 2596, f. 52*r

British Museum
1844,0425.24 (Gold medal of James I)
1849,0626.1 (Marriage ryal of Henry and Mary, King and Queen of Scots)
SLMisc.1778 (Phoenix jewel of Elizabeth I)

Lambeth Palace Library
MS 3206, p. 819
MS 4267, f. 19r

The National Archives
E 23/4, ff. 8v–9r
MPF 1/366
SP 11/4/2, ff. 3Av – 3Br
SP 12/193/54, f. 123r
SP 52/12/38
SP 53/14/30
SP 53/18/53
SP 70/17, f. 81v.

National Portrait Gallery
NPG 359 (Electrotype of figure of Henry Stuart, Lord Darnley)
NPG 6343 (Portrait of George Talbot, Sixth Earl of Shrewsbury)
NPG 6676 (Portrait of Thomas Howard, Fourth Duke of Norfolk)

Victoria & Albert Museum
T.29-1955 (The Marian hanging)

OXFORD

Bodleian Library
MS Add. C. 92, f. 24r

PETWORTH

Lord Egremont, Petworth House
Bird's eye view of Leith

PRESTON ST MARY

St Mary's Church, Preston St Mary, Suffolk
Wooden triptych of the royal arms

ST ANDREWS

Historic Environment Scotland, St Andrew's Cathedral Museum
SAC/x/24 (Sculpture of Head of Christ)

PRIVATE COLLECTIONS
Portrait of the young Elizabeth
Bust portrait of Elizabeth I, c.1567
Portrait of Elizabeth I in her parliament robes
Portrait of Sir Francis Walsingham

SIMANCAS, SPAIN

Archivo General de Simancas
Secretaria de Estado, MS 949, 35

WADDESDON MANOR

Waddesdon (Rothschild Family)
Portrait of Robert Dudley, Earl of Leicester

ILLUSTRATION CREDITS

INDEX